A TROPICAL DEPENDENCY

A TROPICAL DEPENDENCY

An Outline of the Ancient History of the Western Sudan with an account of the Modern Settlement of Northern Nigeria

Black Classic Press
Baltimore

A Tropical Dependency

First published 1906
Published 1997 by
Black Classic Press

Cover Art by Carles Juzang

Library of Congress Catalog Card Number:
97–74312

ISBN: 0–933121–92–X

Printed by BCP Digital Printing, Inc.,
an affiliate company of Black Classic Press

Founded in 1978, Black Classic Press specializes in bringing to light obscure and significant works by and about people of African descent. If our books are not available in your area, ask your local bookseller to order them.

Visit www.blackclassicbooks.com for a full list of our titles, or obtain a list by writing to

Black Classic Press
c/o List
P.O. Box 13414
Baltimore, MD 21203

A Young Press With Some Very Old Ideas

INTRODUCTION

Flora Shaw Lugard's *A Tropical Dependency* was the first general survey of African people in world history and was published at a time when nearly all books on Africa began and ended with slavery. It was a major influence on a select group of African historians because it provided a general overview of African history before and after slavery and examined the circumstances that made slavery possible. *A Tropical Dependency* has been around long enough to be legendary and to have legends surrounding it.

W. E. B. Du Bois first called the attention of Black American scholars to this book because it was one of the reference books he used in *The Negro.* When William Leo Hansberry, a young scholar from Mississippi, heard about this book, he went to a library in Atlanta, but could not find it because the libraries in the Black universities of that day were not adequately equipped. Later, when Hansberry was accepted at Harvard, the first thing he did upon arrival on campus was to go directly to the library instead of the registrar's office. He found the book; and when the library closed that evening, he was still there reading it. Hansberry had not registered and had no place to sleep that night, but he had read the book. The reading of this book not only influenced his outlook on African history, it influenced his future career. The information *A Tropical Dependency* contained was advanced for that day; and for those not well read in African history, it is advanced even today.

When Nnamdi Azikiwe read *A Tropical Dependency* and learned that Africans had ruled themselves and parts of Mediterranean Europe long before the period of slavery and imperialism, he was encouraged and said, "Well if Africans did it once, Africans can do it again." Years later, a young student at Lincoln University, Francis Kwame Nkrumah (later Kwame Nkrumah) said more or less the same thing upon reading the book. Lady Lugard's book influenced more than a generation of Africans fighting to regain the independence of their countries and become their own masters. The irony of *A Tropical Dependency* is that this was not Lady Lugard's intention when she sat down to write it.

In the closing years of the nineteenth century and in the early years of the twentieth, Britain's empire building had reached a point where the British people, who furnished most of the soldiers and the workers that built the empire, began to question what they were getting out of the imperial enterprise. Many workers and soldiers were away from home for long periods of time with little benefit to their families. Those who continued serving the empire found that they could not live on the small pensions they received. They questioned the value of the empire to the British working class since it was the middle class that was getting richer at their expense. They also questioned its long-term value for all Britons.

There were, of course, supporters and opponents of the empire in England. Flora Shaw, one of the first female journalists and a supporter of empire, went out to the British-governed protectorate that would later become Nigeria to write a series of articles in defense of the British takeover of this territory. She met, fell in love with, and married the British governor of the protectorate, who would later become Lord Lugard.

As an aristocratic lady, it was not considered proper form for Lady Lugard to continue in her job as a journalist, or any job for that matter. The Nigerian climate and the prevalence of mosquitos induced the Lugards to divide their time between Nigeria and England. An avid reader knowledgeable in Mediterranean and Arab literature and history, Lady Lugard decided to write a book. She undertook research to learn how Africans had ruled themselves before the coming of Europeans. The information gathered for the preface became the basis of the book. Her research, which was intended to justify Britain's right to rule the territory, proved instead that Africans had ruled themselves just as well and far better at times than the Europeans. In her introduction, she confesses that England and Europe in general are dependent on materials and resources coming from Africa, which explains the title—*A Tropical Dependency*. She further confesses that without the resources of the tropics, European mercantilism could not have functioned as the world-wide enterprise that it had become.

She speaks of slavery as though it is a God-given right of Europeans not only to own slaves in general but to own Africans as slaves in particular. She makes no moral justification for this claim except that in her opinion the European is a bearer of civilization and light to the dark places of the world. In the book's introduction, it is clear that Lady Lugard fell for one of the oldest myths in history: the myth of the invader and conqueror as civilizer. As a matter of historical fact, no one ever brings any civilization to anyone. Invaders and conquerors bring their way of life and suppress or destroy the way of life of the people they invade. This is a universal truth no matter who is invading whom. The truth is that no one came to Africa to do African people any good.

Nevertheless, in spite of the imperialist attitude in her Introduction, Lady Lugard tells us much about independent states in precolonial Africa, about the roles of Africans and Arabs in the conquest of Spain, and about their influence on the Mediterranean from 711–1492. When she speaks of the nations of the Western Sudan in inner West Africa, she refers to some nations as having been ruled by White kings, but this information was corrected by Carter G. Woodson in his book, *The African Background Outlined.* Neither Arabs nor Berbers ever ruled the great nation states of Ghana, Mali, or Songhay. For one thousand years after the fall of the Roman Empire, African ingenuity brought into being one independent state after the other in East Africa, West Africa, and in Central Africa in the Congo.

In 1492 when the Africans and Arabs were expelled from Spain, the Arabs returned to Africa and turned on the Africans, the military arm that had protected their power in Spain and in the Mediterranean. This shifted the Arab slave trade into second gear, mainly in East Africa.

In 1591 the nations in inner West Africa were invaded from Morocco by Arabs and European mercenaries using European weapons of that day. The wreck and ruin of this invasion facilitated the spread of the slave trade inland. In East Africa, the Portuguese, who had been driven out of the West African slave trade by the British, formed a partnership with Arab slave traders that wrecked the east coast of Africa. Thus Africa was in the most tragic bind of the ages, a bind from which she has not recovered to this day.

The value of Lady Lugard's book is that while she is telling us about the interplay of power between religions and other competing forces before slavery, she provides us with a much needed look behind the curtain of slavery. In telling us what African states had been, she is clearly indicating what African states could be. This may not have the intent of her book, but this is the message that came across to more than a generation of African activists.

Since the book was first published in 1906, there has been detailed research on Africa's place in world history. *A Tropical Dependency* was part of the stimulus for this research. New readers of Lugard's book and much new research on Africa before slavery and colonialism will produce a new generation that will say what a previous generation said, "If Africa did it once, Africa can do it again!"

—John Henrik Clarke, 1997

TO

MY HUSBAND

CONTENTS

A TROPICAL DEPENDENCY

CHAPTER I

INTRODUCTORY

It has become the habit of the British mind to think of the British Empire as a white empire. But, as a matter of fact, we all know that ours is not a white empire. Out of an estimated population of 413,000,000, only 52,000,000, or one in eight, are white. Out of a territory of 16,000,000 square miles, which extends over a quarter of the globe, about 4,000,000 square miles, or a quarter of the whole, lies within the tropics.

The administration of this quarter of the Empire cannot be conducted on the principle of self-government as that phrase is understood by white men. It must be more or less in the nature of an autocracy which leaves with the rulers full responsibility for the prosperity of the ruled. The administration of India, where this aspect of the question has been long appreciated, is among the successes of which the British people is most justly proud. The work done by England in Egypt is another proof of our capacity for autocratic rule. We are justified therefore in thinking of ourselves as a people who may face with reasonable hopes of success still vaster questions of tropical administration.

We stand now at an interesting moment in our history. The most pressing questions which are connected with the self-governing colonies would seem to have been settled; attention and interest are set free to turn themselves towards other channels; and simultaneously with this liberation of public sympathy the direction of a new development is indicated by circumstances of almost irresistible significance.

Within the last five-and-twenty years we have acquired in tropical Africa alone territories of which the area exceeds by one-half the whole extent of British India. These, and other colonies and dependencies which lie within the tropics, now call for some of the same care and attention which have helped to make India what it is.

In nearly all the tropical colonies there is much fertile land which already produces some of the most necessary and valuable raw materials of trade. Cotton, silk, rice, rubber, sugar, coffee, tea, oils, drugs, dyes and spices, gold and gems, and other important elements of civilised industry, are home products of our tropics. But in very few of the colonies have these products been developed to anything approaching the natural capacity of their sources of origin. In many parts of the colonies the resources of nature have not been cultivated at all. Valuable commodities produce themselves and grow wild — unsown, unreaped. The increase which might result to British trade by a mere opening of the markets that lie as yet unapproached within the Empire, is past calculation. Such opening would necessarily be reciprocal in its action, and every market of supply over which our administration extended would automatically become a market of consumption for manufactured goods. At home the very prosperity of our trade creates a demand for expansion. And these potential markets are our own. We may do as we will within them.

The cultivation of our tropical lands involves, we are sometimes told, questions of transport and labour which are too difficult to touch. Of these the question of transport within the limits of our own colonies and protectorates is very largely a question of money, and its difficulties may easily be made to disappear whenever a real demand for transport shall arise. The question of abour is more serious. Tropical labour is coloured labour, and we have not yet faced the question of organising free coloured labour. But that this question has not yet been faced is not a reason why the difficulties attending it should be regarded as insurmountable. They must be reckoned among the most interesting problems of tropical administration.

The industrial development of ancient civilisations was largely based on slavery, and, from the earliest periods of which history has any record, countries lying within the tropics—always prolific of population—were raided to supply the slave-markets of the world. It was thought worth while in the great days of Egypt, Persia, Greece, Rome, and mediæval Spain, to be at the expense of sending caravans into the Soudan for slaves, who had to be hunted and caught in the tropical regions further south. Notwithstanding the cost of the overland journey, the expense and waste of slave-hunting, and the large percentage of deaths which occurred in transit, the labour of Africa was considered valuable enough to be worth transporting to any market in which it was required. The trade was continued through the Middle Ages, and under modern conditions of steam shipping and travelling it was still found worth while less than fifty years ago to carry African labour to America.

We have abolished slavery, and, as a consequence, it has been assumed that the labour which once supplied the great industries of the world has ceased to have any value.

This is a curious anomaly, for which, however, many explanatory reasons might be produced. Coloured labour, without the control which the master exercises over the slave, has its peculiar difficulties. In the face of them the civilised communities of the Western world have abandoned the use of coloured labour, and the introduction of industrial and agricultural machinery, which began almost coincidently with the abolition of slavery, has minimised the consequences of the loss. The fact is not altered that African labour had through many ages of the world's history a very high marketable value. That this labour still exists, that it is native to an immense area of the tropical colonies, and that it will rapidly increase in volume under the conditions of peace and security introduced by British administration, are factors of great importance in considering the possible development of the resources of these colonies. To construct a bridge between the old system of civilisation and the new, by finding means to organise as free labour the labour which preceding generations could only use enslaved, would be to lead the way in a very sensible advance beyond the first and necessary step of the abolition of slavery.

In speaking of ancient civilisations, I have not mentioned the ancient civilisations of the Far East, where industry is believed to have been first carried to the highest pitch. The industries of the Far East were supplied with other than African labour. From the earliest times the Chinese have been famed for manual dexterity, and Eastern industries have been based upon yellow labour. Yellow labour was carried to a far higher degree of perfection than black labour ever seems to have attained, and yellow labour has never been thrown out of employment. The products of its industries were always largely imported by the nations which owned black slaves. It retains to-day the dexterity for which it was famous in the period of the Pharaohs. But the kingdoms of the East having risen earlier to a condition of cohesion in which they were able to protect their subjects, and having also from a very early period maintained the policy of exclusion practised by Egypt in its greatest days, yellow labour has never been used to supply the slave-markets of the West. Western communities have felt the same repugnance to the employment of free Chinese labour that they felt to the employment of free African labour, and we have had to wait for the present conjunction of events in order to see yellow labour, under the direction of intelligence as acute as any intelligence of the West, prepare to enter into competition with white labour in the industrial markets of the world.

That Japan, which has now established its military and naval ascendancy on the shores of the Pacific, will proceed to the fuller development of its industrial resources, is scarcely doubtful. The labour of China is under its hand. We have therefore an additional reason to take stock of our imperial and of our industrial position. We have within our Empire a body of coloured labour greater than any which Japan can at present command. There is nothing to prevent us from attracting by immigration as much more as we please. But in order to use our own, or to attract more with profit to the Empire, we must face the whole question of tropical administration. We must study with an open mind the thorny questions of native labour. We must prepare and make known those parts of hitherto undeveloped colonies to which it may be considered desirable to attract labour. We must introduce systems of transport by means of which not only the fruits of labour but labour itself may be able to circulate within the Empire. We must, no doubt, in many instances recast our local labour laws. We must frankly recognise the fact that labour is the foundation upon which development rests.

We may at the same time have the satisfaction, even in our earliest beginnings, of knowing that the development of the tropical colonies, if we undertake it seriously, will not end with industrial development. There are many sides to the history of nations, and in the attempt to introduce order and industry into the at present uncivilised areas of many of our tropical possessions, we shall no doubt meet with innate powers unsuspected now, that in more favourable conditions may blossom into life.

Our fathers, by a self-denying ordinance, did what they could to set the subject populations free. It was nobly conceived, and civilisation has profited by the step in human progress that was made. But the actual enjoyment of freedom is still far from the African native. If we could realise the dream of abolition by carrying freedom to every village, and so direct our administration that under it the use of liberty would be learned, we should be filling a place that any nation might be proud to hold in the annals of civilisation. It is not a mere unworthy dream of gain which turns our eyes towards the tropics. It is a great opportunity which seems to be presenting itself in national life, one which affords scope for the best qualities and highest talents that we can command.

It is not, therefore, surprising that interest in tropical questions should of late have become more general, and it is only when we begin to think about them that we realise how very little we know of some of our newer possessions in the tropics. A recognition of this ignorance on my own part in relation to the interior of West Africa has led me to study such authorities as I could find, and, with a very profound sense of my own incompetence in dealing with a subject which demands the care and attention of an accomplished Oriental scholar, I have put together a little account of the general movement of civilisation in the Western Soudan which may perhaps serve rather as a basis for future criticism than for any of the permanent purposes of history. Fresh information comes almost daily to light in the territories occupied by civilised powers, which will doubtless elucidate many points now left obscure, and rectify mistaken conclusions. In the meantime, what I have been able to gather, in part from original manuscripts, but chiefly from translations of Arab historians, may interest some of those who, like myself, desire to have a connected idea of the civilisations which have preceded our own in our lately acquired territories in the interior of West Africa. I am, of course, chiefly concerned with the territories of the protectorate lying on the watershed of the Niger and the Benué, of which the administration was only assumed by the British Government on the 1st of January 1900. By this occupation an entirely new chapter has been opened in the relations of Great Britain with West Africa.

Nigeria—as we call our latest dependency—is not properly a name. It cannot be found upon a map that is ten years old. It is only an English expression which has been made to comprehend a number of native states covering about 500,000 square miles of territory in that part of the world which we call the Western Soudan. Ancient geographers called the same section of Africa sometimes Soudan, sometimes Ethiopia, sometimes Nigritia, sometimes Tekrour, sometimes and more often Genewah or Genowah—which, by the European custom of throwing the accent to the fore part of the word, has become Guinea; sometimes they called it simply Negroland. Always, and in every form, their name for it meant the Land of the Blacks. Genowah, pronounced with a hard G, is a native word signifying "black." It is so generally used to designate blacks that at the present day, among the Arabs of Egypt and the Moors of Morocco—that is, at both exits from the desert—I have myself heard it applied to the negroes of the Soudan. From the earliest periods of which we have any knowledge, Blackland has stretched, as it stretches now, from the west coast of Africa to the east, along that line of successive waterways which begins with the mouth of the Senegal, and ends only at the southern mouth of the Red Sea.

If the north of Africa be considered as a whole it divides itself into three great main sections, all of which run, like the Land of the Blacks, east and west. There is first, outside the tropics and within the zone of winter rains, the historic coast strip stretching along the Mediterranean shore from the mouths of the Nile to Cape Spartel. A range of mountains at its back receding towards the western end separates it from the deserts and gives to its fertile lands the shelter and the water which they need. These mountains have been as the stronghold of civilisation to the coast. Behind them on the southern slopes there is a belt of land on which the date palm flourishes, salt mines abound, and flocks and herds can find subsistence. In this belt there are even spots of great fertility, and there are parts in which it widens, spreading with fertile promontories into the desert. But in its nature this southern face of the hills, known to the ancients as the Land of Dates, is but an offshoot of the coast strip.

It merges soon into the deserts of the rainless zone which form the second great section of North Africa. From the Atlantic coast to the Nile these deserts, under different names, succeed each other across the continent in a broad belt of desolation. Upon the map they cover an area of between ten and fifteen degrees of latitude. At their narrowest parts the caravans which traverse them count upon a march of fifty days. They are in part composed of drifting sand, through which only long practised local guides can find their way; they are practically waterless, and it is of course only in places where springs are known to exist that the passage of them is possible. Marmol, a Spanish writer of the sixteenth century, gives an interesting description of how these wells were preserved in his day: "They are," he says, "walled inside with camels' bones for want of stones, and they are also covered with camels' skins lest the shifting sands should blow over them and fill them up. The natural consequence is that even when there the wells are often hidden, and the traveller may die of thirst within a few feet of water."

With the hot sands of the deserts the continent passes into the tropics, and here again a natural barrier marks the third great division of North Africa. A straight line drawn upon the seventeenth parallel of latitude will mark the edge of the zone of summer rains. Slightly to the south of it may be traced the great water-belt formed by the courses of the Senegal, the Niger, the Benué, the rivers of Haussaland, Lake Chad, the Shari, the lakes and rivers of Wadai and Darfour, the Bahr el Gazal, and the sources of the Nile, which, with their network of tributaries, fertilise the land from the Atlantic Ocean to the mountains of Abyssinia. Other great lakes and rivers traverse the continent farther south. The waterways that I have named suffice, with the Nile, to arrest the advance of the northern deserts and to place round them a border of luxuriant vegetation.

Thus in silent prehistoric ages the rough outlines of the destiny of North Africa were traced. There was a fertile strip in the temperate zone, and near an easily navigable sea; there was a great barren strip in the waterless desert near to nothing which could encourage human occupation; there was another fertile strip in the tropic zone well watered, but sealess—save at its western and eastern extremities, where on the western coast a lack of good harbourage discouraged navigation—miasmic, of a climate very different from that of the strip upon the northern coast; and, running north and south, connecting these three which lay parallel to one another, there was the wonderfully fertilised Valley of the Nile.

It was almost a foregone conclusion that one race should inhabit the coast and a wholly different race the tropics; and that civilisation of a no less different sort should spring up in both zones. Separated as they were by the deserts, it was natural that connection between them should be maintained by that Valley of the Nile which has made itself immortal in the name of Egypt.

It is accordingly to Egypt that we look for all our earliest information concerning the Land of Blacks, and it is to Egypt, and through Egypt to Asia Minor and Arabia, that the blacks themselves trace their oldest traditions.

As it is impossible to appreciate the position of Western Negroland in the history of the world without reference to the movements of other civilisations by which it was influenced, it may be useful, at the risk of repeating very familiar facts, briefly to recall some of the commonly accepted dates relating to the rise and fall of the early civilisations of the Mediterranean.

The great period of Egyptian civilisation, including that of the southern end of the Nile Valley, under its Ethiopian, Coptic, and Libyan Pharaohs, extends from an antiquity which recent excavations tend to show ever more remote, to the conquest of Egypt by Cambyses, King of Persia, B.C. 527. Egypt then became a province of the Persian Empire. It was in the early period, before the time of Herodotus and Cambyses, that Egypt would seem to have given the first inspiration of civilised life to Western Negroland. It remained a dependency of the Persian Empire for two hundred years, but during the whole period was constantly at war with its conquerors. In 332 B.C. Egypt was invaded by Alexander of Macedon as a part of his campaign against Persia. It submitted willingly, and on his death in 321 the dynasty of the Ptolemies was founded and continued, until, on the death of Cleopatra, who was the last sovereign of that dynasty, Egypt became a Roman province, B.C. 30. On the division of the Roman Empire it was included in the Prefecture of the East, and it remained a province of the Byzantine Empire until it was conquered by the Arabs in 638 A.D.

The civilisation of the Phœnicians, contemporary at least in part with the history of Egypt, dates also from the earliest periods of which civil history has any record. The Phœnicians are believed to have migrated from Erythrea on the coast of the Red Sea, about the year 2000 B.C., to the Mediterranean, where they were first established on a strip of Syria between the chain of Lebanon and the sea, and afterwards took possession of a portion of Greece, of some of the islands of the Mediterranean, and of the principal promontories along the coast of Africa to the Straits of Gibraltar, and as far down the western coast as the mouths of the Senegal. They also colonised Spain and spread up the coast of Western Europe, navigating as far as the Baltic and the English Channel. They were never permitted to have a colony on the Egyptian coast, because it was a fundamental maxim of the early Egyptians to suffer no vessel to enter the mouths of the Nile; but the Phœnicians had a large settlement in the very heart of Egypt itself—an entire quarter of Memphis being devoted to them. Tyre and Sidon on the Syrian coast were among the most famous of their early cities. The overthrow of Sidon by Joshua, it will be remembered, took place about 1400 years before Christ. Carthage, of later growth, is believed to have been founded about 853 B.C. Other Phœnician cities on the coast of Africa were of far greater antiquity than Carthage, and Phœnician trade in the Gulf of Sallee on the west coast of Morocco was famous for many centuries before the Romans gave to that part of the coast the name of Sinus Emporicus, or Merchants' Bay.

An even more interesting maritime trade than that of the Phœnicians with the West seems to be clearly established as having existed from a very early period between the coasts of the Persian and Arabian Gulfs, the east coast of Africa as far south as Delagoa Bay, and possibly to the southern coast of the African continent, the western coast of India as far south as Ceylon—the Taprobane of the ancients—and beyond Ceylon to China. By means of this commerce intercourse between India and Africa was regularly carried on during the earliest Egyptian era. The Ethiopian ports for the Indian trade were Azab and Adule within the Straits of Bab-el-Mandeb on the Red Sea; and the Phœnicians, after their land trade had penetrated to India, had colonies upon the Persian and Arabian Gulfs. They also fitted out ships at Suez for the navigation of the Southern seas. The three well-known names of Thule, Tarshish, and Ophir, would appear to have been used generically to indicate these three fields of maritime activity—Thule covering the Atlantic ports, Tarshish the Mediterranean, and Ophir those of the Southern seas. It may be interesting in this connection to note that the words which are translated in the English version of the Bible as "ivory, apes, and peacocks," are not Hebrew but Tamyl words—a circumstance which serves to confirm historic evidence that the commerce of Solomon extended at least as far as Ceylon. The participation of the Phœnicians in the trade of Ophir seems to have dated from the period of their friendship with the Jews under Solomon, or about 1000 years before Christ, but the trade itself was much older.

Through a considerable portion of their history the Phœnicians appear to have acted as commercial agents for Egypt. It was by the orders of Necho, King of Egypt, that about the year 612 B.C. Phœnician sailors, playing for this famous king a part analogous to that which Columbus played 2000 years later for Ferdinand and Isabella of Spain, started from the Red Sea to explore the Southern Ocean, and, according to the tradition related by Herodotus, proved the fact that Africa was surrounded by water on all sides but the strip of land which bound her to Asia, arriving in the third year from their departure once more in Egypt by way of the Straits of Gibraltar. As they sailed, it is related that they landed on the coasts, sowing the land and waiting for harvests. Thus a tradition of them lingers on the west coast as well as on the east; and to them it is in some quarters believed that the legend of the first white men in Western Negroland may be traced. It is the fashion to doubt this statement of Herodotus with regard to the circumnavigation of Africa; but, in the light of many remarkable facts concerning African history which have of late become known, it may be worth while to remember that the achievement spoken of, if it really occurred, would have been almost within the memory of an old man at the time at which Herodotus wrote. Carthage had intercourse across the desert with Negroland, and drew thence its supply of elephants, as well as gold and carbuncles.

Later accounts of the immense quantities of gold which abounded in Negroland render it not improbable that some of the gold so lavishly used by Phœnician artificers in the decoration of Solomon's Temple may have been brought from the Valley of the Niger.

Greek influence in Africa was much later than that of Egypt and Phœnicia, and the colony of Cyrene, which afterwards became the province of Cyrenaica, between the borders of what is now Tripoli and Egypt, was not founded till 620 B.C., about 100 years before the conquest of Egypt by Cambyses. It became subject to Egypt in 323, and afterwards shared in her fortunes.

Libyan, or, as we should call them, Berber tribes, held the extreme west, or divided it with the Carthaginian colonies until the conquest of the northern region by the Romans, during the two hundred years which immediately preceded the birth of Christ. It may be remembered that Scipio received the surname of Africanus in recognition of his triumph over Hannibal in the year 202 B.C. Africa proper, the territory owned by Carthage which corresponds to the modern Tunis, was created a Roman province in 146 B.C. But Egypt and Cyrenaica did not become Roman provinces until 30 B.C. Mauritania, in the north-western corner, also became a Roman province in 33 B.C. When the Romans completed the nominal conquest of Africa, they divided it into six provinces, of which Ethiopia or Negroland was one. But though the northern strip was well known to them, and flourished under their rule, and they made some military expeditions to the south, they had little if any recorded intercourse with Negroland.

Thus from the earliest dawn of Western history the northern coast strip of Africa was the scene of civilised occupation. The introduction of the previously existing Berber or Libyan inhabitants into Africa belongs, says Ibn Khaldun, their great historian, to "a period so remote that God only knows the epoch of it." And as one race of conquerors displaced another, there was a perpetual pressure driving the Libyan inhabitants with the dispossessed peoples across the borders. The natural borders were the hills, and the hunted populations taking refuge in them were forced down the southern slopes upon the deserts. Gradually through the ages the deserts became the home of nomad peoples, who learned, wandering upon the inhospitable face of their drifting sands, to pluck subsistence from widely scattered patches of fertility. These wandering tribes, known under many names, from the Toucouleurs, Tuaregs, Kabyls, Amozighs of the West, to the Tibboos, Berdoas, and others of the eastern borders of the desert, are generally classed as Berbers. It is under the name of Berbers that they are most frequently alluded to by Arab historians, from whom, at a much later period, we derive our principal knowledge of them. Between the coast strip and Negroland the desert itself became in this manner sparsely inhabited by a race which, though it is held to have had one Libyan origin, suffered in the course of history so many invasions and infusions of new blood, that it has broken into almost countlessly diverse tribes, cherishing many and widely differing traditions.

Speaking in roughly general terms, the Berbers are a white people who, having a tradition that they once were Christian, now profess Mohammedanism. North Africa, in the centuries which elapsed between the birth of Christ and the appearance of Mohammed, was the favoured home of Christianity. The names of its saints and martyrs stand high upon Christian rolls. St. Cyprian suffered at Carthage. St. Augustine was born at Hippo. Tertullian and Lactantius, if they were not African, bore eloquent testimony to the fervour of the African Church. In the many contests of early Christian councils it was the African divines who finally triumphed and gave to Christianity its Western form. The African, like the Syrian desert, was at one time honeycombed with the cells of hermits and self-torturing monks. There was no heresy that had not its counterblast in Africa. Proselytism was perhaps nowhere more active. There is, therefore, nothing to surprise us in the Christian tradition of the Berber tribes. They have presumably been, in turn, of the religion of every great invader. Their language has been classed among the Hamitic languages, but they have traditions of Arabian descent. One among many stories of their original introduction into Africa is that five colonies were introduced from Arabia Felix by a certain leader Ifrikiah, or Afrikiah, who gave his name to the continent; and that from these are descended no less than six hundred clans of Berbers. Amongst their many tribes is not, however, to be counted a race wholly distinct from the Berbers, but also nomad in the eastern desert, who are said by those learned in these matters to be the true gypsy of the East. The tradition of the Zingari, as they are found in Northern Africa, is that they came originally from India. This tradition is to be met with again, though faintly and uncertainly recalled, amongst some of the races of Western Negroland.

While the northern strip pressed thus upon the desert, the desert, there can be little doubt, pressed equally upon the fertile belt to the south. Quite indirectly the influence of Tyre and Sidon, Rome and Carthage, must have been brought to bear from the very earliest periods upon Negroland. But besides this indirect influence of pressure by the superior race along the whole course of their borders—an influence which, as will presently be seen, was very potent in modifying the character of the leading black races of Negroland—there were also channels of direct influence which, though Europe has ceased to use them, remain unchanged to this day. These are the caravan routes across the desert. Nature laid them down, and has marked them by certain spots where water can be obtained. The springs have not changed their position within any period of which history has preserved a record, and it is an interesting illustration of the continuity of custom which strikes the imagination in these remote regions of the earth, that the roads trodden by the caravans which this year visit Kano and Timbuctoo, are the same which offered themselves to the first civilised footprints that crossed the desert.

There are two principal roads across the desert, one through Tripoli and the Fezzan running due south towards what is now Nigeria, taking the shape of a forked stick, to rest upon Lake Chad and the Niger; the other through Morocco, running again due south towards Timbuctoo and the western end of Negroland. These two roads, as a glance at the map will show, mark the two narrowest parts at which the desert can be crossed, for in both instances the fertile land of the coast strip runs down in important promontories into the arid sands. Both these roads were counted as a fifty days' journey from edge to edge of fertile land. They are, I believe, so counted still. It hardly needs to be added that one was the channel of Eastern and the other of Western influence upon Negroland.

It is difficult now, when we are accustomed to regard the west coast ports as the natural channels of entrance into the Western Soudan, to remember that throughout the early history of Europe, and up to the period of the discovery of the passage of the Cape of Good Hope at the end of the fifteenth century, the approach to Negroland was by land. In the early periods of African history the navigation of the Atlantic was for all practical purposes unknown. Equatorial Africa faced civilisation on the north. It looked northwards for all its finest inspiration. The south represented to it only barbarism and obscurity. This fact, although difficult now for the imagination to grasp, is of first importance in endeavouring to construct any true conception of Soudanese history. The Soudan was regarded as occupying the edge of the then known world. Homer, first of Europeans to mention it, speaks of the Ethiopians as "the farthest removed of men, and separated into two divisions." Later Greek writers, borrowing their information from Egypt, carry the description somewhat further, and characterise the two divisions as Western and Eastern—the Eastern occupying the countries eastward of the Nile, and the Western stretching from the western shores of that river to the Atlantic coast. One of these divisions, we have to acknowledge, was perhaps itself the original source of the civilisation which has through Egypt permeated the Western world. Both divisions alike faced north, and had their frontage to the great civilisations of their day, along what may be described as the shore of the desert, fringing the 17th parallel of north latitude. Across this desert the native camel was the ship which bore their merchandise and maintained their intercourse with outer life. The caravan roads were the trade routes marked for them as clearly as the trade winds marked the route to be taken on the ocean by later sailing ships. The tonnage of the big caravans was greater than the tonnage of the vessels by which at a subsequent period Drake and Magellan circumnavigated the globe, and England, Portugal, and Holland maintained a prosperous trade with the East Indies. It was sufficient for the purposes of a considerable commerce, and there can be no doubt that from a very early period the communities of the coast were in close and constant communication with Negroland.

When the history of Negroland comes to be written in detail, it may be found that the kingdoms lying towards the eastern end of the Soudan were the home of races who inspired, rather than of races who received, the traditions of civilisation associated for us with the name of ancient Egypt. For they cover on either side of the Upper Nile, between the latitudes of 10° and 17°, territories in which are found monuments more ancient than the oldest Egyptian monuments. If this should prove to be the case, and the civilised world be forced to recognise in a black people the fount of its original enlightenment, it may happen that we shall have to revise entirely our view of the black races, and regard those who now exist as the decadent representatives of an almost forgotten era, rather than as the embryonic possibility of an era yet to come. Be this as it may, the traditions of the Eastern Soudan of the present day would seem to be derived from the same sources as those of Egypt and Arabia, while the nations lying towards the western end of the fertile belt have been more strongly imbued with the influence of the Western Arabs, who in comparatively modern times carried civilisation into Spain. This theory, amply illustrated by the history of the Western Soudan, receives further support from the philological studies of M. Fresnel, who asserts that the alphabet of the Eastern Soudan is the regular alphabet of Arabia, while the alphabet of the Western Soudan is the alphabet of Morocco.

In addition to the influence of the Western Arabs, there was, at a period shortly after the Hegira, an immigration from Arabia under a leader called Abou Zett, which appears to have crossed the Red Sea at the Straits of Bab-el-Mandeb, and to have spread westward along the fertile belt. The tradition of this immigration is vivid in Kordofan, Darfour, and Wadai. It is said to have extended through the entire belt of Negroland, and, as a later chapter will show, some members of it are believed to have reached the bend of the Middle Niger, but the tradition grows fainter in the territories west of Chad.

The influence of Egypt, also perceptible in the Western Soudan, is naturally strongest in the territories which lie nearest to the eastern caravan route across the desert. The meeting ground in which it would appear to have overlapped with the more modern influence of the Western Arabs may perhaps be placed geographically upon the Bend of the Niger. Es-Sadi, a native writer born in Timbuctoo in the sixteenth century, states in his "History of the Soudan" that "the town of Kuka was in existence under the Pharaohs." The only town of Kuka now known to us is in Bornu, but as late as the sixteenth century A.D. there were two Kukas, one of them on the middle Niger—and it is to this latter Kuka that Es-Sadi refers.

In any case this neighbourhood has a special interest, for the first spot in Negroland of which European history preserves any record would seem to have been the site of this very Kuka, or Kaougha, which stood near the present Gao. Herodotus, writing something more than five hundred years before Christ, gives an account in his second book of an attempt which was made by certain Nasamonians, occupying the territory on the Mediterranean coast behind Tripoli, to penetrate into the desert by the eastern road, afterwards so well known and used by the caravan trade of Negroland and the coast. According to his account there were among these people "certain daring youths, sons of powerful men, who, having reached man's estate, formed many extravagant plans, and chose five of their number by lot to explore the deserts of Libya to see if they could make any further discovery than those who had penetrated the furthest." The Nasamonians related that when the young men deputed by their companions set out, well furnished with water and provisions, they passed first through the inhabited country, and having traversed this they came to the region infested by wild beasts, and after this they crossed the desert, making their way towards the west; and when they had traversed much sandy ground during a journey of many days they at length saw some trees growing in a plain, and that they approached and began to gather the fruit that grew on the trees; and while they were gathering it, some "diminutive men, less than men of middle stature, came up," and, having seized them, carried them away. The diminutive men conducted them through vast morasses, and when they had passed these they came to "a city in which all the inhabitants were of the same size as their conductors, and black in colour; and by the city flowed a great river running from the west to the east, and crocodiles were seen in it."

Herodotus does not mention the date of this discovery of the Niger by the Nasamonians. It may have taken place before or after the reported circumnavigation of the continent by the Phœnicians. It may have happened within the memory of those who related the facts, or it may have been a tradition of much earlier events. In the incidents of the discovery there is an indication which the further history of Negroland supports, that the races which now inhabit equatorial regions further south, at one time extended towards the northern edge of the fertile belt. The "diminutive men," whose city existed on the middle Niger some hundreds of years before Christ, are presumably the dwarfs who in our own day were found by Stanley in the Congo forests. Their displacement illustrates the movement under the influence of which the aboriginal inhabitants of the fertile belt were pushed backwards towards equatorial Africa by that pressure of superior races from the desert of which I have spoken. Greek historians of a later date than Herodotus establish the fact that between the purely black people known as the Western Ethiopians, and the Mauritanian inhabitants of the north-western corner of Africa, there were tribes, known as the Pharusii and the Nigretes, who used bows and arrows, and had chariots armed with scythes. The description of the Nigretes, who evidently knew at least the use of iron, would appear to imply a somewhat superior race occupying a position between the black dwarfs and the Northern Libyans. Thus it would seem that in quite ancient times the existence of different races within the belt of Negroland was established. There were evidently superior and inferior tribes; and without attempting to follow the question in detail, it is interesting, though not surprising, to observe that along the whole line of the fertile belt the superior races, modified by intercourse with the white pressure from the north, gradually established themselves in possession of the uplands bordering more nearly upon the desert and civilisation, while the inferior races were driven back towards the then impenetrable regions of barbarism and equatorial Africa. This movement of all that was inferior towards the south is a fact of supreme importance to the subsequent history of the Negro belt.

In the later history given to us by Arab records of every one of the superior black kingdoms which established themselves upon the borders of the desert from Kordofan to the Atlantic, there is to be found at some point in the description the information that to the south of this country lies the country of the "Lem-Lems," or it may be of the "Yem-yems," or the "Dem-dems," or the "Rem-rems," or the "Gnem-gnems," and after the double name comes invariably the same explanation, "who eat men." In following the history of kingdom after kingdom it becomes clear that a belt of cannibalism, of which the Nyam-nyams of the Congo may be counted among the present survivors, extended along the south of the Negro belt across the whole breadth of Africa. M. de Lauture, a French writer of much knowledge and acquaintance with his subject, takes the latitude of 10° north as forming in his day, 1853, the northern limits of habitation of the debased pagan negro. Between 10° and 17° he places the finer races, which he qualifies generally as Mussulman negroes. To-day I believe it will be found that there has been a still further recession southwards of the inferior races, and 9° north would perhaps be nearer to the limit of their northern extension. It is interesting to observe that Northern Nigeria stretches from 7° to 14°, thus including within its limits both classes of natives.

The modern history of Negroland may be said to date from the period at which it accepted the Moslem religion, but the finer black races had established their domination over the inferior, and ruled by force of superior intelligence and cultivation long before that time. Es-Sadi, the same writer who speaks of Kuka as a town which existed in the days of the Pharaohs, speaks also in turning to the west of a kingdom extending to the Atlantic Ocean of which Ghana was the capital, and adds: "They say that twenty-two white kings had reigned over this country before the year of the Hegira. Their origin is unknown." It is also in this neighbourhood, about the sources of the Senegal, that the original home in Africa of the Fulain, who count as a partly white race, is placed. The movement of this remarkable people in Africa within historic time has unquestionably been from west to east, but this does not preclude the theory of some more remote eastern origin which may have preceded their African immigration. Whether Phœnician, Egyptian, Indian, or simply Arab, they are evidently a race distinct from the negroid and other black types by which they have been surrounded, and notwithstanding the marked effect produced on some portions of their people by intermarriage with negro women, they have kept the distinctive qualifications of their race through a known period of two thousand years. The Fulah of to-day is as distinct from the pure Negro as was the first Fulah of whom we have record. How long they may have existed in Africa before any record of them was made it is with our present knowledge impossible to say. The Haussa and the Songhay are other races which, though black, are absolutely distinct from the pure negro type.

In accepting as an historic fact the gradual migration southwards of all that was least valuable in the elements composing the mixed and widely varying populations of the Negro belt, it is to be also recognised that this migration, though doubtless accentuated by the outside pressure of civilisation from the north, was a natural movement initiated by the native populations and carried on by them throughout the known period of their history. Not only were the uplands bordering upon the desert the most desirable portions of the Negro belt, and as such likely to pass into the hands of the strongest who could hold them, but, as they were also the healthiest, the races which inhabited them were maintained by climatic conditions on a higher platform of mental and moral activity than the more supine inhabitants of the denser tropical regions to the south. Hence every cause, natural and artificial alike, has combined to the one end, of establishing the superior races in the northern and the inferior races in the southern portions of the fertile belt.

The result as we see it to-day is strikingly illustrated in British territory by a journey from the Niger mouth to Sokoto. The river in its windings makes a sectional cut of which the general direction is from north to south, and leaving the nude savage of the coast to prowl in dusky nakedness through the mangrove swamps of Southern Nigeria at its mouths, the traveller who enters the river sees the natives on the banks ever increasing in decency and dignity as the latitude recedes from the equator. At Lokoja no native is unclothed. A little farther north, at Bida, where the town is approached by avenues of trees, and native brass and glass manufactures add to the usual industries, Moorish dress is already common. In the markets of Sokoto and Kano the scene is as varied and as dignified as in any market of the Mediterranean coast.

CHAPTER II

CONQUEST OF NORTH AFRICA AND SPAIN BY THE ARABS

THE Roman occupation brings the history of North Africa to the Christian era. The subsequent decline of the Roman Empire was marked by a corresponding decline of the Roman colonies in Africa. The Vandals, who occupied Spain and gave it its name of Vandalusia or Andalusia, followed the Romans and effected establishments upon the coast. But they left the interior untouched, and the conquest which was of supreme interest to Negroland was that which was carried out in the seventh century of the Christian era by the Arabs.

The Arabs conquered Egypt in 638, and their victorious forces spread rapidly, as was to be expected, across the provinces of North Africa. And, as might also be expected, they did not occupy the prosperous northern provinces without endeavouring to find out something of what lay behind them in the desert. Tripoli was taken by them in 643, and expeditions were immediately sent across the hills to the slopes upon the south and as far as Wadan in the western desert. A very little later, 666, Okbar ibn Nafe made a military progress of a still more complete description, and inquiring always of the inhabitants of each conquered tribe—"What lies beyond you?" he marched as far as Kawar, the country of the Tibboos to the north of Lake Chad, which to this day does not appear to be substantially altered from the condition in which he found it. The people of Kawar, either not knowing or not choosing to tell that there was anything beyond them, replied in answer to his questions that the country beyond was unknown. He turned back to Tripoli, and thus just missed entering the fertile belt. Fifteen years later, 681, the same Okbar attacked the south-western part of Morocco, a very fruitful district then occupied by Europeans and Christian Berbers, and made himself master of the whole. The principal town, Medina Niffis, is spoken of by Arab historians as a town of great antiquity. It lies, however, on the other side of the mountains which separate Morocco from the desert, and he still did not enter the fertile belt of Negroland. But Okbar was only a forerunner of the more celebrated Musa Nosseyr, who was appointed Governor of Africa under the Caliphs in 698, and made his administration for ever famous by that Arab conquest of Spain which so profoundly affected the civilisation of the West.

It is interesting, and important to the history of North Africa, that Musa did not immediately undertake the invasion of Spain. Upwards of ten years elapsed, during which he had time to make his presence felt in the province which was at that time known by the name of Afrikyah, or, as it was more generally spelt, Ifrikyah. This province of the Arab domination corresponded not to Africa as we know it, but to the Carthaginian and Roman Province of Africa Propria, which stretched from Barca to the borders of Morocco and extended southward to the edge of the desert. It held the head of the eastern road into the desert through the Fezzan, while the head of the western road through Morocco appears, notwithstanding Okbar's partial conquests, to have remained in the hands of the Europeans and Christian Berbers who held the country which corresponds to the modern Morocco.

Musa's first act on arriving at Cairouan to take up the governorship, was to make a speech to his soldiers which, interpreted by the light of succeeding events, had almost a prophetic note: "I know well," he said, "what sort of commander you want," and after describing to them an ideal soldier "doubly cautious after victories, doubly brave after defeat, trusting ever in the righteousness of his cause," he lifted his hands to the mountains in the shadow of which they stood, and cried: "You may safely rely upon me as your commander, for I shall seize every opportunity of leading you on to victory; and, by Allah! I will not cease making incursions into yonder high mountains and attacking the strong passes leading into them, until God has depressed their summits, reduced their strength, and granted the Moslems the victory. I shall lead you on until God Almighty makes us the masters of all or part of the territories lying beyond them, and until we have subdued the countries which His immutable decrees have already allotted to us."

His own province was far from being at that time in a state of complete subjection. His first campaign was against the Berbers of Arwah, who made forays towards Cairouan. He overthrew them and took 1000 prisoners. These were the first Berber captives taken to Cairouan. Then he sent one of his sons against the tribes. His son was successful, and returned with 100,000 captives. He sent another son in another direction, who was successful, and returned with 100,000 captives. He himself went in a third direction, and was successful, and returned with another 100,000 captives. In all, upwards of 300,000 captives resulted from this campaign. The Caliph, we are told, would hardly believe it when he was informed that his fifth of the captives amounted to 60,000. Musa, encouraged by his success, despatched his troops farther and farther into the desert. The Western Berber tribes of the Hawara, the Zenatah Kotamah, and even as far south as the Senhajah, were in turn taken by surprise. He fought with them—in the words of his historian—"battles of extermination, he killed myriads of them, and made a surprising number of prisoners, with great booty of cattle, grain, and articles of dress." These conquests took place in the years 699 and 700 A.D. The fame of Musa spread so far and wide that all soldiers desired to serve under him in

Africa, and the numbers of his army increased so much that they were doubled. Conflict was constantly renewed with the more warlike of the desert tribes, but "God was pleased to permit that the Moslems should have everywhere the victory." By the year 702, Musa was joined by the van of the Egyptian army, and a great battle was then fought in the west, in which the Berbers were commanded by their famous king Koseylah. The Moslems were entirely victorious, and with the spoils there were taken from the Berbers "innumerable maidens inestimable by their beauty and accomplishments." The maidens were distributed amongst the soldiers as wives. This battle was the prelude of many further African conquests, including the conquest of the territory of Morrekosh. (The town of Morrekosh or Morocco was not founded till near the end of the eleventh century.)

The territory of Northern Africa being conquered, and Arab armies driving all before them to the southern edges of the desert, where, as will presently be seen, the harried tribes found refuge in the fruitful plains of Negroland, Musa turned his ambition to the sea. He ordered the building of a dockyard at Tunis, and himself sailed thither. From the moment of the completion of the dockyard the port of Tunis became "a place of safety for ships when the winds blew at sea and the waves were high." Musa ordered the construction of a hundred vessels, and in these preparations passed the remainder of the year 703.

In the year 704 all the best of his army embarked in an expedition which was called "The Expedition of the Nobles." They spoiled Sicily and returned safe.

In 705 another expedition against the Berbers was followed by their total submission. In the same year Syracuse was attacked by sea and spoiled. Three years afterwards Sardinia was attacked and immense spoil taken. A great expedition inland to the territory to the south of Morocco, lying on the slopes of the mountains between it and the desert, and commanding the western road to

Negroland, resulted in the submission of that country. There was also a sea expedition to Majorca, which was conquered.

By this time (708) Musa was fairly master by sea and land of the whole of North Africa from the Mediterranean to the borders of Negroland. His influence upon the Berber tribes whom he displaced or overthrew was twofold. One effect of his conquests was to drive them from their old habitations in the fruitful northern edge of the desert to find new habitations in the no less fruitful but already occupied southern edge, where to make room for them disturbance was necessarily produced among the existing black populations. The other effect was in an exactly opposite direction. It was to draw them into the circle of Arab influence and even to incorporate them with the nation of their conquerors. It is related of Musa that on his return to Egypt at a later period he was on one occasion asked by the Sultan to describe the various peoples whom he had conquered. It came to the turn of the Berbers, and of them he said: "The Berbers, O Commander of the Faithful, are of all foreign nations the people who resemble most the Arabs in impetuosity, corporal strength, endurance, military science, generosity, only that they are, O Commander of the Faithful, the most treacherous people upon earth." The Berbers themselves had various traditions purporting to show that they were sprung from the same stock as the Arabs. It has already been seen that the innumerable maidens who were taken with the spoils of Musa's many conquests were regarded as "inestimable by their beauty and accomplishments," and were distributed among his soldiers for wives. Musa's own sons had sons by Berber wives who rose to high repute. But it was not only by intermarriage, nor by the revival of traditions of a common stock, that the two races were mixed. It was also Musa's habit to spend the immense sums with which the Sultan rewarded his victories largely in the purchase of captured Berbers. This he did, his biographer relates, in the interests of religion. "Whenever after a victory there were a number of slaves put up for sale, he used to buy all those who, he thought, would willingly embrace Islam, who were of noble origin, and who looked, besides, as if they were active young men. To these he first proposed the embracing of Islam, and if, after cleansing their understanding and making them fit to receive the sublime truths, they were converted to the best of religions, and their conversion was a sincere one, he would then, by way of putting their abilities to trial, employ them. If they evinced good dispositions and talents he would instantly grant them their liberty, appoint them to high commands in his army, and promote them according to their merits." If they showed no good dispositions, he returned them to the common stock of captives belonging to the army.

The effect of such a system in bringing about an amalgamation of the two races and in inducing the acceptance of Mohammedanism by the Berbers does not need to be insisted upon. The races became by degrees so mixed that in many cases the Berber could hardly be distinguished from the Arab nor the Arab from the Berber. In all that was subsequently done by the Arabs leading Berbers had their share.

The amalgamation of the Arab and the Berber peoples, which could not have taken place but for the similarity in their dispositions noted by Musa, was very shortly to be illustrated in that conquest of Spain which has left Musa's name enshrined in the sacred places of Arab history.

Having assured himself of the necessary command of the sea, Musa sent ' the Berber Tarik, one of his freedmen," to possess himself of Tangiers and the strong places of the neighbouring districts with a view to crossing over into Spain. Tarik accordingly marched thither and took the strong places and cities of those Berbers. This being done, Tarik wrote to his master, "Musa, I have found here six vessels." Musa told him to take them and to sail for Spain. Tarik did so in the year 710, and was joined by Musa himself in the year 711. As is well known, the mountain by which the expedition entered Europe bears to this day the name of the military commander—the Mountain of Tarik, Jebr el Tarik or Gibraltar—while the spot, a little further along the coast, on which a lesser detachment landed, is known as Tarifa from the name of its leader Tarif, another of Musa's Berber freedmen. What is not perhaps so generally recognised is that the men who led this civilising expedition into Spain were of the same race as those who, driven by the same compelling cause to another fate, carried the banner of civilisation into Negroland. The capacity for taking high command which Musa recognised in the Berbers was a capacity of race which was sure to find its satisfaction under circumstances of the most diverse kind. North or south, it mattered ittle in which direction they were forced by the resistless, pressure of a higher fate. Alike in Spain and Negroland, where they went in misfortune they were to remain in triumph, until that mysterious decadence which attends the fate of peoples marked them for decay.

CHAPTER III

ARAB CIVILISATION IN SPAIN

THE fascinating story of the conquest of Spain by the Arabs and of the development of a civilisation far in advance of anything known at the time to Western Europe, lies outside the scope of this book. Yet the history of Negroland and of Spain were in their early days so closely interwoven through the links of the Arab and Berber connection that the records of Arab civilisation are not altogether foreign to the history of West Africa.

The conquest took place at the beginning of the eighth century, and was for all ordinary purposes complete. It was carried out almost entirely by Berber troops whom Musa continued to convert, to organise, and to draft into Spain. Tangiers, which had always been a Berber stronghold, became for this purpose his military headquarters, and he was enabled perpetually to recruit his conquering armies with fresh troops. Tarik took 12,000 of these converts with him on his first landing. There was a tradition lingering from the Greek occupation of the country that Spain would be conquered only "by two nations composed of peoples unaccustomed to the luxuries of life, hardened by privation and fatigue." The Arabs and the Andalusians alike translated the prophecy to apply to the Arabs and the Berbers. "For a long period," says one of their historians, "the Berbers and Andalusians had hated each other across the Straits, but Berbers being more in want of Andalusians than these were of them, owing to certain necessaries not to be procured in Africa, which were imported from Andalus, communication necessarily existed between the people of both countries." The Berbers had long wanted Spain: Spain had long feared the Berbers. The conquest of Spain was therefore to some extent regarded as a fulfilment of the destiny of both nations.

But while the Berbers claimed to be of the same stock as the Arabs, and were admitted, as has been seen, to some degree of comradeship, they were at a very inferior stage of civilisation. The sense of difference of the cultivated Arabs was expressed by a comic poet, who suffered under a subsequent Berber dynasty for his readiness of speech. "I saw Adam in my dream," he makes one of his characters declare, "and I said to him, 'Oh, Father of Mankind! Men generally agree that the Berbers are descended from thee.' 'Yes,' replied Adam, 'it is true, but none dispute that Eve was at that time divorced from me.'" Brothers, but brothers of divorce, very fairly represents the relation which for a long time existed between Berber and Arab.

Shortly after the whole of Spain was reduced there was a general Arab migration to it, and it was with this Arab migration that the high civilisation came. For about fifty years the Berbers in fitful revolution struggled against the Arabs for the sole possession of a country which they claimed that they and they alone had won. The conflict between the dynasties of the Ommeyades and the Abbassides in the East gave opportunities for the disaffected in Spain. But about the middle of the eighth century, when the Abbassides succeeded in overthrowing the dynasty of the Ommeyades in the East and possessing themselves of the Caliphate, one son of the Ommeyades escaped into North Africa, and, after many adventures, established himself under the name of Abdurrahman I. upon the throne of his fathers in Spain. He ascended the throne in 757, thus separating the Caliphate of the East from the Caliphate of the West, and brilliantly opened the chapter of cultivated Arab rule in the West.

The dynasty of the Ommeyades lasted in Spain for upwards of two hundred and fifty years, and may be thought of as coming to an end, in power at least, about the year 1000 A.D.; when, after an interval of misrule, it was succeeded in the latter part of the eleventh century, that is, shortly after the Norman conquest of England, by the purely Berber dynasty of the Almoravides. During the first two centuries of the rule of the Ommeyades the Arab dominion in Spain reached its highest point. The court of Abdurrahman and his successors became the centre of all the art, the learning, the refinement, and the elegance of the known world. Commerce brought to the shores of Spain the best productions of every land. Science was honoured. Arab travellers penetrated to the furthest limits of the Eastern hemisphere. All that India and China had to teach was known to them.

They had a common saying that "Science came down from heaven and lodged itself in three different parts of man's body: in the brain among the Greeks; in the hands among the Chinese; and in the tongue among the Arabs." Unfortunate in the fate that subsequently befell them, the Arabs were fortunate in this, that during the period of their prosperity they had historians and poets capable of preserving for posterity records of the high level of civilisation that was reached. Religious fanaticism, which made a duty at a later period of sweeping the infidel out of Spain, made it no less a matter of conscience to destroy the admirable literature which centuries of enlightenment had amassed in the libraries of his forefathers. Fortunately, however, the writings were so copious that many escaped destruction, and the industry of modern research has brought again to light learning which was indignantly rejected by the religious Europe of the Middle Ages.

To appreciate in any degree the debt which Europe owes to the Arab civilisation of Spain, we have to remember the condition of barbarous ignorance, sloth, and superstition in which the Continent was plunged after the break-up of the Roman Empire. What the Berber was to North Africa, such was the Scythian, in the many divisions of Goths, Gauls, Huns, &c., to Europe. What the cultivated northern strip lying between the mountains and the sea was to North Africa, such on the Continent of Europe was the strip lying also between the mountains and the sea which is known to us under the names of Italy, Spain, and Greece. To both these famous districts the Mediterranean had given life and the mountains defence. Beyond the mountains, equally on the north and on the south, countless hordes of nomads unacquainted with the gentler arts of civilisation, but vigorous and active in their barbarism, awaited nothing but the opportunity of conquest. The Scythians and the Berbers were, in their original condition, pastoral tribes of migratory habits, feeding exclusively on meat and milk, and clothing themselves in the skins of animals. Of many of them it is said that they had never even seen bread ; this, as well on the plains of Europe and Asia as in the African desert. They had no dwelling-houses and no domestic arts. Leather tents or straw huts served all their temporary purpose. But they were hardy, abstemious, expert riders, brave, brutal, and proficient in all the ruder military virtues. Nothing strikes the student of Berber history more than the resemblance to be noted between the characteristics of the Berber tribes and the descriptive traits recorded by Tacitus, and quoted by Gibbon from earlier authors, of the primitive inhabitants of Northern Europe. The cannibalism which distinguished the extreme barbarism of Africa was not wanting, as we know, among the aboriginals of Northern Germany.

In Europe the decadence of Rome and the downfall of the Byzantine Empire gave opportunity for the northern tribes to possess themselves of all the outlying territories of the Empire, and from the forced wedlock of decadence and barbarism the states of modern Europe took their rise.

In Africa the strong intellectual impulse of the Jews and Saracens dominated the brute forces of barbarism by which it was surrounded, and the southern tribes, instead of conquering, became the instruments of conquest directed by a higher mind. While Europe fell to the level of her conquerors, Arabian civilisation rose, and, spreading through Africa to Spain, it maintained for the Western world the moral ideals and the intellectual enlightenment which, without the refuge afforded them in Spain, had perhaps been wholly lost.

Medieval Arabian achievements in the higher paths of learning are well known. There is no branch of scientific development among the Western nations upon which the Arabs have not set their mark, either by original research, or by the service which they rendered in transmitting to their European posterity the learning accumulated by other generations in other lands. They initiated the Renaissance in Europe by preserving and translating at a much earlier period the great works of the Greeks. They gave a vivifying impulse to all the intellectual life of the West by introducing to it the hoarded knowledge of the East. In mathematics they imported much from India, amongst other things the numerals known to us as "Arabic" numerals, and with them the advantages of the decimal system. The word cypher, with all its derivations, is an Arabic word. They translated from the Greek Euclid and the earlier geometers; but it was to the original studies of an Arab geometer—Ben Musa—of the ninth century, that Europe owed its use of the improved science to which the Arabs gave its modern name of algebra. Ben Musa was the inventor of the common method of solving quadratic equations, as well as of the substitution of sines for chords in trigonometry. His system was the system commonly adopted by the Arab schools. The Arabs were ardent students of mathematics, and a long list of astronomers and physicists, from Al Maimon, who determined the obliquity of the ecliptic in 830; through Ebn Junis, who constructed the Hakemite tables of the stars in 1008; Avicenna, the well-known physician and philosopher, who wrote, amongst other things, in the early part of the eleventh century, an encyclopædia of human knowledge in twenty volumes;

Al Gazzali, who in 1058 was the forerunner of Descartes; Al-Hazen, the optician, who established the modern theory of vision, basing it on clear anatomical and geometrical evidence, and who was the first to trace, about the year 1100, the curvilinear path of rays of light through the air, deducing from his theory of refraction a determination of the height of the atmosphere; to El Idrisi, the geographer of Roger of Sicily; the famous Averrhöes, the commentator of Aristotle, who lived at the end of the twelfth century; and the brilliant schools of medicine and surgery which adorned the thirteenth century: all serve to demonstrate that in the application of the abstract principles of science to natural phenomena, the Arabs luminously opened the path of modern progress. Their studies in chemistry were profound. Geber, or Djajar, who lived in the ninth century, and of whom Roger Bacon speaks at a much later period as the *magister magistrorum* of chemical science, was the first to describe nitric acid and *aqua regia*. Before him chemistry had no stronger acid than concentrated vinegar. The properties and preparation of sulphuric acid and phosphorus soon followed. For the composition of gunpowder we get towards the end of the eighth century the following prescription: "Pulverise on a marble mortar one pound of sulphur, two of charcoal, and six of saltpetre." Any one who may have visited the royal gunpowder works at Waltham Abbey will know how little the prescription has altered, except in varying proportions, to the present day. In geology, also, Arabian investigations were on the sound path of reason. Avicenna says of mountains that they may be due to two different causes. "Either they are the effect of upheavals of the crust of the earth . . . or they are the effect of water which, cutting for itself a new route, has denuded the valleys, the strata being of different kinds—some soft, some hard." The Arabs were early acquainted with the properties of the magnet and the theory of gravitation. True conceptions of geology and astronomy led naturally to truer conceptions of the age of the earth and the lapse of historic time than have ever prevailed before the scientific era of the present day.

History and geography were no less brilliantly represented than the natural sciences. Ibn Said, who wrote in the middle of the thirteenth century, has preserved for us a vivid description of the attainments of the Arabs of Spain. There is no department of science or literature in which he does not claim pre-eminence for them, and supports his claim by lists of names, strange now to the European ear, but, if we may judge by the manner in which they are introduced, familiar enough to the learned of his time. Ibn Said himself is described by his successors as "the truthful historian." He was the descendant of a line of distinguished men, and tells us that the history of Andalusia, which he carried down to the year 1247, had taken no less than 125 years to write and six authors tc complete it. It was conceived and carried to a certain stage by his great-grandfather; it was taken further by his grandfather; his two great-uncles worked upon it; then "came my father Musa, who certainly was the most learned and experienced of all my ancestors in these matters"; finally, Ibn Said himself completed the work. It is said that a better history of Andalusia was never written. Contemporary with the earlier part of this composition was the geography of El Idrisi, who wrote about the year 1153. Nearly the whole of this work is still extant. For the purpose of contrasting the state of knowledge of Arabic Spain with the ignorance of the Christian countries of the North, who had yet to wait nearly four hundred years for a true knowledge of the conformation of the earth, the following passage from it may be quoted:—

"What results from the opinion of philosophers, learned men, and those skilled in observation of the heavenly bodies, is that the world is round as a sphere, of which the waters are adherent and maintained upon its surface by natural equilibrium. It is surrounded by air, and all created bodies are stable on its surface, the earth drawing to itself all that is heavy in the same way as a magnet attracts iron. The terrestrial globe is divided into two equal parts by the equinoctial line. The circumference of the earth is divided into 360 degrees each of 25 parasangs. This is the Indian calculation. . . . From the equinoctial line to each pole there are 90 degrees, but there is no habitable land farther north than the 64th degree." The earth, he says elsewhere, is essentially round, but not of a perfect rotundity, being somewhat depressed at the poles. His description of the countries upon the earth, including England to the west and China to the east, is extraordinarily full, and in many essential particulars remains accurate to the present day. America alone appears to have been unknown to the Arabs, and when we remember that modern Europe had to wait for the journey of Magellan round the world in the opening years of the sixteenth century to be quite sure of the shape of the globe, we must admit that in the learning of the Arabs of Spain, Negroland had sources of information far purer than any of which England at that time could boast.

In every branch of science the theoretic conquests of the Arabs gave practical results. Spectacles and telescopes resulted from their study of optics. Ebn Junis, the astronomer, was the first to apply the pendulum about the year 1000 to the measure of time, and from his abstruse studies in astronomy clocks became a domestic possession. The use of the astrolabe and the compass, revived again at a later period in Europe, were common to Arab navigation. Gunpowder has already been mentioned as a result of chemistry, and military science was revolutionised by the introduction of artillery and firearms. Improvement in agriculture and the introduction and acclimatisation of new plants were an even more important result of the same study, combined with that of botany, to which the Arabs were passionately addicted. Studies in the effects of drugs and the nature of plants were the basis of their medicine, while physiology and anatomy gave to their surgical schools the wide renown which they enjoyed.

For seven centuries the medical schools of Europe owed everything they knew to Arabian research. The Arabic impression is still to be traced in the derivation of such words as syrup, julep, &c. Vivisection as well as dissection of dead bodies was practised in their anatomical schools, and women as well as men were trained to perform some of the most delicate surgical operations. Their studies of the functions of the human body and the cure of its diseases enabled them to establish hygienic systems which were perhaps among the greatest of the many boons which they conferred upon medieval Europe. Every court and household of importance had at one time its Jewish or Saracen physician. Amongst other very eminent names may be quoted for surgery Albucasis of Cordova, and for medicine Ibn Zohr.

Ibn Zohr, more generally known as Avenzoar, was regarded as the great authority in Moorish pharmacy. He lived in the first half of the twelfth century, and was contemporary of another and almost equally eminent physician, Al Far. A story is told of these two which is not without application to the dietetic controversies of the present day. Ibn Zohr was very fond of green figs, and ate them freely. Al Far never ate them, and he used to say to Ibn Zohr: "If you eat figs to that extent you will have a very bad abscess." Ibn Zohr replied: "If you don't eat them you will be subject to fever and die of constipation." Ibn Zohr was right. Al Far had fever and died of constipation. But Al Far was also right. Shortly after Al Far's death, Ibn Zohr was attacked by a bad abscess and died of it in Seville in 1161. The daughter and granddaughter of this Ibn Zohr were both accomplished female doctors. Avempace was another physician of the twelfth century whose reputation was European. Averrhöes, also deeply versed in medicine, was a personal friend of Ibn Zohr.

In the higher departments of jurisprudence and political economy, as well as in the literary fields of grammar, logic, poetry, and biography, the Arabian schools excelled. Their schools, colleges, and universities were the resort of the learned of all nations; but it was perhaps specially in the material development of their civilisation that their prosperity had its most direct effect in stimulating commercial intercourse with Negroland.

An Arab historian, writing in the sixteenth century, says of Cordova, where Abdurrahman I. established his court: "One thing is certain, namely, that trade and agriculture flourished in this place during the reigns of the sons of Ommeyah, in a degree which has scarcely been witnessed in any city of the world. Its market was always over-stocked with the fruits of the land, the productions of every district, and the best of every country. No robe, however costly, no drug, however scarce, no jewel, however precious, no rarity of distant and unknown lands, but was to be procured in the bazaar of Cordova, and found hundreds of purchasers." There were 471 mosques and 300 public baths, of which the numbers afterwards increased. One "trustworthy writer" counted the number of houses under the Caliph Al Mansur, and found 63,000 of the "great and noble, and 200,077 of the common people"; there were at the same time upwards of 80,000 shops. Water from the mountains was conveyed to the royal palace of Cordova, and "thence distributed through every corner and quarter of the city by means of leaden pipes into basins of different shapes, made of the purest gold, the finest silver, or plated brass, as well as into vast lakes, curious tanks, amazing reservoirs, and fountains of Grecian marble beautifully carved."

The town in the time of the Ommeyades measured twenty-four miles by six, the greater part of which area was covered by mosques, palaces, and the houses of the great standing in beautiful gardens. These houses were palaces of luxury, magnificently decorated, cooled in summer by ingeniously arranged draughts of fresh air drawn from the garden over beds of flowers chosen for their perfume, warmed in winter by hot air conveyed through pipes bedded in the walls. There were bath-rooms supplied with hot and cold water. There were boudoirs, drawing-rooms, libraries, halls, corridors, and galleries lighted by windows of clear and coloured glass. Clusters of columns of marble, either plain or incrusted with more precious substances, supported roofs of mosaic and gold. The walls were decorated with mosaics, or covered with arabesque and floral paintings. The furniture was of the most precious and varied description. It was made of sandal and citron and other woods brought from the tropics, and curiously inlaid with mother-of-pearl, ivory, silver, and gold. There were tables of gold, set with emeralds, rubies, and pearls. In winter the walls were hung with tapestry, the floors were covered with thick Persian carpets, of which the most magnificent were embroidered with gold and pearls. There were luxurious couches piled with pillows. Vases of porcelain and crystal were filled with flowers. Rare and curious objects from all parts of the world were brought together to satisfy the eye and taste. In the evening the rooms were lit by wax candles, which were distributed by groups of hundreds in chandeliers that hung from the ceilings. Great skill and taste were devoted to the design and workmanship of these chandeliers. They were often made from the metal found in the bells of Christian churches, and when this was the case, there seems to have been a special pleasure in designing them for use in the mosques. One famous chandelier is mentioned which held no less than 1804 candles. The gardens in which the great houses stood are described by every writer in terms of rapture. Bowers of roses; orange and pomegranate groves; shaded walks, over which lemon-trees were trained, so that the fruit when ripe "hung down like little lamps"; successions of colour and perfume, to procure which plants were brought from all parts of the world. Sometimes, to please a favourite wife, a whole hillside would be planted with her chosen colour. The use of water was thoroughly understood Fountains, cascades, and lakes gave coolness and moisture to the air, and also provided opportunities for the keeping of fish and the special cultivation of water-plants. Garden fruits and vegetables were cultivated in rare perfection and variety. In the gardens there were labyrinths, and marble playing-courts. There were menageries of curious animals, and aviaries of foreign birds. Botany, horticulture, zoology, and ornithology were passions no less of the learned than of the rich.

In the town of Cordova, for a distance of ten miles, the streets were lit at night by lamps placed close to one another. The descriptions of the mosques and buildings of Cordova—including the famous mosque with the 360 arches, and the even more famous palace of Azzahra, which took forty years to build, and contained the Hall of the Caliphs, roofed in pure gold, and lighted at will by fountains of quicksilver, which, when they were set in motion, caused the room "to look in an instant as if it were traversed by flashes of lightning"—are so elaborate as to fill many volumes. The size of the Azzahra palace may be imagined from the fact that it had 15,000 doors. It had amongst its many beauties remarkable fountains and terraces of polished marble, which overhung "matchless gardens." It was filled with works of art, and, according to one writer, it was such that "travellers from distant lands, men of all ranks, following various religions, princes, ambassadors, merchants, pilgrims, theologians, and poets, who were conversant with edifices of this kind, and had surveyed this, all agreed that they had never seen in the course of their travels anything that could be compared to it."

The other cities of the Arabs in Spain were no less remarkable. In the garden of one of the palaces of Toledo there was an artificial lake, in the centre of which there was a kiosk of stained glass adorned with gold. "The architect so contrived this that by certain geometrical rules the water of the lake was made to ascend to the top of the dome, and then, dropping at both sides, join the waters of the lake. In this room the Sultan could sit untouched by the water, which fell everywhere round him, and refreshed the air in the hot season. Sometimes, too, wax tapers were lighted within the room, producing an admirable effect on the transparent walls of the kiosk." It is worth remembering that glass was not introduced into English domestic architecture until the reign of Queen Elizabeth, and that the period at which this kiosk is described was contemporary with the Saxon Heptarchy.

Seville, with its famous gardens, its noble squares, its great observatory, its suspension bridge, was regarded as one of the most important of Arab towns. Granada was the Damascus of Andalusia, very famous under the Almohade Sultans. Malaga, with its numerous towers, had the advantages of land and sea. It was famous very early in its history for the manufacture of forbidden wine. Its oil and its figs were known all over the world, so were its silks, especially the brocades, for which it had beautiful designs. Its export trade extended to India and China. Almeria was another of the rich coast towns. It had a dockyard in which very fine vessels were built. It was, according to an Arab author, Ash-shakandi, the "greatest mart in Andalusia: Christians of all nations came to its port to buy and sell, and they had factories established in it, where they loaded their vessels with such goods as they wanted, owing to which, and to its being a very opulent and large city, filled with passengers and merchants, the produce of the tithe imposed upon the goods and paid by the Christian merchants amounted to very considerable sums, and exceeded that collected in any other seaport."

Almeria gained this trade largely by its famous manufactures of silk, and especially of brocades and damasks and tissues of gold and silver. Thousands of hands were engaged in each branch of the silk trade. It was also famous for the manufacture of pottery and glass and what we should in the present day call hardware. Ships from the East brought to its ports all the finest wares of India and China. "Almeria," says the author already quoted, "is an opulent and magnificent city, whose fame has spread far and wide. God has endowed its inhabitants with various gifts, such as a temperate climate and abundance of fruits; they are handsome, well-made, good-natured, very hospitable, very much attached to their friends, and are above all things very refined in their manners, and very elegant in their dress. Its coast is the finest in all the Mediterranean as well as the safest and the most frequented." Its inhabitants were said to be the wealthiest in all Andalusia, and they would appear to have somehow solved the problem of creating a manufacturing town without loss of beauty, for all authors vie with one another in extolling the charm and picturesqueness of the town. It had no less than a thousand public baths, and for forty miles the course of the river, "which contributed no little to the ornament of the city and the environs," was "through orchards, gardens, and groves, where singing birds delight with their harmony the ears of the traveller."

All the towns of the Arabs had public gardens planted with groves of fine orange, pomegranate, and other trees, of which the remains are still to be seen in the Alamedas of Southern Spain. Abdurrahman I. was "passionately fond of flowers." He planted beautiful gardens, to which he brought all kinds of rare and exotic plants and fine trees from foreign countries. He introduced good systems of irrigation. His passion for flowers and plants led him to send agents to Syria, India, and other countries with a commission to procure him all sorts of seeds and plants, many of which he successfully acclimatised in the royal gardens, and this custom, followed by his successors and adopted by the rich, led to the introduction of many fruits and plants previously unknown even to cultivated Rome. Among these, cotton, rice, the sugar-cane, the pomegranate, and the peach may be mentioned, but many of our garden vegetables have also come to us from the same source. It may be worth noting that the peach, to which we are in the habit of attributing a Persian origin, was found by the Persians, according to Strabo, in the eastern part of Negroland, where it was cultivated by the Ethiopians at the period of the conquest of Egypt by Cambyses. It does not seem to be native to Negroland, and the presumption is that it may have been introduced into the valley of the Nile from India. Nevertheless we may accept it as a pleasant fruit of the early intercourse of Egypt with Negroland.

Among the vegetables which we owe to the Arab passion for gardening is asparagus. This was introduced somewhat later than the peach by a certain courtier and epicure of the name of Zaryab, who came to Andalusia in 821. This Zaryab, who, like Tarik, Tarif, and others, was a freedman, was a celebrated musician. He improved the lute, adding a fifth string to the four which up to his time had sufficed, and founded a great school of music. He was renowned throughout Spain, enjoyed a public pension, and on one occasion, when he came to Cordova, the Sultan himself, to show the respect which he held to be due to talent, rode out to meet him. Zaryab appears to have been a remarkable as well as an extraordinarily popular person. He was not only talented but learned. He was an astronomer and geographer. He had a prodigious memory. "He was, moreover, gifted with so much penetration and wit, he had so deep an acquaintance with the various branches of polite literature, he possessed in so eminent a degree the charms of polite conversation and the talents requisite to entertain an audience . . . that there never was either before or after him a man of his profession who was more generally beloved and admired. Kings and great people took him for a pattern of manners and education, and his name became for ever celebrated among the inhabitants of Andalusia."

Zaryab, who is worth quoting individually as having been evidently a leader of fashion in the most civilised court of Europe in the early half of the ninth century, appears to have disdained no detail of daily life. Asparagus is not the only dish which he added to the menus of his day. He was fastidious about cooking, and invented many good things. He also introduced the fashion of being served on crystal instead of on gold or silver, with other refinements of the table. The manufacture of glass was introduced into Spain by an Arab of the name of Furnas at about this period. Zaryab also set the fashion of changing dress for four seasons of the year instead of for only two, as was the custom before his day. The curious in such matters may read in the Arab chronicles what was worn—silks and muslins, wadded clothes and furs, according to the time of year. The ladies were also extremely fond of jewels, and wore even jewelled shoes, for which they would give as much as £120 a pair. But in dress as in food, Zaryab specially valued the refinement of cleanliness. Before his time the Kings of Andalusia, we are told, used to have their clothes washed in water of roses and other garden flowers, the consequence of which was that they never looked quite clean. Zaryab taught them a method in which, by adding salt to the mixture, "the linen could be made clear and white." The chronicle gravely records that the "experiment having been tried, every one approved of it," and Zaryab was much praised for the invention. It was the reputation of the Arabs that they were "the cleanest people upon earth" in all that related to their person, dress, beds, and the interior of their houses. Indeed, we are told, "they carried cleanliness so far that it was not an uncommon thing for a man of the lower classes to spend his last coin in soap instead of buying food for his daily consumption, and thus go without his dinner rather than appear in public in dirty clothes." By way of contrast in habits we may recall certain Irish earls, who, towards the end of the Desmond rebellion about 1581, are described as sleeping with their ladies and all their servants in a hall so dirty as to be "not fit for a hog cote," while the only toilet that the ladies made in the morning was "to get up and shake their ears." Zaryab flourished some seven centuries before the ladies whose toilet was so simple. He was the contemporary of Egbert and Charlemagne.

The contrast between Arab civilisation and the civilisation of Northern Europe of that date is sharply accentuated by the fact that, while the literature of the Arabs was such as to remain for our instruction to this day, Charlemagne, the greatest monarch of the West, could not write. Spain under the Arabs truly deserved, as we have seen, its name as the "noble repository" of learning. One of the four principal things in which Cordova was said to surpass all other cities was "the sciences therein cultivated." It was reputed to be the city of the earth where the greatest number of books was to be found, One of the Ommeyade Sultans was "so fond of books that he is said to have converted Andalusia into a great market whereto the literary productions of every clime were brought immediately for sale." He also collected round him, and employed in his own palace, the most skilful men of his time in binding, transcribing, and illuminating books. He amassed such literary treasures as no sovereign before or after him, to the knowledge of his biographers, had ever possessed. It is said of him that he was so fond of reading that he preferred the pleasure of perusing his books to all the enjoyments which royalty could afford. He himself wrote a voluminous history of Andalusia. His collection of books founded the great library of Cordova, which remained until the taking of the city by the Berbers in A.D. 1010. The catalogue alone consisted of forty-four volumes.

Every wealthy man in Cordova had his own library. To such an extent did this rage for collection increase, says Ibn Said, that any man in a prominent position considered himself obliged to have a library of his own, and would spare no trouble or expense in collecting books. Books were an expensive luxury too. A story is told of a certain writer, richer in learning than in other goods, greatly desiring a book, and watching for it daily in the market till it came, "a beautiful copy, elegantly written." He immediately bid for it and increased his bidding, but to his great disappointment he was outbid, though the price was beyond the value of the book. The book went to his competitor. He approached to congratulate the learned owner, but the man who had acquired it said: "I am no Doctor; neither do I know what the contents of the book are; but I am making a library, and there is a vacant space which, as my means are ample, I resolved to fill with this volume." The reader echoes with sympathy the reply of the Doctor: "It is ever so; he gets the nut who has no teeth."

Cordova was not singular in its literary reputation. All the great towns had good libraries, and the Arabs in Andalusia had a handwriting of their own which they adopted at some period subsequent to their arrival in Spain. It has already been mentioned that one of the distinctions by which it has been made possible to learned French research to trace the different origin of the civilisation of Eastern and Western Negroland is the employment of the Eastern alphabet of Arabia and Egypt in the one, and the Western alphabet of Morocco and Spain in the other. In addition to the geometricians, astronomers, geographers, mechanicians, botanists, chemists, physicians, who appear to have collected all that was known in Asia as well as Europe, and who wrote voluminously—the works of many of them amounting to fifty and sixty volumes—every branch of literature was represented. There were histories, essays, poems; there were treatises upon arithmetic, grammar, poetry, rhetoric, canon and civil law, jurisprudence, logic. Lists of distinguished writers have been preserved in biographical dictionaries which have escaped destruction, and it is therefore possible to some extent to reconstruct the intellectual life of the day. It would appear to have been active, charming, polished. The Arabs claimed for their children and their women that they had a natural gift for poetry, narrative, and repartee. They appear to have had a sufficient number of poets to furnish matter for biographies of poets, of which one is mentioned as having been in ten volumes. Philosophy, theology, metaphysics, were richly represented, and fiction was not neglected.

The minor arts, as we have seen, were warmly encouraged. Seville, which was the special home of music, had a large export trade in musical instruments, which it sent to Africa. In this town it was said that every musical instrument was to be obtained. Toledo was the centre of steel and metal work. In Cordova, the famous Cordovan leather, of which the skins were imported from Negroland, was worked into many designs and extensively used in beautiful book bindings. All the arts to which elaborate architecture and luxurious domestic life gave rise were, of course, highly developed. Painting appears to have been restricted chiefly to decorative work, but we are repeatedly told that the palaces of southern Spain were filled with works of art.

It is interesting to note that in the great days of Mohammedan Spain, Arabian women were not confined, as in the East, to harems, but appeared freely in public and took their share in all the intellectual, literary, and even scientific movements of the day. Women held schools in some of the principal towns. There were women poets, historians, and philosophers, as well as women surgeons and doctors.

A national life, so varied and active, having a commerce which reached to the confines of the known world, naturally drew material for its consumption from every source with which it was acquainted. Negroland offered to Saracen Spain many of the same sources of supply which our tropical colonies offer to us, and it will presently be seen how deeply the development of Negroland was affected by the high civilisation of the Peninsula.

CHAPTER IV

THE EMPIRE OF "THE TWO SHORES"

THE dynasty of the Ommeyades lasted nominally in Spain until the year 1031; but the visible decay of its power may be placed about the year 1000.

Abdurrahman III., one of the greatest of the Western Caliphs, reigned for fifty years, between the dates of 911 and 961 A.D. He was the first to assume the title of Commander of the Faithful in the West, and his reign may be taken as marking the highest epoch of Mohammedan authority in Europe. The Christian nations of the North represented to the Mohammedans of that day nothing more than barbarism, and in levying successful war upon them, Abdurrahman took the place of the champion of civilisation. Every year he renewed his attacks. He carried war by land across the Pyrenees, and his fleets dominated the Mediterranean.

"In this manner," says his chronicler, "the Moslems subdued the country of the Franks beyond the utmost limits reached during the reigns of his predecessors. The Christian nations beyond the Pyrenees extended to him the hand of submission, and their kings sent costly presents to conciliate his favour. Even the kings of Rome, Constantinople, Germany, Sclavonia, and other distant parts, sent ambassadors asking for peace and suspension of hostilities, and offering to agree to any conditions which he should dictate." The most elaborate receptions were accorded to these embassies, and it is rather interesting to note incidentally in a description of the reception of the embassy from Constantinople, which took place with extraordinary magnificence in the year 949, that amongst other things brought by the ambassadors there was a letter enclosed in a gold case, with a portrait of the Emperor Constantine, "admirably executed" in stained glass.

Abdurrahman, moved, it is said, by the consideration that he could not afford to have any hostile power so close to the borders of Spain as Western Africa, subdued also a great portion of Africa. He thus established the power of the Western Caliphate from the borders of Negroland to the Pyrenees, and this double kingdom was known by the name of Adouatein, or "The Two Shores." In the course of all his wars he suffered but one serious defeat, and he had the surname of "the Victorious." "Never," it is said, "was the Mohammedan Empire more prosperous than during his reign. Commerce and agriculture flourished; the sciences and arts received a new impulse, and the revenue was increased tenfold." It was under this Abdurrahman that cotton manufacture was first established in Europe in the year 930. The Arabs also introduced the art of printing calicoes from wooden blocks.

Abdurrahman is described as the mildest and most enlightened sovereign that ever ruled. His meekness, his generosity, and his love of justice became proverbial. None of his ancestors surpassed him in courage in the field; he was fond of science, and the patron of the learned, with whom he loved to converse, spending those hours that he stole from the arduous labours of the administration in literary meetings, to which all the eminent poets and learned men of his court were admitted.

It is an interesting comment on this half-century of glory and prosperity that, after Abdurrahman's death, a paper was found in his own handwriting, in which those days that he had spent in happiness were carefully noted down, and, on numbering them, they were found to amount to fourteen!

Before the nominal end of the Ommeyade dynasty a usurper, Al Mansur, "called in Berbers and Zenatahs, whom he divided into companies according to their tribes," and made himself Sultan. Al Mansur became one of the great Caliphs, and established a splendid dominion in Western Africa. But the fact that he was a usurper held in power by African tribes introduced a dangerous element of disruption into the body-politic of the Caliphate in Spain. The Berbers of Africa began to recognise their power. The descendants of the original Berbers who, with the Arabs, had effected the conquest of Spain, were growing soft with the pleasures and the luxury of a high civilisation. Their ruder brothers in Africa had kept their vigour, and began to realise the possibilities which it opened to them. A great African revolt was organised, the result of which was that Al Mansur gave Fez in sovereignty to the Berber chiefs of the Zenatah tribes, together with a good bit of Western Africa, including the southern province of what we now call Morocco. Side by side with the dominion of the Caliphs, local sovereignties in Africa acquired importance, and the ambitions thus partially gratified were not long limited to Africa.

Al Mansur died in 1002, and Arab historians are in practical agreement that from this time the Mohammedan Empire in Spain began to show signs of decay. Perpetual claimants of the throne of the Caliphs employed African troops in Spain. Between 1020 and 1030 the whole of Andalusia submitted with revolts and civil wars to the Berbers. It became the habit of the reigning Caliph to employ a black bodyguard drawn from Negroland, and, instead of maintaining the old attitude of united hostility to the Christians on their northern borders, each faction in turn called in Christian help.

It was not long before the Christian armies dominated the situation. The limits of the Arab Empire became narrower, and the power of the Caliphs was broken. Cordova, Granada, Malaga, Seville, became separate principalities. Here is a view of the situation as presented by an Arab historian of the sixteenth century: "In Africa as well as in Andalusia the possessions of the

Ummeyah were broken up into petty provinces, thus giving an opportunity to the cruel enemy of God to attack in detail the divided Moslems, and to expel them at last from those countries which they had so long held in their power." Alfonso VI. took Toledo in 1081. In the following year Al Mutammed, the Arab king of Seville, refused to pay him tribute, and Alfonso swore to drive the Arabs into the sea at Gibraltar. In this extremity Al Mutammed looked across the straits for help, and Africa once more intervened directly in the affairs of Spain.

To understand the position which had been reached in Africa, it is necessary to go back for a few years. It has been mentioned that of the two main roads by which communication between Negroland and Northern Africa was maintained, one lay across the western deserts in a direction almost due south of the territory now known as Morocco. The consequence of many wars in Northern Africa had been to force down certain Berber tribes upon the western confines of Negroland. "From time immemorial," says Ibn Khaldun, "the Molet-themim (or Wearers of the Veil) had been in the Sandy Desert. As brave as they were wild, they had never bowed under a foreign yoke. Having increased their numbers in the vast plains of the desert, they formed several tribes—the Goddala, the Lemtunah, the Messonfah, the Outzila, the Tuareg, the Zegowah, and the Lamta. These people were all brothers of the Senajah, who lived between the Atlantic and Ghadames," that is, in the western half of Northern Africa.

The Lemtunah were already a powerful nation obeying hereditary kings when the Ommeyade dynasty reigned in Spain, and the western portion of the desert over which they ruled was known as the "Desert Empire." At that time also the Negro nations of the West were very powerful, but at a later period, after the Lemtunahs had subdued the lesser tribes, the Western kingdom of the Negroes began to decay. The Lemtunah made war upon them and forced them partially to accept Islam. Under Tiloutan, a

Lemtunah king who died in the year 837, the Desert Empire reached its height. Twenty Negro kings paid tribute to him. It is said of his kingdom that the climate was so healthy that men commonly reached in it the age of eighty. The sons and successors of Tiloutan reigned successfully until the year 918, when the dynasty was overthrown by the Senajah. After this there was confusion mixed with conquest for about 120 years, until there came to the throne a Senajah ruler of the name of Yahya, under whom there took place a union of the tribes which resulted in the foundation of the Empire of Morocco.

In 1048 Yahya made the pilgrimage to Mecca, and brought back with him for the instruction of his people a religious teacher, Ibn Yasin. The united tribes had never wholly abandoned the nomad habits of their ancestors. They were a hardy, active people, who had kept the abstemious customs of the desert. Their principal wealth consisted in their flocks. They were among those of whom it was said that many of them passed their lives without ever seeing bread. They had long since embraced Islam, but they had apparently strayed from the true path, and the reformation preached by Ibn Yasin was stern. Severe penalties were imposed on wrong-doing. The man who told a lie was beaten with eighty strokes; the man who drank wine was beaten with eighty strokes; serious offences were more heavily punished; and every stranger who joined the sect was required to forfeit one-third of his property by way of redemption for any injustice by which he might have acquired the rest.

The pressure of these doctrines in application produced a revolt. Ibn Yasin with a few of his followers withdrew to an island in the Senegal, the river which formed the southern frontier of the Desert Kingdom. Here he practised in rigid seclusion all he taught. The fame of his doctrine spread through the West, and thousands flocked to him, till at last, seeing the number of his followers daily increase, he declared to them that it was not enough to accept the truth themselves, they must also constrain the world to accept it. He gave to his disciples the name of "Morabites," or "Champions of the Faith," afterwards known as "Al Moravides," and proceeded to preach a Holy War. To "maintain the truth, to repress injustice, and to abolish all taxes not based on law" was the formula of faith with which this religious movement started from the extreme south of the then known Western world. The Emir Yahya assumed command, and under his leadership the Almoravides began that triumphant march to the north which was to end only on the throne of Spain. Yahya died in 1056 after a successful campaign which established his power in South-Western Morocco. He was succeeded by his brother Abou Bekr, who led the Almoravides to further conquest. Their dominion spread across the Atlas Mountains to the sea, and they subdued all the territory to the western coast.

In 1061 dissensions breaking out amongst the tribes in the south, Abou Bekr returned to his Desert Kingdom, leaving his cousin Yusuf Tachefin in command in the north. This proved to be a final division. Abou Bekr succeeded in reconciling his unruly tribes, and to give an outlet to their energies he led them to the conquest of Negroland, the northern border of which he overran for a distance of ninety days' march from his own territory. This should have carried him to the Haussa States. But he returned no more to take command in the north. In the year 1062 Yusuf laid the foundation of the town of Morocco with his own hands, and not long afterwards declared the independence of the northern kingdom of which it was to become the capital. Abou Bekr acquiesced, and Yusuf, left to himself, continued the conquest of North-Western Africa. By the year 1082 he had long been the supreme ruler of that portion of the world. His court had begun to attract the learning and civilisation which civil war was driving out of Spain, and we are told that it was filled with Arabs from the frontier towns which had submitted to Alfonso. These men, "with tears in their eyes and sorrow in their hearts, had come to Yusuf to implore his protection." It was to this court and to this man that Al Mutammed of Seville came in 1083 to ask for help against the Christians.

Yusuf is described as a "wise and shrewd man, neither too prompt in his determinations, nor too slow in carrying them into effect." He had passed the greater part of his life in his native deserts exposed to hunger and privation, and had no taste for a life of pleasure. It is expressly said of him that he did not speak Arabic. When, therefore, he consented to cross over to Spain, and in the course of time drove back the Christians and established once more a supreme Sultan upon the throne of Andalusia, his conquest and the dynasty which he founded must be regarded as an African conquest and an African dynasty. The Almoravides ruling in Spain were identically the same race as that which, moving from the West, imposed Islam on the races of Negroland, and established kingdoms, of which we shall presently hear, along the courses of the Niger and the Senegal.

It is stated that when Yusuf crossed to Spain there was no tribe of the western desert that was not represented in his army, and it was the first time that the people of Spain had ever seen camels used for the purpose of mounting cavalry. Forming part of the army which fought at Zalakah in 1086 there were also some thousands of blacks armed with Indian swords and short spears, and shields covered with hippopotamus hide. This battle drove the Christian forces out of southern Spain and laid the foundation of Yusuf's Spanish Empire. When, after fighting it, Yusuf marched to Seville, the comforts and luxury of that town, far from raising in his mind the admiration and astonishment that might have been expected, impressed him with very different sentiments. His councillors and courtiers pointed out to him the advantages which power conferred in a civilised country. "It strikes me," he replied, "that this man (meaning the King of Seville) is throwing away the power which has been placed in his hands. Instead of giving his attention to the good administration and defence of his kingdom, he thinks of nothing else than satisfying the cravings of his passions."

Not long afterwards, when Yusuf had returned to Africa, his generals informed him that the whole of the fighting against the Christians was left to them, while the Kings of Andalusia remained sunk in pleasure and sloth. They asked for his instructions, and were ordered to conquer the Kings of Andalusia, and to appoint to every city or town as it fell into their power a governor from among the officers of Yusuf's army. Town after town fell to the army of the Almoravides, till Seville itself was taken, and the King sent a prisoner into Africa, where he died in 1095.

Yusuf died in 1106. His son succeeded to the Sultanate of North Africa and Spain; and the Almoravide dynasty continued to reign with a double court, one in Africa and one in Spain, the Sultan residing alternately in either until the African dominion was overthrown in 1142, and the Spanish dominion three years later, in 1145. The last Almoravide sovereign of Africa and Spain was, according to Ibn Khaldun, executed in the presence of the Almohade conqueror in 1147. During the whole of this period, as under the dynasty of the Ommeyades, intercourse between Spain and Negroland was freely maintained.

CHAPTER V

AFRICAN RULE IN SPAIN

ALTHOUGH the Almoravides on their first entrance into Spain came as reformers from the desert, preaching a stern doctrine of abnegation, they yielded rapidly to the seduction of Spanish luxury, and in little more than half a century they are spoken of by Arab historians as having become soft and effeminate like their predecessors. The probability is that the body of the Moors in Spain remained what they had been before the Almoravide invasion, and the course of history was not altered, but only delayed, by the African conquest.

In the same spirit of religious reform which had stirred the founder of the Almoravide sect, a Mahdi arose in the early part of the twelfth century in the northern provinces of Ifrikiah, and preached a doctrine so stringent that he excited a revolt among the populace, and was obliged to fly from the anger of the Sultan. He appeared first in Bugia in 1118, and preached his ascetic reforms in Telemçan, Fez, Mequinez, and Morocco. Everywhere he excited the anger of the people, and towards 1121 he withdrew into the desert, where gradually disciples began to join him in great numbers. The authorities persecuted him here also, and he then called upon the Mesmudian Berbers to rally to his cause, to defend his person, and to declare a Holy War in defence of the doctrine of the Unity of God. He declared himself to be the Mahdi, and he gave to his followers the title of Almohades or Unitarians. He entrenched himself in the Mountain of Tinmelel in the southern fastnesses of the Atlas chain, and this spot remained the stronghold of the sect until their final extinction as a political power about a hundred years later. The original Mahdi died in 1128, but this event had little effect upon the sect. In 1130 a war began between the Almohades and the Almoravides in Africa, which ended in 1147 by the capture of Morocco and the execution of the reigning Almoravide sovereign.

No sooner was the province of Morocco subdued than the Almohades crossed into Spain, and after a determined contest with the Christian armies, who were only with the greatest difficulty prevented from taking Cordova, Mussulman Spain swore fealty in 1150 to the Almohades. Thus for a second time a purely African dynasty reigned upon the most civilised throne of Europe. This same Almohade conqueror reconstructed the Moorish fleet, and added to it no less than 460 vessels. His reign, which lasted until 1163, was a period of constant war, during which he was compelled to put out all his strength against the Christians. He succeeded in holding his own with difficulty, and his successor united all the tribes of North Africa in a Holy War against the "infidels of Spain." It is curious to read in the Arab chronicles the history of the Crusades told from the other side. It will be remembered that the famous Saladin took Jerusalem in 1187. In 1189 this Caliph of the Eastern Arabs appealed to the reigning Almohade Caliph of the West, El Mansour, to assist with his maritime forces in the sieges of Acre, Tyre, and Tripoli, and according to one historian 180 ships sent by the African Sultan prevented the Christians from landing in Syria.

Under the great Almohade sovereigns the glory of the Arabs in Spain was well maintained. Monuments of their civil activity remain in the Castle of Gibraltar, which they built in 1160, and in the great mosque of Seville, which was begun in 1183. The Giralda or tower of Seville—not, alas! now perhaps to be spoken of as existing—was built as an observatory under the superintendence of the mathematician Geber in 1196. The Almoravides had fixed their Spanish Court at Seville. The Almohades imported to their African Court in Morocco workmen from all parts of Spain. Ibn Said describes Morocco in the thirteenth century as the "Baghdad of the West," and says that it was never so prosperous as under the early Almohades. Both dynasties had two courts, one in Africa and one in Spain. Thus, whatever was the prosperity or greatness of one part of their empire, it was shared by the other, and under the Almohades there was a shifting towards the African centre.

A good deal of jealousy seems to have existed between the natives of the "Two Shores" as to the merits of their respective territories. A certain distinguished citizen of Tangier, Abu Yahya, arguing on one occasion with the Sheikh Ash-shakandi of Cordova—who flourished under the later Almohades and died 1231—on the advantages of their respective countries, provoked Ash-shakandi to say: "Were it not for Andalusia, Africa, thy country, would never have been known." "Do you really mean," replied the African, "to say that excellency and power reside anywhere in such degree as amongst us? Prove it!" The Caliph, who was listening to the dispute, interposed. He said that it was too serious to be decided by extempore speaking, and ordered each disputant to put his views in writing. Hence the celebrated epistle of Ash-shakandi, written under the last of the Almohades, to which we are indebted for a great deal of contemporary information. It states the case for the civilisation of the Spanish half of the empire. Unfortunately the counter-statement of Abu Yahya, maintaining the claims of the African half, has not been preserved.

"He pretends to make Africa superior to Andalusia!" exclaims Ash-shakandi in derision of his opponent. "It is as much as to say that the left hand is better than the right, and that night is lighter than day." No claim is allowed to be based on the fact that the Sultans of the day kept their chief court in Africa. "We too," says Ash-shakandi, "have had our Sultans," and he speaks of the Ommeyades as "Sultans who succeeded each other as pearls in a necklace united by the thread." The break-up of their empire was as the cutting of the string. As the Ommeyades are the objects of his panegyric, so the Africans are of his disdain. Yusuf Tachefin, the founder of the Almoravides, owed his fame, he says, wholly to Al Mutammed, King of Seville. "Otherwise, I ask you, would he have been known, ignorant and rude Bedowi as he was?" Among the limitations of Yusuf it is recounted that on various occasions he jeered at the poets and their fine metaphors, declaring that he understood nothing of their writings except that the writers wanted bread! But Ash-shakandi proceeds: "Since Africa dares to dispute the superiority in the sciences, can you produce such men as these?" He then gives a list of scholars eminent in the ranks of science, philosophy, and literature, which is now valuable for the service it renders in rescuing the names of great men from oblivion and preserving a record of their works. This list contains geometers, philosophers, theologians, historians, men distinguished in philology, literature, geography, medicine, and all the natural sciences, also grammarians, musicians, poets, and orators. Ash-shakandi also distinguishes the scholar kings of the lesser courts of Spain, men who could still devote their minds with ardour to the study of science in the midst of all the tumult of civil war.

He proceeds to the description of Spain itself, its principal towns and monuments. Much that was said of Cordova in a previous chapter was taken from this epistle. Though himself a native of Cordova, he says of Seville, where the later court of the Almoravides and Almohades was fixed, that it was one of the finest cities of Spain, and praises at great length its magnificent buildings,—especially the famous mosque—its good streets, its spacious dwelling-houses,—of which the courtyards were planted with orange, citron, lemon, and other fruit-trees—and its generally excellent arrangements. The river at Seville was navigable for large vessels, and was always filled with pleasure boats kept by the inhabitants of the town, "who were very luxurious and dissipated." It was held to be a delightful boating river. The environs of Seville were very picturesque—olives, figs, and sugar-cane abounded, and the banks of the river were covered with fruit-trees "forming a sort of canopy, so that it was possible to sail sheltered from the rays of the sun, and listening to the melody of singing-birds along the banks." The river ran for a course of thirty miles through clusters of buildings and farmhouses, high towers and strong castles, forming a continued city. The mildness of the temperature, the purity of the air, the abundance of provisions and commodities which were to be found in its markets, made it an agreeable place of residence. There was a saying, common in Andalusia, "If thou seekest for bird's milk, by Allah! thou shalt find it in Seville." The love of music of its inhabitants has been already mentioned. They were, Ash-shakandi says, "the merriest people upon earth, always singing, playing on instruments, and drinking wine, which among them is not considered forbidden so long as it is used with moderation." Amongst its many manufactures Seville was as famous for oil as Malaga was for wine. Beja, a town in its territory, was famous for its cotton manufactures.

Other Spanish towns—Granada with its magnificent chestnut trees, Toledo, Valencia rich in trade and noted for the paper manufactories of Xatina in its neighbourhood; Jaen, so famous for its silk manufactures that it was called "Jaen of the Silk"; Murcia, Xeres, Malaga, Lisbon, each famous for their special products; Saragossa, afterwards the seat of Empire of the Huddites, in which there was a wonderful palace with a golden hall of extraordinary beauty of design and workmanship, and many more, are described by Ash-shakandi in detail enough to present a vivid picture of the wealth, importance, and refinement of civilisation which distinguished the Spain of the thirteenth century. If his opponents in the literary contest had anything like the same account to give of the African half of the Arab Empire, the condition of this portion of the Western world under the African dynasties which administered it for nearly two hundred years, must have been extraordinarily prosperous.

We may add to Ash-shakandi's account a statement of Ibn Said, made also in the thirteenth century, that in his day Andalusia was "so thickly populated that if a traveller goes any distance through it he will find at every step on his road hamlets, farms, towns, orchards, and cultivated fields, and will never meet, as is more or less the case in other cultivated countries, with large tracts of uncultivated land or desert. This, united to the habit of the Andalusians, who, instead of living together as the Egyptians do, grouped in towns and villages, prefer dwelling in cottages and rural establishments in the midst of the fields, by the side of brooks, and on the declivities of mountains, gives altogether to the country an aspect of comfort and prosperity for which the traveller will look in vain elsewhere. Their houses, too, which they are continually white-washing inside and out, look exceedingly well by the side of the green trees."

This picture of country life speaks much for the general order and security which prevailed, and indicates that the measures taken by Almoravide and Almohade sovereigns to maintain a general respect for law had been successful. During the disorders preceding the Almoravide conquest brigandage had become rife, and a quaint story is told of a certain brigand, Greyhawk by name, who was brought before Al Mutammed, King of Seville. This Greyhawk, having committed atrocious crimes, was condemned to be crucified, and while he hung on the cross watched by his devoted wife and daughter, he managed still to beguile an unwary traveller into leaving his laden mule to search for treasure in a well, upon which Greyhawk instructed his wife to make off with the mule and its burden. The traveller meanwhile died in the well, and Greyhawk was taken down from the cross and brought again before the King. "Tell me, O Greyhawk," said the King, "how couldst thou be guilty of such a crime as that now imputed to thee, being as it were under the very clutch of death?" "O King," replied the robber, "if thou knewest how strongly nature impels me to the perpetration of such acts, and how great is the pleasure I enjoy while I commit them, I have no doubt but that thou wouldest relinquish the royal power and embrace my profession."

That story and the state of affairs which it illustrates belong, however, to another period. The reign of the Almohade el Mansur, which lasted till 1214, marks the greatest period of Almohade prosperity. It was during this reign, in the year 1195, that the three Christian kings of Arragon, Castile, and Leon were overthrown in the celebrated battle of Alarcos, at which it was said that the loss of the Christians amounted to 146,000 men, besides 30,000 prisoners and an incredible amount of spoil. It would seem to be after this battle, though it is variously related and placed by some historians in the reign of one of the Almoravide sovereigns, that the Christian population of Granada, accused of intriguing with the governments of Christian Spain, was transported by the Moors in a body to Africa and settled by thousands in Mequinez, Sallee, and other towns of the western coast. An Arab historian who visited Sallee in the year 1360 says that at that time the town of Rabat, not far distant, was almost wholly inhabited by families from Granada.

Thus began in the twelfth century, after a long period of African domination in Spain, a reaction of Europe upon Africa which has continued to the present day. This expulsion of the Christians from Granada may be taken as the first of the great religious expulsions for which Spain became famous in later years. It is just to remember that the system was initiated by the Moors, and it is perhaps worth noting that the celebrated Averrhöes, one of the most famous among the many names associated with the enlightenment which Arab civilisation spread through the dark ages of medieval Europe, was so warm an advocate of the measure, that he took the trouble to cross from the Spanish Court to the Court of

Morocco for the purpose of urging his views upon the Sultan. He appears to have spent a considerable part of his life at the court of Morocco, which was at that time a centre of learning. He died there in 1198, and, in recording his death, Morocco is mentioned as "the capital" of Adouatein. The mere existence of this geographical expression, used, as has been said, by the Arabs to signify the two kingdoms of Spain and Africa, shows how very closely the interests of the two countries had become bound together. In connection with the residence of the learned Averrhöes at the court of El Mansur in Africa, it may be worth mentioning that the praises of the same sovereign were sung in his court at Seville by the "learned and celebrated poet, a black of Soudan, Abu Ishak Ibrahim al Kanemi." The circumstance, though slight, is interesting, as serving to show that at the end of the twelfth century Negroland contributed, not only its commercial wares, but also its quota of art to the stores of Europe.

From the beginning of the thirteenth century onward, the decay of the Mussulman power in Spain is marked. The Christian Powers made constant and successful onslaughts upon the Almohade possessions. Town after town of importance fell into their hands. They were assisted by internal divisions among the Mussulmans; and in 1230, after nearly a century of brilliant rule, the Almohade dynasty was brought to an end by the deposition of the reigning sovereign. The Moslem portion of the continent declared itself independent under Ibn Hud, also a leader of African origin. Valencia fell into Christian hands, 1238; Cordova, 1239; Seville, 1260. A little later the whole of the Moslem population was driven to the coast between Ronda, in the west, and Almeria, in the east. In Africa the province of Ifrikiah, which stretched at one period from the confines of Egypt to those of Morocco, at the same time declared itself independent under a Sultan of the Hafside dynasty. In 1269 the Merinites possessed themselves of the throne of Morocco and its surrounding provinces, and fixed their capital at Fez. When nothing was left to the Almohades but Tafilet and a small part of Ifrikiah, they returned to their stronghold of Tinmelel, to maintain for a few years only a "phantom Caliph," Ishak, last of his race, who, when the successful siege of Tafilet in 1274 had given all that remained of Moroccan soil to the Merinites, was brought before the ruling sovereign of that dynasty and executed. It is interesting to note that at this siege of Tafilet, which put an end to even such empty pretence as still remained of the Dual Empire of Spain and Africa, mention is made of the use of firearms, or "fire-engines," which threw out iron gravel. The shot, it is said, was forced from the piece by means of a burning powder, "of which the singular properties work effects that rival the power of the Creator."

CHAPTER VI

DECLINE OF MOHAMMEDAN POWER IN SPAIN

THUS, before the end of the thirteenth century, the dual Mohammedan Empire or "Adouatein," or "The Two Shores," had ceased to exist, and in its place there had grown up three distinct Moslem powers. In Spain the Huddites, who afterwards fell under the Hafside leadership of the celebrated Ibn Ahmar, the builder of the Alhambra, formed a Moslem kingdom within the restricted limits still left to them, scarcely extending beyond the province of Granada. Upon the northern coast of Africa, in the ancient province of Africa Propria, or Ifrikiah, embracing Tunis and Tripoli, and henceforward generally known as Barbary, an independent Hafside dynasty was established, of which the subsequent history is one long succession of war. In Morocco the dynasty of the Merinites, ever at war with the Hafsides of the coast, was to hold its own until, at the beginning of the sixteenth century, it was overthrown by the Sherifs, whose descendants now reign in Morocco. Almost simultaneously with this break-up of the Caliphate of the West, the Caliphate of the East was overthrown by the Tartars in 1258.

Notwithstanding the ceaseless wars to which all these dynasties were exposed, the Courts of Tunis, Fez, and Granada maintained a high reputation for learning, refinement, and civilisation. The most brilliant period of Arab domination had come to an end, but the Arabs continued for two hundred years to represent the highest standard of knowledge and enlightenment which existed in modern Europe. Their universities were the founts of learning to which Christian ignorance went for its early education. Their courts were homes envied openly by the most distinguished of European kings. Among the celebrated pupils of Arab teachers, Roger Bacon, Peter the Venerable, Pope Sylvester II., are illustrious names which occur at once to the memory, and up to the end of the fifteenth century there was scarcely a man of eminence or learning in the schools of England, France, or Italy, whose biography, when it has been preserved, does not acknowledge the debt which he owed directly or indirectly to Arab learning. Arabian knowledge of the physical conditions of the Universe remained far in advance of anything known to Europe until near the end of the fifteenth and the beginning of the sixteenth centuries. The entire medical faculty of the Continent was trained in Arab schools. That they maintained this high place in the front rank of science through all the decadence of their later history, is sufficiently illustrated by the fact that when, at the moment of the final expulsion of the Moors from Spain, the Catholic Cardinal Ximenes ordered the destruction of the libraries of Granada, he reserved from the general condemnation three hundred medical works, to which Europe recognised its obligation.

There is no department of our daily life upon which the Arabs have not left their mark. Not only our learning, our laws, our justice, our naval and military science, our agriculture, our commerce, our manufacturing industries, have been profoundly impressed by Arab influence maintained in Europe for upwards of 800 years, but our daily customs, our domestic life, have been no less intimately touched. It is from the Arabs of Spain that we have learned to wash, to dress, to cook, to garden. They improved our musical instruments; they gave us new poetic metres; they gave us the imaginative pleasures of narrative fiction. From them France and Italy borrowed the lighter play of wit and repartee, which has since radiated through the northern races. From them modern Europe learned to associate with the emotions of love the grace and joy of cultivated life. It was from their hands that the growing life of the young nations of the West received its happiest direction. We have but to turn to the vocabularies of Europe and to trace in them the many important words of Arabic origin in order to appreciate to some extent the debt of which we have lost sight.

I have no intention of entering into the history of Spain during the centuries which led to the conquest of Granada by Ferdinand and Isabella, and the final expulsion of the Arabs from Europe in 1502. My purpose in briefly relating the outlines of the Arab-African conquest of Spain has been merely to indicate the nature of the national life to which Negroland owed the impulse of its medieval civilisation. If the impression made by Arab-African civilisation upon Europe has been indelible, it is only natural that the same impression should have been strong upon the nations which were brought in contact with it—even though in some instances they were of a wholly different race—in the continent from which it sprang.

Here is a picture quoted by Ibn Said, the "truthful historian," to whom allusion has been already made, from a previous writer, the truth of whose words he endorses, of the immediate effect upon Africa of the downfall of the Almohade dynasty in Spain. Ibn Said was born in Granada in 1214; he died in Tunis in 1287, and was therefore a personal witness of the condition of things which he describes.

"Africa," he quotes, "may be said to have derived its present wealth and importance, and its extent of commerce, from Andalusians settling in it. For when God Almighty was pleased to send down on their country the last disastrous civil war, thousands of its inhabitants, of all classes and professions, sought a refuge in Africa and spread over Maghreb el Aksa (Morocco), and Africa Propria (Barbary), settling wherever they found comfort or employment. Labourers and country people took to the same occupations which they had left in Andalusia. They formed intimacies with the inhabitants, discovered springs, made them available for the irrigation of their fields, planted trees, introduced water-mills, and other useful inventions. In short, they taught the African farmers many things whereof they had never heard, and showed them the use of excellent practices whereof they were completely ignorant. Through their means the countries where they fixed their residence became at once prosperous and rich, and the inhabitants saw their wealth increase rapidly, as well as their comfort and enjoyments. . . . There was no district in Africa wherein some of the principal authorities were not Andalusians. . . . But it was in the class of operatives and workmen in all sorts of handicrafts that Africa derived the most advantage from the tides of emigration setting towards its shores."

Ibn Ghalib, from whom the quotation is made, wrote at an earlier period than Ibn Said. After making the quotation, Ibn Said continues: "Perhaps some of my readers, in perusing the accounts I have just given in the words of Ibn Ghalib of the revolution created by the Andalusian emigration in the trade and agriculture of Africa, will say to themselves: 'This author was undoubtedly partial towards his countrymen, and he exaggerated their merits'; but let them plunge into his book, let them weigh every one of his expressions, and compare his narrative with those of other writers, and they will soon feel convinced that he spoke the truth."

Of these same Andalusians the author, Ibn Ghalib, who is quoted, says, at an earlier period: "They are Arabs by descent, in pride, in the haughtiness of their temper, the devotion of their minds, the goodness of their hearts, and the purity of their intentions. They resemble them in their abhorrence of everything that is cruel or oppressive, in their inability to endure subjection or contempt, and in the liberal expenditure of whatever they possess. They are Indians in their love of learning, as well as in their assiduous cultivation of science, their firm adherence to its principles, and the scrupulous attention with which they transmit to their posterity its invaluable secrets. They are like the people of Baghdad in cleanliness of person and beauty of form, in elegance of manners, mildness of disposition, subtlety of mind, power of thought, extent of memory, and universality of talent. They are Turks in their aptitude for war, their deep acquaintance with every one of its stratagems, and their skilful preparation of the weapons and machines used in it, as well as their extreme care and foresight in all matters concerning it. They have been further compared with the Chinese for the delicacy of their work, the subtlety of their manufactures, and their dexterity in imitating all sorts of figures. And, lastly, it is generally asserted that they are of all nations that which most resembles the Greeks in their knowledge of the physical and natural sciences, their ability in discovering waters hidden in the bowels of the earth and bringing them to the surface; their acquaintance with the various species of trees and plants and their several fruits, their industry in the pruning and grafting of trees, the arrangement and distribution of gardens, the treatment of plants and flowers, and all and every one of the branches of agriculture. Upon this last subject their proficiency is proverbial. The Andalusians, moreover, are the most patient of men and the fittest to endure fatigue."

Such was the estimate made by contemporary writers of the people whom civil war and religious intolerance drove from the cities of southern Spain, to spread through the northern part of Africa and to found new homes upon its shores. But to these descriptions it may be well, in this place, to add another, made a hundred years later, by a very competent historian, who, looking from a distance at the events which had taken place, was perhaps able to form a truer opinion of the causes of the national downfall. Ibn Khaldun, who was born at Tunis in 1332, and died in Egypt in 1406, and whose "History of the Berbers" is held to contain the most authentic information of the internal history of North Africa, thus summarises, on his opening page, the fate of the Arab nation to which he belonged: "Raised to the height of power in Asia Minor under the dynasty of the Ommeyades, formidable still under that of the Abbassides, attaining the highest fortune in Spain under the second dynasty of the Ommeyades, the Arabs found themselves in possession of such glory and prosperity as had never been the lot of another people. Surrounded by luxury and devoted to pleasure, they yielded to the seductions of idleness, and, tasting the delights of life, they fell into a long sleep under the shadow of glory and of peace. Then the soldier was no longer to be distinguished from the artisan, except by his ineptitude for work; their hardy habits were gone, and they were overthrown, not in the first instance by strangers, but by their own Caliphs. They were enslaved, then broken and dispersed."

Allowing for the somewhat over-flowery rhetoric of Arabian writers, the facts would seem to justify both sides of this description. The later decadence of the Arabs, when, after the final expulsion of 1502, they entirely lost touch with the progressive life of Europe, can only be accounted for on the assumption that they had, as Ibn Khaldun perceived, lost their early vitality, and that they carried with them into Africa the elements of their own decay. They were overthrown, not, in the first instance, by strangers, but by themselves.

Yet, without a doubt, their influence upon Africa, when the civil wars first drove them out of Spain, was that described by Ibn Said.

CHAPTER VII

SPANISH ARABS IN AFRICA

FROM the break-up of the Arab Empire of "The Two Shores" in the middle of the thirteenth century to the moment of the final severance of North Africa from Europe in the sixteenth century, the growth and spread of civilisation in the independent kingdoms of North Africa was very marked. Throughout the dark period of the Middle Ages, when the Catholic Church was asserting its claim to dominate the conscience of the Western World, and to direct not only the action but the thought of Christendom, all that was independent, all that was progressive, all that was persecuted for conscience' sake, took refuge in the courts of Africa. Art, science, poetry, and wit found congenial homes in the orange-shaded arcades of the colleges of Fez, in the palaces of Morocco, and in the exquisite gardens of Tripoli and Tunis.

The charm of life which had been so sedulously cultivated in the Mohammedan towns of Spain was transported to the coast of Africa. The beautiful palaces of southern Spain were reconstructed upon African soil. The gardens of El-Mostancer, a Hafside sovereign of Tunis who reigned from 1252 to 1277, rivalled those of the Ommeyades in Cordova. After describing the beauties of the gardens, Ibn Khaldun says of the court of this monarch, that it was always filled with distinguished persons. "Here," he says, "were to be seen numbers of Andalusians, amongst them distinguished poets and other eloquent writers, illustrious men of science, magnanimous princes, intrepid warriors." Here, too, we may note, in the year 1237, amidst all the brilliancy of such surroundings, a deputation from the king of the black countries of Bornu and Kanem, who sent amongst other gifts a giraffe, which so interested and delighted the inhabitants of Tunis that it excited the greatest enthusiasm.

At Fez, which now became the capital of the Merinite sovereigns, beautiful palaces and gardens were constructed, and the life of the higher nobility was conducted with much state. Learning also was encouraged, and it is interesting to observe, as the result of a "Holy War" successfully carried on against the Christians in Spain by one of the greatest of the Merinite sovereigns of Morocco, that among the conditions of peace imposed by the Moslem king was the surrender of all scientific works which had fallen into the hands of the Christians in the capture of Mussulman towns. Unfortunately only about 1100 volumes had been saved. These were afterwards conveyed to the University of Fez.

Ibn Khaldun says that literature presently declined at the court of Fez, owing to the too great materialism of the Merinite sovereigns. This was not the opinion of the celebrated traveller Ibn Batuta, but Ibn Khaldun was probably the better judge.

Ibn Batuta, who, like Ibn Khaldun, was born in North Africa of Arab parents, though about thirty years earlier (1303), distinguished himself by spending five-and-twenty years in travel, which extended over the greater part of the known world, and included Europe, India, China, and Thibet. He entered the "white town of Fez" on the 8th of November 1349, and decided there to lay aside his pilgrim's staff, because, for reasons which he sets forth at length, his judgment was convinced that the noble country over which its sovereign ruled was the best country and the best administered of all those that he had visited. Here he found the conditions of life better than in any other country. Food was more plentiful, varied, and cheap; life and property were more secure, law was milder, justice was more assured, charity more fully organised, religion more truly maintained, and literature, science, and art more honoured than in any other centre of civilisation. He mentions, in regard to the organised charities of the country, that free hospitals were constructed and endowed in every town of the kingdom. As regards the endowment of science and literature, he describes the great College of Fez as having "no parallel in the known world for size, beauty, and magnificence." He speaks of the deep interest taken by the sovereign in all that related to science and literature, the very considerable literary achievements of the sovereign himself, and of the generous protection which he gave to all persons who were devoted to the study of science. Here also, before the date of Ibn Batuta's visit, we are brought into touch in the year 1338 with the political life of the Negro kingdom of Melle. Mansa Musa, a black sovereign, of whom we shall presently hear more, and the seat of whose empire was in the territory now known as the Bend of the Niger, sent an embassy on the occasion of the conquest of Telemçan by the Merinites to congratulate the Merinite sovereign, who was his nearest white neighbour. His embassy was accompanied by an interpreter from Masina in the Upper Niger, where the Fulanis had then a principal seat of occupation. Abou el Haçen—the king so warmly praised a few years later by Ibn Batuta—received them very cordially, and sent back by their hands a very handsome present to Mansa Musa.

In the lists which are given of the presents exchanged between monarchs on state occasions, interesting glimpses of the condition of the nations concerned may be obtained. The present made by Abou el Haçen to Mansa Musa is not described, but here is the description of a present sent by him to the reigning Sultan of Egypt on the same occasion of the taking of Telemçan from the Hafsides in 1337.

First on the list is placed a copy of the Koran written by the monarch's own hand, and most beautifully bound at Fez. The binding, which is described in great detail, was made of ebony, ivory, and sandalwood, "inlaid with admirable art," and decorated with fillets of gold and pearls and rubies. There was also an outside leather case, which was solidly worked and decorated with fillets of gold. Next after the book there came upon the list five hundred thoroughbred horses, of which the saddles were embroidered in gold and silver, and of which the bridles and bits were some of them of pure gold and some of them plated. Also there were five hundred loads of objects made in Morocco—or Maghreb, as the portion of Africa now known to us as Morocco was then called. There were arms, and beautiful woollen stuffs; cloaks, robes, burnooses; turbans, striped and plain stuffs of silk and wool; silks plain and in colours, embroidered and brocaded with gold. Also shields brought from the countries of the desert, made of the skin of the lamt, and "covered with that famous varnish which renders them so hard." Also many pieces of furniture "which is made in Maghreb and much sought after in the East."

A country which can count all these objects amongst its manufactures is evidently in a very fairly high condition of industrial prosperity. A monarch who can transcribe a copy of the Koran in his own hand in such a manner as to render it worthy of being placed in so precious a binding at the head of a present of this value must evidently have at least some appreciation of the charms of literature. It is said of Abou el Haçen that he performed the feat of transcribing the Koran with his own hand three times.

After this conquest of Telemçan intercourse between Morocco and Negroland appears to have increased, which is not unnatural, as already a very considerable trade existed between Telemçan, which was one of the principal ports of embarkation for Spain, and the countries of the Negro belt. The king of Melle was at that time the greatest of the black sovereigns, and Abou el Haçen, desiring to cultivate pleasant relations with him, sent him an embassy with handsome presents, a compliment which in 1360 the reigning king of Melle returned to Abou el Haçen's successor. Unfortunately the details of this present are not recorded. It is only stated that Mansa

Suleiman of Melle, "wishing to return the good treatment of the Merinite sovereign, collected various products of his country, all extremely rare and curious, and sent them to Fez." He also added to his presents a giraffe, which gave great pleasure to the Court of Fez. The embassy was received with the greatest possible honour at Fez, the place being thronged and people standing on each other's shoulders in the crowd to see—while the Sultan, seated in his golden kiosk, received and returned the assurances of friendship sent to him by the black king.

An incident of the developed intercourse between Morocco and Negroland which is of more interest to posterity than the exchange of presents between their respective sovereigns, was the decision arrived at by Ibn Batuta to take up again his pilgrim's staff, and quitting the lettered luxury of Fez, to add another chapter to his travels by journeying through Negroland. He accordingly crossed the frontier of Morocco on his southward journey on February 18, 1352, and spent upwards of eighteen months in a journey through the principal countries of the Nigerian watershed, re-entering the kingdom of Morocco in December of 1353. The record of this journey, which he has added to the four volumes of his travels, is especially interesting, as giving a picture of the Negroland of that day written from personal observation. The earlier Arab writers, from whom our information is principally drawn, were not themselves personally acquainted with the countries of which they write. They described them generally from the hearsay of travellers and traders, and though this has its value as representing the volume of common knowledge which existed concerning Negroland, other descriptions lack the vividness which Ibn Batuta gives to his.

CHAPTER VIII

THE SOUDANESE STATES

We come now to the history of Negroland itself, which began to be known in its relatively modern development from about the period of the Arab conquest of Africa and Spain. The sources of information regarding it are mainly Arab, and the earliest records which have been preserved carry us only vaguely back beyond the seventh century of the Christian era. The records which exist make it clear that the Empire of the Two Shores established by the Arabs in North Africa and Spain was the commercial field of Negroland. This was also the case with the territories included in the dominion of the Eastern Caliphate, and intercourse was frequent between the principal countries of Negroland and the towns of North Africa, Spain, Egypt, Syria, and Arabia. Negroland was therefore in closer touch than many of the countries of Northern Europe with the highest civilisation of the period, and the effect of this closer relation is of course traceable in its history. Throughout the whole period it would seem that the ancient tradition of civilisation, which had come to it from the East, so far prevailed that the kingdoms of Negroland were disposed to acknowledge the political supremacy of the Eastern, rather than of the Western Caliphate. More than once in later times there are instances of their sovereigns accepting investiture from the Sultan of Egypt, even after the overthrow of the Caliphate by the Turks. But their intellectual and commercial intercourse would appear to have been more active with the West than with the East; and in tracing the course of civilisation in their kingdoms from the seventh to the seventeenth century, at which latter period the whole underwent a chaotic change, it is to be observed that the tide of progress spreads steadily from the West eastward, not from the East westward. In saying this I allude especially to those countries to the west of Lake Chad, which, taken collectively, may be said to form the Western Soudan. There is one other general observation which it is, I think, interesting to make with regard to the civilising influence exercised by the Empire of the Two Shores upon Negroland. It is that between the seventh and the seventeenth centuries; though there were many local wars and conquests of black kingdoms by Berbers and Berber kingdoms by blacks, there was never any military conquest made or attempted by Spanish Arabs of the black countries with which they traded. At the beginning of the seventeenth century, when the Spanish Arabs had themselves been expelled from Europe, this policy was reversed with disastrous results, and the conquest of the country by the decadent Moors put an end to the prosperity of Negroland.

In order to follow with any interest the historic development of this little known portion of the world, it is well to glance at a map of Africa and note the more salient physical features which have to some extent determined here, as they determine elsewhere, the political distribution of the country. It has already been mentioned that the latitude of 17° N. may be taken as the edge of the summer rains, and that between 10° and 17° all the finest races of this part of Africa are to be found. This is M. de Lauture's limit of distribution. Later experience would lead us perhaps to draw the southern line a little lower. Probably the parallel of 9° would be found more accurate. If two blue pencil lines be drawn upon these parallels on a map of north-west Africa, it will be seen that they include within their limits the whole course of the Senegal from its rise in the mountains north of Sierra Leone to its mouth in the Atlantic Ocean, and the course of the Upper and Middle Niger from its rise in the same mountains to its most northerly bend, almost on the parallel of 17°, and its descent in a south-easterly direction to that fall in its bed which has been rendered famous by Mungo Park's death in the rapids which are caused by it near Boussa. The same limits include Lake Chad and all the tributaries which drain to it from the highlands of the Haussa States. It will be observed that towards the northern portion of this territory the country has a general tendency to open into level plains; while towards the southern portion hilly regions, drawing together, form a natural dividing-line from the countries of the coast. It will also be observed that the line drawn upon the parallel of 9° excludes from the area occupied by the fine races every one of those territories hitherto occupied by the nations of modern Europe in the maritime settlements made upon the southern portion of the coast, except the French settlement of the Senegal.

It becomes apparent, in looking broadly at the lines thus traced upon the map, that the country which lies between them is cut by its main watercourses into four principal divisions. There is the territory lying south-west of the Senegal, between the course of that river and the sea; there is the country lying north-east of the Senegal, between that river and the Niger to the point where the Niger presses upon the desert at Timbuctoo; there is the country lying south of the Niger enclosed in the bend of the river, and generally known now by the geographical expression—the Bend of the Niger; and there is the country stretching from the eastern bank of the Niger to Lake Chad. Allowing something for the always too arbitrary nature of geographical boundaries, it will be found that the history of Negroland tends also to group itself within these four divisions.

The very earliest records which we have in point of date, exclusive of the tradition of ancient Egypt in the East, relate to the north-east of the Senegal, between that river and the Niger. This territory was known by a confusingly different number of names; but the name of its principal town, and the name by which the territory itself was most generally known in the first days of its medieval prosperity, was Ghana or Ghanata. At a later date the territory was called Walata, and the principal town became Aiwalatin.

We are told that white kings had reigned over Ghana before the year of the Hegira; but when the Arabs visited the country in the eighth century they found it in the possession of a black monarch, to whom the Berbers or white people of the more northerly desert towns paid tribute. The town of Ghana lay towards the eastern portion of this district, and at one time the territory over which it ruled extended to the sea.

The district to the south-west of the Senegal, between that river and the sea, is regarded by early writers as the original place of settlement of the Fulani in Africa. The Djolfs, who inhabited it during the Arab period, are described in the *Tarikh-es-Soudan* as "the best of men." "By their acts and their character," the author says, "they differ essentially from all the other Fulanis. God by a special grace has endowed them with a generous nature, and He inspires in them fine actions and conduct worthy of all praise. For valour and bravery they have no equal. . . . In all that we have ever heard about them, loyalty and fidelity to their engagements appear to be innate, and to have reached the highest expression in them." It will be noticed that this praise of the Djolfs is given at the implied expense of "all other Fulanis." There can be no doubt that from the beginning of their history there has been a wide variation in the endowments of this people. They are, however, so remarkable, and from our earliest knowledge of them have maintained the character of their own race so exclusively of the life and history of the other races of the Soudan, that the account of their progress as a ruling power from the extreme western corner upon the Atlantic coast, in which we first hear of them, to the eastern regions between the Niger and Lake Chad, where, at the beginning of the nineteenth century, they established their domination over the Haussa states, will best be given later in a separate chapter.

The history of Ghana and of the Empire of Melle which superseded it constitute the two first chapters of the native history of Negroland. Melle, which extended at one period of its history over the territory of Ghana and also over the Bend of the Niger, gives way in its turn to the extraordinarily interesting history of Songhay—an empire which from the middle of the fifteenth to the end of the sixteenth centuries extended over the entire Bend of the Niger, and even carried its domination for a time to the Atlantic on one side and to Lake Chad upon the other. Contemporaneously with the rise of Melle and Songhay, the Haussa States and Bornu rose to prosperity between the Niger and Lake Chad, while the native states of Nupe, Borgu, Mossi, and some others, appear to have maintained an independent existence from a period of considerable antiquity upon the Niger. To the south of these territories, during the whole period of which we have the record of their history, the country was inhabited in a continuous belt by Pagan cannibals.

As civilisation in the medieval epoch of Negro history would seem to have arisen in the west, and gradually to have crept across towards the east, meeting, in the Bend of the Niger and the Haussa States, that other wave of civilising influence which in earlier days had inspired its life from the east, so it will not be surprising to find that decadence spreads also along the same path and in the same historic order. When the Arabs first visited Negroland by the western route in the eighth and ninth centuries of our era, they found the black kings of Ghana in the height of their prosperity. The countries bordering upon Lake Chad are then spoken of contemptuously as the "country of the idolaters." But the black kings of Ghana had long passed into oblivion when Edris, one of the greatest of the kings of Bornu, was making gunpowder for the muskets of his army at a period contemporary with Queen Elizabeth.

CHAPTER IX

NEGROLAND AND THE WESTERN ARABS

It has already been mentioned that the whole of the Fezzan and the south-western province of what is now Morocco were conquered by the Arab general, Okbar, in the middle of the seventh century, but that he did not penetrate at either end of the Western Soudan to the territories of the fertile belt. There was not for nearly a thousand years any direct military conquest of these territories by the Arabs. But the Berber tribes, dispossessed and driven southwards by the Arabs, made room for themselves at different periods in the fertile belt, and in doing so necessarily fought with and overthrew or were overthrown by the blacks. As in the case of the conquest of the British Isles by Saxons, Danes, and Normans, this resulted in a very great admixture of blood, and though the black strain would seem generally to have prevailed in point of colour, the characteristics of the races occupying the fertile belt were in the course of centuries so modified that in speaking of them it will perhaps be more accurate to employ the word "black" than the in many ways misleading term of "negro."

The true negro is hardly to be found amongst these races of the northern inland belt—the cast of face, even when jet black in colour, being frequently European in form, with the high nose, thin lips, and deep-set eyes, characteristic still of the Arab of the Mediterranean coast. The aristocratic thin hand, and the slight, somewhat square shoulders of the Arab of the coast are also frequently noticeable. As a consequence of many invasions from the north this blood no doubt penetrated as far as climatic conditions would allow. I shall also hope to show that from any time of which history has note, the northern belt of the Soudan has been occupied by races of a higher than negroid type. The operation of these types upon the purely negroid races was to drive them southwards into the tropical swamps of the coast belt in which the higher type could not live.

The pressure of the tribes of the desert upon Negroland dates of course from a very much earlier period than the Arab conquest of North Africa, but it was renewed and accentuated by that conquest. The earliest Arab writer who is known to make any allusion to Arab dealings with Negroland in the west is Abd el Hakem, who died in Egypt in 870, but he merely alludes to a military expedition against the Berbers in the south-west, undertaken about the year 720, which reached the Soudan and brought back as much gold as the soldiers wanted. The next writer in point of date whose writings have been preserved is Ibn Haukal, the geographer, who wrote about the year 930. But he confines his writings chiefly to "those lands which are the seat of Islam and the residence of true believers," and though these extended in the tenth century from Spain to China, through Trans-Oxiana, Tibet, and Hindostan, the black countries of the Western Soudan are regarded as being still at that date outside the pale. "As for the Land of Blacks in West Africa," he says, "I make but slight mention of them, because naturally loving wisdom, ingenuity, religion, justice, and regular government, how could I notice such people as those or exalt them by inserting an account of their countries." It is evident that this haughty writer had but a small acquaintance with the Land of the Blacks which he despises, and that he knew only its northern edge. "The Land of the Blacks," he says, "is a very extensive region, but *extremely dry*. In the mountains of it are to be found all the fruits which the Mohammedan world produces." He tells us also that it extends to the ocean on the south and is bordered on the north by deserts which reach across Africa to Zanzibar. In his day the Tripoli-Fezzan route would appear to have been closed. "Whatsoever they get," he says, "comes to them from the western side, because of the difficulty of entering their country from any other quarter."

This scant notice is only interesting as showing that, although intercourse with the Arabs had already begun by the western route, it was not in the middle of the tenth century sufficiently active to be regarded in the higher circles of the learned as having serious importance.

The step from this writer to the next who has preserved for us any contemporary knowledge of Negroland, is the more remarkable. Ibn Haukal died in 968. Just a hundred years later, in 1067, a book was written that gives us a description as vivid as the description of Ibn Haukal is bare. The name of the book is usually translated as "Roads and Realms." It treats of the whole of North Africa, but of Negroland in special detail, and the intimate knowledge which it displays serves to indicate the development of intercourse with the Soudan which must have taken place under the Ommeyades. The author, whose long Arabic name is usually shortened to El Bekri, was the son of a prince of Huelva, who, as a consequence of civil war in Spain, sold his principality to the Prince of Seville in or about the year 1051. He then went as a rich man to live at Cordova, taking with him his son, the famous El Bekri. The exact date of El Bekri's birth is doubtful, but the best authorities put it at 1028. It was the moment of the break-up of the Ommeyade power in Spain, when petty courts were establishing themselves in the principal towns. On the northern frontier of Mohammedan Spain the Christians, gaining daily strength, were before the end of the century to be led to victory by the immortal Cid, while in the far south of Western Africa that army of the Al Moravides was drawing together upon the banks of the Senegal, which was first to bring regeneration to unconscious Spain.

In the meantime the life of the pleasant courts, which

the weakness of the declining power of the Ommeyades had permitted to erect themselves into independence, was gay, cultivated, splendid, and refined. El Bekri knew them all. After his father's death in 1066 he went to that of Almeria, then one of the first cities in importance of Southern Spain. It is claimed by some Arab writers that the commercial greatness of the Italian republics had its foundation in trade with Almeria, and through Almeria with the East. In Almeria El Bekri was the favoured guest of El Mutassim, the reigning prince. From Almeria he afterwards went to take up his residence at Seville, the home of art and science, where also he was honoured of the great. He loved the good things of life; he enjoyed the society of the learned, and, eminent among all that was most eminent of his day, he was remarkable for his own great attainments and intellectual industry. He died in 1094. It is not recorded of him that he ever left Spain. It is true that his geographical works can therefore only be regarded as compilations, but this renders them for our purpose in one sense the more important, as serving to show how much was known at that time of West Africa in the cultivated circles of the courts of Spain.

It is evident from El Bekri's account that the trade of the Soudan with Spain and the countries of the Mediterranean coast had for a long time been important enough to attract attention and interest. He notes the two principal caravan roads into the western and eastern end of the Soudan, but describes the western road by Morocco and Tafilet as being that in most frequent use. Kanem, lying at the eastern end of the Western Soudan, is to him a "country of idolaters very difficult to reach," while the country to the south of Morocco is evidently as well known as the provinces of Spain.

Tafilet—known to the Arabs and always spoken of under the name of Sidjilmessa, the last town at which the road to the Soudan left the fertile territories of Morocco—was, according to El Bekri. founded in the year 757 of our era. He describes it as being situated at the junction of several streams, in a plain of which the soil was impregnated with salt and was extraordinarily fertile. Among their crops the people grew "Chinese wheat." The town was large, containing some very splendid buildings, and was surrounded by extensive suburbs and gardens. Grapes, dates, and all kinds of fruits were very plentiful, and amongst other industries the town was celebrated for drying raisins. There was a gold currency, and it was regarded as a peculiarity that gold pieces at Sidjilmessa were received by count and not by weight.

The founder and first governor of this town was black. It seems contrary to modern ideas that white people should under any circumstances consent to be ruled by blacks, but it will be seen that in the history of the Western Soudan this objection was not universally felt. Instances are common, especially in the western portions of the territory of the Soudan, of Berbers paying tribute to black sovereigns. The Fulani, who counted themselves a white race, were constantly subject to black rulers, and it is related of the black women of one of the kingdoms of the Soudan, that when their monarch was overthrown by a contemporary Berber king, they, "too proud to allow themselves to fall into the hands of white men," preferred to commit suicide.

Sidjilmessa was already Mohammedan in El Bekri's time. It was the meeting-place of many roads: those leading from Wargelan and other places in the Barbary States which were marts of the trade of the Soudan, and also from Morocco, Telemçan, and the coast. For all these roads it formed the most westerly entrance to the desert.

From Sidjilmessa to Ghana in the Land of Blacks there was a march of nearly two months to be made across a practically uninhabited desert. Throughout this vast region only nomad tribes were in El Bekri's day to be met with, having, he says, no town for their headquarters, with the exception of the Wadi Dra, at five days' distance from Sidjilmessa, which was the meeting-point of the Masmouda Berbers, a fraction of the Senajah tribe. For the accurate geography of this road the reader who is interested should refer to Cooley's "Negroland of the Arabs," in which he will find a learned and most careful examination of the ancient geography of the country. From the conclusions drawn by Cooley it would seem quite clear that the road described by El Bekri coincides almost exactly with that shown in modern maps as connecting El Harib on the south-western frontier of Morocco with Timbuctoo, *viâ* Mabruk, which encampment Cooley identifies with the Audoghast of the Arabs. The only difference would appear to have been that the meeting-point of Tamedelt mentioned by El Bekri as being eleven days west of Sidjilmessa, was slightly to the west of El Harib. Cooley fixes it at lat. 28° 45′ N., long. 7° 10′ W. Dr. Barth disagrees with Cooley, and would place Audoghast somewhat to the west of Mabruk.

To reach Negroland by the western route there were, however, two possible variants of the road, both of which have been so accurately described by El Bekri, and after him by Ibn Batuta and other travellers, as to leave little room for doubt as to their direction; one led *viâ* Audoghast, the other, as pursued by Ibn Batuta at a later date, ran more directly south *viâ* Tegazza to Aiwalatin or Walata. Both would appear to have been equally well known and equally used from the earliest times. Both required a journey of about two months from Sidjilmessa; but the one skirted the western and the other the eastern border of the desert of Tizer or Ayawad. Both traversed the desert, using as guides the nomad Berbers of the locality. Ibn Batuta describes the portion of it just north of Aiwalatin as "a vast plain, beautiful and bright, of which the air is so invigorating that the spirits rise and the lungs dilate." It is, however, quite waterless for many days, and in order to reach Aiwalatin the custom was to send a practised guide seven days ahead to give warning of the approach of a caravan, which messengers from the town were then sent to meet, carrying water into the desert for a four days' march. Without this precaution caravans frequently perished of thirst. Like all great plains in which the mirage is common, this desert had the reputation of being haunted by demons. On the more westerly route, at a distance of twenty days from Sidjilmessa, lay the great salt-mine of Tegazza, which is described in detail by every writer.

CHAPTER X

BERBER AND BLACK

THESE two roads, forming together the great western caravan route to the Soudan, led each to a separate and typical objective. The stopping-place of the easterly branch was Audoghast; the stopping-place of the more westerly branch was Aiwalatin. Audoghast was about fifteen days north of the present position of Timbuctoo. It lay, therefore, between 21° and 22° N. lat., and whether Cooley or Barth is right as to its exact position, it was well outside the belt of the Soudan proper, while Aiwalatin, or Walata, between the seventeenth and eighteenth parallels, lay on the edge of the summer rains, and was the frontier town, and at one time the capital of the great black kingdom of Ghana. These two towns represented two elements in the life of the Soudan, and are therefore worth dwelling upon. The one represented the Berber, the other the black, element, which are to be found constantly side by side. Audoghast was a type of the Berber state, lying not in but on the northern edge of the Soudan, fronting the black races and having intercourse with them, but preserving a semi-separate existence. Aiwalatin was a type of the purely black state lying in the heart of the fertile belt. Each of these states in turn would seem to have paid tribute to the other; each in turn was ruled by princes of the opposing race; each had its periods of independence. The Soudanese author of the *Tarikh-es-Soudan* tells us that forty-four white princes had ruled over Ghana before the great black princes arose. In the early part of the eleventh century Audoghast was tributary to

Ghana, and was ruled, as Sidjilmessa had once been, by a black prince.

El Bekri has preserved an interesting description of both towns as they were known to the travellers and merchants of Mohammedan Spain.

Before reaching Audoghast, he tells us, the pure desert of drifting sand gave way to sandy but wooded uplands, where a succession of wells furnished an ample water supply. Amongst these woods a rubber or gum tree was plentiful, of which the produce was exported to Spain, and much used in the manufacture of silk. From these wooded uplands the road led down to Audoghast, which was a large and thickly populated town, built in a sandy plain and surrounded by gardens and date-groves. Its pastures were well stocked with sheep and cattle, and meat was very plentiful, but wheat was cultivated as a garden crop. The rich alone indulged themselves in the use of it. The common grain used by the people was dourra. Fields of henna bore heavy crops. The town had several mosques and other fine public buildings, and the houses generally were "very elegant." The people were rich and lived in great comfort. There was a large and extremely busy market, where, notwithstanding the distance, wheat, fruit, sugar, and dried raisins from the Mohammedan countries were regularly sent. Honey, which was very plentiful, came from Negroland. Luxuries of all kinds were to be obtained for gold dust, which was the medium of exchange. There was no proper currency. Amongst the trade imports El Bekri mentions worked copper and dress stuffs, and amongst the exports amber and refined gold run into the form of gold wire. The refined gold of Audoghast had the reputation of being purer than that of any other country in the world. The population of Audoghast was very mixed, but was mainly Berber, consisting of natives from the Barbary coasts and members of the surrounding Berber tribes. There were also to be seen, El Bekri says, but in smaller numbers, people from all the great Mussulman towns of Spain, and amongst the white women many were remarkable for their beauty. The service of the households would appear to have been done by negroes, and the rich merchants of Audoghast owned sometimes as many as a thousand slaves. There were especially clever negress cooks who were worth £100 apiece, and who knew how to prepare most appetising dishes, the flesh of camel calves stewed with truffles, maccaroni dressed with honey, nut cakes, and all kinds of sweetmeats.

Between the years 961 and 971, that is, a hundred years earlier than the date of El Bekri's writing, Audoghast formed the centre of a Berber state which was ruled by a prince of the Senajah tribe whose name was Tin Yeroutan. More than twenty black kings acknowledged his rule and paid tribute to him, and his empire extended over an inhabited country which it required two months to march through from end to end. He was able to put in the field an army of no less than 100,000 men mounted upon trained camels. When the King of Macina, a Berber frontier state situated south of his territory upon the Niger, asked for help against a powerful black neighbour, he sent him 50,000 mounted men. The whole country from Audoghast to the Atlantic coast was in those days in the possession of the Berbers. Certain tribes, amongst whom were the Beni Goddala and the Lemtunah, destined afterwards to give the dynasty of the Almoravides to Spain, retained their independence on the western coast, and as nomads continued for a long time to haunt the more westerly of the two roads to Negroland. All these tribes of the desert wore the double veil, the *nicab*, which concealed the upper part of the face, and the *litham*, which concealed the lower in such a way that only the orbit of the eyes was visible. "Never," El Bekri says, "in any circumstances did they take off the veil, and if by accident a man's veil had been taken off he would have been quite unrecognisable by his parents." When it happened in battle to a warrior the body could not be identified. "The veil," he adds, "is a thing which they no more take off than their skins, and to men who do not dress as they do they apply the nickname of 'fly-traps.'"

The Berber Tin Yeroutan had ruled in Audoghast a hundred years before El Bekri wrote, and in that time much had happened. The black kingdom of Ghana, already famous in the eighth century, had risen in prosperity and importance, and had spread northwards, conquering amongst other territories the kingdom of Audoghast. In the year 1054 the town of Audoghast, still rich and flourishing, not only acknowledged the rule of Ghana and paid tribute, but was also a place of residence of the black monarch. But in the following year, 1055, the Almoravides, already setting out upon their northward march, made a first example of this town. They took it by assault and sacked and pillaged it, exposing it to every horror of barbaric warfare, and it is especially stated that "they treated the population of Audoghast with this extreme rigour because the town had acknowledged the sovereignty of the black king of Ghana."

The actual position of the town of Ghana, of which no certain trace now remains, has been much disputed. Leo Africanus, by a careless phrase, confused it with the town of Kano, upwards of 1200 miles distant in the Haussa States, and as a consequence, in the very unenlightened condition of European knowledge, the traditions of the one town were commonly associated with the other until Cooley, in his "Negroland of the Arabs," demonstrated once and for all the absurdity of such a geographical transposition. That the town of Ghana was somewhere in the west, situated between the Niger and the sea, and near to the issue of the western caravan road from Morocco, is not questioned. The exact locality is uncertain, but it is generally held that it was some days to the south-west of Timbuctoo. Taking into consideration that it is constantly spoken of as the capital of the kingdom of Ghana or Ghanata, and that that capital is also sometimes spoken of as Biru and Walata, Ghanata and Walata being interchangeable, and that Walata, Biru, and Aiwalatin are one, also noting the points of resemblance between the geographical description given by El Bekri of the position of Ghana, and by Ibn Batuta 300 years later of Aiwalatin, it scarcely seems to be doubtful that the Ghana of the eighth century was identical with the Aiwalatin of the fourteenth, and with the Walata of to-day.

We learn by extracts from a Haussa record, of which the original has unfortunately been destroyed, that the people of Ghana were anciently known by the name of Towrooth or Taurud, and that they claimed to have come from the territory lying between the Tigris and the Euphrates. In other words, they claimed descent from the Assyrians or the Babylonians, both peoples who had their origin in the Taurus Mountains, and reached their highest development in the Valley of the Euphrates and the Tigris. If the migration of the people of Ghana formed part of the movement impelled by the Chaldean conquest of Babylon, this would carry their settlement in Africa back to the seventh century before Christ. It may have been much earlier. When Alexander the Great took Babylon, he sent back for the information of Aristotle records of Babylonian astronomical observations extending over 1903 years.

Among the peoples ruled by Ghana in the Arab period, one of the most important was known by the name of Ungara, Wangara, or Wakore, of whom many were Fulani. The Wangara, at a later date, migrated eastward into the Haussa States. This people claimed on their part to have descended from the Persians. When, at a later period, they moved eastward from Ghana to Haussaland, the province which they founded was called indifferently Wangara or Ungara. It is, therefore, interesting to find that in the Ramayana, the Indian epic, a Rajah of Ungar is mentioned among those who paid tribute to the famous Desaratha. Commentators who were in no way concerned with African history, have agreed that Ungar must have been a province of Persia on the northern frontier of India. We get, therefore, somewhere about the time of Moses a spot in Persia whence the Wangara may have originated. The fact that Persian influence extended at a very early period to the black countries of Africa is also attested by the ruins of Persepolis, where amongst the bas-reliefs believed to have been carved in commemoration of the glories of Cyrus and his immediate successors, there is one which shows the king in the act of receiving tribute from the ambassadors of subject nations, and amongst them there is a negro. Niebuhr tells us that the profile is unmistakable, and that the hair of the negro is so carefully carved that it is impossible to mistake it for the hair of an Asiatic. Cambyses, son of Cyrus, conquered Egypt in 527 B.C., and his army perished in marching into Ethiopia. There is nothing impossible in the supposition that fragments of that defeated army may have remained and settled in the Soudan.

Further information of the remote antiquity of Ghana seems unfortunately to be at present unattainable. So far as we are aware, no monuments remain to confirm the traditions of the people. I give these surmises, therefore, for what they may be worth, and have myself found nothing to connect the Taurud of Ghana with the ancient Babylonians except two characteristics mentioned by El Bekri: one is that they were workers in gems, the other is that their notables indulged a passion for fine dogs. Both of these, as we know, were also characteristics of the people of Babylon.

We are on safer ground when we return to the medieval records of Arab writers.

In the years 1067 Ghana was still the principal black kingdom of the Western Soudan. The name of its reigning sovereign was Tenkamenin, who ascended the throne in the year 1062, in succession to his maternal uncle, Beci. It was the custom amongst these blacks for the succession to go always to the son of the king's sister.

The town of Ghana, which, after the sack of Audoghast by the Almoravides, became the royal residence of the kings, was composed, according to El Bekri, of two towns situated in a plain. One town was Mussulman and the other pagan. The king himself was a pagan, and lived in the pagan town. The Mussulman town was very large, and contained no less than twelve mosques. All these mosques had their *imams*, their *moweddins*, and their salaried readers. There were also schools and centres of learning, and according to the author of the *Tarikh-es-Soudan*, the town, besides being the meeting-place of commercial caravans from all parts of the world, was "the resort of the learned, the rich, and the pious of all nations." They came, he says, from Egypt, from Augila, from the Fezzan, from Ghadames, from Taouat, from Dra, from Sidjilmessa, from Sus, from Bitou, and other places. This account is fully borne out by later writers. El Edrisi, writing in 1153, describes the king's residence as being a well-built castle, thoroughly fortified, decorated inside with sculptures and pictures, and having glass windows. El Bekri makes no mention of glass, but says that the king's residence in the pagan town consisted of a "castle" surrounded by native huts. He mentions that the buildings generally were composed of stone and acacia wood. The native town was six miles distant from the Mussulman town, but the whole space was covered by suburbs, consisting of stone houses standing in gardens. In the native town there was one mosque for the use of Mohammedans occupied on duty round the king. The king's principal ministers and advisers were at this time Mohammedans, and he and his heir-presumptive wore Mohammedan dress, but the religion of the country was still devoutly pagan, and all other persons of native religion, except the king and his heir, wore robes of cotton, silk, or brocade, according to their means. The local religion, evidently different from the paganism now practised among the lower class tribes upon the coast, had yet certain points of resemblance.

The royal town, says El Bekri, was surrounded by groves jealously guarded, which were sacred to the worship of the gods. Here dwelt the priests who directed religious worship. No other person was allowed to enter or to know anything of what happened within their precincts. Here were the idols of the nation. Here also were the tombs of the kings, and the royal prisons, in which, if a man were once confined, he was never heard of again. From the description of royal funerals it may be inferred that a new grove was planted for each tomb. On the death of a king, the custom was to construct a great dome of wood on the spot which was to serve as his tomb. The body was then laid upon a couch covered with drapery and cushions, and placed within the dome. Round the dead were laid his decorations, his arms, the dishes and cups from which he was in the habit of eating and drinking, and various kinds of food and drink. With the body of the sovereign were enclosed several of his cooks and attendants. The edifice was covered with cloth and mats. The assembled multitudes then threw earth upon the tomb until a great hill was formed. When this was done the monument was secured from defilement by a ditch which left only one passage of approach. Sacrifices to the dead were also made.

This system of burial recalls a description given by Macrizi, in his "Historical Description of Egypt," of the burial of Misraim, who died seven hundred years after the Flood, and who is said to have given the ancient name of "Misr" to Lower Egypt. Misraim being dead, they prepared for him, Macrizi tells us, a hollow place most richly decorated, with a pedestal in the midst of it. On the pedestal they engraved an inscription: "He never worshipped idols, neither was he ever old, nor sick, nor downcast, nor morose. His strength was in the Most High God." The body, in a coffin of marble and gold, was laid near the pedestal, and on the pedestal—of which, perhaps, the translation should be platform—was heaped every kind of precious possession, emeralds, pearls, gold talismans, perfumes, &c. The whole was then covered with rocks, over which earth was heaped, between two mountains, and his son took the reins of government.

The descent from this form of sepulture to that of Ghana, and again from that of Ghana to that now practised among the fetish worshippers of the coast, is illustrative of the decadence which an ideal may undergo as it passes from its original source into the keeping of lower orders of comprehension.

Magic and trial by ordeal were also in use among the people of Ghana. El Bekri is the latest of the Arab authors who refers to these native rites. Shortly after the period at which he wrote the whole country would appear to have become Mohammedan.

Ten days to the south of Ghana was the country of the Lem-Lems or cannibals, whom it was the custom to raid for slaves. Within the kingdom there was a district of which the inhabitants were naked pagans, very expert in the use of the bow and arrow. There was another district entirely inhabited by the descendants of the soldiers sent by the Ommeyade Arabs against Ghana in the first years of the Hegira. These people kept their light complexions and the fine features of their race.

In nearly all the important towns of the country, Mussulman traders from the countries of the north were to be met. In some of the towns Mussulmans did not take up their residence, but they were always well received.

Tenkamenin, besides having already adopted Mohammedan dress, was much governed by Mohammedan opinion. He is described as the master of a vast empire, and of a power which rendered him very formidable. He could put in the field an army of 200,000 men, of whom more than 40,000 were armed with bows and arrows. The wealth of the country was very great. The soil was fertile, and gave generally two crops a year. Gold was abundant. The custom, according to El Bekri, was that all nuggets found in the mines of the Empire belonged to the sovereign, while the public was allowed to keep the gold dust. "Without this precaution," El Bekri gravely states, "gold would become so abundant that it would have hardly any value." The nuggets found in the mines of Ghana varied usually in weight from an ounce to a pound; some were much larger. The king had one which weighed thirty pounds. There was a part of the country called El Ferouin, in which gold was so plentiful and salt so scarce, that salt was sold for its weight in gold. The king had further sources of wealth in a very large customs revenue raised on salt, copper, and foreign merchandise.

When he gave audience to the people, Tenkamenin appeared in great state, seated under a pavilion round which were ranged ten horses caparisoned in gold. Behind him were ten pages bearing shields and swords mounted in gold. On his right stood "the sons of the princes of the Empire, magnificently dressed." The governor of the town and all the ministers sat upon the ground before the king. The door of the pavilion was guarded by pure-bred dogs, whose collars were of gold and silver, with bells of the same metal. It was the custom for these dogs never to leave the spot occupied by the king. On the days of audience the grievances of the people were inquired into by the king. El Bekri tells us little of the system of justice of the country, except that it was organised by the Mohammedan ministers of the king.

Mohammedanism had made such evident progress in the middle of the eleventh century, that it is not surprising to learn a century later from El Idrisi, that the King of Ghana and the notables of his day were Mohammedan, and that the king accepted investiture from the Eastern Caliph. There had, however, intervened between the period of the two writers a Mohammedan conquest of which we have yet to hear.

CHAPTER XI

THE TRADE OF GHANA

THE constant allusions made by early writers to the trade of Ghana leave no doubt that its commercial relations with the outside world had already become very important during the period in which the Ommeyades ruled in Spain. Gold, slaves, skins, ivory, kola-nuts, gums, honey, corn, and cotton, are among the articles of export which are most frequently named. Hardly a town is mentioned in the states of Northern and North-Western Africa of which it is not said that it carried on trade with the Soudan. Augila, in the back country of Tripoli, Wargelan or Wargla, in the back country of Algiers, with Sidjilmessa in the back country of Morocco, were all known by the name of "Gates of the Desert." Augila was the special entrance of the trade with Egypt and the East; Sidjilmessa, which was the entrance for the trade of the West, has already been described; Wargelan, which lies on the parallel of Bugia, is specially mentioned as being inhabited by very rich merchants, who made their fortunes from the gold of the Soudan, brought to Wargelan in the form of gold dust, and "coined" there for export. From Wargelan to Ghana was, we are told, a journey of thirty days.

At a somewhat later date, towards the end of the period of the Ommeyades, we have a circumstantial account of how the ancestors of the historian Al Makkari carried on a trade between Europe and the Soudan, by which the fortunes of the house of Makkari were laid. An ancestor of his, writing in the fourteenth century, says: "From time immemorial my family had exercised the profession of commerce in the countries where they settled, deriving no small share of influence and riches from it. They furrowed the sands of the desert in all directions; they dug wells and facilitated travelling in the Sahara, thus affording security to merchants and travellers. They took a drum, and marching always preceded by a banner, they headed the numerous caravans which from time to time penetrated into the country of the blacks. . . ."

A certain Abdurrahman, one of the family, having died and left behind him five sons, "they determined upon forming a partnership, carrying on the trade conjointly, and dividing between themselves the profits of their mercantile speculations." They accordingly threw together in a "common fund all their father's inheritance, and having held a consultation together as to the means of carrying on the trade to the greatest advantage," it was "agreed" that two should remain and establish themselves at Telemçan, at this time a principal port upon the Mediterranean for European trade; that one should fix his residence at Sidjilmessa; and lastly, that two should go to Aiwalatin in the desert.

"It was done as agreed between them. Each reached his place of destination, settled there, married and had a family, and they began to conduct their trade in the following manner: those in Telemçan sent to their partners in the desert such goods and commodities as were wanted in those districts, while these supplied them in return with skins, ivory, and kola-nuts. In the meanwhile the one stationed at Sidjilmessa was like the tongue of the balance between the two, since, being placed at a convenient distance between Telemçan and the desert, he took care to acquaint the respective parties with the fluctuations of trade, the amount of losses sustained by traders, the overstock of the markets, or the great demand for certain articles;" and, in short, to inform them of the "secret designs of other merchants engaged in the same trade, as well as of the political events which might in any way influence it. By these means they were enabled to carry on their speculations with the greatest success; their wealth increased, and their importance waxed every day greater."

An account is then given of how on one occasion in Aiwalatin, when the neighbouring Sultan of Tekrour attacked and took the town, the property and lives of the Arab merchants, including those of the Makkari company, were placed in great danger. "But my ancestors, being men of great courage and determination, would not consent to witness their ruin. They assembled all their servants and dependents, and such traders as happened to be in Aiwalatin at the time, and having distributed arms among them, they shut themselves up in their warehouses, and decided to fight, if necessary, for the defence of their goods and chattels."

Catastrophe was averted, however, by an interview between the senior partner and the invading king, who agreed to extend his protection to the company, and who treated them from that time with the utmost favour and distinction. "He frequently after this wrote to the partners at Telemçan, applying directly for such goods as he wanted for his own consumption, or such as were most sought for in his dominions." This political development seems to have greatly enlarged the scope of the operations of the Makkari firm. "The moment my ancestors perceived that they could trust and rely on kings, such difficulties as might have existed before were speedily removed. . . . The desert and its dangers seemed no longer the scene of death and misery, and they began to frequent its most lonely and dangerous tracts, their wealth thereby increasing so rapidly that it almost surpassed the limits of computation. Nor," says the account, "were these the only advantages arising from their enterprise; the natives with whom they traded were considerably benefited by it. For it must be understood that the trade with the desert was in the most deplorable state before the people of Makkareh engaged in it. Merchants, totally unacquainted with the real wants of the inhabitants, carried thither articles which were either of no use or of no value to them, taking in exchange objects which were a source of profit and wealth. This even went so far that an African sovereign was once heard to say: 'Were it not that I consider it a bad action, I would, by God! prevent these Soudan traders from stopping in my dominions; for thither they go with the most paltry merchandise, and bring in return the gold which conquers the world.' However, when my ancestors had once established a direct trade with those countries, the scene changed, and the blacks were better and more abundantly provided with such articles as they stood most in need of. They also were furnished with goods which they had never seen before, and they obtained a better price for their returns."

The writer of this account was a Judge of the Supreme Court of Fez in the year 1356. Presumably, therefore, he may have been born about the year 1300, and he counts himself sixth in descent from Abdurrahman, the founder of the firm. Allowing thirty years for a generation, this would get us back near to the year 1100, or not very far distant from the period at which the life of Ghana has been described. As all writers agree that the trade of Ghana was important in the eighth and ninth centuries, we must assume that, with the approaching decline of the kingdom, the trade had already fallen into some decay, from which it was revived by the exertions of the Makkari firm. The account is interesting for the indication which it gives that, in the early period of Arab trade with the Soudan, companies found it necessary, as European companies have found at a later date, to acquire political as well as commercial influence, and also that the better class of traders exercised a wise discretion as to the class of articles which they introduced to the notice of the natives.

The allusion made in the incidents which have been related to the successful attack upon Ghana by a neighbouring king may be taken, perhaps, to presage the conquest of Ghana, first by Susu and then by Melle, events which took place, the first in the twelfth, and the second in the thirteenth century.

Many lesser kingdoms, both black and Berber, surrounded Ghana. Amongst the black, El Bekri mentions specially Tekrour and Silla, both of which, though black, already in the middle of the eleventh century professed Mohammedanism. Silla, which was situated on the banks of the Niger, where the river skirted the south-eastern frontier of the Empire of Ghana, was, when El Bekri wrote, a country of some importance, able, he says, to maintain its independence against Ghana, and was a centre of the cotton industry. At Terensa, a town within the limits of this country, he remarks, "that no house is without its cotton plantation."

Among the lesser kingdoms, also, south and east of Ghana, one which deserves special mention is Masina, of which the inhabitants were largely Fulani. This little state is particularly interesting as having in its origin submitted by agreement to draw its rulers equally from Fulani and Berber sources, and as having succeeded in maintaining its integrity if not its independence for many centuries against the invasion of surrounding black peoples. It has been already mentioned as having solicited with success the assistance of Tin Yeroutan, the Berber king of Audoghast in the tenth century, against its black neighbours of Aougham. After passing through many vicissitudes, including submission to the black dynasty of Melle and the Songhay dynasty of Timbuctoo, it is mentioned again by the author of the *Tarikh-es-Soudan*, as refusing any longer, in 1629, to accept the investiture of its rulers from the hands of the decadent and Moorish Timbuctoo.

But it does not fall within the scope of this book to attempt to deal with the many nations of the Western Soudan who arose and fell within a period of a thousand years. For the purpose of tracing the course of civilisation through the fertile belt it is enough to mention a few of the most important. Amongst these Melle followed most closely upon the footsteps of Ghana, but at the end of the eleventh century it was a mere town, mentioned by El Bekri, under the name of El Melel, as occupying a position of no great importance on the Bend of the Niger. Its kings were at that date already Mohammedans, but the mass of its people were "still plunged in idolatry."

Little would seem to have been known to the Spanish Arabs in El Bekri's days of the countries lying eastwards of the Bend of the Niger. El Bekri gives, however, a very accurate account of the course of the Niger throughout the northern portion of the Bend, describing some of the principal towns, though not all, which were at that time in existence on the part of the river known as the "Rasel-Ma," or "Head of the Waters," where, near to the present position of Timbuctoo, the river, according to El Bekri's description, "leaves the Land of the Blacks" and runs eastwards for six days to a place which he calls Tirca before turning south by the famous city of Kagho or Kaougho. El Bekri tells us little of the place, of which the author of the *Tarikh-es-Soudan* says "that it was a city in the days of the Pharaohs." It has been generally identified as occupying the position of the present town of Gao. El Bekri's knowledge of it went no further than to enable him to say that its king was Mohammedan though the people were still pagan, and that from this point the Niger ran southward into the country of the Dem-Dems or cannibals.

In the immediate neighbourhood of this place there were, he tells us also, "a great quantity of mines which furnished gold dust." Of all the countries of the blacks it was the richest in gold, and foreign and black merchants, whom he designates by the name of Noughamarta, were constantly occupied in carrying this gold into all countries. All that El Bekri appears to know of the country lying between the Niger and Lake Chad is, that first there came a great kingdom, extending for more than an eight days' march, of which the sovereigns bear the title of "Du," beyond which comes Kanem, a country of the idolaters. The names of the early kings of Bornu all began with "Du." It is therefore presumable that El Bekri was correctly informed as to the position of Bornu, which at that time probably overran Haussaland ; but he gives us no information with regard to it. This silence on the part of a Spanish Arab, so generally well informed as El Bekri, seems to confirm the theory that the countries eastward of the Bend of the Niger derived their civilisation largely from Egypt *viâ* the Tripoli-Fezzan route, scarcely used at this time by the Western Arabs.

El Bekri makes no mention at all of Nupe, one of the oldest and most important of the purely native kingdoms, nor of Borgu, also a kingdom of great antiquity, which is said to have derived an early Christianity from the Copts of Egypt.

The waters of the Niger at the northern part of its course divided the Land of the Blacks, he tells us, from the territories of the Berbers on its northern banks. As the operations of these Berber tribes precede, in point of date, the rise of the kingdom of Melle, it may be well to turn for a moment to the eastern development of that Desert Kingdom which gave the Almoravide dynasty to Spain.

CHAPTER XII

MORABITE CONQUEST OF THE SOUDAN

It will be remembered that the population of the Desert Kingdom was composed of united Berber tribes, whose occupation of the desert was of immemorial antiquity. The united tribes were ruled, in the very healthy part of Africa which spreads inward from the Atlantic coast to the Sahara, by hereditary Berber kings. It has already been mentioned that Tiloutan, who died in 837 A.D., was one of the first of these to exact tribute from the black kingdoms of the Western Soudan, and that his descendant, Tin Yeroutan, was ruling in Audoghast between the years 961 and 971. This Berber rule having been overthrown by the black monarch of Ghana, it was by an act of natural retribution, when the Almoravides formed themselves into a religious fighting force in the heart of the desert kingdom, that one of the first incidents of their Holy War was the sack of Audoghast and its restoration to Berber rule. But the taking of Audoghast was indicative of a movement which was in some sort to decide the fate of the Desert Kingdom. At the moment at which El Bekri wrote, this ancient kingdom was about to divide itself permanently into two sections, of which one, moving northwards under the Morabite commanders, was to renew the power of Africa upon the throne of Spain, while the other, breaking away from its brethren of the north, was to follow the road suggested to its armies by the taking of Audoghast; and, having carried the banners of the Crescent from the shores of the Atlantic to the Nile, was to scatter itself eventually in divided communities along the southern edge of the Sahara Desert. The Desert Kingdom itself disappeared, but in Africa the northern branch of the Almoravides left a permanent mark upon history by the foundation of the town of Morocco, while the southern branch left a no less permanent record in the foundation of Timbuctoo. These two towns came into existence within twenty-five years of each other. They were born of the same Almoravide parents, and were the outcome of the same religious and political upheaval.

El Bekri, safe in the seclusion of the court of Seville, to which before his death the Almoravides were to march as stern deliverers from the Christian yoke, was aware of the formation of the sect on the southern frontier of the Desert Kingdom. He had heard of the taking of Audoghast and of the advance to Sidjilmessa in 1056. But after the taking of the latter town he had evidently received only imperfect rumours of the reorganisation of the Almoravides under their new leader Yusuf. He makes no mention of the foundation of the town of Morocco, which took place in 1062; and writing—as he expressly says—in the year 1067, he no doubt gave the latest information possessed at Seville, when he says: "The present Emir of the Almoravides is Abou Bekr, but their Empire is broken up and their power divided. They now maintain themselves in the desert."

It is to Ibn Khaldun that we turn for the fuller history of this movement.

The northward march of the Almoravides has been related in an earlier chapter. It will be remembered that when, after the death of the original leader, success had crowned the arms of Abou Bekr, he was recalled from the northern provinces by the report of dissensions which had broken out between the tribes of the kingdom in the south, and that, placing full power in the north in the hands of his cousin Yusuf (or Joseph) Tachefin, he himself returned southwards with the object of reconciling his turbulent subjects. To effect this reconciliation he initiated a new campaign to the east, in the direction thrown open by the taking of Audoghast, and, as a matter of fact, he never again returned to the north. By a friendly partition agreed to in 1062, the northern provinces to the Mediterranean were ceded to Yusuf, while Abou Bekr retained for himself the old regions of the desert in the south. He retained also the old licence to extend these regions as far as force of arms could carry them.

We first hear of him as leading the armies of his followers on a victorious march across the southern borders of the desert, fighting with the pagan nations of the Soudan for a distance of ninety days east of the most easterly frontier of the Desert Kingdom. In these territories, as he conquered them, he assigned areas for the habitation of the principal tribes who had united beneath his banners. But these territories were not in the Soudan proper, as we know it. They were north of the Great River, and Ibn Khaldun, describing the position occupied by their descendants who were still all "Wearers of the Veil" 300 years later, especially tells us that they had never territorially occupied the Soudan, but remained in the desert, changing nothing in their ways. "Always divided and disunited by the diversity of their habits and their interests, they formed," he says, "a cordon of desert nations upon the northern frontier of the Soudan, separating its territory from the sandy regions that lie between it and the States of North Africa and Morocco."

By the end of the fourteenth century, when Ibn Khaldun wrote, this cordon of desert nations stretched from the Atlantic to the Nile; but by that date the people comprising it were subject to the black kings of the Soudan, paid them tribute, and furnished contingents for their armies.

Under Abou Bekr, at the end of the eleventh century, the united tribes marched as conquerors, and their campaign did not abandon its character as a Holy War. If they made no territorial confiscations, they claimed tribute from the vanquished peoples, and they imposed the Moslem faith upon all infidels who submitted to their arms. In some cases the necessity of accepting the faith was commuted for payment of a subsidy; but historians are practically in agreement that the conversion of the northern belt of the Soudan to Mohammedanism became general at about this date. The Almoravides did not confine their requirements to a purely nominal conversion. Doctors of divinity and Moslem teachers were sent into the black countries to teach the true faith, and no doubt the increase of communication which at this time took place with Spain opened the way for the acceptance of more enlightened religious views.

Although the cordon of natives spoken of by Ibn Khaldun in the fourteenth century extended at that period as far eastward as the Nile, the march of Abou Bekr in the eleventh century does not appear to have been carried beyond the deserts lying to the north and north-east of the Bend of the Niger. The Berber nations which completed the cordon are distinctly stated by other writers to have come down from Tripoli and the East.

Two important political incidents marked the campaign of Abou Bekr. In 1076 he carried the vengeance of Audoghast to the gates of Ghana, and, overthrowing the reigning black dynasty, placed a Berber on the throne. The life of the country does not seem to have been profoundly affected at the time by this revolution. El Idrisi, writing nearly a hundred years later, still speaks of it as being the greatest kingdom of the blacks. He mentions the fact that it is ruled by a king of Berber descent, who "governs by his own authority, but gives allegiance to the Abbasside Sultan of Egypt," and that the king and people are now Mohammedans; but he does not speak of it as having become in any respect a Berber kingdom.

Here is his account: "Ghana . . . is the most considerable, the most thickly populated, and the most commercial of the black countries. It is visited by rich merchants from all the surrounding countries, and from the extremities of the West. Its inhabitants are Mussulman. . . . The king governs by his own authority, but he does obeisance to the Abbasside Commander of the Faithful"—that is, the Egyptian Caliph. Then follows a description of the palace already mentioned, and the date of its construction, 1116 A.D. "The territory and domains of this king," Edrisi continues, "are conterminous with Wangara, or the country of gold." The king's nugget, weighing 30 lbs., is mentioned, and we are told that it was "an entirely natural production, which has been neither melted nor worked by the hand of man, except for the fact that a hole had been made through it in order that it might be fastened to the king's throne." It was regarded as a curio, unique of its kind, and the king was proud of its fame in the Soudan. Other writers give more fabulous weights to this famous nugget, and it appears to have remained among the royal treasures for upwards of two hundred years; for Ibn Khaldun mentions, at the end of the fourteenth century, a degenerate monarch of the conquering dynasty of Melle who sold the nugget for the value of its gold. Edrisi describes the King of Ghana, who was contemporary to himself, as "one of the most just of men," whose custom it was to ride once daily into the poorest and most wretched quarters of the city, and there to dispense justice to all who had ground for complaint. On all other occasions he rode with great pomp, magnificently dressed in silk and jewels, surrounded by guards preceded by elephants, giraffes, and other wild animals of the Soudan, and no one dared to approach him. The territory of Ghana proper was bounded, Edrisi tells us, by "Mazzawa on the west, by Wangara on the east, by the desert plains of the Soudan and the Berbers on the north, and on the south by the pagan countries of the Lem-lems and others." Mazzawa must be taken to represent the territory which was the seat of the Desert Kingdom, a country over which Melle was soon to extend its authority. Of Wangara Edrisi gives the following description: "From the town of Ghana to the frontier of Wangara is an eight days' journey. This latter country is renowned for the quantity and the quality of the gold which it produces. It forms an island of about 300 miles in length by 150 in breadth, which the Nile [Niger] surrounds on all sides, and at all seasons. Towards the month of August, when the heat is extreme and the Nile overflows its bed, the island, or the greater part of the island, is inundated for a regular time. When the flood decreases, natives from all parts of the Soudan assemble and come to the country to seek for gold during the fall of the water. Each gathers the quantity of gold great or small which God has allotted to him, no one being entirely deprived of the fruit of his labour. When the waters of the river have returned to their bed every one sells the gold he has found. The greater part is bought by the inhabitants of Wargelan, and some by those of the extreme west of Africa, where the gold is taken to the mints, coined into dinars, and put into circulation for the purchase of merchandise. This happens every year. . . . In Wangara there are flourishing towns and famous fortresses. Its inhabitants are rich. They possess gold in abundance, and receive productions which are brought to them from the most distant countries of the world." Like the inhabitants of Ghana, they wore mantles and veils. They were entirely black. The whole of the country owed allegiance to Ghana, in the name of whose sovereign the Khotbah was read and government was carried on.

The change of dynasty in Ghana between the eleventh and twelfth centuries altered little, therefore, in the habits or prosperity of the country. It serves principally to illustrate the alternating rule of black and white sovereigns, which was apparently accepted without difficulty in the Soudan.

It was perhaps rather in the other political event of the campaign to which allusion has been made than in the substitution of Berber for native rule in Ghana that a prophetic eye would have seen the little cloud destined some day to overspread the fair horizon of Ghana's future. This was the foundation of Timbuctoo by the Tuaregs in the year 1087.

CHAPTER XIII

GHANA AND TIMBUCTOO

It was indeed a fine movement of historic fate which caused the conqueror of Ghana to become the instrument of the foundation of Timbuctoo. "The prosperity of Timbuctoo," says the author of the *Tarikh-es-Soudan*, who was himself born in that town in the year 1596, "was the ruin of Ghana." Before the great days of Timbuctoo, Ghana, he tells us, "was the centre of the Soudan." After the rise of Timbuctoo all was gradually transferred. Timbuctoo drew to itself not only the wealth but the learning and enlightenment of the civilised world, and became the home of all that was "pure, delightful, and illustrious" in the Soudan. But the days of Timbuctoo's greatness were not yet; queen of the Soudan, as she was afterwards proudly to become, she was born, if not in a manger, yet under circumstances nearly approaching to the lowest conditions of humility. Abou Bekr was not himself the founder of the town. The Tuaregs of his train, to whom were allotted for their occupation the portion of the desert opposite to the most northerly reaches of the Niger, would seem to have chosen the site some nine years after his death. They were, like all the nomads of the desert, a pastoral people, and used to feed their flocks in the summer season upon the northern or left bank of the Niger. They never crossed the river to the Soudan side, but withdrew in the autumn and winter months to the interior uplands of the desert. The spot on which Timbuctoo now stands was the extreme limit of these summer wanderings. At first they had only an encampment there; gradually their encampment became a meeting-place for travellers coming from different parts of the country. Then they made of it a store where they left food and other objects of necessary use, and they placed the store under the care of an old female slave called Timbuctoo. So homely, according to the apparently best-informed writers, was the origin of the afterwards famous name. But if Timbuctoo had the homeliness, she had also the purity of a simple origin. The town, founded by Mohammedans, was never sullied by pagan worship. "Upon its soil," we are told, "no knee was ever bent, except to the Most Merciful"—a curious commentary, alas, upon certain subsequent passages of its history. At first the dwellings of the town were constructed simply of thorns and straw, later they grew into clay huts. Later still low walls were built all round them. Finally a mosque was erected large enough for the needs of the inhabitants. But though the site was never altered, and the foundation of Timbuctoo, the stronghold of Mohammedanism in the Soudan, may therefore be regarded as the direct outcome of the religious campaign of Abou Bekr, it was not for two hundred years that the real town of Timbuctoo, as it was known in its greatness to posterity, was built by one of the kings of Melle, himself a Mohammedan, though black, and two more centuries were added to these before Timbuctoo reached the summit of its prosperity and fame as the capital of the Songhay empire.

However much it may flatter the pride of the historians of Timbuctoo to represent it as the cause of the downfall of Ghana, it is evident that the rivalry between the two towns must have been of much later date than the Almoravide conquest of Ghana. Ghana was in a position to bear a very active part in such rivalry for many generations after its conquest by the Berbers of Abou Bekr's train. The conquest by which the independence of Ghana was overthrown was not in fact the conquest of Abou Bekr. Between the Almoravide campaign of the end of the eleventh century and the development of the greatness of Timbuctoo under the Songhay dynasty, a very important chapter of Soudanese history was to intervene. This was the rise of the kingdom of Melle, the first of the black Mohammedan native states to be recognised on terms of equality by the other Mohammedan kingdoms of North Africa. It was the conquest of Ghana by Melle which really put an end to the independence of Ghana, and merged its history in that of the more civilised empire.

We have seen that at the end of the eleventh century, when Ghana submitted to the vengeance of Abou Bekr, Melle was but a town of second-rate importance in the bend of the Niger. A place of more distinction mentioned by El Bekri was Tekrour. Whether the Tekrour of El Bekri was identical with Jenné, a town of which the history is famous, and which was founded by Songhay pagans about the year 800 of our era, I leave for the more learned to decide. There are grounds for believing that this may have been the case; but "Tekrour," of which the literal meaning is "black," is one of the names that create confusion in the history of the Soudan. It has evidently been applied at different periods to different peoples. However this may have been, Ghana was at a period subsequent to the Almoravide conquest attacked and apparently for a time overwhelmed by the neighbouring black kingdom of Tekrour. In the earlier period of its history, Ghana had ruled over the Wangara. When Idrisi speaks of it in the middle of the twelfth century, though still the greatest of black kingdoms, with a trade extending to Egypt, North Africa, and Spain, its territory had apparently diminished, for Idrisi describes it as limited on the east by the territory of the Wangara, —whom he calls also by the alternative name of Mandingoes—and they, instead of forming part of the kingdom, were only tributary. Ibn Khaldun says that before the rise of Melle, Ghana was conquered by the Su-Su. The Su-Su, as they now exist, are of Mandingo origin. It is therefore possible that the Wangara, once the subjects of Ghana, became its rulers. No historian, however, dwells with any detail upon these early conquests. They are interesting merely as indications of the approaching disappearance of the supremacy of Ghana. While Timbuctoo, which was destined to represent the great centre of Mohammedanism in the Soudan, was growing, Ghana, the great centre of paganism, was passing away. It had maintained itself from a period long antecedent to the Hegira. After an existence of perhaps a thousand years, the term of its decadence had arrived, and toward the beginning of the thirteenth century of our era it had reached a condition in which, being at once rich and weak, it could scarcely fail to become the prey of stronger neighbours. By the end of that century it had become subject to its Mohammedan neighbour Melle.

So silently, and without dramatic rites, the gods of paganism disappear from the front rank of the history of the Soudan. No dome was built for them in Ghana. No ditch was dug. No sacred grove was planted. They simply fell back into the dark and barbarous country to the south—the land of the Lem-Lem, which Arab historians dismiss contemptuously as the land of idolaters "who eat men." The memory of these pagan gods lingered long amongst the lower orders of the northern states; but whatever their worship had brought with it of enlightenment from the antiquity of eastern civilisation was finally extinguished in the barbaric caricature which is the memorial preserved of them to the present day by certain tribes of the southern coast.

CHAPTER XIV

THE MELLESTINE

THE empire of Melle and its dependencies, known to the Arabs as "The Mellestine," which rose in the thirteenth century on the ruins of Ghana, was the first of the great black Mohammedan kingdoms of the Western Soudan to claim intercourse on equal terms with contemporary civilisation. In the days of its greatest prosperity the territories of the Mellestine extended from the coast of the Atlantic on the west to the Niger boundary of Haussaland on the east, and from the country of the cannibals on the south its protectorate extended into the desert as far as the frontier of Wargelan.

In 1353, when the fortunes of Melle were at their highest, Ibn Khaldun, who was then employed on a political mission at Biskra, met one of the notables of Tekadda, an important Berber town of the desert, which, "like all other towns of the Sahara," at that time acknowledged the sovereignty of Melle. Amongst other details of the caravan trade which Ibn Khaldun learned from this man he mentions that caravans from Egypt, consisting of 12,000 laden camels, passed every year through Tekadda on their way to Melle. The load of a camel was 300 lbs.: 12,000 camel loads amounted, therefore, to something like 1600 tons of merchandise. In the comparison which has so often been made of a caravan of the desert to a ship, it is worth while to remember that, at this date, there was probably not a ship in any of the merchant navies of the world which would carry 100 tons. At the time of the Armada, 250 years later, when English and Spanish merchant ships were scouring the Eastern and the Western seas, the average tonnage of the vessels which composed the Spanish force was 500 tons, and that of the English ships much less. The largest ship which Queen Elizabeth had in her navy, the *Great Harry*, was 1000 tons, but it was considered an exception and marvel of the age.

The western half of the desert was no less active in trade with Melle than the eastern. All the desert towns, we are told, from Twat westward, were halting-places for caravans passing between Morocco, the Barbary coast, and Melle. Tementit, a community of about 200 villages, lying to the west of Twat, was a great centre of this passing trade. These desert towns of the back country of Algiers possessed the inestimable boon of artesian water. The method of obtaining it was to sink a deep well, of which the sides were carefully built up. This was carried down to the rock under which water was expected to be found. The rock was cut away with picks and axes until nothing but the thinnest layer was left. The workmen were then taken out of the well, and a great mass of iron was dropped upon the rock, which, giving way, the water leaped up, "sometimes with such force as to carry everything before it," into the receptacle which had been prepared, whence, overflowing, it formed a little stream upon the ground. Not only the artesian water of Twat, but also the great salt-mines of Tegazza, lay within the limits of the Mellestine.

The first sovereign of Melle to accept Islam was Bermandana, who made the pilgrimage to Mecca—a custom afterwards adopted by his successors. The date of this pilgrimage does not appear to have been preserved, but it may be gathered from a list of ten kings descending from one of his successors, Mari Djata, to the famous Mansa Musa, who made the pilgrimage in 1324, that his conversion must have been rather before than after the Morabite invasion of Negroland at the end of the eleventh century.

Leo Africanus, whose history, however, is not usually

trustworthy, says that the people of Melle embraced the law of Mohammed when "the uncle of Joseph, King of Morocco"—that is, Abou Bekr, the Morabite leader—was then prince. He also says that the government of Melle remained for some time in the posterity of that prince. If Melle in the beginning took its rise, as Leo Africanus suggests, under Berber princes, it is but one instance the more of the profound impression made by the Morabite invasion upon Negroland. But there can be no doubt that in the days of its greatness the kings of Melle were black, and ousted the Berber descendants of the Morabites in the desert.

In the early part of its history Melle consisted of three principalities claiming equal rights. The first of its kings who would appear to have consolidated the kingdom and enlarged its boundaries to any appreciable extent was Mari Djata, who overthrew the Su-Su and conquered Ghana in the early part of the thirteenth century. The name of Ghana from this time is no longer heard, Ghana being properly the title of the ruler, not the name of the kingdom. The country heretofore known as Ghana now becomes Ghanata or Walata. Mari Djata's name of Djata meant Lion. His hereditary title Mari was something less than king, confirming the theory that he was the first of the rulers of Melle to consolidate its possessions under one sovereign. He reigned for twenty-five years, and his descendants and successors are all known by the full title of Mansa, or king, the succession going, as in the old pagan succession of Ghana, in female descent, not to the king's son but to his sister's son.

The pilgrimages made by these kings to Mecca are the dates by which we are usually able to fix the period, if not the exact limit, of their reigns. The son of Mari Djata made his pilgrimage as king in 1259. A famous usurper, Sakora, who greatly extended the dominions of Melle towards the east, made his pilgrimage in the year 1310.

Under Sakora the territories of Melle were as much extended in the east as they had been by the conquest of Ghana in the west, for he conquered Gago or Kaougha, the capital of Songhay, of which the site was the present town of Gao. This town was, at the beginning of the fourteenth century, the centre of a rich and important territory shaken for the moment by internal convulsions, and therefore open to conquest by a powerful neighbour. In the twelfth century it was described by El Idrisi as a "populous, unwalled, commercial and industrial town, in which were to be found the produce of all arts and trades necessary for the use of its inhabitants." Ibn Said, in the thirteenth century, speaks of it also with respect. It was throughout its history celebrated for the great quantity of gold with which its markets abounded; it will be remembered that this peculiarity was noted by El Bekri.

The Mohammedanism of Songhay, having presumably come to it by the eastern and not by the western road, dated from an earlier period than that of Melle and Ghana. The first of the Songhay kings to accept Islam was Za-Kosoi, whose conversion took place in 1009. The early kings of Songhay were all known by the title of "Za," which was afterwards changed to Sonni, and at a later period still to Askia or Iskia. The "Zas" were still reigning when Songhay was conquered in the early years of the fourteenth century.

Mansa Musa, the next great king of Melle, completed the conquests made by Sakora, and Songhay remained subject to Melle until about the year 1356. Although in its state of unwalled prosperity it fell a comparatively easy prey to the military strength of Melle, it is probable that Songhay regarded itself even at that period as possessing a higher civilisation than that of its conquerors. In including it within the territories of the Mellestine and causing its princes to be brought up at his own courts, the Sultan of Melle unconsciously played the part of one who takes to his hearth a slave destined eventually to become his master. For about fifty years Melle ruled Songhay. At the end of that period Songhay recovered its independence, and a hundred years later it reared upon the ruins of Melle an empire which outdid in splendour and enlightenment the most glorious epoch of the Mellestine.

CHAPTER XV

MANSA MUSA

MANSA MUSA, who completed the conquest of his predecessor Sakora, was a prince whom all historians combine to praise, celebrating his justice, piety, and enlightenment. He was the friend of white men, and entertained pleasant relations with the kings of Morocco and the Barbary coast, at whose courts, as has been mentioned, the Arab civilisation of Spain had already in great part taken refuge. He exchanged presents with them, and kept himself well informed of the political developments of their kingdoms.

He made a celebrated pilgrimage to Mecca in the year 1324, of which the details, preserved by more than one contemporary witness, furnish an interesting illustration of the condition of his country and the state preserved by its monarchs.

The caravan consisted on this occasion, we are told, of no less than sixty thousand persons, a considerable portion of whom constituted a military escort. The baggage of the caravan was carried generally by camels, but twelve thousand young slaves formed the personal retinue of Mansa Musa. All these were dressed in tunics of brocade or Persian silk. When he rode, five hundred of them marched before him, each carrying a staff of pure gold, which weighed sixty-two ounces. The remainder carried the royal baggage.

The caravan was accompanied by all essential luxuries, including good cooks, who prepared elaborate repasts, not only for the king, but for the king's friends, at every halting-place. To defray the expenses of the journey,

Mansa Musa took with him gold dust to the value of upwards of a million sterling. This was carried in eighty camel loads of 300 lbs. weight each. His Songhay historian says of him that, notwithstanding all this magnificence, he was not generous in the gifts which he made in the holy cities. Others say that, on the contrary, he was so lavish in his gifts, that the large provision which he had made for his journey was insufficient, and that he had to borrow money for his return, which, as his credit was good, he had no difficulty in doing, and that the debt was afterwards punctually paid.

He made of his pilgrimage something more than a religious journey to Mecca. It was also a state progress through his dominions. Instead of starting eastward, as might have been expected, he started in a westerly direction, going first through the conquered territory of Ghana to the town no longer spoken of by that name, but by the modern name of Walata, or Aiwalatin. On his way thither, at Mimah, one of the conquered towns, a characteristic little incident occurred. There was in the Sultan's train a white judge to whom he had given four thousand ducats to meet the expenses of the journey. At Mimah this white judge complained that his four thousand ducats had been stolen. Mansa Musa sent for the governor of the town, and ordered him, on pain of death, to produce the robber. The governor caused the town to be vigorously searched, but he found no robber, "because in that town there were none." He went to the house occupied by the judge and cross-examined the servants. A slave of the judge then confessed: "My master has lost nothing; but he himself hid the money in this place." He showed the place to the governor, who took the ducats, and reported the circumstances to the Sultan. Mansa Musa sent for the judge, and, after trial, banished him to the country of the pagans "who eat men." He remained there, the historian states, for four years, at the end of which time the Sultan allowed him to return, not to Melle, but to his own native country. "The reason," it is added, "why the cannibals did not eat him is that he was white. They say that the flesh of white men is unwholesome because it is unripe. Black flesh alone, in their opinion, is ripe."

The caravan proceeded from Walata by the westerly route northward to Twat, and here suffered a very considerable diminution by an affection of the feet which attacked a large portion of the caravan. This malady, of which no descriptive account is given, was, it is said, called in their language *touat*. There is no hint that it was caused by "jiggers," but the event, important enough to have been preserved in subsequent chronicles, of half a caravan incapacitated by an epidemic of the feet, suggests the widespread devastation of the "jigger," and it would be interesting, were it possible, to ascertain whether any surviving word in the Melle language connects *touat* with the destructive insect. The author of the *Tarikh-es-Soudan* says that the name of the oasis of Twat was bestowed upon it in consequence of this catastrophe. Commentators reject, however, this derivation of the name.

From Twat the caravan would seem to have pursued the usual road to Egypt, where it camped for a time outside Cairo, and passed on to Mecca and Medina. Here Musa made a profound impression on the peoples of the East, who have left in their annals, says one historian, a record of his voyage, and of their astonishment at the magnificence of his empire. But it appears that he gave only 20,000 gold pieces in alms in each town, and in comparison with the immense extent of the territories he governed, this was not considered munificent. The same author, however, mentions incidentally that throughout his journey, wherever he halted on a Friday, he built a mosque. The funds required for such a purpose, even though some of the mosques were but small, must have been considerable.

At Mecca the Sultan of Melle made literary acquaintances, and persuaded the Spanish poet and architect,

Abu Ishak, better known by the name of Toueidjen, to return with him, and to take up his residence at the court of Melle. Every kind of royal favour was afterwards, it is said, showered upon the family of Toueidjen, who established themselves permanently at Aiwalatin. The caravan returned from Mecca by the eastern route, and at Ghadames, in the desert, it was met by a certain El Mamer, a chief who, being at the time out of favour with the powers of Tunis, was anxious to conciliate Mansa Musa, "whose authority extended over the desert." Mansa Musa received him very hospitably, and took him also in his train to Melle. El Mamer relates how he and the Spanish architect travelled together in the royal cortège in great comfort. Precedence was given them over many of the native chiefs and viziers. "His Majesty," El Mamer says, "seemed to take pleasure in our conversation." And at every halting-place their table was provided from the royal kitchen with food and sweetmeats. On its way to the capital the caravan passed through Songhay and stopped at Kagho, where the emperor caused a mosque to be built. It was apparently a mosque of some importance, and it was still in existence three hundred years later. Mansa Musa also took the two young sons of the Songhay monarch, by name Ali Kolon and Suleiman Nare, to educate at his court.

Having thus made the complete round of his empire, Mansa Musa re-entered his capital and immediately employed his Spanish architect to design for him a hall of audience, built after the fashion of Egyptian architecture. Abou Ishak, it is said, displayed all the wonders of his genius in the creation of "an admirable monument" which gave great satisfaction to the king. The hall was square and surmounted by a dome. It was built of stone, covered with plaster, and decorated with beautiful coloured arabesques. It had also, we are told, two tiers of arched windows, of which the windows of the lower tier were framed in gold, plated upon wood, and the windows of the upper tier were framed in silver, plated upon wood.

This hall of audience communicated by an interior door with the palace. In expression of his satisfaction, the Sultan gave Abou Ishak 12,000 mitkals of gold dust, a sum amounting in our money to about £8000. But to this, which seems to us a relatively moderate reward, must be added, says the historian, the high favour of the prince, an eminent place at court, and splendid presents made from time to time.

Upon his return from this great pilgrimage, Mansa Musa turned his arms against Timbuctoo, and after a severe conflict with the Sultan of Mossi, who sacked the town in or about the year 1330, Musa became master, in 1336, of the future capital of the Soudan. This town offering fresh opportunity to the young architect, it was embellished by a royal palace and mosque. Both buildings were of cut stone, and the remains of the palace exist at the present day, though they are now used only as a slaughter-house. The Great Mosque, which had a remarkable minaret, was afterwards rebuilt about the year 1570 by a pious governor of Timbuctoo in obedience to advice from Mecca, where it was stated that the prosperity of Timbuctoo was closely associated with the prosperity of the minaret, then apparently in a dilapidated condition. Some portion of the old mosque still remains, and when Barth saw it in 1855 it was perfectly distinguishable from the later construction.

The first Imaums of this mosque were all learned blacks, many of whom made their studies in the University of Fez. One of these, Katib Moussa, who was a jurisconsult and very learned, had also extraordinary health. He lived to a great age and filled the position of Imaum for forty years without a single day's illness. Being asked to what he attributed his good health, he gave three simple hygienic rules, of which the last, at least, if not the other two, is still worthy the consideration of white men in West Africa. He never slept, he said, exposed to the night air; he never missed anointing himself at night and taking a hot bath in the morning; and he never went out without breakfast.

The Great Mosque continued to be the centre of religious life in Timbuctoo until the conquest of the town by the Moors in 1591, while the still older Sankoré Mosque was the centre of university life. A teacher of this mosque, who also returned with Musa from the East, found Timbuctoo full of black jurisconsults, whose knowledge of law was greater than his own. He accordingly went to Fez, where he studied law for some years, and then returned to found a chair of law at Timbuctoo.

In 1337, the year after Musa's conquest of Timbuctoo, Abou el Haçen, the reigning monarch of Morocco, effected that conquest of Telemçan which has already been mentioned in a previous chapter, and Mansa Musa sent a deputation to congratulate him. Abou el Haçen, on his part, being, it is said, "animated by a proper pride," had "adopted the habit of interchanging presents with all monarchs his equals." The King of Melle was at that time the greatest of the black kings, and his territories were nearest to Morocco. Abou el Haçen therefore determined to send him a "truly royal" present of the finest products of his kingdom. We are not told of what it was composed, but we are told that he carefully chose all the objects which it included himself, and that he confided it to the care of a highly honourable chief, Ibn Ghanem. A deputation composed of the most eminent persons of the empire was selected to accompany it. The magnificence of the offering, Ibn Khaldun says, was the subject of general comment, and we may draw from this circumstance our own inference as to the importance of the place occupied by Melle among the states of Africa. But the splendid gift never reached Mansa Musa. While it was on its way he died. It was delivered to his successor, who sent the handsome return present once before mentioned, composed of products of his own country all extremely rare and curious, and it became the habit of the sovereigns of Melle and Morocco to interchange presents by the medium of the great officials of their kingdoms. The amiable relations thus established between them were maintained by their successors for several generations.

During the reign of Mansa Musa the limits of the Mellestine were extended over the desert until they became practically conterminous with those of Morocco and the westernmost portion of the Barbary States. They were separated from them only by a belt of shifting sands, of the breadth of a three days' journey, known to the Arabs under the name of "El Areg," or "The Dunes," which, uninhabited by any peoples, stretched more or less continuously across the continent from the Atlantic to the Nile. The Mellestine had by this time become so important that all its towns were frequented by the merchants of Morocco, Barbary, and Egypt. The capital is described by a contemporary writer as a place of considerable extent, very populous and commercial. Numerous streams watered the cultivated lands which surrounded it. Merchandise from all countries was sent to it, and it was the meeting-place of caravans from Morocco, North Africa, and Egypt. The system of government and justice established by Musa would seem to have been that which animated the political existence of Melle during the prosperous period of its history.

Mansa Musa himself reigned twenty-five years, and his death, which took place between the sending of his deputation to congratulate Abou el Haçen on the conquest of Telemçan in 1337 and the arrival of the return present of Abou el Haçen, must have been presumably not later than 1339, more probably 1338. Ibn Khaldun says of him: "Mansa Musa was distinguished by his ability and by the holiness of his life. The justice of his administration was such that the memory of it still lives." This was perhaps not much to say at the end of the fourteenth century, when he had hardly been dead for sixty years; but nearly 300 years later his Songhay historian, writing with no bias in his favour, in the middle of the seventeenth century, repeats the praise and speaks of him as a pious and equitable prince, unequalled for virtue or uprightness.

CHAPTER XVI

IBN BATUTA IN MELLE

It was at the court of Abou el Haçen, the conqueror of Telemçan, that Ibn Batuta, as we have seen, resolved in the year 1349 to rest from further exploration, and though, like Marco Polo, he wrote nothing himself, to dictate to his scribes a record of the voyages he had made. Intercourse between the sovereigns of Melle and Morocco had within the ten years preceding his arrival received a great development. The fame of Mansa Musa's journey to Mecca, his admirable and upright character, and the opening of his country to the commerce of North Africa, formed at the time subjects of fresh interest at the court of Fez. That a king so enlightened and intelligent as Abou el Haçen should wish to know more of the countries lately opened to Moorish influence was natural, and having at his court a traveller so experienced as Ibn Batuta, it is not surprising that the idea of still further voyages should have been suggested to the explorer.

Notwithstanding his intention of travelling no more, Ibn Batuta was, as we have already seen, infected by the general enthusiasm, and in 1352 he started on the journey which gives us, from the lips of an eye-witness, a picture of the court and kingdom of Melle as they existed within ten or fifteen years of the death of Mansa Musa. Mansa Musa's son had had only a short reign of four years, and the succession had passed to his uncle, Mansa Suleiman, a brother of Musa. This Suleiman reigned twenty-four years, and was the sovereign of Melle at the time of Ibn Batuta's visit.

Ibn Batuta travelled south by the road already described by El Bekri, taking the westernmost branch which led through the "Salt City" of Tegazza. It is unnecessary to reproduce his description, to which allusion has been made in an earlier chapter. It is chiefly interesting as serving to prove the accuracy of El Bekri's description given from the reports of Spanish merchants three hundred years earlier, and to illustrate incidentally the continuity of life and tradition which left the conditions of travel upon the road practically unchanged after the lapse of so long a time. El Bekri's account, gathered from the experience of travellers passing over the road in 1052, might equally have been written by Ibn Batuta in 1352, and the account given by Ibn Batuta have been given by El Bekri. Indeed, in one respect, Ibn Batuta's account carries the imagination even further back, for his description of the town of Tegazza, in which the houses and the mosque were built of slabs of salt, recalls the description given by Herodotus of the salt towns of the "Land of Dates."

The whole of these desert stopping-places lay within the limits assigned by Ibn Khaldun to the Mellestine. Ibn Batuta crossed the frontier of Melle proper at Aiwalatin, the capital of the old kingdom of Ghanata. But the Ghana of El Bekri's day had fallen low. Ibn Batuta found it occupied largely by Berbers, descendants of the Morabites, whose degeneracy gave him cause for amazement. Mohammedan as they called themselves, they had fallen into habits which scandalised him. He felt, as unfortunately many a white man since then has had sorrowful occasion to feel in similar circumstances, that these white men did not sustain the dignity of their race in the presence of the blacks by whom they were surrounded and to whose rule they bowed.

The black viceroy who received the merchants of the caravan with which Ibn Batuta travelled remained seated while they stood before him. He spoke to them through an interpreter, not because he did not understand, or because they were not close enough for him to hear, but "solely to indicate his disdain for them." The experience stirred in Ibn Batuta such wrath that he regretted to have entered the country of black men who were thus ill-mannered, and who treated white men with so little respect. His disgust and indignation were for several days overpowering. He could hardly prevail with himself to continue his journey, and he had nearly resolved to return with the caravan with which he had come. However, a stay of seven weeks in Aiwalatin appears to have modified his views. Possibly what he observed there of the degeneracy of the Berbers led to more sympathetic reflections upon the attitude assumed towards them by the blacks, and he determined to carry out his intention of travelling at least as far as the court of Melle.

It is evident from what he says that the Berbers of Ghana, though Mussulmans, and observing all the religious customs of their faith, studying jurisprudence and theology, and devoting a considerable portion of their time to learning the Koran by heart, had to a very great extent assimilated themselves to the customs of the blacks. The domestic privacy of the Moslem was not observed, and they had adopted the native habit of tracing their genealogy in the female line through a maternal uncle. The inheritance, as with the native royal dynasties in pre-Mohammedan days, went to the son of a sister. This was a practice which, though it is known to be common in Negroland, Batuta says that he had never seen, except amongst pagan Indians in Malabar.

The climate of Aiwalatin, Ibn Batuta says, was exceedingly hot. Food was abundant there, and the inhabitants were very prettily dressed, in clothes imported for the most part from Egypt. The women were beautiful, and, in Ibn Batuta's opinion, very superior to the men.

He found occasion for much criticism of their domestic conduct, but with regard to the strictures, of which he is not sparing, it is possible that there may be another side. Mohammedan women, in the great days of the Ommeyades in Spain, were not confined to harems, but went unveiled, and enjoyed the society of men as freely as do the English and American women of the present day. The Mohammedans of the desert may have preserved the custom of this freedom after it had been abandoned by the more cultivated Moslems of the towns, and may have felt that in doing so it was they, and not the orthodox, who had maintained the purer traditions of the faith. There is a hint of something of this sort in an argument which took place between Ibn Batuta and the leader of the caravan with whom he travelled—a rich man who possessed a house of his own in Aiwalatin. "The companionship of men and women in this country," urged the caravan leader, "is respectable and good. There is no harm attaching to it, and no unpleasant suspicions are aroused by this freedom of which you complain." But Ibn Batuta remained unconvinced. "I was surprised at his folly," he says, "and went no more to his house, though he invited me several times."

From Aiwalatin to the capital of Melle was a twenty days' march, for which, Ibn Batuta says, it was hardly necessary to have a guide or companions, as the road was perfectly safe. He travelled himself with three companions. All along the road they found immense and very old trees, of which one would have been enough to shelter a large caravan. Many of the trees had hollow trunks, in which, during the rains, water accumulated, and they served as cisterns for the passers-by. Others were much used by bees to build in, and men took the honey. In one a weaver had established his loom, and was weaving when Ibn Batuta passed.

The country between Aiwalatin and Melle would seem to have been wooded and thickly interspersed with villages. Amongst the trees of the wooded country Ibn Batuta notes fruits "resembling plums, apples, peaches, and apricots, but not quite like them." He also notes plantains; and ground nuts, of which the oil was employed for many purposes, formed a prevailing crop. Spices, salt, beads, and aromatic gums appeared to be the currency of the smaller villages. Everything required for a journey was easy to buy on the way. There was no need, Ibn Batuta says, to make any provision: food was plentiful, villages succeeded each other at short distances, and the inhabitants were always willing to sell anything that was required.

About half-way between Ghana and Melle Ibn Batuta and his companions reached the large town of Zaghari, principally inhabited by black merchants called *Ouandjaratah*, who remind us of the *Noughamarta* mentioned by El Bekri. In most of the towns there was a white quarter—in all of them Ibn Batuta notes the presence of white men. Zaghari was the centre of a great corn country, whence millet was exported to the frontier. From it the party struck the Niger at the point at which Segou now stands.

We get at this stage of the journey a description of the course of the Niger which is worth quoting. Some of the principal towns upon the river are first mentioned, including Zaghah. This town had adopted Islam, Ibn Batuta says, at a very early period. It had a king of its own who paid tribute to Melle, and its inhabitants were distinguished by their great zeal in the study of science. "From Zaghah," he continues, "the river flows down to Timbuctoo and Gao; thence to Muri or Muli, a place which forms part of the country of the Sêmiyyown (or Cannibals) and is the most distant limit of Melle. The river then flows down from Muri to Nupe, one of the most important countries of the Soudan, whose sovereign is among the greatest kings of the country. No white man enters Nupe, because the blacks would kill him before he arrived there." The course of the Lower Niger, where the river flowed through the territories of the cannibals and entered the swampy districts of the coast, was wholly unknown to Arab geographers, and Ibn Batuta accepted the common theory, which supposed that the Benué was a continuation of the Niger, and that below Nupe the river turned eastward to join the Nile.

There is a noticeable increase of respect in the tone

adopted by the traveller as he approaches the capital of Melle.

Quitting the Niger at Segou, "we travelled," he says, "towards the river Sansarah, which is about ten miles from Melle. The custom is to forbid the entrance of Melle to any one who has not obtained permission, but I had written beforehand to some of the principal personages in the white community of Melle to engage a house for me, and no objection was made to my entrance."

He went at once to the white quarter of the town, and found that one of his friends who was a lawyer had hired a house for him just opposite to his own. Ibn Batuta took possession of the house without delay. Food and wax candles were supplied to him, and on the following day he received visits from distinguished persons, of whom he subjoins a list. Amongst these there were men of letters, lawyers, jurisconsults. One black judge is specially mentioned as a man of merit, "adorned with most noble qualities." The royal herald Dougha, also a "black of great distinction," and holding one of the principal positions at court, was among his early visitors. These men and others all sent him presents and compliments, and caused him to feel at once that in the capital of the kingdom he was treated with the consideration which was his due.

The reigning king was somewhat miserly, and seldom gave presents of any value. He at first paid no attention to the arrival of the distinguished traveller, but during the period of Ibn Batuta's stay in the town the sorrowful news was received of the death of the Sultan of Morocco, Abou el Haçen. The king on that occasion gave a "banquet of condolence," and Ibn Batuta was invited. The governors, the jurisconsults, the judge, and the principal preacher of the mosque, are mentioned as being present. Caskets containing chapters of the Koran were apparently taken by the guests, and the entire Koran was read through on the occasion. Prayers were offered for the soul of Abou el Haçen, that the Almighty might have mercy upon him. Prayers were also offered for Mansa Suleiman.

It was after this ceremony that Ibn Batuta was first presented to the sovereign, who received him with a gravity befitting the occasion. A purely formal "gift of hospitality" was subsequently sent to him, which consisted only of meat and bread, and for two months he had no further private audience of the sovereign. He, however, continued to attend the public audiences, of which he describes the ceremonial in some detail. They were held sometimes in the Hall of Audience, designed by Mansa Musa's Spanish architect; sometimes outside in the Place of Audience, an enclosed square upon which the palace opened, and which was approached from the town by a wide and long boulevard, planted with trees. Whether they were held indoors or in the open air, a very strict and pompous ceremonial was observed. The boulevard was lined by detachments of soldiers armed with bows and lances, each detachment having its own commandant and military band. The bands were composed of drums and trumpets, horns made of ivory, and other instruments made with reeds and gourds, which gave a "most agreeable sound." The commandants were mounted, and armed with bows and arrows, each bearing a quiver full of arrows at his back, and carrying his bow in his hand. The soldiers were some on foot and some mounted. The general public, and all persons who had business to lay before the Sultan, waited in this boulevard. On occasions when the Sultan held his audience within the hall, the square outside was occupied by 300 servants of the palace, who stood to left and right in double rows, the front row seated on the ground armed with little shields and short spears, the back row standing and armed with bows and arrows.

No one entered the Hall of Audience itself till the curtains of the windows, which were usually kept closed, were, on the entrance of the Sultan, drawn back. At the same time a handkerchief or little banner was waved, which served as a signal to the public, and there was a burst of music from the bands. Then on receiving the summons of the King, certain officials, including the military governor, the preacher, and the jurisconsults, took their places in the Hall of Audience, seating themselves to left and right before the King's arm-bearers and the royal herald or interpreter placed himself in the doorway. This official was a personage of the greatest importance. He was "superbly dressed" in stuff of the finest silk, with a very handsome turban. He was booted and spurred, and wore hanging from his neck a sword in a gold scabbard. In each hand he carried a short spear, one of gold and one of silver, tipped with iron. Any one who had a cause to present then approached the open door and laid their case before the herald. He in turn repeated it to the lieutenant of the King, and this official repeated it to the King.

When the audience was held outside, a throne was erected for the King on a platform under a great tree in the square. The platform, which was approached by three steps, was covered with silk and cushions, and over it an immense silken umbrella "resembling a dome" was opened, on the summit of which perched a large golden bird.

The Sultan, preceded by his own private band, then issued in state from the palace. His band was composed of singers who accompanied themselves upon gold and silver instruments, of which the native name was a word signifying "larks." The band marched first. Then came the Sultan, dressed usually in red velvet with a golden helmet upon his head, a bow in his hand, a quiver full of arrows slung across his back. Behind him marched 300 armed slaves. The Sultan walked slowly. When he reached the platform, his custom was to pause to look at the public, and then very slowly to mount the platform "as a preacher mounts the pulpit." As he took his seat the military bands broke out, and the same ceremony was then observed as for the other audiences.

On occasions of public festivities these ceremonials were immensely increased, the whole crowd wearing only fine white clothes, public prayers and thanksgivings being offered up, and magnificent gifts presented by subjects to the Sultan and by the Sultan to subjects whom he wished to honour. On the breaking of the fast of the Ramadan, it was the custom to present arms to the Sultan in a more literal sense than that usually conveyed by the term; and on the occasion of that ceremony when Ibn Batuta was present, "squires" offered to the Sultan for his acceptance arms which are described as "magnificent." "They were," Ibn Batuta says, "swords ornamented in gold, with scabbards of the precious metal; spears of gold and silver; quivers made of gold and silver; and clubs made of crystal." On these occasions there were dramatic displays, including dancing, fencing, and gymnastic performances, which Ibn Batuta, having experience of similar performances in India, declared to be extremely good. There were also poetic recitations of an apparently comic kind.

Poets wearing masks and dressed like birds were allowed to speak their opinion to the monarch. Ibn Batuta states that this practice was of great antiquity, long anterior to the introduction of Islam amongst these people. The description which he gives in some detail can hardly fail to recall similar practices inherited from the Tezcucans by the Aztecs, who in nearly the same latitude on the American continent were at this very moment, in the middle of the fourteenth century, making good their position upon the Mexican plateau.[1] Ibn

[1] See likeness to Aztec performance at contemporary date. Prescott, in his account of Aztec literature and civilisation previous to the conquest of Mexico by the Spaniards, says: "They are said to have had also something like theatrical exhibitions of a pantomimic sort, in which the faces of the performers were covered with masks, and the figures of birds or animals were frequently represented."—*Conquest of Mexico*, vol. i. p. 98.

For a fuller account of these mummeries Prescott refers his readers to *Acosta*, lib. 5, cap. 30; and also Clavigero, *Stor-del-Messico*. See also for Aztec customs, Toribio, *Hist. de los Indios*, MS., parte 3, cap. 7.

Batuta also notices with censure the extreme servility which the Sultan of Melle exacted from the nobles and others by whom he was surrounded, and here, too, there is a resemblance to Aztec manners which is striking. "When the Sultan, seated in the Hall of Audience, calls any one before him," says Ibn Batuta, "the person summoned immediately divests himself of his fine clothes, puts on shabby garments, and, taking off his turban, covers his head with a dirty cap. He then enters the presence barefooted, with his trousers rolled half-way up his legs, listens with an air of profound submission to what the Sultan has to say, and covers his head and shoulders with dust, exactly as one might do who was performing his ablutions with water." Ibn Batuta's commentator, Ibn Djòzay, adds to this passage a note to the effect that the Secretary of State, who was present when Mansa Musa's ambassadors were received at Fez by Abou el Haçen, told him that on all state occasions, when the ambassador had audience of the Moorish Sultan, he was accompanied by an attendant carrying a basket of dust, and every time that the Sultan said something gracious to him he covered himself with dust. Prescott, in describing the ceremonial of the court of Montezuma, the Aztec Emperor of Mexico, at the time of the Spanish conquest, says that when ambassadors from foreign states were introduced, "whatever their rank, unless they were of blood royal, they were obliged to submit to the humiliation of shrouding their rich dress under the coarse mantle of *nequen,* and entering barefoot, with downcast eyes, into the presence." This custom of taking off the sandals and covering fine clothes with a mantle of the coarsest stuff which was made in Mexico, was imposed equally on all the nobility of Montezuma's capital. The Mexican's mode of obeisance was not to throw dust upon the head, but, bowing to the earth, to touch it with the right hand. The Aztecs were, it will be remembered, though not negroes, a dusky or copper-coloured race, apparently of the tint which Barth describes as that of the "red races" of the Soudan. They had other customs which correspond to those of the Soudanese. The Aztec crown was transmitted, like that of Melle, in collateral descent, though in both kingdoms exceptions to the rule occurred. The practice of keeping the sons of subject princes as a sort of honourable hostage at the court of the monarch was perhaps too general to be worthy of special note, though it also was common to the two peoples. The more terrible custom of propitiating the gods with human sacrifice which was so extensively practised by the Aztecs, was, it will be remembered, only the other day brought to an end under British rule in Benin, and is probably still practised in less accessible portions of the pagan belt. Such heathen rites were, of course, unknown in the Mohammedan Melle of the thirteenth, fourteenth, and fifteenth centuries. The custom of wearing the heads of animals as a head-dress, which was also common to the Aztecs, was preserved amongst the pagans of the West African coast at the time of the first occupation of the Gold Coast by the Portuguese in 1481.

On festive occasions the servants of the rich at Melle would seem to have worn livery. The royal herald Dougha's thirty servants are mentioned as being all dressed in red cloth, with white caps. Music evidently formed a prominent part of every entertainment. The women are described as wearing pretty clothes, and having their hair dressed with bands of gold and silver.

We get an indication of social etiquette from the experience of Batuta. The treatment which he had received from the Sultan was not considered by his friends to be sufficiently honourable, and about two months after his arrival in Melle he was presented a second time. This was done on the advice of the herald, Dougha, who told the traveller that he must rise and call attention to himself at one of the public audiences, and promised when he did so to explain matters.

Accordingly, Ibn Batuta rose at the audience and said: "Surely I have travelled in the different countries of the world, and I have known their kings; but I have been in your country four months, and you have not treated me as a guest. What shall I say of you to the other kings?"

The Sultan replied: "I have not seen you, nor known you." Then the judge and other important persons rose and said: "He has already saluted you, and you have sent him food!" After this the Sultan ordered him to be lodged at his expense, and on the distribution of gifts at the end of Ramadan did not forget him.

The customs of the town were very devout. Prayer was regularly said in private houses. There was a cathedral mosque to which all fashionable people went on Fridays, and it was habitually so crowded that the worshipper who was late could find no place. The practice of the rich was to send their slaves in good time to spread their seat in the place to which they considered themselves to have a right, and the slaves kept the place till the master arrived.

At this mosque one Friday Ibn Batuta had the pleasure of seeing vengeance fall on the head of one of the black officials of Aiwalatin, who had so offended him on his first crossing the frontier of Melle. "I was," he said, "taking part in the prayers, when a Berber merchant, also a student and a man of letters, rose and cried: 'Oh, you who are present in this mosque, be my witnesses that I accuse Mansa Suleiman' (the Sultan), 'and I cite him before the tribunal of God's envoy, Mohammed.' Immediately there came from the Sultan's grated gallery messengers who approached the complainant, and asked: 'Who has committed an injustice? Who has taken anything from you?' He replied: 'Mancha Djou, the governor of Aiwalatin, has taken from me goods worth 600 ducats and he has given me in compensation only 100 ducats.'"

The result of the incident was the arrest of the governor of Aiwalatin, who was brought to the capital, and having been tried before the regular tribunal, was found guilty. The merchant recovered his money, and the governor was deprived of his functions.

CHAPTER XVII

ADMINISTRATION OF THE MELLESTINE

I HAVE lingered, perhaps, too long over the personal experiences of Ibn Batuta in Melle, but they serve to illustrate, as a drier chronicle of historic events might fail to do, the actual life of the town and the degree of civilisation which had been reached.

Politically, as we have seen, the Empire of Melle was divided into Melle proper and the Protectorate, which extended into the desert until it met the boundaries of the civilised states of the north and west. The empire would appear to have been further divided into provinces, each ruled by a "Ferba" or viceroy of the sovereign, while each town had its "Mochrif" or inspector, who was responsible to the viceroy for the maintenance of order, the suppression of crime, and, presumably, for the collection of the taxes.

The "Ferba" is spoken of by Ibn Batuta as the viceroy of the Sultan, but there existed another dignitary, known as the "Koï," who was apparently a native and subject king, not dispossessed, but holding his possessions as tributary to Melle. In some instances, he would seem to have been confirmed by Melle in the occupation of an old position; in others, he was apparently appointed by the Sultan. In speaking of the Timbuctoo Koï, a little later, at the beginning of the fifteenth century, the author of the *Tarikh-es-Soudan* says that it was customary for the Koï to receive one-third of the total taxes, and that in Timbuctoo he had all administrative and financial powers in his hands. It is evident that if the Koïs were petty native kings, who, on submission to the Sultan of Melle, were by him confirmed during good behaviour in certain powers, and on occasion superseded by his appointment, it would be necessary to make some fairly ample provision for their revenues. A certain semi-independence on their part would seem to be argued by the fact that when the Tuaregs took Timbuctoo from Melle in 1434, they confirmed the existing Timbuctoo Koï in his powers. At one time there were thirty-six Koïs in the empire of Melle. As the empire extended it is probable that their number may have increased, and, at a later period, as the central government weakened, the power and self-assertion of the Koïs grew, and contributed, doubtless, to the disruption of the empire.

Unfortunately, though the finances of the country in the middle of the fourteenth century would appear to have been flourishing, no special accounts have been left to us of the revenue or system of taxation. We can only assume from incidental allusions that taxation continued to be based, as in the kingdom of Ghana, on a system of royalties on minerals and taxes on foreign merchandise. We hear of the great wealth of the country and of the kings, but we get no hint from Batuta of taxation which was felt to be oppressive by the people. He mentions that Mansa Suleiman was unpopular because of his avarice, but this would appear to apply rather to his personal thriftiness than to any system of government. A narrative which abounds in anecdote, and is not animated by any sentiment of friendliness for the government, would have been likely to incorporate any instance of oppression which reached the author's ears. But, after a residence of several months in the country, Ibn Batuta not only brings forward none; his evidence is given in a contrary direction.

The judicial system of the country, though not described in detail, would seem to have been carefully and fully organised. The frequent reference which is made in all chronicles to judges, black and white, to lawyers and jurisconsults, indicates that men of this profession occupied a very prominent position in the social organisation of the country. The fact that it was the custom of the Sultan to send cases in which he was appealed to for justice, to be tried at the "proper tribunal," would seem also to indicate a severance of the executive and judicial powers which it is the habit of civilisation to regard as one of the guarantees of justice. But the condition of the country itself is, perhaps, the best testimony which can be borne to the efficacy of the system by which crime was punished and repressed. Amongst the admirable things which Ibn Batuta feels it to be his duty to praise, when, at the end of his visit, he summarises his opinion of the people of Melle, is, he says, the rare occurrence of acts of injustice in the country. "Of all people," he thinks that "the blacks are those who most detest injustice. Their Sultan never forgives any one who has been guilty of it." He also praises the "complete and general safety which is enjoyed in the country. Neither those who travel nor those who remain at home have anything to fear from brigands, thieves, or violent persons." "The blacks do not," he says, "confiscate the goods of white men who die in the country, even though it may be a question of immense treasure. On the contrary, their goods are always placed in charge of some white man, trusted by the community, until those who have a right to them can apply and take possession of them."

The organisation of the Church was orthodox, every town having its mosque or mosques with salaried readers and teachers; and in the principal towns, such as Melle, Timbuctoo, and Gago, mention is made of a "Cathedral Mosque." Schools are mentioned in many towns, and some, as in Zaghah, are specially spoken of as centres of distinguished learning. Ibn Batuta mentions with praise the religious assiduity of the people—the custom of celebrating regular prayer, not only in the public mosques, but in private meetings of the faithful—and the care with which children were brought up to observe similar practices. All educated children were expected to learn the Koran, and were either whipped or had fetters placed upon their feet when they were negligent in doing so. In the house of the principal judge he one day saw all the children chained up, and was told that it was a punishment for not having learned their Koran. On another occasion he saw a magnificent young black, superbly dressed, who had shackles on his feet, and on inquiring whether he had committed a crime, was told laughingly that he was only being forced to learn his Koran. The principal preacher of the cathedral mosque and the principal judge of the town of Melle were constantly in the presence of the sovereign, and would seem to have occupied a recognised position as ministers and the heads of their respective professions.

The army, which is spoken of as very large, was an organised military force, composed partly of cavalry and partly of infantry, armed with bows and arrows, swords, and long and short spears. It was divided into units, each commanded by a captain or commandant, and it is interesting to note in relation to the appointment of these commandants that it was the custom, on the occasion of their selection for command, for the viceroy or governor of the town to cause the new commandant to be placed upon a shield and raised above the heads of the soldiers in exactly the same manner as was common in Northern Europe. It will be remembered that the Merovingian and Carlovingian kings were always raised on a shield as part of the ceremony of their enthronement, and as late as the Latin Conquest of Constantinople in 1204, when Baldwin of Flanders was elected Emperor of the East, he was, we are told, raised upon the buckler by the hands of his rival candidate. The smaller military units led by the commandants were apparently grouped into a larger formation, which in its turn was commanded by a military chief or general, and these larger formations were again united into two divisions, one forming the army of the south, and the other of the north. The two generals-in-chief commanding these divisions were very high personages, who occasionally gave to the reigning sovereign all that he could do to keep them in order. The strength of the army of Melle receives indirect testimony from the fact that Jenné, a territory which, though lying within the limits of the Mellestine and paying tribute to Melle, had its own king, and was never conquered until 1468, thought it necessary, in order to preserve the much-cherished independence of its town, to keep no less than twelve army corps always on foot charged solely with the duty of watching the military movements of Melle and of guarding against any approach of the Melle troops which was not authorised by the king.

Beyond the general indication that the country was fertile, cultivated, and very populous, Ibn Batuta gives no satisfactory account of its agriculture nor of the numbers of its population. Other writers dwell, however, on the fact that it was rich in cattle, corn, and cotton, which last was exchanged freely in its markets for the woollen cloth of Europe. That it was very populous may be inferred from a fact mentioned by the author of the *Tarikh-es-Soudan* in relation to Jenné, through whose territory Ibn Batuta travelled without mentioning that it was more populous than any other portion of the country. The territory of Jenné extended for a journey of several days. If the king, it is said, desired to send a message, though it might be to the farthest limits of the territory, the royal messenger simply mounted upon the rampart near one of the gates of the town and called aloud the message with which he was charged. The people from village to village repeated the call, and it was delivered in the farthest village to the individual to whom it was addressed. This custom not only illustrates the density of population in a country in which it could be practised, but it also suggests an explanation of the extraordinary rapidity with which news is even now sometimes transmitted among natives in countries where no mechanical means for the purpose exist. A message so delivered from voice to voice might pass with almost the rapidity of a telegram, and doubtless the calling of royal messages was not left to the chance of any hearer. There must have been an organised system of public criers to make the practice effective. Of this, however, no indication appears to exist, and it would be interesting if light could be thrown upon the subject.

Ibn Batuta is equally unsatisfactory on the subject of the trade of Melle. Though he travelled with a caravan of merchants, he tells us nothing that is interesting upon the subject, and we are left to learn from other sources the great importance which it had assumed. All European goods, it would seem, were welcomed in the markets of the Mellestine, and were paid for apparently in gold, cotton, slaves, ivory, skins, and kola-nuts. A good deal of corn would seem to have been exported to the frontier, but presumably this was destined rather for the towns of the desert than for Europe. At a somewhat later period the trade in "written books" from Barbary was said to be one of the most profitable. Ibn Batuta mentions an interesting copy of a book called "The Marvellous,"[1] which was lent to him by one of his many hosts, in a place of which he had forgotten the name, and there must already in his day have existed a very considerable demand to satisfy the needs of the many schools which are mentioned. When the King of Jenné, somewhat later, at the end of the twelfth century, adopted Islam, and desired that all the Ulemas of his territory should be present at his abjuration of the gods of paganism, they assembled to the number of 4200. If the relatively small territory of Jenné produced so large a number, it is evident persons of some degree of Mohammedan learning must have been numerous in the countries of the Soudan. There can be no doubt that gold abounded with which to pay for all desired luxuries. In the market of Gago it is said that the inhabitants frequently brought in more gold than they could exchange for commodities. All travellers allude to the golden arms and utensils frequently

[1] Perhaps "The Choice of Marvels," composed at Mossul by a writer of Granada in 1160, a copy of which Felix Dubois found at Timbuctoo.

used by persons of importance. This perpetual testimony to the quantity of gold in the country begins, it may be remembered, in the eighth century, when, according to Abd el Hakem, the first military expedition of the Arabs brought back "all the gold it wanted," and continues through the testimony of El Bekri in the eleventh century, El Idrisi in the twelfth, and all subsequent writers of the thirteenth, fourteenth, fifteenth, and sixteenth centuries, up to the moment of the overthrow of native independence by the Moors in the conquest of 1591. Allusions to the cotton trade are scarcely less constant, though less prominent and less important, and there must have been a considerable local consumption. Ibn Batuta mentions amongst the good qualities which he ascribes to the blacks of Melle, that they never failed to dress in fine white robes on Friday, and the dressing of many millions of persons must have needed a large supply.

The other never-failing supply of wealth which would seem to have persisted throughout the history of the Soudan was the slave labour raided from the pagan belt to the south. The attitude of the Mohammedan black towards those people seems to have been almost identical with that of the Spaniards towards the natives of the New World. They were idolatrous, and had no rights. Probably the occupation of raiding the little known and unhealthy regions of the pagan belt gave occupation in times of peace for the immense armies which were kept on foot. But, beyond the actual cruelty of the raid, the slave does not appear to have been badly treated. He served in the armies of the conquerors and performed the duties of the house and farm. He seems to have received little more consideration than a domestic animal, but he does not appear to have been persecuted. All rich people in Melle were proud of possessing a very large number of slaves. Ibn Batuta mentions that he gave twenty-five ducats for a good woman slave, but the price of the ordinary slave was much less. In the sixteenth century Leo Africanus mentions that the price of a Barbary horse in Bornu was fifteen slaves. In Ibn Batuta's day a Barbary horse cost one hundred ducats at Melle ; but no deductions can be legitimately drawn from these two facts as to the money value of the ordinary slave.

The vast body of slaves no doubt represented the labour power of the country, and that they existed within its boundaries without disturbance and without the multiplication of crime, if it says much for the organisation and the administration of justice, says also something for the manner in which they were treated.

After a stay of several months in the capital of Melle, Ibn Batuta visited some of the minor towns, in most of which he mentions the black governor with respect, and in nearly all of them received hospitality from "persons of merit" who had made the pilgrimage to Mecca.

Amongst these minor towns he mentions Timbuctoo, which was still far from the height of its fame. He disposes of it in a sentence, as a town situated at a distance of four leagues from the Niger, and occupied chiefly by Berbers. It was here that he witnessed, on the occasion of the appointment of the captain of a troop, the ceremony of lifting him on a shield above the heads of his men. He mentions incidentally that this captain was a Berber. Berbers and blacks seemed to enjoy at the time perfect equality throughout the kingdom—all being alike Mohammedan. The only class distinction seemed to be idolater or orthodox, slave or free. He does not mention either the mosque or palace of Timbuctoo, though as they were at the time of his visit only fifteen years old, and as we know from previous and subsequent descriptions that they were handsome buildings of cut stone, they might have been expected to attract his attention. He does, however, mention the tombs of several distinguished persons, amongst them that of the young poet and architect from Granada who designed the mosque, and who had not lived long to enjoy the favour of his black patrons, the monarchs of Melle.

From Timbuctoo Ibn Batuta, having evidently resolved

to see the whole of the Mellestine, travelled eastward by water to Gago. On the way, amongst other incidents of travel, he made the acquaintance of the black governor, who lent him the book already alluded to, who spoke Arabic fluently, who had made the pilgrimage to Mecca, and who impressed him as "one of the best and most generous of men." In the cordial expression of the respect and sympathy awakened in his mind by friendly intercourse with this and other black dignitaries of the kingdom of Melle, it becomes clear how greatly he had modified his opinion with regard to the inhabitants of the Soudan since he first crossed the frontier at Aiwalatin.

He remained a month at Gago, the capital of Songhay, which he describes as "one of the finest cities of the blacks." It evidently occupied in his estimation a far higher position than Timbuctoo. It was, he said, one of the largest and one of the best-supplied towns in the Soudan. Food was very plentiful, especially rice, milk, fowls, fish, and he mentions a particular kind of cucumber, which he held to be "unequalled." The currency amongst the natives in the market both here and at Melle was still in cowries. He mentions a "white man's mosque," and gives a list of distinguished persons from whom he received attentions and hospitality.

Gago and Aiwalatin were evidently regarded as the extreme limits east and west of Melle proper. The authority of Melle was respected vaguely to the south in the country of the cannibals and amongst other minor kingdoms of some importance, which are confusingly enumerated under different names by different authors. Amongst these Mossi was one of consequence enough to inflict very heavy blows upon Melle itself at a later date. Borgu was another which had preserved its independence from a period of great antiquity. Nupe, on the opposite bank of the river, was, as we have seen, also an independent native state of importance, though practically unknown to the Mohammedans of the West. Melle, however, never extended beyond the limits of the Niger in the East. Haussaland and Bornu drew their civilisation more directly from Eastern sources, and belong to another chapter of history, with which we have yet to deal.

The Mellestine took a wider extension as it spread north into the desert, and Tekadda, which is on nearly the same parallel as Aiwalatin, may perhaps be taken as forming, at the end of the fourteenth century, its most easterly development in the desert. Here, as will be seen, the frontier of the Mellestine trenched upon the territory of Gober and the Haussa States, and the authority claimed over Tekadda was at a future period the cause of the friction.

Ibn Batuta, who confined his journey entirely to the Mellestine, went from Gago north-eastward to Tekadda, where he gives some description of the copper mines. At Tekadda he received an order from the new Sultan of Morocco, who had succeeded Abou el Haçen, to return to court and give an account of his wanderings. He turned his steps north-westward, abandoning the Tripoli-Fezzan road where it branched off towards Ghat, and made his way with a friendly caravan to Touat, thus reversing the road which the Emperor Musa had followed on his famous pilgrimage. From Touat the road to Sidjilmessa and Fez was easy, except for the incident of a very heavy snowstorm which overtook the caravan shortly after leaving Sidjilmessa; and having seen practically the whole of the black empire, which at first he so much despised as to have been tempted to turn back on the frontier, Ibn Batuta re-entered Fez in the early days of January 1354.

The curiosity which his travels excited at the court of Fez was, it is said, so great that the Sultan himself wished to hear his adventures, and after listening to him for several consecutive nights, ordered that the whole should be drawn up and made into a book. This was done, and the account, as it now exists, was finished on December 13, 1355.

This may be regarded as the period at which Melle

reached its greatest prosperity. Mansa Suleiman reigned for twenty-four years, but he was succeeded by Mansa Djata, a vicious tyrant, during whose reign of fourteen years the decadence of the kingdom began. Mansa Djata, far from practising the frugality of his ancestors, had a passion for expenditure which he carried to madness. He spent, it is said, in every kind of folly and debauchery, the immense wealth which had been amassed by the kings his predecessors. It was this king who sold the famous nugget which was regarded, we are told, as one of the rarest of the public treasures. He died finally of sleeping-sickness. Ibn Khaldun describes the malady as being very common in the country, but as this is the first instance which we have of it historically, the symptoms as then recognised are perhaps worth noting. It was specially apt, Ibn Khaldun says, to attack the upper classes of the people. It began by periodic attacks, and finally brought the patient to such a state that he could not remain awake for a moment. It then declared itself permanently, and ended sooner or later in death. The King Djata suffered for two years from periodic attacks before he died in 1374.

This was practically the end of the kingdom of Melle. The Songhay kingdom had already asserted its independence in 1355, within two years of Ibn Batuta's visit. The Tuaregs took Timbuctoo in 1434. In 1468 the overthrow of the empire was begun by Sonni Ali, the Songhay precursor of the great dynasty of the Askias, and the conquest of Melle by the Songhays was completed in a twelve years' war carried on by Askia the Great, from 1501 to 1513. It is interesting to note that in this very year, 1513, a map was published in Strasburg in which the kingdom of Melle appears under the title of Regnum Musa Melle de Ginovia.

CHAPTER XVIII

MEETING OF EASTERN AND WESTERN INFLUENCE UPON THE NIGER

It has been said that civilisation flowed to the Soudan from two sources. There was a civilisation of the East, and a civilisation of the West. The two streams flowed in from different ends of the country, and there was a point at which they met and overlapped. We have now come to that very interesting point.

We have seen in the fall of Ghana under Mohammedan influence the final extinction at its most westerly limit of an order of civilisation which belonged to a different epoch of the world's history. It is probable that the civilisation of Ghana may have drawn its original inspiration also from the East. But historical documents are wanting. The care of students has not been devoted to this point, or if it has, the results of their labours have been unfortunately lost in the many holocausts made by ignorant conquerors of learned libraries. The Christians distinguished themselves in Spain by destroying Arab libraries wherever they conquered Arab towns, and at a later period their example was unhappily imitated in the Soudan by Moors and Fulahs in relation to the documents of local learning.

Hence of the antique civilisation which preceded that of the Middle Ages under the Tropic of Cancer in West Africa we know but little. What we know either by document or direct tradition is first connected with the rise of the Songhay people, and it is at a point farther east than Ghana, and at a period subsequent to the Mohammedan domination of that town, that the advancing

L

waves of West and East may be discerned as clearly meeting each other in the Soudan. In the shock and amalgamation of the two forces, black civilisation attained the greatest height which it has ever reached in modern Africa. The gentle nature of the Soudanese black, inoculated with intellectual germs from a long forgotten civilisation, would seem to have allied itself in the Songhay race with the virility of the Arab, and a result was produced unlike anything which the world had seen.

The sixteenth century, so full of interest to contemporary Europe, was the period of fulfilment of this development. The halcyon days of the modern Songhay Empire lay between the years 1492 and 1592. The rise of the Songhay people dates, however, from a much earlier period. Though in the order of the great kingdoms of the Soudan as they came into touch with the outer world Songhay succeeds to Melle, it was as a matter of fact a far older kingdom. The first true chapter of its history, though lost to us, had been lived in the aspiration and the efforts of its people, and had resulted in its own conquest, long before modern influences had reached it, of a level of civilisation higher than that of any of the surrounding countries.

Hitherto we have taken the historians of the Western Arabs for our principal guides. In opening this new chapter of the history of the Soudan we abandon them and turn to local literature. From this point onward the Soudan has its own historians. Chief amongst them in regard to the history of Songhay is the author of the *Tarikh-es-Soudan*, or "History of the Soudan," which has within the last few years been translated into French by M. Houdas, the eminent French Professor of the Oriental School of Languages. The book is a wonderful document, of which the narrative dealing mainly with the modern history of the Songhay Empire relates the rise of this black civilisation through the fifteenth and sixteenth centuries, and its decadence up to the middle of the seventeenth century. Barth, who obtained some fragments of an Arabic copy when he was on his way to Timbuctoo, goes so far as to say that the book forms "one of the most important additions that the present age has made to the history of mankind." But it is not merely an authentic narrative. It is for the unconscious light which it sheds upon the life, manners, politics, and literature of the country that it is valuable. Above all it possesses the crowning quality, displayed usually in creative poetry alone, of presenting a vivid picture of the character of the men with whom it deals. It has been called the "Epic of the Soudan." It lacks the charm of form, but in all else the description is well merited. Its pages are a treasure-house of information for the careful student, and the volume may be read many times without extracting from them more than a small part of all that they contain.

Its chief author, Abdurrahman Es-sadi, was a black of Timbuctoo, who was born in that town in the year 1596. He came of learned and distinguished ancestors, and his genealogy is interesting because he united in his own person three of the most important strains of blood in the Soudan. His mother was a Haussa woman. His great-great-grandfather, he tells us, was the first white—that is, Berber—Imaum of Mansa Musa's mosque, and succeeded that Katib Moussa whose remarkable longevity and health were mentioned in a previous chapter. This ancestor married a Fulani woman, and from the combination of Berber and Fulani blood his father was descended on the maternal side. Es-sadi was himself Imaum of the university mosque in Timbuctoo, but he also exercised the functions of a notary at Jenne, where he would seem generally to have lived. In this capacity he was frequently called upon to prepare state papers. He was also entrusted on various occasions with public missions, and seems to have had very special opportunities for acquiring information. He first relates as an historian the history of the country up to the period of his own manhood, and from that time continues to write as a contemporary of the events which he records up to the year 1656, when presumably he died. But a great part of the charm of the *Tarikh* consists in the fact that it is not the work of one hand alone. Nor is it always easy to distinguish when Es-sadi has ceased to write and has given place to some other distinguished contemporary. Among those whose chronicles are thus incorporated with his own is Ahmed Baba, the well-known historian of the Soudan, who at the period of the overthrow of the Songhay Empire by the Moors was carried as a captive into Morocco, but was so profoundly respected there for his learning and philosophical demeanour that he was allowed in 1607 to return to Timbuctoo, where he died twenty years later. Though an older man than Es-sadi, Ahmed Baba was writing in Es-sadi's lifetime, and his work is so freely incorporated in the *Tarikh* that when Barth had the book in his hands in Gando he took it to be the work of Ahmed Baba.

From Ahmed Baba, who was the descendant of a long line of learned ancestors, we get some charming biographical sketches; amongst them many of his own family, which enable us perfectly to reconstruct for ourselves the cultivated and dignified life of letters in the palmy days of Timbuctoo, when Sultans, however great, felt themselves to be honoured by the presence of the learned, and to do justice was recognised as the first quality of a gentleman. Ahmed Baba tells us of his father that he had "a fine and sagacious mind and a sensitive heart," that he was as firm in his dealings with kings as he was with other men, and so earned their profound respect, that he had no hatreds and did justice to all. He was widely read, and very fond of books. His well-furnished library contained many rare and precious works, and "he lent them willingly." This last-mentioned form of generosity, greater in that day than we can easily now imagine, is frequently noted in relation to the rich and learned men of Timbuctoo. Indeed, Ahmed Baba confesses that it sometimes amazed him to observe to what extent it was carried. "But this," he adds, "they did for the love of men." His father died in 1583, and the son mentions that he had studied under him for some years, and had obtained from him his diplomas as a licentiate in several subjects. He was himself born in 1556. His life and that of Es-sadi, therefore, cover a hundred years of a very important period of the history of the Soudan, of which they were able to write as contemporaries.

We turn now to the people with whom the *Tarikh* is principally concerned. The ancient capital of the Songhay Empire stood where Gao now stands upon the Eastern Niger, and was generally called Kaougha or Kaukau by the ancients. It was situated within the edge of the summer rains upon the course of the river, where, having turned southward from its most northerly extension, the Niger flows steadily from west, south-eastward towards the Gulf of Guinea. The *Tarikh* tells us that, according to tradition, it was from this town that Pharaoh obtained the magicians who helped him in the controversy which is related in the Twentieth Sourate of the Koran as having taken place between him and Moses. Barth, travelling through this neighbourhood in the middle of the nineteenth century, also heard at Burrum, a little town near Gao, that it had once been a residence of the Pharaohs. An older authority than either the *Tarikh* or Barth also, it will be remembered, speaks of a city in this place inhabited by black dwarfs, not, it is true, at a date so remote as that of Moses, but still at a period of very respectable antiquity; for it is here that the young men of the adventure related by Herodotus found a city built upon a river which flowed from the west towards the east.

But the history of the dwarfs is hidden from us as completely as the history of the magicians. If the dwarfs of the Congo forest ever did inhabit the vicinity of Gao, all that we know of them now is that, in common with other lower types of black humanity, they were driven by superior pressure from the north, backwards and southwards towards the equator. As for the magicians and the link which they may have been supposed to establish between the contemporary history of Kaougha and the Egypt of the Pharaohs—if the tradition of this is preserved in the annals of Egypt, it is all that we have. Knowledge of the country in which they lived vanishes, alas, in that chapter of Songhay civilisation which is lost to us. The religion of Egypt, the art of Egypt, the intellectual fertility of Egypt, even the policy of Egypt, while they are at times to be traced as a tradition carried in the blood of this half of the Western Soudan, and expressing itself unconsciously in customary life, offer yet a scarcely more definite outline to description than the impression of a ghostly hand laid by the past upon the present, and visible in short glimpses only to the eyes of faith.

It is perhaps most continuously observable in the physical characteristics of the Songhay race. Their skin is black like that of the negro, but there is otherwise nothing negroid in their appearance. A modern writer, who has had ample opportunity for observation, describes them thus:[1] "The nose of the Songhais is straight and long, pointed rather than flat; the lips are comparatively thin, the mouth wide rather than prominent and thick; while the eyes are deeply set and straight in the orbit. . . . It is to the south of the island of Philæ that we find a similar race."

In speaking of the people of ancient Egypt, Herodotus informs us that they were "black, with curly hair"; and though modern investigations of Egyptian monuments have led to the conclusion that there were three races,

[1] Felix Dubois, "Timbuctoo the Mysterious," p. 97, Eng. trans.

of which one was probably red, like the still existing red races of the Soudan, and another yellow, or practically white, we yet draw from the history of that Ethiopian people who dwelt to the south of Philæ a very different conception of the possibilities of black achievement from any furnished by our knowledge of the negroid native of Africa. The language of the Songhay is also different from that of the dialects of the Western Soudan, and gives proofs of Nilotic extraction.

The modern history of this people is supposed to date from about the year 700 A.D., and it is with this alone that the historian can deal.

The story which the Songhays themselves tell of the period which preceded this, and included the foundation of the first recorded dynasty of this era, is that at a period when they were still pagans and worshipped a river-god, there arrived one day at their city two brothers out of the East. They were weary, travel-stained, and in so piteous a condition that they had almost lost their human form. Their nakedness was only hidden by the skins of wild beasts thrown upon their shoulders, and to the question whence they came, the reply was made by one brother for the other: "*Dia men el Yemen*" (he comes from Yemen). This by the Songhays, who did not speak Arabic, was taken to be a proper name, and the elder stranger was known by the name of Dia, afterwards corrupted to "Za" al Yemen. He was, according to the legend, a prince who had left his native land, attended only by his brother, with the intention of travelling over the world. Destiny had brought him to Gao. He accepted the decree of fate and remained in the city. But perceiving that his hosts were the worshippers of false gods, he killed the river-god, and "was himself worshipped in its place." This was the beginning of the dynasty who, like their founder, were all known by the title of "Za."

I give the legend as commonly repeated in Songhay. It is perhaps worth mentioning in connection with it the tradition preserved in the history of Egypt that when the descendants of Misraim divided the land of Egypt between them, a territory which stretched from the present position of Alexandria to the borders of Tripoli fell to the portion of a well-beloved younger son called "Sa." "Sa" devoted himself with the greatest interest to his kingdom, and made it very prosperous. He built towns full of marvels; he constructed baths; he had palaces with stained glass windows and exquisite gardens. He erected statues bearing burning-glasses, and other marvels, along the Mediterranean coast. His explorations extended to the Atlantic on the west, and far into the desert on the south.

Macrizi, writing in the fifteenth century, says of the towns which he constructed in the desert: "The dwellings have disappeared, their inhabitants are scattered, but the vestiges remain; and all travellers who have penetrated into those regions relate what they can still see among those marvellous ruins."

This kingdom of "Sa" covered the Tripoli-Fezzan caravan road into the desert. If we may judge from all that is related of its monuments, it must have endured for many generations. It is no more difficult to believe that two of the princes of this Egyptian house of "Sa" should have reached Gao by marching southwards through the desert, than to accept the story that they came from the still more distant Arabia. The change of sound from "Sa" to "Za" is less than from "Dia" to "Za."

Whatever was their origin, the "Zas" reigned for many generations over Songhay, and "none of them believed in God," till in the year 1009 A.D. Za Kosoi accepted Islam. It will be observed that this was nearly a hundred years before Islam was generally accepted throughout the Soudan.

The fact is corroborated by El Bekri, who, writing in 1067, says that the inhabitants of Kaougha were then Mussulman, though the surrounding populations were pagan.

Under the pagan "Zas" Songhay influence extended as far west as the town of Jenné, which was founded by them in the eighth century, though afterwards cut off from their possessions and isolated on the westerly frontier of the "Bend of the Niger" by the Morabite invasion of the Soudan. Jenné, it will be remembered, maintained its paganism until the twelfth century in the midst of surrounding Islam, and, though tributary to Melle, kept the independence of the town until, as will be seen, it was once more incorporated with the Songhay Empire in or about 1477. The most westerly manifestation of the influence of ancient Egypt in the Soudan is placed by the talented author of "Timbuctoo the Mysterious" in this town of Jenné, where, when he visited it at the end of the nineteenth century, he found, to his amazement, "a colony of ancient Egypt" in the heart of the Soudan. He describes the architecture of Jenné as "neither Arabic nor Byzantine, Greek nor Roman, still less Gothic nor Western." "At last," he says, "I recall these majestically solid forms, and the memory is wafted to me from the other extremity of Africa. . . . It is in the ruins of ancient Egypt, in the valley of the Nile, that I have seen this art before."

Jenné may be taken as marking the limit of pagan Songhay development, though at a later period of conquest the dominion of the Songhays included the whole of the Western Soudan from the Atlantic to Lake Chad. The Songhay kingdom flourished exceedingly under the Mohammedan Zas. Their capital was, of all the cities of the blacks, that which had most gold. It had also abundance of cotton and rice, and it is at this period that Idrisi says of it that "it was populous, commercial, and industrial, and that in it was to be found the produce of all arts and trades necessary for its inhabitants."

After Za Kosoi there were twelve more Mohammedan "Zas" before the country was conquered by Mansa Musa, and the two sons of the reigning Za Yasiboi were taken by him to be educated at his court. After that four more Zas were allowed to occupy the throne, presumably in the position of tributaries of Melle, while the young princes grew up at the court of the Mansas. The elder of the young princes, Ali Kolon, was destined to throw off the yoke of Melle and to found the new dynasty of the Sonnis upon the throne of Songhay.

CHAPTER XIX

RISE OF THE SONGHAY EMPIRE

When, on his return from his great pilgrimage in 1326, Mansa Musa stopped at Gago and ordered the construction of a cathedral mosque, he took away with him, according to the custom of the kings of Melle in dealing with the children of vassal potentates, the two young sons of Za Yasiboi, the conquered sovereign, to finish their education at his court. These boys, of whom the elder was called Ali Kolon, were the sons of two sisters, wives of Za Yasiboi, and were both, as it happened, born in the same hour on the same night. But being both of them in the darkness laid side by side, and not washed until the morning, it was never certain which of the two came actually first into the world. Ali Kolon was, however, the first washed, and therefore it was determined that he should have the honours of the firstborn. By all he was accepted as the elder, and by none with more faithful devotion than by his younger brother Selman, or Suleiman.

These brothers, inspired, perhaps, by the legend of the two other brothers to whom their dynasty owed its foundation, resolved in their state of honourable captivity at Melle that they would some day return and free Songhay from the yoke of the conqueror. Ali Kolon as he grew up showed himself to be a man of sense and intelligence, and was trusted by Mansa Musa and his successor with the conduct of occasional raids, presumably against the cannibals of the pagan belt, which gave him cause for traversing the empire in various directions. He profited by the opportunity to make himself acquainted with all roads leading to the east, and to make deposits of arms and provisions at important points. When the time was ripe, he communicated to his brother his design to make good their escape from Melle. To this end they carefully trained their horses, preparing them to endure long marches, and at last boldly left the capital of Melle, riding in the direction of Songhay. The king, hearing of their flight, gave orders that they should be pursued and killed. But they had doubtless prepared friends for themselves, as well as arms and resting-places along the roads, and with many hairbreadth escapes they eluded their pursuers, and succeeded in reaching their own country.

They succeeded, too, in their larger design. Ali Kolon was hailed as king by the Songhays. For some reason which is not given, possibly connected with the uncertainty of his birthright, he caused himself to be proclaimed by the title not of "Za" but of "Sonni," thus founding a new dynasty—and under his leadership his people were delivered from the yoke of Melle. This result was achieved in 1355, nearly thirty years after he had been taken as a child to the court of Mansa Musa. On his death he was succeeded by his faithful brother Suleiman; and there were in all seventeen kings of this dynasty, who continued to reign independently during the gradual decadence of the Empire of Melle. But though the Songhay kings succeeded in maintaining their independence, and resistance to Melle became an inherited policy of the race, there was no important extension of the limits of Songhay beyond the immediate neighbourhood of the capital until the last and greatest prince of the dynasty ascended the throne. His name was the same as that of the first of the Sonnis. He also was Sonni Ali, and he began to reign in 1464.

At this time the Tuaregs were again in possession of Timbuctoo. They had for a long time ravaged the country with impunity up to its walls, and under a chief called Akil they had been tempted by the feeble condition of Melle to make an effort to recover their ancient town.

"A prince," says the *Tarikh*, "who cannot defend his possessions, does not deserve to keep them." Melle had accordingly been forced in 1434 to abandon Timbuctoo, and at the date of Sonni Ali's accession to the Songhay throne the Tuaregs had been masters of the town for upwards of thirty years.

Rude people as they were, their conquest does not seem at first to have carried with it any disastrous consequences to the life of Timbuctoo. There had been no convulsion. The sovereignty of Melle had simply been withdrawn, and the existing Timbuctoo Koï, a man of eminent piety and learning of the name of Mohammed Naddi, had continued to exercise his functions. It is expressly stated that he had all powers in his hands, that under the domination of the Sultan of Melle he was already the chief of the city, and that his title alone was changed by the change of government. Up to the time of his death all went well, but shortly before the accession of Sonni Ali, Mohammed Naddi died. A new Koï was appointed whose authority was not respected, and Timbuctoo then became a prey to the "odious exactions" of the Tuaregs. An epoch of violent tyranny ensued, during which desolation spread within its walls.

While the Tuaregs had thus shorn Melle of power on its desert frontier, the King of Mossi was ravaging its territories from the south; and the Fulanis of Massina towards the west, forced to defend themselves against the inroads of Mossi, were also incidentally strengthening their independence of an empire which could no longer give them adequate protection. Jenné, with its 7000 villages, rich and famous as the centre of an extremely flourishing cotton industry, remained, as ever, independent. Aiwalatin—or Biro, as it is usually called by Songhay historians—was fast becoming, on the far north-western frontier, the safest place of residence in the empire for persons of peaceful disposition. The disturbances in Timbuctoo were restoring Aiwalatin to the distinction enjoyed by the Ghana of old days as the nearest point of junction between the Soudan and the civilisation of the Western world. It is accordingly to Aiwalatin that hasty migrations of wealth and learning are directed in the yet more troublous days about to fall upon the once flourishing Empire of Melle.

This was the general position of the western portion of the Soudan when Sonni Ali, last of his race, but first of the great Songhay kings of modern times, ascended the throne. He was one of the born soldiers of the world, and the moment was favourable to the gratification of military ambition.

The hereditary enemy of his country, attacked by rude and vigorous foes on all her borders, was paralysed by internal decay, and a great sceptre was falling from a hand too weak to hold it. A lesser mind might perhaps have been content to join the ranks of the enemies of Melle, and revenge old wrongs by helping forward a work of sheer destruction, but Sonni Ali would seem to have had wider views. Whether, as is probably the case with many a constructive genius, his work grew under his hand till he himself was surprised at the dimensions it assumed, or whether he knew from the first at what he aimed, the result is the same. The Empire of the Soudan was the heritage which the petty kings in revolt against Melle purposed to divide. Sonni Ali resolved to keep it intact, and to take it for himself. To this end it was necessary to overthrow, not only Melle, but all her foes.

He early perceived the strategic value to him who would rule the Soudan of that command of the water which on wider fields has brought about the creation of great navies. The Niger was the ocean of the desert, and his first object was to possess himself of its shores. Fortune favoured his desires. Shortly after his accession an incident occurred at Timbuctoo which gave him the opening that he required. It was the custom, as has already been mentioned, for the Koï to receive one-third of the taxes. The Tuareg Chief Akil, who was growing old and infirm, forbade this third to be paid. "Who is the Timbuctoo Koï?" he contemptuously asked on one occasion of the puppet of his own creation. "What is the meaning of him? What good is he to me?" And he distributed among his followers the revenue which had been set aside for the Koï. The town was already seething with discontent, and the Koï, now at the end of his endurance, sent secretly a messenger to Sonni Ali informing him of the condition of affairs, and promising to deliver the town into his hands if he would march against Timbuctoo. Timbuctoo is on the north side of the river. In marching across country from Gao, boats were needed to transport an army across the stream. These it would seem that the Timbuctoo Koï undertook to provide. Sonni Ali richly rewarded the messenger who brought him the welcome invitation, and marched upon the town. But for some reason the Timbuctoo Koï was unable, or at the last moment unwilling, to fulfil his promise of delivering Timbuctoo into Sonni Ali's hands. The boats were not ready, and the first approach from the south side of the river was unavailing. A second attack had to be made from the direction of Haussaland, on the north bank of the river, where no crossing had to be effected and no boats were needed. By the time this could be done, the town had had full warning of Sonni Ali's approach. Opinion was much divided as to the gain likely to result from a change of rulers. Measures were apparently taken for defence, and there was a great exodus of the learned and cultivated towards the haven of Aiwalatin.

The Tuareg Chief Akil making, it is said, no attempt to defend himself, headed a caravan of a thousand camels with which went, besides much valuable property, the greater number of the jurisconsults of the university. Eminent names are mentioned in the lists, and some who lived to return at a later period to Timbuctoo, and to lead lives of high distinction under the succeeding reign, took part in the exodus as children of only five and six years old. The craven Koï fled also to Aiwalatin.

In connection with the departure of this caravan, scenes are described which throw a curious light upon the habits of the learned in the remote universities of the Soudan at that day. "On the day of departure," it is said, "there were to be seen bearded men of middle age trembling with fright at the prospect of having to bestride a camel, and falling helplessly off as the animal rose from its knees." This came, we are told, from the custom which existed amongst the "virtuous ancestors" of the people of Timbuctoo of "keeping children so close to their apron-strings, that, having while they were young never learned to play, they grew up without knowing anything at all of the affairs of life. Now games in the season of youth," the chronicle gravely continues, "form the character of man and teach him a very great number of things." After the exodus to Biro this was recognised. "Parents regretted from this time to have acted as they had done, and when they afterwards returned to Timbuctoo they relaxed the constraint which they had been accustomed to impose, and the children of the learned were allowed the time to play."

The middle-aged professors who tumbled off their camels because they had not practised athletics in their youth, must have suffered considerably on the road to Aiwalatin, which was a rough ride of 500 miles across the desert. Their children—still the degenerate children who had not learned to play—were carried the whole way on the backs of faithful slaves. But, having arrived safely at Aiwalatin, the members of the caravan had reason to congratulate themselves upon their flight, and upon the safety of such precious books and manuscripts as they had brought with them.

For Sonni Ali, enraged at the unexpected resistance of the town, took it by assault, sacked and burnt the principal buildings, and put many of the leading inhabitants to death.

Three times in the course of its native history Timbuctoo, says the *Tarikh*, has suffered the horrors of being taken by assault. Once by the Sultan of Mossi before it passed into the safe keeping of Mansa Musa, once by Sonni Ali, and once more again when at the end of its period of prosperity it was sacked by the Moors in 1591. The author of the *Tarikh*, whose account of the siege we are following, was the historian of the Askias, and as such was bound to justify them at the expense of Sonni Ali. A distinct bias is observable in all that he has to say of him, and the actions of that "tyrant and libertine," as he usually calls him, receive no merciful interpretation at his hands. Of the three assaults which Timbuctoo had to sustain, this, he says, was the worst. Sonni Ali spared neither age nor sex, and "seemed to take pleasure in destroying or dishonouring all that was most cultivated in Timbuctoo." It was perhaps the better classes of Timbuctoo who had inspired and organised the resistance of the town, and it was upon them that Sonni Ali determined to let his vengeance fall.

He took the town in 1468, and it is said that for three years he continued to persecute the learned. Many succeeded in leaving Timbuctoo, and all the members of the university who had remained during the siege fled to Aiwalatin. Others were not so fortunate as those who went with the first caravan. On one occasion the new Timbuctoo Koï appointed by Sonni Ali was ordered to pursue and destroy a flying caravan, and a massacre took place at Tadgit in which some of the most eminent lost their lives. The same fate overtook many of those who fled to different towns. It seemed for a time as though the conqueror had determined to extirpate learning from the Soudan. But after three years the persecution ceased, and the theory that it was intended as a punishment for a definite offence is supported by the fact, admitted even by the author of the *Tarikh*, that notwithstanding the persecutions which Sonni Ali caused the learned to endure, he did, nevertheless, recognise their merits. He was heard to say that "without learning life would have neither pleasure nor savour," and "if he injured some, he did great good to many, and loaded them with favours." Amongst other favours, in keeping with the rude character of the conqueror, was the presentation on one occasion to the more favoured "notables, saints, and sages" of Timbuctoo of a number of Fulani women whom he had captured in a military expedition against a settlement of this people in the north of Gurma. One of the favoured was the Imaum of the cathedral mosque, the great-great-grandfather of the author. To him was sent a very charming Fulani girl of the name of Aïcha, whom, contrary, it would appear, to the usual custom of Sonni Ali and his profligate favourites, he married. From this marriage, as has been already stated, was descended the family of Es-Sadi.

The conqueror's religion was no more orthodox than his morals. He was the son of a pagan woman of the neighbourhood of Sokoto, and was deeply imbued, it is said, with the superstitions of the race. He was nominally Mohammedan, and like Henry IV. of Navarre, knew the value of a mass. But he cared nothing for these things. In private he habitually left his five daily prayers to be said when it was convenient, either in the evening, or perhaps not till the following day. He would even profanely call the prayers one after another by their names, and without more ceremony dispose of them, saying: "You know my sentiments, you can divide them between you." His temper was violent, and he would order men to be executed for trifling offences; sometimes this would happen even to those who were his best friends and to whom he was most attached. In such cases he frequently repented, and in his court it became the custom, when the order appeared unreasonable, to hide the victim of his indignation for a time, and when the fit of remorse followed upon anger to produce the culprit.

All this gave occasion for great horror and dismay in those circles of Timbuctoo where it was felt that in exchanging the nominal rule of the Tuaregs—accompanied though it had been with occasional outbreaks of disorder—for the heavy hand of Sonni Ali, they had exchanged freedom for a yoke which was almost too heavy to be borne.

The only circumstance which rendered their fate tolerable was the interposition of Sonni Ali's prime minister, a man for whose counsels he had a great regard, and who acted as a moderating influence upon him. This man, whose name was Mohammed Abou Bekr Et-Touri, was a pure-blooded black of Songhay. He was born of well-known parents in the island of Neni, a little below Sinder, in the Niger, and though he first made his fame as a soldier, being one of the most distinguished generals of Sonni Ali's army, he was more remarkable for the qualities which usually characterise great civilians. He appears to have been a man of liberal principles and large views, naturally humane, and disposed to temper justice with mercy, more than usually cultivated, active, wise, and firm. He had been fortunate in the circumstances of his youth. He came of good stock. His father was a man universally respected. His mother was a woman of remarkable piety, who brought up her children with care. A brother of his is mentioned by Leo Africanus—who was by no means disposed to be a gentle critic—as "black in colour but most beautiful in mind and conditions." Mohammed himself had been brought up in the strictest orthodoxy, and throughout his life he adhered closely to the faith of his youth. He took no part in the luxuries and the loose living of Sonni Ali's court. Possibly the purity of his life contributed no less than the well-balanced power of his mind to the creation of the remarkable friendship which existed between him and the wild monarch, so unlike himself in every particular, except that of a certain greatness which they had in common. Sonni Ali, with all his faults, had qualities which won him friends. When his name was mentioned with blame before them, they would say, "He has been good to me; I will speak neither praise nor blame." His prime minister would seem to have been one of these. For thirty years their friendship, though often severely strained, never gave way. The minister would seem to have had the rare power of understanding the strength and the weakness of the character with which he had to deal. He appreciated the genius of Sonni Ali, and entered into his great designs. His constant care was to assist him in carrying them out. At the same time he endeavoured to save both him and the country from the consequences of the madness with which in this case genius seems to have been closely allied.

It was this minister who instituted at Sonni Ali's court the practice of concealing for a time culprits capriciously condemned to death. He had the courage frequently to disobey the unjust orders of his master, and thus, while he risked his own life, stood between the monarch and the defenceless people over whom he ruled. He was enabled to do this, says his chronicler, because God had endowed him with a special force of character.

He had the wishes of the people on his side, and often, when his struggles with the conqueror became critical, his mother, it is said, would cause prayers to be offered in Timbuctoo that the Almighty would sustain him in his opposition. The picture is curious, of a prime minister sustained by public prayer in opposition to a friend and tyrant whose lightest word had power to end his life. It serves to illustrate the typical relation of Mohammedan to pagan greatness in the country where each commands, even to this day, its own form of respect. Sonni Ali, though nominally Mohammedan, was in truth of the pagan type. He was the last of the great pagans, and in the double strain of conflict and affection which existed between him and his minister, may be seen reflected the conflict between enlightenment and natural instinct, between law and tyranny, between reason and force, which form the elements of the eternal conflict between the higher and the lower life of peoples.

Yet through all the conflict it reflects also the natural affection of man to the race from which he springs, to the customs amongst which he was born, to the aims and aspirations which are the aims and aspirations of his blood. Standing as they do side by side on the field of history, Sonni Ali and his great minister must be taken as representing in the Soudan the genius of paganism and the genius of Islam clasping hands in a last salute before their respective roads cross and part.

CHAPTER XX

MILITARY CONQUESTS OF SONNI ALI

WHILE by the exertions of Mohammed Abou Bekr the worst evils which might have resulted from Sonni Ali's administration were averted, the military genius of the monarch himself extended the limits of this administration year by year. To meet the requirements of the army he imposed a general military service upon the people, and his reign of nearly thirty years was one long series of campaigns. From Timbuctoo he marched on Jenné. That town, which had successfully resisted, it is said, no less than ninety-nine sieges from Melle, cost him a siege of seven years, seven months, and seven days, during which time his army camped and cultivated the fertile fields by which Jenné is surrounded. At the end of the siege the town yielded by honourable capitulation. No injury of any kind was done to its inhabitants, and the seven days which are added to the period of the siege were consumed, it is said, by festivities on the occasion of the marriage of Sonni Ali with the widow of the ruler of the town, who had died during the siege. Thus, after about four hundred years of separation, Jenné became once more a portion of the Songhay Empire.

The exact date of the fall of Jenné is not given, but it was presumably towards the year 1477, and in the meantime the troops of Sonni Ali had not been idle. The entire course of the Middle Niger was in their general's hands. From Gago to Jenné he commanded the great highway of the Soudan. He had repulsed Mossi in the south. He had conquered Hombori in the Bend of the Niger, and Kanta, and other countries in the east. A little to the north of Jenné on the west, and again to the south of Gago on the east, he had successfully encountered the semi independent Fulani rulers, on whom he had imposed his suzerainty. Either at this time or later—I have been unable to ascertain the exact date—he constructed and placed upon the Niger a great fleet under the supreme command of an officer of high naval rank, corresponding to an admiral, whose headquarters were at the port of Kabara near Timbuctoo. In 1477–8–9 we find him free to devote his principal efforts to the western province and to encounter his chief enemy, the King of Mossi, who, having been driven from the Bend of the Niger, had crossed the river, and, to the terror of the unhappy professors of Aiwalatin, was making his way over the ravaged territories of Melle towards that town. The campaign which ensued in the province of Walata practically placed Melle in the hands of Sonni Ali, although in the year 1480 Aiwalatin was taken and occupied for a month by the King of Mossi. Mossi was unable to hold it, and was compelled to withdraw and to abandon the booty which he had seized. The result of the fighting would seem to have convinced Sonni Ali of the difficulty of holding and defending a frontier town in the isolated position of Aiwalatin as a part of an empire of which the river Niger was the base, for he conceived and put into partial execution the daring scheme of connecting Aiwalatin by water with Timbuctoo by means of a canal which he proposed to construct across the desert.

The fame of Sonni Ali by this time had spread beyond the limits of the Soudan. He was recognised in Northern Africa as the most powerful of the black sovereigns of the West, and he is mentioned in European annals under the name of Sonni Heli, King of Timbuctoo, whose power was acknowledged as extending to the West Atlantic coast.

It was a moment in which African affairs were beginning to be regarded with interest by European powers. The Portuguese, under Prince Henry the Navigator, had in the early part of the century begun that career of exploration and settlement which was to lead to the discovery of the passage of the Cape of Good Hope, and so to revolutionise European history. A curious theory still prevailed amongst the ignorant that at the Equator the sea ran dry, and that the passage of ships would be found barred by sand. No sailor having as yet dared like Columbus to put boldly out to sea, the Portuguese movement crept round the African coast, and the sandbanks of the West African harbours served during the early explorations to confirm the common view. Each was taken in turn to represent the last step which could be safely made. It was considered a great feat when a man in Prince Henry's service courageously doubled Cape Bogador, and two others explored the coast at Angra de Cintra in 1435. But Cape Blanco followed in 1441. The banks of Arguin were discovered in 1443, and Cape Verde and the mouth of the Senegal in 1444 and 1445. Trade was opened on the Senegal with the natives, and after this the Portuguese discovery of Gambia, Sierra Leone, and the Gold Coast, rapidly followed. The last-named coast was explored by two Portuguese sailors in 1471, and the quantity of gold which they obtained was so great as to give to their first landing-place the name which it has always kept of The Mine or Elmina. Within a few years the Portuguese had established trading stations along the coast, and in 1486, having built a first fort and church at Elmina, the King of Portugal took the title of Lord of Guinea. In 1481, at the moment when Sonni Ali had driven the King of Mossi out of the province of Walata, and was preparing to strengthen his own hold upon the capital of that province by the construction of a canal from Timbuctoo, the Portuguese had taken to Lisbon and were receiving there with great honour a certain prince of the Joloffs, or black branch of the Fulani people, who inhabited the territory to the south of the Senegal, lying between that river and the Atlantic coast. This visit is interesting, as giving one of the earliest authentic descriptions which we possess of the Fulah in his most westerly African home. The prince, whose name was Bemoy, is described as "a man of about forty years of age, of a fine figure and generally well made. He had a long and well-trimmed beard, and did not appear to be a negro, but a prince to whom all honour and respect were due." He was received by King John with the utmost distinction. Fêtes, bull-fights, and other entertainments were given in his honour, and he had many audiences of the king and queen. In these interviews he spoke well, and gave the king most interesting information about Negroland, and especially about the King of Mossi, of whose defeat by Sonni Ali he had not then heard, and whom he described as "neither pagan nor Mohammedan, but as conforming in many things to the views of the Christians." Mossi was at that time regarded by the pagans of the coast as the greatest of the kings of the interior—so little did they know of the life and civilisation of the Nigerian Soudan. Bemoy, who would seem to have been himself better informed, gave it as a proof of the important position held by Mossi that he had not been conquered by the King of Timbuctoo.

The outcome of all this knowledge gained by the Portuguese was that they conceived the idea of carrying their trade from the coast to the interior of the country, and that they desired to gain the friendship of the King of Timbuctoo. They accordingly despatched an embassy to Sonni Ali, asking for his permission to establish a trading station at Wadan in the back country of Cape Blanco, within the western borders of the Mellestine. Sonni Ali acceded to their request, and a Portuguese trading station was actually established within his territories at the oasis of Hoden or Wadan in the western desert. The place was unsuitable, and it was afterwards abandoned. The fact of its having existed for some time with the friendly recognition of the Songhay king is an interesting indication of the intercourse with Europe, which might have been developed along the northern trades routes of the Soudan, but for the approaching events in Spain, of which the immediate result was to close the interior of Northern Africa for four hundred years to Christian enterprise.

At the same time that the Portuguese sent embassies to the King of Timbuctoo they also sent an embassy to Mossi. They wished to conciliate his goodwill for their trade upon the southern coast. But the glory of Mossi was at an end. After driving him from Walata in 1480, Sonni Ali devoted himself for two years to the work of constructing the canal which was to join Timbuctoo with Aiwalatin. He was himself engaged in superintending the operations at a place in the desert called Chan-Fenez, when word was brought to him in 1482 that the King of Mossi had assembled all his forces, and was marching against Timbuctoo. Sonni Ali immediately abandoned the canal, and the place which it had reached when the news was brought to him was, we are told, the farthest point in the desert which it ever attained. Placing himself at the head of his troops, he marched against Mossi, and completely overthrew him in the year 1483. He followed up the victory by pursuing him to the farthest limits of his territories, and in 1485–86 he conquered the mountain territory to the south. By this conquest he carried Songhay arms far into the pagan belt. But the mountain range in which the Niger and the Senegal have their sources, at the back of Sierra Leone and Senegambia, and which runs from west to east between the tenth and eighth parallels of latitude, until it passes on to become the mountains of the Cameroons in German West Africa, would seem to have been always regarded as the natural southern boundary of the Nigerian Soudan. On the southern side of this range, usually known by the name of the Kong Mountains, the country assumes that swampy and tropical character which renders it apparently unfit for the habitation of the higher races. Its rivers run through belts of oil-palm and mangroves to the coast, and it has ever been the habitation of pagans and cannibals. Sonni Ali carried his arms no farther. The pagans of the Gold Coast were left unmolested by his victories, and it is probable that the naked savages who received the Portuguese at Elmina and Achem, with heads surmounted by the grinning masks of wild beasts, and no other covering but a palm-leaf fringe, were as ignorant a hundred years later of the existence of Songhay as they were in 1486. The Benins were at this time the most powerful and the most civilised among the coast natives, and they were known to the Portuguese as "an extremely cruel people who lived upon human flesh."

The conquest of Mossi placed Sonni Ali in the position of having subdued all those enemies of Melle whom he found in arms at the time of his accession. He was virtually the master of the Mellestine, though Melle itself still preserved a nominal independence, and the town of Aiwalatin enjoyed a quasi-separate position apart from the subdued province of Walata upon the frontier. He now turned his arms against the east. A campaign against Borgu, which lies south of Gurma on the Eastern Niger, was only partially successful. Details are wanting, but the people of Borgu were able at a later period to boast that they had never been conquered. Some other conquests took place, of which it is difficult to identify the localities, and in 1492 he undertook a campaign against the Fulani of Gurma, lying also in the bend of the Eastern Niger, between Borgu and his capital of Gago.

This was his last campaign. Here, though successful, he lost his life. He died, not as so great a soldier would have wished to die, under the spears of his enemies, but by a trivial accident of fate. He was drowned in the sudden flood of a stream on his return from his victorious expedition. His death occurred far from the capital, and the hand of ancient Egypt is for a moment visible in the circumstance that his sons, who were present, immediately disembowelled the body and filled it with honey, that it might be safely transported to take its place in the tombs of his fathers.

In summing up Sonni Ali's military career, the chronicle says of him: "He only suffered two reverses, one at Duoneo[1] and the other in Borgu. He surpassed all the kings his predecessors, in the numbers and valour of his soldiery. His conquests were many, and his renown extended from the rising to the setting of the sun. If it is the will of God he will be long spoken of."

[1] Dounna, a mountainous country in the West, which had resisted Sonni Ali, and afterwards fought Mohammed El Hadj so well, that neither of them could achieve anything against its inhabitants.—*Tarikh*, p. 81.

CHAPTER XXI

ASKIA MOHAMMED ABOU BEKR

Sonni Ali was succeeded by his great minister, Mohammed Abou Bekr—not without fighting. There was a minority who upheld the claim of one of Sonni Ali's many sons, and two great battles were fought near Gago. The second battle decided the question without any further doubt, and Mohammed ascended the throne, supported by the good wishes of every important section of the people. He seems to have felt himself fully justified in thus taking the supreme power, and it is said that the title by which he and the dynasty that he founded were known for the next hundred years had its rise in his calm acceptance of the position. After the battle in which the fate of Sonni Ali's dynasty was decided, the news of Mohammed's accession was brought to the daughters of Sonni Ali. They received it with a cry of "Askia!" or "the Usurper!" The incident was related to him, and instead of showing any resentment, he said, "By that title I will be known." By his command his sovereignty was accordingly proclaimed under the title of "Askia Mohammed Abou Bekr," and Askia became the royal title of the Songhay kings until their empire was overthrown by the Moors.

Sonni Ali had conquered an empire. The great work of the Askias was to organise it, and to bring it to a condition of peace, prosperity, and cultivation, which was little suspected as existing in the heart of the Soudan during that century which witnessed in Europe the expulsion of the Moors from Spain, the crusade of Charles V. against the Saracens, the victory of Lepanto over the Turks, and the closing of the principal ports of the Mediterranean to the infidels.

The lately subjected portions of Askia Mohammed's empire not unnaturally seized the opportunity of a change of dynasty to rebel, and in the course of the long reign which lay before him he fought perhaps as many campaigns as Sonni Ali. Nevertheless his reign was, to the majority of his people, a reign of peace. Almost his first act was to issue orders for the organisation of a standing army—a scheme which had no doubt been long matured—and by this separation of the fighting element from the people he saved the country, says his chronicler, from the desolating effects of war. The industrial and learned life of the towns went on without interruption, and one end of the empire hardly knew whether the other end was at peace or war. Simultaneously with his reform of the military forces of the empire, he gave his attention to the Church. The orthodox and pious, whose voices had not been heard during the late reign, now came from their obscurity. Mohammed consulted frequently with the heads of the Mussulman communities in all the towns, and everything that could be done to improve the religious position of the country was undertaken. Schools were founded, mosques were rebuilt. A new activity was felt throughout the empire.

Sonni Ali died in November of 1492. Mohammed was occupied for nearly three years with these first necessary reforms, and with the subjugation of outlying and rebellious populations. But though he had accepted with such apparent calm the irregularity of his own position, it is clear that he was not indifferent to the importance of affirming his power by a sanction stronger than that of popular acclamation. As soon as the immediate necessities of the situation had been dealt with, and it was possible for him to contemplate a temporary absence from the country, he appointed his favourite brother to be regent in his place, and proceeded to Mecca to make the pilgrimage and to seek at Cairo a formal investiture at the hands of the Caliph of Egypt. The Turks had, it will be remembered, long since overthrown the political supremacy of the Caliphs, and had affirmed their own position by the taking of Constantinople in 1453. But the Caliphs of Egypt still kept their position as the religious head of the Mussulman world.

This pilgrimage of Askia Mohammed, which has kept a place in the annals of the country side by side with the pilgrimage undertaken nearly two hundred years before by Mansa Musa, was made the object, like that earlier pilgrimage, of the display of some magnificence. But there is a distinct progress observable in the nature of the display. The pilgrimage of Askia Mohammed does not involve the march of an army of 60,000 persons, accompanied by a baggage train of thousands of camels, to be moved in a slow royal progress round the empire. The king went accompanied by a brilliant group of the principal notables and the most holy and learned men of the Soudan. It is probable that he moved with some state, for both Marmol and Leo Africanus inform us that he kept a magnificent and well-furnished court. But a military escort of 500 cavalry and 1000 infantry was considered sufficient for the protection of his caravan, and there is no mention that he caused himself to be preceded, like Mansa Musa in procession across the desert, by slaves dressed in silk brocade and carrying golden wands. Neither did he take with him eighty camels laden with gold dust. Three hundred thousand gold pieces are mentioned as his more portable and convenient provision for financial necessities. It was not in barbaric splendour like that of Mansa Musa that the fame of Askia's pilgrimage consisted, but rather in the distinction of the persons who accompanied him, of whom Ahmed Babà gives us some of the biographies, and in the great number of learned doctors and noble friends whom Askia had the opportunity of meeting in Cairo and in the Holy Cities. The friendships which were here formed lasted for the rest of his life, and correspondence with some of the most distinguished men of letters of the East, which was at this time entered into, was never dropped.

Es Soyouti, the famous Arabian encyclopedist and scholar, was one of those who met Askia Mohammed during this visit to the East, and with whom the Songhay king continued to correspond. It is said that he never afterwards undertook a reform of importance in the State without previously consulting Es Soyouti. All who met the king were impressed with the keen interest which he displayed on many subjects, his readiness to listen to the best opinions, his diligent discussion with the learned, and his anxiety to acquire information on practical questions. Askia Mohammed remained for two years in the East, during which period he devoted much time to study. Amongst subjects named as arresting his special attention we find: "Everything that concerned the government and administration of peoples;" "principles of taxation, and especially land tax and the tithe or tribute to be taken from newly conquered peoples;" "verification and inspection of weights and measures, regulation of trade, laws of inheritance, laws for the suppression of fraud, customs duties;" "laws for the suppression of immorality, and measures to be taken for the introduction of better manners among the people." The limits of religious tolerance and persecution also appear to have occupied his mind, and it is mentioned of him by one or two of his biographers that he allowed himself to be influenced by orthodox marabouts in the direction of the persecution of the Jews.

There can be little doubt that to a man of his age, having had already thirty years of practical acquaintance with affairs, but having now for the first time the sense of security in his own position and of power to carry his views into operation, the visit under the circumstances which seem to have accompanied it must have been one of extraordinary interest and importance. Mohammed Abou Bekr was already a distinguished soldier at the time of the conquest of Timbuctoo in 1468. He cannot have been less than fifty years of age in 1495. He had been educated in an island of the Niger, and such portion of his life as had not been spent in attendance upon Sonni Ali at one or other of his rough courts had been spent in the hardest form of active campaigning in the tropics. It throws a remarkable light upon the vigour of his mind and the natural distinction of his character, that at this age, and having lived the life which he had lived, he was able to apply himself with the eagerness of youth to the sources of learning, and, undeterred by differences of colour, to form friendships on equal terms with men of the greatest enlightenment and highest intellectual activity which a centre of civilisation like that of Egypt could produce.

The phases of development of a despotic monarch have a wide-reaching influence, and it is hardly too much to say that the course of history in the Soudan was profoundly modified by this visit of its sovereign to the East.

He accomplished the political and religious purposes for which he went. The cities of Mecca and Medina were visited, and vast sums given in charity in both towns. In Mecca he bought a garden and established a charitable institution for the benefit of all future pilgrims from the Soudan. In Cairo he received investiture at the hands of El Motawekkel the Fourteenth, Abbasside Caliph of Egypt. The ceremony included a solemn abdication on Askia's part for three days of the Songhay throne. On the fourth day the Caliph appointed him to the position of Lieutenant of the Abbasside Sultans in the Soudan, and invested him, in sign of this authority, with a turban and cap. Thus politically, but far more intellectually, was Songhay restored to its ancient position as a child of Egypt.

It is an interesting coincidence that 1493, the year in which Askia formed the resolution to seek the religious sanction of the head of the Mohammedan Church to his occupation of the throne of the Soudan, was the year in which, in consequence of the discoveries made by Columbus in the western hemisphere, and the differences which had arisen between Spain and Portugal with regard to their respective rights in the new world opening to exploration, the two great powers of Southern Europe resolved to settle their controversy by reference to the head of the Christian Church. Already, under a Papal Bull of Martin V., Portugal had acquired supreme rights over all non-Christian territories which she might discover between Cape Bogador and the Indies. Greek and Arabian geographers, although so well informed on the general geography of the eastern hemisphere, had, up to the period of the discoveries of Columbus, laid down the dictum that the "Ocean Sea" which washed the western borders of Europe and the eastern borders of Asia, surrounded one-half of the world without interruption, and that in it there existed absolutely no habitable land. This view was accepted by enlightened opinion in Europe. The claim was therefore put forward by John II. of Portugal—the same king who, in 1486, had received the Fulani Prince Bemoy with so much honour in Lisbon—that Columbus, in sailing westward till he came to land, was likely to trespass upon territories already granted to Portugal in the east. To obviate the difficulties which might arise from such undetermined rights, Ferdinand and Isabella appealed to the Pope to give the sanction of the Church to their occupation of lands discovered in America; and, in response to their request, Pope Alexander VI. issued, in May 1493, the famous Bull by which all territories, not already in the possession of Christian powers, and situated to the east of an imaginary line drawn from pole to pole through what was then believed to be the immovable point of non-variation of the compass, were given to Portugal, and similar territories to the west of it were granted to Spain. The grant was accompanied by an injunction to subdue and convert the barbarous nations with whom either power should come in contact, and plenary indulgence was accorded for the souls of all those who should perish in the conquest. The exact position of the dividing-line was decided by a commission which met at Tordeçillas in January 1494, and after much discussion the point through which the line should pass was fixed at 370 leagues west of Cape Verde.

Thus it happened that while Spain was about to expel the Moors entirely from her dominions, and to close the ports of the Mediterranean, so far as lay in her power, against them, Portugal was invested by the Pope with supreme authority over those territories of the Western Soudan which the Spanish Arabs had always regarded as their natural though unconquered appanage in Africa.

As the resolution conceived by Askia in 1493 was not carried out till 1495, it is possible in point of time that he may have been already acquainted with the movements that were taking place in the Western world, and that his investiture by the Egyptian Caliph was part of a general drawing together of the Mussulman forces in the East. But of this, if it was so, we have no trace. I have been unable to find any allusion to interest expressed or felt in the Soudan in the great discoveries of Columbus and Vasco da Gama. Rather it would seem that the conquest of the Moors by Ferdinand and Isabella in 1492, shortly followed as it was by the total expulsion of that people from Europe, must be regarded as closing the connection of the Moors, and through them of the Soudan, with the progressive life and science of the West.

Yet it was from Cairo, only a few years before the visit of Askia, that news had been sent to King John II. of Portugal of a south Cape of Africa with which Arabian mariners, who had long been accustomed to the use of compass, quadrants, and sea-charts, were well acquainted. It was a matter of common knowledge to their seamen that the African continent terminated with a cape, and that there was no difficulty in the way of sailing round it to the west. Two Jews took the information to King John that it could be easily doubled from the west, and to prove their statement took also with them an Arabic map of the African coast. In consequence of this information, King John was preparing the expedition of Vasco da Gama at the time that Askia was in Cairo. The interest aroused by the discoveries of Columbus must have been great in Arabian as well as European circles. The geographers of the East must have believed that he had reached the eastern shores of Asia, and as they were well acquainted with the geography of Asia to the farthest limits of China and Japan, they must have been greatly exercised to account for the discrepancy apparently displayed in the size of the world as long since measured by the astronomers of India, and corrected and accepted by the scientific observations of Greeks and Arabs. These matters must have been subjects of discussion in intelligent circles in Cairo during the visit of the Askia, and he must presumably have shared in the general interest which they excited.

He returned to the Soudan in 1497, too early to have heard of the result of the expedition of Vasco da Gama, which in November of that year attained the object for which it was despatched, and succeeded in doubling the Cape of Good Hope. This last event was one of supreme importance to the history of the Soudan, for it opened the passage of the Atlantic to European commerce; and, in conjunction with the almost simultaneous closing of the northern ports of Africa to Christian intercourse, it determined the fact that the subsequent approach of Europe to West Africa should be from the south by sea, instead of, as in all the previous chapters of Soudanese history, from the north by land. The frontage of the Soudan upon civilisation was reversed.

But, as has been seen, the southern portion of West Africa, following the sinuosities of the Gulf of Guinea, is cut off from the healthier uplands by a swampy belt of densely wooded malarial jungle, backed by a continuous range of hills. This swampy belt was, at the end of the fifteenth century, as it had been from immemorial antiquity, the habitation of pagans, who, in the estimation of their Arab chroniclers, represented the lowest types known to humanity. They were for the most part cannibals, idolaters, and barbarians; their country had been for centuries the place of exile for all that was basest in the Arabian Soudan; their people, from the earliest ages of history, had been regarded as the lawful prey of the slave-hunter, only differing by the lesser value that was placed upon them from the elephants which they hunted in the impenetrable recesses of their tropical jungle. The territory of these lower tribes, extending for a couple of hundred miles inland from the coast, offered, under their existing conditions of transport, a practically impassable barrier to civilised exploration. The character of the inhabitants, and the deadly nature of the climate, did not encourage the expansion of European settlement. As will presently be shown, the coast settlements of Europe for four hundred years spread no farther than a few miles from the sea. Direct commercial intercourse with the interior was never established over the difficult and unfrequented roads which penetrated towards the higher lands, and from this period the relations of Europe with West Africa were confined mainly to trade in three lucrative products of the coast —gold, ivory, and slaves. None of these required any high state of civilisation to produce. All were to be obtained in profusion in the belt which lay between the mountains and the sea. The knowledge of what lay beyond the mountains was lost to Europe by the cessation of intercourse between Africa and Spain. Approach, which could not be seriously attempted from the south, was rendered impossible from the north. The Soudan of the Arabs was visited no more by the outer world, and a civilisation which had been in touch for nearly a thousand years with the most highly cultivated centres of European life was silently buried in the sands of Africa.

CHAPTER XXII

SONGHAY UNDER ASKIA THE GREAT

ASKIA THE GREAT, in returning from Cairo to the Soudan in 1497, had little knowledge of the strange destiny which lay before his country. He knew, indeed, that the last stronghold of the Moslems in Western Europe had been conquered five years before by the Christian sovereigns of Spain. But the expulsion of the Arabs from the Spanish Peninsula had not yet taken place. He was probably acquainted with the authority given to Portugal to prosecute a career of exploration and conquest on the African coasts. But the coast territory interested him little. It was a matter of no great moment to him whose armies raided with his own upon the prolific populations, of whom the experience of history served to prove the slave supply to be inexhaustible. No wisdom could have enabled him to foresee that the whole current of European life would flow to the channel opened by the maritime enterprise of the Atlantic nations, that the supremacy of the East was at an end, and that his own people, isolated in the heart of Africa, were to be left untouched by the tide of a civilisation sweeping past them to fertilise the shores of continents then unknown.

To himself it must have seemed that the work which lay before him of reforming the administration of his vast empire, and raising the life of the populations committed to his care to the level which reflection and experience led him to believe to be attainable, was a labour of absorbing interest, and demanded the whole activity of his mind.

Already past the zenith of middle age, he must have

doubted whether the portion of life which still remained would be enough to permit him to carry his many schemes to a point at which their success would ensure stability. It was, perhaps, with this thought in his mind that he had caused himself to be accompanied to the East by his eldest son and heir, as well as by a picked band of chosen counsellors and ministers. This group of persons who had shared his experiences, and had no doubt been admitted to his confidence, offered not only a guarantee of the continuance of the reign of enlightened principles in the event of his death, but also a number of trained instruments, by whose co-operation his ideas of government might be brought into effect. Amongst these he appears to have been fortunate in possessing for his principal minister just such a faithful friend and counsellor as he had been himself, during a term of thirty years, to Sonni Ali. Ali Folen—sometimes called Fulan or Fulani—mentioned amongst the foremost of those who accompanied him on the pilgrimage of 1495, remained absolutely devoted not only to him, but to his ideas, throughout the long reign which, though neither of them knew it, lay still before him. At the end they were separated only in the old age of the then blind monarch by the jealousy of others, who could not tolerate the "mutual understanding and support which was perfect between these two." The man who had been himself a loyal friend was able to accept and to appreciate the loyalty of others. He freely trusted and freely used the service of his friends. He was more than a wise monarch, he was the founder of a school, and so long as his inspiration lasted, enlightenment, order, and prosperity were enjoyed in the Soudan.

The institution of a standing army, recruited, no doubt, largely from the slave and subject populations, had already relieved the people from one of their most intolerable burdens. This was of the utmost importance, as Askia found himself obliged to sustain an almost continuous state of war. In the first year of his return from Mecca, he undertook a war, formally invested with all the characteristics of a "Holy War," against the Sultan of Mossi, whose paganism it was resolved no longer to tolerate within the empire. The circumstances of this war, and the devotion of Mossi to his idols, are related with some detail, and serve to dispose of the Portuguese rumour that Mossi was a Christian after the manner of Egypt. The result of the war was a complete conquest on the part of Askia, and the acceptance of Islam by the conquered people. This, it is expressly stated, was the only "Holy War" of Askia's reign. He conquered all that remained unconquered of the West as far as the Atlantic Ocean, and reasserted his authority to the utmost limits of the salt mines of Tegazza and the old north-western frontiers of the Mellestine. Immediately after subduing Mossi, he subdued the Fulani of the south-west. In 1501 he entrusted his brother with the command of an army destined for the overthrow of Melle, but the campaign proving unsuccessful, he himself took the field in the following year, and, having completely defeated the armies of Melle, sacked the capital and carried the family of the reigning prince into captivity. Amongst the captives was a girl of the name of Miriam, who became the mother of his son and subsequent successor, Ismail.

It is mentioned that after this campaign there was no more fighting for three years, and Askia remained for some time in Melle studying the country, and devoting his attention to the amelioration of its condition, and to its reorganisation upon a new political footing. His system would seem to have been, as was the universal custom in the confines of the Soudan, to allow the country to remain quasi-independent—that is, governed by its own rulers under the suzerainty of Songhay, to whom tribute was paid and obedience in certain respects was given. A Melle-Koi is spoken of from this time forward up to the period of the overthrow of the country by the Moors. But Askia's measures of reorganisation, whatever they may have been, can hardly have satisfied himself, for we read of further campaigns, or perhaps more properly punitive expeditions, against Melle, which recurred with sufficient frequency to be described by some historians as a "twelve years' war," before Melle was finally subdued.

After Melle came Borgu, and here again a captive was taken who became the mother of another of the sons of the great Askia. These marriages or connections which resulted in the birth of princes, recognised as royal, are worthy of mention, as they represent a custom of the Soudan, where, amongst terms of peace, the demand of a wife for the conqueror from the royal family of the conquered almost invariably appears. They also indicate a gentle method by which the amalgamation of conquered provinces was made secure. There was no province of the empire from whom the future Emperor or Caliph of the Soudan might not be taken. Askia the Great lived, as will be seen, to an unusual old age. There reigned after him in succession four of his sons. The mother of the eldest of these, Askia Moussa, was taken from the household of the Hombori Koï, a conquest made in the Bend of the Niger while Mohammed was still minister of Sonni Ali. The mother of the second of his successors, Askia Ismail, was the Wankori girl first mentioned, very probably Fulani by birth, who was taken from Melle. The mother of the third, Askia Ishak, was from Tendirma, also the result of a conquest of the western province. The mother of the fourth, Askia Daouad, came from Sana, and was the daughter of the subject King or Koï of that province. Other marriages, although they did not give successors to the throne, gave personages of high importance and influence in the political administration of the country. Viceroys, governors, generals, admirals, inspectors, cadis, and officials whose functions it is not now easy to determine but whose titles were so eagerly sought as to show them to have been accompanied by considerable emoluments and power, were frequently selected from the sons and nephews of the kings. Oriental history has demonstrated that such a system has its serious inconveniences, and the Soudan was no exception to the rule, for if on the one hand the honours of the kingdom were opened freely to the best blood of every province, the system also created an excessive number of claimants for all preferment, and gave rise to labyrinths of intrigue, which not infrequently upset for personal motives the wisest plans. Successions were too often accompanied by the private murder or public massacre of superfluous co-heirs.

After the campaign against Borgu, which would appear to have been very severe, there followed further campaigns against Melle, and in 1512 there arose in the West a Fulani false prophet, Tayenda, against whom the Askia marched with success. Tayenda was killed. His son Kalo fled with the remnant of his troops to the Fouta Djallon, a country which at that time belonged to the Djolfs, and founded a second Fulani kingdom, which continued to exist even after the Moorish conquest of the Soudan. Towards the end of the same year, 1512, the Askia marched into the Haussa states.

The very meagre account which we have of the campaigns which appear to have occupied his troops in that region for the next few years, constitute the first mention of any importance of the Haussa States from the point of view of the Songhay Empire. These states, which at the present day constitute the greater part of Northern Nigeria, have a history of their own which dates back as far as that of Songhay itself.

At the time of the Askia's conquests in the first half of the sixteenth century they were an agricultural and commercial people who, situated as they were between the two powerful empires of Songhay on the one hand and Bornu on the other, had already suffered the tide of conquest to sweep over them more than once in the course of their long existence. Yet always as the waters of war subsided, they had emerged with independence, and by means partly of a not despicable courage and partly of payments, which were called either tribute or subsidy according to the ·humour of those who received and those who paid, they had sustained the continuity of their history and the individuality of their political life.

Katsena and Zaria, two of the states, would seem to have had some cause of quarrel with their more powerful neighbour Kano, and to have in the first instance solicited the intervention of the Askia. There are hints of some shadowy claim of suzerainty on the part of Songhay, which may have been the survival of previous and unrecorded conquests. Whatever the cause, Askia marched first against Katsena and took it in 1513. He also made himself master of Zaria and Zamfara—this last province being mentioned as especially rich in cotton and other crops—and proceeded to march against Kano and Gober. The conquest of Kano cost him a long siege, but both states fell to his arms, nnd were made tributary to Songhay. He then marched against the Sultan of Aghadez, a Berber kingdom lying north of the Haussa States, and stated by some authors to have been tributary to Songhay. Tekadda, in the desert to the west, was at one time, as we have seen, tributary to Melle, and causes of dispute between border provinces were not difficult to find. After a campaign which lasted for two years Aghadez yielded, and an annual tribute of 150,000 ducats was imposed upon it.

In Aghadez in the sixteenth century we have the counterpart of Audoghast in the eleventh century, and it furnishes again an example of a rich white town ruled by blacks. Aghadez was, we are told, at the time of the Songhay conquest, a wealthy town inhabited by white people, in which the houses were stately mansions, built after the fashion of Spain and Barbary, and the greater part of the citizens were either foreign merchants, artificers, or government officials.

It was on the return of the Askia's armies from this campaign that Kanta, an important chief of territory, conquered, as has been mentioned, some thirty years previously by Sonni Ali, dissatisfied with the treatment which had been accorded to him, revolted, and established an independent province, still known as Kanta, on the eastern side of the Niger. At a later date the whole of the province of Kebbi became subject to him. A campaign directed specially against him in the year 1517 was unavailing. The independence of Kebbi was maintained against all succeeding Askias, though its territory was enclosed in the territory of Songhay and its tributaries on all sides, and ultimately Kebbi became the bulwark which saved Haussaland from the encroachments of the Moors, when they attempted to overrun it from the west. During the years 1517–18 there was further successful fighting in the western portion of the empire. From this time to the end of the Askias' reign in 1528 peace would seem to have prevailed.

Askia the Great reigned altogether thirty-six years, during the whole of which time his minister, Ali Folen, continued to be the faithful assistant of his counsels and the interpreter of his wishes to the people.

I have thought it well very briefly to summarise the military history of the reign in order that the borders of the empire over which the rule of the Askia extended might be defined, but war was far from being the principal subject either of the Askia's or of his people's thoughts. The administrative organisation of the empire occupied his immediate care, and a parallel of the system which he partly adopted, and partly developed, from the already existing sytem of Melle, may perhaps be most nearly found in our own early administration of India. Native rulers continued to occupy positions of dignity and quasi-independence, and would seem to have been even permitted in some cases to levy troops, on the understanding that they furnished a regular quota to the imperial army. But the representatives of Songhay were supreme in all parts of the empire, and over the heads of the native rulers there was a complete network of Songhay administration.

By the acquisition of the Haussa States the territory of the empire was carried from Bornu on the borders of Lake Chad to the Atlantic. The southern limits had been securely extended, by the final conquest and conversion of Mossi and the subjection of Borgu, to the mountains which divide the uplands of the interior from the jungle of the coast. Its northern frontier was re-established on the old limits of the Mellestine, being so far enlarged in the north-east by the conquest of Aghadez as to command the Tripoli-Fezzan route into the desert. It already commanded the routes entering on the west from Sidjilmessa and Wargelan. Thus Songhay held the southern side of the three already mentioned "gates of the desert," and in language of latitude and longitude the empire may be described as extending, in the middle of the sixteenth century, from about 17° west to 13° east, and from about 10° to between 25° and 30° north. Its shape, however, was not that of a parallelogram, but rather that of a figure enclosed within a great semicircle, of which the base, extending from the country south of Lake Chad to the Atlantic, measured about 2000 miles, while the greatest diameter, taken at right angles to the base due north in the neighbourhood of Twat, measured a little over 1000 miles.

For the purposes of administration this vast empire was divided into the home provinces and the vice-royalties. There were four vice-royalties. Beginning at the west, the first vice-royalty was called Kormina, and was composed of the south-western provinces, including what remained of the dismembered Melle, the Fulani State of Masina, the country of the pagan Bambaras, and the territory lying between the Niger and the Atlantic, up to the limit at which it met the frontier line of the second vice-royalty known as Bal or Bala. The vice-royalty of Bal took in the north-western provinces, including Ghanata, and extended from Timbuctoo to the salt-mines of Tegazza. The frontier of Bal was conterminous in the desert with the frontier of the third vice-royalty of Bankou, which covered the country extending north-east from the river between Timbuctoo and Kagho or Gao. The eastern frontier of Bankou was again conterminous in the desert, probably about the limits of Tekadda, with that of the great vice-royalty of Dandi, which seems to have had an extension in the east equal to that of Kormina in the west. It reached from the eastern end of the southern mountains, in the neighbourhood of the province now known as Yoruba, at the back of Lagos, and after including Borgu and the country as far north as Gao on the western side of the Niger, it spread over the eastern side of the river as far as Aghadez in the north-east, and across the Haussa States to the borders of Wangara and Bornu near Lake Chad.

The exact frontiers of the vice-royalties are unknown. Presumably they did not always remain the same. But roughly speaking, if the Niger be divided into the four sections which have been indicated, that is, from the sources of the river in the west to Jenné, from Jenné to Timbuctoo, from Timbuctoo to Gao, and from Gao to a point above the junction with the Benué, which might perhaps be fixed at the Boussa rapids above Jebba, radiating lines drawn from the meeting points of those four sections to the circumference of the empire will serve to give a fairly definite impression of the political division of the outlying provinces.

The territory which remained, and which was enclosed between the river and the southern mountains in the area now known as the Bend of the Niger, was divided into the home provinces. Of these there were several of importance. Amongst them may be named Hombouri, Sansanding, and Bandouk. The old capital of the empire, and the residence always preferred by the great Askia, was Kagho, now represented only by the unimportant little town of Gao. But the true centre of political, religious, and commercial life was Timbuctoo.

CHAPTER XXIII

SONGHAY UNDER ASKIA THE GREAT (*continued*)

To cross the dominions of the Askia was, we are told, a six months' journey. Yet so effective were the measures taken by him for its administration, that before the end of his reign, the result is thus summarised by his historian: "He was obeyed with as much docility on the farthest limits of the empire as he was in his own palace, and there reigned everywhere great plenty and absolute peace."

He laboured unceasingly to introduce the reforms which he thought desirable, and to appoint to every position of importance men whom he could trust to supervise his measures. The reformation of the army and the church, which had occupied the opening years of his reign, represented but the beginning of the care which he continued to bestow upon these two great institutions. The evolution of systems of government suitable to the widely differing peoples over whom he ruled, the development of trade, the protection of letters and the opening of communications, were among questions to which he gave much of his time. Moslem judges were appointed in the lesser towns, which up to this time had been content with the services of scribes or conciliators; and among the biographies of upright judges given to us by Ahmed Baba or Es Sadi, the comment is not infrequent: "He was one of those appointed by Askia the Great." There was a state prison for political offenders, which seems to have served a purpose similar to that of the Tower of London, and the courtyard of the prison of Kanato was no less famous in local annals than

Tower Hill. The general rule would seem to have been a rule of mildness, but it is to be noted that inhuman punishments which, in their survival, shock the sentiment of the twentieth century, were used on occasions which called for exceptional severity. Among these, burying alive in bottle-shaped holes, which were closed over the head of the victim, and sewing up in the hides of oxen or wild beasts, are two which connect the criminal code of Songhay with the past and with the present. The sewing up of victims in the skins of wild beasts was, it may be remembered, practised in Rome under the Emperor Makrinus, and was still in use at a much later period. The practice of burying alive remained among the punishments of the Soudan, and was only abolished in the states acknowledging British rule by the expedition to Sokoto and Kano in 1903. Askia the Great does not seem to have gone the length of codifying the Songhay laws, but the attention which was given to the study of law, and the long lists of distinguished lawyers who are mentioned in the annals of this and the succeeding reigns, would seem to indicate that Mohammedan law was generally accepted and practised through the Songhay Empire, with only such local modification as experience may have suggested. The system of local law existing at the present day in the Haussa States is admirable in theory. In the decadence of the country it is the administration of it which has failed.

Askia also introduced a reform of the markets. A unification of weights and measures was drawn up. Inspectors of the markets — an office which already existed under the Sultans of Melle—were selected with special care. They were enjoined to keep close watch over the introduction of the new system, and any falsification was severely punished. The markets were, it is said, rendered so honest, that a child might go into the market-place and would bring back full value for value sent. The Niger was, of course, the great highway of commerce, and the towns situated upon it were the principal centres of trade. Jenné, which continued to be enriched by a great cotton industry, was looked upon as the principal market for internal trade. Timbuctoo governed the trade of the west and north-west, including relations with Morocco and the coast. Kagho, or Gao, governed the trade of the east and north-east, including relations with Egypt and Tripoli, but in the Haussa States Kano had long been an important trading centre; and Gober, Zamfara, and Zaria—all rich in local produce, especially cotton, for which their soil and climate was said to be particularly fitted—possessed a well-established and busy trade. Aghadez formed a very wealthy station on the main north-eastern trade route, and it is not improbable that the cause of the war which occupied the armies of the Askia for two years had its origin in the commercial rivalry of that town with the town of Tekadda, on the borders of the vice-royalty of Bankou.

Systems of banking and credit, which seem to have existed under the kings of Melle, were improved. Banking remained chiefly in the hands of the Arabs, from whom letters of credit could be procured, which were operative throughout the Soudan, and were used by the black travelling merchants as well as by Arab traders. Commerce, as was to be expected, developed greatly under the encouragement and security given to it by the Askia's measures.

With the increase of commerce and luxury came also the gradual refinement and softening of manners which accompany wealth in a community where military service is no longer a universal obligation. The reforms of the great Askia did not neglect the department of morals. The great freedom prevailing in the intercourse of men and women was among the scandals for which he would seem to have endeavoured, but without much success, to legislate. He seems to have instituted a body of correctional police, who were charged with the prevention of any infringement of the laws. Women were placed on the same footing as in the harems of the East, and obliged to veil themselves when they appeared in public. Nevertheless, Timbuctoo remained ever celebrated for the luxury of its habits and the gaiety and licence of its manners. Music, dress, dancing, and amusement formed, say its indignant chroniclers, the principal objects of life to a large portion of the population. The immense domestic establishments of the East would seem to have excited in the Askia no displeasure. He was himself the father of a hundred sons, of whom the youngest was born when he was ninety years of age. But his influence appears to have been strongly and indignantly excited against forms of licence which exceeded the bounds of this very liberal standard of morality. His adviser, in respect to these reforms, was a learned fanatic of the name of El Mocheili, whose writings remain to attest the workings of the royal mind. The Askia's own sons, less rigid in their principles than their father, did not escape when punishment seemed to him to be due to their offences. El Mocheili, whose advice was at times more enthusiastic than discreet, was among those who are said to have influenced the Askia in the direction of the religious persecution of the Jews.

Another great counsellor of the Askia, whose name has been preserved, was a Marabout of the name of Mohammed Koti, a scholar and writer of great eminence, the author, amongst other things, of a history of the kingdoms of Ghanata, Songhay, and Timbuctoo, called "The Fatassi," which has unfortunately been lost. M. Felix Dubois, who, after diligent search, was able to recover a few fragments of this valuable work, gives an interesting account of the destruction of the only existing copy of the history by the Fulani, as late as the middle of the nineteenth century. The author was born in 1460, and survived Askia the Great by fourteen years, being connected during the whole period of the reign with public affairs. Under the influence of Koti and other distinguished scholars, letters received well-directed sympathy and encouragement.

After the siege of Aiwalatin in 1480, there began a gradual but steady flow of learning and cultivation from that decadent capital of Ghanata to Timbuctoo. The death of Sonni Ali and the accession of Mohammed gave confidence to this movement, which soon gathered force and volume, and we are enabled to reconstruct from the writings of Ahmed Baba, who was himself born during the reign of Askia Daouad, the fourth and last reigning son of the great Askia, some picture of the intellectual and literary revival of Timbuctoo.

The University of Sankore would seem to have been a very active centre of civilisation. It was attached to the mosque of the same name, and was in correspondence, both by letter and by the frequent visits of its professors, with the universities of North Africa and Egypt. It was already in existence under the rule of Melle, and at that time was in touch with the universities of Spain. The latter source of knowledge was now, of course, cut off, by the cessation of intercourse between Spain and Africa. But, as the first result of the expulsion of the Moors was to drive the more learned Arabs of Spain into the recesses of the University of Fez, the full effect of the measure had not yet been felt. On the contrary, the life of Timbuctoo had probably received some stimulus from the influx of learning to Morocco. The historians of Timbuctoo distinctly state that civilisation and learning came to it from the West. In the middle of the sixteenth century there existed in the town, side by side with the luxury of the court and the frivolity of fashion, a large and learned society, living at ease, and busily occupied with the elucidation of intellectual and religious problems. The town swarmed also with Soudanese students, of whom we are optimistically told that they "were filled with ardour for knowledge and virtue."

The more distinguished professors would seem to

have had schools in which they gave courses of lectures, attended by students, who afterwards received diplomas from the hands of their masters. In the biographical sketches of Ahmed Baba, the master from whom diplomas were received is mentioned as regularly as the school or university in which a man receives his education is mentioned in similar English works. A sketch which Ahmed Baba gives of one of the principal professors under whom he himself had studied, may serve to indicate the type of sage who was revered by the youth of Timbuctoo, and incidentally presents a picture of local scholastic life.

Mohammed Abou Bekr of Wankore, his pupil tells us, writing himself as an old man forty or fifty years later, was "one of the best of God's virtuous creatures. He was a working scholar, and a man instinct with goodness. His nature was as pure as it was upright. He was himself so strongly impelled towards virtue, and had so high an opinion of others, that he always considered them as being so to speak his equals, and as having no knowledge of evil. He did not believe in the bad faith of the world, but always thought well of his fellow-creatures until they had committed a fault, and even after they had committed a fault. Calm and dignified, with a natural distinction. and a modesty that rendered intercourse with him easy, he captured all hearts. Every one who knew him loved him." He taught during the whole of a long life, while at the same time he continued to take an active interest, and even some part, in public affairs. The Sultan, who shared the general respect for him, offered him the lucrative appointment of Governor of the Palace, but he refused it—"God having," he said, "delivered him from such cares." He was also offered the appointment of principal preacher to the great mosque, but that also he prayed the Sultan to excuse him from accepting. He was apparently wealthy, and possessed a fine library. "His whole life was given," says Ahmed Baba, "to the service of others. He taught his pupils to love science, to follow its teachings, to devote their time to it, to associate with scholars, and to keep their minds in a state of docility. He lavishly lent his most precious books, rare copies, and the volumes that he most valued, and never asked for them again, no matter what was the subject of which they treated." Sometimes "a student would present himself at the door and ask for a book, and he would give it without even knowing who the man was." Ahmed Baba recalls with affection an instance when he himself wanted a rare work on grammar, and the master not only lent it, but spent a long time searching through his library for other works which might help to elucidate his pupil's difficulties. "It was astonishing to see him," says Ahmed Baba; "and he acted thus, notwithstanding the fact that he had a passion for books, and that he collected them with ardour, both buying and causing them to be copied." It is not, alas! surprising to hear that "in this way he lost a great quantity of his books."

His industry in teaching was equalled only by his patience. "When I knew him," says Ahmed Baba, "he used to begin his lectures after the first prayer, and continued them until the second prayer at half-past nine, varying the subjects of which he treated. He then returned home for the prayer, and after it usually went to the cadi to occupy himself with public affairs. After that he taught at his own house till mid-day. He joined the public mid-day prayers, and then continued his lectures at home till the fourth prayer. Then he went out and lectured in another place until twilight. After the sunset prayer, he taught in the mosque until the last night prayer, and then returned to his own house. No pupil was too stupid or too ignorant for him. He never allowed himself to be discouraged, or to despair of gaining an entrance into the understanding of his hearer. Sometimes, indeed, his patience with the stupid was so great, that the more intelligent members of the class were moved to wonder and impatience. "He must have drunk the water of Zem-Zem to be able to stand it," was the comment of one of Ahmed Baba's fellow-pupils on such an occasion. But Ahmed Baba, in faithful remembrance, forgets the impatience of youth, and keeps only admiration. "His like," he says, "will never be found again." The mind of this teacher is described as "subtle, sagacious, ready, swift to comprehend. His intelligence was broad and luminous. His usual manner was taciturn and grave, but he would occasionally break into sallies of wit. He occupied himself with what concerned him, listened to no gossip, and took part in no frivolity, but "wrapped himself in a magnificent mantle of discretion and reserve. His hand held fast the standard of continence."

In the atmosphere of laborious calm which is pictured by such a rule of existence, the sages of Timbuctoo would seem to have lived and carried on their labours to advanced old age. It is impossible not to be struck by the long periods of activity which are assigned to distinguished scholars. Ahmed Baba himself was born in 1556, and did not die till 1627, writing industriously during the greater part of his grown-up life. Nor was his career exceptional in this respect. Seventy, eighty, and even ninety, are ages at which men were still frequently to be found at work.

The study of law, literature, grammar, and theology would seem to have been more general at Timbuctoo than that of the natural sciences. We hear, however, of at least one distinguished geographer, and allusions to surgical science show that the old maxim of the Arabian schools, "He who studies anatomy pleases God," was not forgotten. At a later date (1618) the author of the *Tarikh* incidentally mentions that his brother came from Jenné to Timbuctoo to undergo an operation for cataract at the hands of a celebrated surgeon there—an operation which was wholly successful. The appearance of comets, so amazing to Europe of the Middle Ages, is also noted calmly, as a matter of scientific interest, at Timbuctoo. Earthquakes and eclipses excite no great surprise. In the sketch which has just been quoted of Mohammed Wankore, the teachers under whom this professor himself learnt Arabic are named, showing that Arabic was by no means considered to be the language of Timbuctoo. That language was Songhay, and if the civilisation of Timbuctoo came from the West, it was wedded within the city walls to the traditions and the forms of expression of the East.

Travellers give us a picture of the town as it existed in the early part of the sixteenth century. The houses, which would seem to have been fairly spacious, were built, some say of clay, and some of wood covered with plaster—the roofs, like the Dutch buildings of South Africa, being universally thatched. The mosques are described as stately buildings of cut stone and lime, and there was a "princely palace," of which the walls were also of cut stone and lime. There were a great many shops and factories, "especially," says Leo Africanus, who was there in 1526, "of such as weave linen and cotton cloth." The court maintained by the Askias is described by Marmol as being so well ordered that it yielded in nothing spiritual or temporal to the courts of Northern Africa. Under the successors of Askia the Great, the palace was enlarged and greatly embellished, the court being then thronged with courtiers in ever-increasing numbers. The habits of dress became sumptuous, and it would seem from incidental allusions that different functionaries had their different uniforms and insignia of office, to the wearing of which great value was attached. The dress and appointments of women became also extravagantly luxurious. They were served on gold. In full dress their persons were covered with jewels, and the wives of the rich when they went out were attended by well-dressed slaves.

Amongst the possessions of the rich, large libraries and good horses would seem, in Askia the Great's time, to have been the most valued. The libraries of wealthy and learned citizens are frequently mentioned, and horses from Barbary would always fetch their price. The king was specially fond of horses, paid for them liberally, and always caused himself to be informed when good ones were brought into the town for sale. Gold plate was also apparently remarkable. Leo Africanus says that "the rich king of Timbuctoo had many plates and sceptres of gold, of which some weighed as much as 1300 lbs." As we are not told that the Askia was waited on by a race of giants, we may permit ourselves to doubt the statement that he caused himself to be served on trays that weighed 1300 lbs. Yet we may remember the famous *missorium* or dish for the service of the table, which in the sixth century was found by the Franks in the Gothic palace of Narbonne, and of which even the grave and careful Gibbon accepts the statement that it weighed 500 lbs. of massy gold. Taken in conjunction with previous accounts of the gold plate of the sovereigns of Melle and the magnificent arms of their retainers, this statement may at least be accepted as showing that the court of the Askias was well supplied with the precious metal.

Among the amusements of the town, music held always a high place, and under Askia the Great's successors, orchestras, provided with singers of both sexes, were much frequented. Of Askia the Great himself, it is said that "his mind was set towards none of these things." Chess-playing, of a kind which is particularly described as "Soudanese chess," was sometimes carried to the extreme of a passion. We hear of a general in the reign of one of the succeeding Askias, who gave it as an excuse for allowing himself to be surprised by the enemy's cavalry, that he was so much absorbed in a game of chess as not to have paid attention to the reports of his scouts. The whole town in Askia the Great's day was very rich, the people living with great abundance, and trade was active. The currency was of gold, without any stamp or superscription, but for small objects in the native markets shells were still used.

A very great trade was done both here and at Kagho in cotton, which was exchanged for European cloth. Unfortunately their relative value is not mentioned. We are told only that the money price of fine European cloth was reckoned at fifteen ducats an ell, and for scarlet of Venice or Turkey cloth, Leo says they would give as much as thirty ducats an ell. In Kagho he says that it was "a wonder to see what plenty of merchandise is daily brought hither, and how costly and sumptuous all things be." Marmol, who wrote about thirty years later than Leo, specially dwells upon the cotton trade of Jenné, Melle, Timbuctoo, Gober, Kano, Zamfara, and Bornu. Both Leo and Marmol, who are worth quoting, as being writers professedly antagonistic to the Soudan, speak of the great trade done in manuscripts and written books from Barbary, which, they say, "are sold for more money than any other merchandise"; and Leo was at least so far aware of the literary life of Timbuctoo as to note that "Here are great store of doctors, judges, priests, and other learned men."

It is interesting and remarkable that while Timbuctoo undoubtedly dominated the life of the Songhay Empire, and was the first town of the Soudan, many other towns are almost equally noticed by travellers for their trade and for the learning of which they were the centre. Marmol, writing in the reign of Askia Daouad, speaks of Melle as not only rich in trade but also in learning, having its own schools of science and religion. The writers of Timbuctoo themselves make frequent allusions to learned doctors of Melle, Aiwalatin, Jenné, and Katsena. In Masina also there were an "immense number of distinguished men of letters and divines." Even the far distant Tekadda is named as the seat in which El Mocheili chose to establish his school, when, as a consequence of his fanatical hatred of the Jews, he was driven from the western part of the Soudan. Marmol says that in his day Songhay was the language commonly spoken in Ghanata, that is, the most westerly of the provinces of the empire. The statement sounds improbable, as seventy-five years of a mild foreign rule would hardly suffice to change the language of a people; but it is possible that Songhay may have been the officially adopted language of the empire.

CHAPTER XXIV

THE LATER ASKIAS

Askia the Great reigned for thirty-six years. It is sorrowful to have to relate that he was not allowed to finish his life upon the throne which he had so conspicuously adorned. In 1528 he, being by that time blind, and being supposed to have fallen too completely under the influence of Ali Folen, was deposed by his eldest son, who ascended the throne under the title of Askia Moussa, and reigned only for three years. During his reign the old Askia lived in comfort in his favourite palace and farm near Kagho; while Ali Folen, after a first flight to Aiwalatin, made his way to Kano with the intention of performing once again the pilgrimage to Mecca, but, falling ill, died and was buried in that town. On the death of Moussa the throne of the Askias was usurped by a nephew, Mohammed Benkan, the son of the great Askia's favourite and profoundly trusted brother. The son did not repay with gratitude the many favours which his dead father had received. Not content with sitting on the Askia's throne, he removed the blind old man from his palace, and confined him in miserable quarters on an island in the Niger. But his ill-doing brought deserved punishment in its train.

In an interview which is related as taking place between the deposed monarch and his son Ismail—a young man of twenty-seven years of age, who came to visit him one night in the island in which he was confined—we see the vigour which had inspired the life of the old Askia still unextinguished. Ismail sat down before his father. The Askia, taking hold of his son's arm, said: "Heavens! how can an arm like this allow mosquitoes to devour me, and frogs to leap upon me, when there is nothing which so revolts me?" Ismail, the son of that Miriam who was married after the great campaign of Melle, was an upright but not brilliant representative of his father's stock. He replied with grief that he could do nothing. The Askia answered by telling him where there was a secret stock of money; who were the men that he could trust; how he was to come into touch with them; and, sitting in his miserable dungeon in all the feebleness of blind old age, the still unconquered monarch planned and dictated a scheme by which his unworthy nephew was removed from the throne he had usurped, and Ismail was seated upon it in his place. Under the protection of Ismail the old Askia returned with honour to his palace, and died there in 1538 at an age which cannot have been far short of a hundred.

Ismail reigned only two years, and was succeeded in 1539 by his brother Ishak, a cruel but very able prince, who, after a reign of nearly ten years, was succeeded in his turn by another brother, Askia Daouad, the most distinguished of all the great Askia's sons. Askia Daouad reigned from 1548 to 1582. After him three more Askias of the next generation brought this brilliant period of the history of the Soudan to an end. When Ishak, the son of Askia Mohammed, was at the height of his power, Muley Hamed, the Sultan of Morocco, called upon him to give up his right to the great western salt mine of Tegazza. His spirited answer, read by the light of subsequent history, has a prophetic ring. "The Hamed who makes such a demand," he replied, "can hardly be the great Emperor of Morocco; the Ishak who can listen to it is not I. That Ishak has still to be born." The Ishak who would listen was born in the next generation of Askias, and it was under Ishak II. in 1591 that the salt mines were taken, and the Empire of Songhay was overthrown by the Moors.

Under Askia Daouad we hear of the murder of the Songhay governor of Tegazza by the instigation of the Emperor of Morocco. Work at the salt mines became so dangerous, and the interruption of the salt trade was so frequent, that Askia Daouad was led to authorise the opening of another salt mine which was found in the desert; but Askia Daouad abated nothing of the claims of his father, although he and a succeeding Muley Ahmed came to a friendly understanding. Before the end of the sixteenth century, conflict between the troops of Songhay and the troops of Morocco, on the question of the salt mines, was clearly becoming inevitable.

Under Askia Daouad military expeditions were renewed on all the borders of the empire. Melle and the Fulani provinces of the west—Mossi, Borgu, Boussa, Gurma, all in turn gave occasion for the exercise of military activity. It is during the military expeditions of Askia Daouad that we get definite accounts of the contingents furnished by subordinate Koïs. Two Koïs are mentioned in one of the western campaigns as furnishing 12,000 men each, which, it is said, was their regular contingent. An expedition was sent also into the Haussa States, and the campaign against Katsena in 1554 was remarkable for an incident which did equal honour to both sides. In an encounter between the Songhay and the Haussa troops, twenty-four picked cavaliers of Songhay sustained a long and desperate struggle against a regiment of 400 Haussa soldiers. They were at last overpowered, fifteen of them being killed. The remaining nine, all badly wounded, were taken prisoners, and the Haussa soldiers were so impressed by their courage that they dressed their wounds, nursed them with the greatest care, supplied their wants, and then set them at liberty, sending them back to Askia Daouad with the courteous assurance that "men so brave should not be allowed to die." Other expeditions occupied the greater part of this reign. As a result of a successful campaign in Melle in 1559, Askia Daouad, like his father, married a daughter of the house of Melle. Here is the description, given by the *Tarikh*, of her bridal train: "He caused the princess to be conducted to Songhay in a sumptuous equipage. She was covered with jewels, surrounded by numerous slaves, both men and women, and provided with an abundant baggage train. All the utensils of the household were of gold—dishes, pitchers, pestle and mortar, everything." Under Askia Daouad the town of Timbuctoo was much embellished. The great mosque of Mansa Musa was restored and enlarged. Two other mosques were also rebuilt, and the restoration of the Sankoré Mosque was begun. These works were all undertaken and carried out under the inspiration of a very public-spirited cadi, whose name, El-Aquib, deserves to be remembered as a representative of illustrious learning, fearless justice, and disinterested devotion to public duty. Askia Daouad himself contributed handsomely to the rebuilding of the great mosque.

The last military expedition of Askia Daouad's reign was a campaign conducted by his son, the Viceroy of the south-western province, against the Fulani of Masina. A lawless portion of the population of Masina had ventured to attack and pillage a royal boat laden with merchandise, which was on the way from Jenné. Such a thing, it is said, had never happened before under the dynasty of Songhay, and the indignant Viceroy resolved to make a terrible example of Masina. He ravaged the country with fire and sword, allowing his troops to massacre indiscriminately; and in the general slaughter there perished, we are told, a great number of distinguished scholars and divines. The Sultan of Masina fled to a place of safety till the storm had passed, and then returned to his estates. Askia Daouad entirely disapproved of the policy and conduct of his son. The massacre of Masina happened, however, in the spring of 1582, and before Askia Daouad had time to take any action in the matter, he died on his favourite estate near Kagho, on the 21st of August of that year. With him died the last of the great Askias. He was succeeded by his son, who, in consequence of having made the pilgrimage to Mecca, was known, like his illustrious grandfather, by the name of "El Hadj." He was an estimable prince, but an invalid, and he reigned only four years. He was succeeded in his turn by his brother, Mohammed Bano, a mere nullity, who occupied the throne for two years; and in 1588 that second Ishak, also a son of Askia Daouad, who lives in the tradition of the Soudan as "the worst of the Askias," closed the line of the independent sovereigns of Songhay.

In bringing to an end this notice of the most remarkable dynasty of which we have any record in the Soudan, it is perhaps worth while to draw attention to the length of the reigns not only of the two most distinguished monarchs of this line, but generally of the more remarkable native sovereigns of the Soudan. The reign of Askia Daouad lasted for thirty-four years, that of Askia the Great for thirty-six years. Sonni Ali, whose life and whose reign were brought to an end only by an accident, reigned for thirty years. The great Mansa Musa reigned for twenty-four years. His brother, who after a short interval succeeded him, reigned for twenty-six years. In the Desert Empire the son of the famous Teloutan, who had himself a very long reign, reigned from 837 till 910, that is, upwards of seventy years, and was then killed in battle. Nor was this longevity confined to the rulers of the country. It has already been mentioned that the common age to which men lived in the Desert Empire was eighty years, and the great age of the teachers and writers of Timbuctoo has been noticed. Public men not only lived to a great age, but kept their offices for long periods of time. The great Askia, after having been a successful general, was Prime Minister for thirty years before he became a monarch for thirty-six years. Ali Folen, his Prime Minister, already a chosen councillor whose fidelity had been approved in 1492, held office till the end of the sovereign's reign in 1528. Mohammed Goddala, the first Cadi of Timbuctoo appointed by the great Askia, a man highly distinguished both for learning and justice in the annals of his country, lived to the age of eighty-four, and was Cadi for fifty years. The Cadi el Aquib, who rebuilt the mosques of Timbuctoo under Askia Daouad, held his functions as Cadi for eighteen years. Mohammed Naddi, the famous Timbuctoo Koï, who, having held office under the Sultan of Melle, was reinstated by the Tuaregs on their capture of the town, had held office for more than thirty years when he died in 1464. It is needless to multiply examples; but the longevity of the individual is an element of so much importance in the development of the race that, in view of the opinion usually entertained with regard to the climate and institutions of the Soudan, it seems interesting to establish the fact that there is nothing in the health conditions of the country which, for those who are acclimatised, is opposed to long and active life. As regards the institutions, continuity of office in the individual is nearly always coincident with stability in the state. Short reigns, short ministries, short military commands, are symptoms which seldom fail to indicate an unsettled and unsatisfactory condition of public life. Prosperity and permanence go hand in hand; and where we find judges, generals, viceroys, kings, holding their public positions for periods varying between twenty-five and fifty years, we may fairly argue a peaceful and prosperous condition of the country.

The history of the Soudan offers no contradiction to the assumption that the life of the nation will correspond to the life of the individual. The duration of the Soudanese empires will bear comparison with that of others which are better known to fame. Ghana enjoyed an independent existence of about 1100 years—that is, a period nearly equivalent to the period of existence of our own British monarchy from the abolition of the Saxon Heptarchy to the present day. Melle, who succeeded her, had a shorter national life of about 250 years. Songhay counted its kings in regular succession from about 700 A.D. to the date of the Moorish conquest in 1591—a period which almost exactly coincides with the life of Rome from the foundation of the republic, 509 B.C., to the downfall of the empire in the first half of the fifth century of our era. The duration of the Empire of Bornu was, as will be seen, no less respectable.

The civilisation represented by these empires was no doubt, if judged by a modern and still more by a Western standard, exceedingly imperfect. The principles of freedom, as we understand them, were probably unknown. Authority rested upon force of arms. Industrial life was based on slavery. Social life was founded on polygamy. Side by side with barbaric splendour there was primeval simplicity. Luxury for the few took the place of comfort for the many. Study was devoted mainly to what seem to us unprofitable ends. These are grave drawbacks. Yet the fact that civilisation, far in excess of anything which the nations of Northern Europe possessed at the earlier period of Soudanese history, existed with stability enough to maintain empire after empire through a known period of about 1500 years, in a portion of the world which mysteriously disappeared in the sixteenth century from the comity of modern nations, is interesting enough to merit recognition, and, it seems to me, to justify some study of the new chapters of history presented to our consideration.

CHAPTER XXV

ANCIENT CONNECTION OF HAUSSALAND WITH THE VALLEY OF THE NILE

THE next great event of importance in the history of the Soudan is the conquest of the country by the Moors, but before approaching the narrative of this catastrophe it will be well to bring the history of Bornu and the Haussa States — which fill the last remaining section of the country lying between the Atlantic and Lake Chad—up to the point of their contemporary development in the sixteenth century. These portions of the Soudan are especially interesting to us, as they constitute at the present day the northern portion of the British Protectorate of Nigeria.

It has been said, in entering upon the history of the Songhay Empire, that in it we reached that part of the history of the Western Soudan in which the influence of the West and of the East visibly met and overlapped. In crossing the Niger, and passing to the territories which lie still farther east, we come to that part of the country in which the influence of the East begins more distinctly to predominate.

To establish the grounds on which such influence may be presupposed, a short digression is necessary into what is known of the geographical connection of the countries of Northern Africa with each other during a very early period of their history.

The ancient civilisation of Egypt spread, as we know, from south to north, and without venturing to accept or to reject the assumption of some learned writers that it came originally by way of the Arabian Gulf from India, there is seemingly no doubt that the earliest seat of civilisation in Africa was the country watered by the Upper Nile, which was known by the name of Ethiopia to the ancients, and which lay in an easterly direction, between the very latitudes of 10° and 17° that on the western side of Lake Chad fixed the limits of habitation of the higher races of the Soudan. Monuments, of which a more or less consecutive chain can be traced from Nubia to the Straits of Bab-el-Mandeb, point to the existence in this territory, at a period of great antiquity, of a people possessing many of the arts of a relatively high civilisation. The principal state of this Ethiopian country bore the well-known name of Meroë. It occupied the territory watered by the Nile and its tributaries, of which the most northerly point is marked by the meeting of the Atbara and the Nile. The capital of Meroë was a city of the same name, which stood a little below the present Shendy, under 17° N. latitude, and in 32½° E. longitude. That is to say, Meroë stood, like Ghana, on the extreme edge of the summer rains. The limits of the State of Meroë extended probably at one time to the north of 17° and to the south of 10°. Those parallels may, however, be taken as indicating its permanent limits.

This is not the place, nor am I competent to discuss the arguments which form the ground of belief that the civilisation of Meroë preceded that of Egypt. It is enough to say very briefly, that on the site of the city of Meroë there exist remains of temples and pyramids, from which archæologists have drawn the conclusion that the pyramid was a form of architecture native to Meroë, and only afterwards brought to perfection in Egypt. It is evident, from the decoration of the temples, that they were dedicated to the worship of Ammon. It is believed that the remains of the temple of the most famous oracle of Jupiter Ammon are to be found in ruins at about eight hours' journey to the north-east of Shendy. This temple of the oracle was known to exist within a few hours' journey of Meroë, and the priestly traditions of

Ethiopia and Egypt assert that the worship of Ammon and Osiris, with its feasts and processions, was first settled at the metropolis of Meroë. This remarkable spot is regarded by the ancients as the "cradle of the arts and sciences, where hieroglyphic writing was discovered, and where temples and pyramids had already sprung up while Egypt still remained ignorant of their existence." From this temple the worship of Ammon and his attendant gods would seem to have spread to Egypt, and through the oasis of Siwah to Carthage and the Mediterranean coast.

The carvings of the monuments of Meroë show a people in possession of the arts and luxuries of civilisation, and having some knowledge of science. On the base of one of the monuments a zodiac has been found, and in the more northerly monuments of Nubia, which portray the conquest of Meroë by Rameses the Great of Egypt at a much later date, the conquered nation is shown as being not only rich, civilised, and important, but also as possessing tributary states, presumably in Central Africa, whence came giraffes and other Central African produce. We learn from the same monuments that the women of Meroë were frequently armed, and appeared to live on equal terms with men. They are constantly portrayed as queens. The Empire of Meroë had its settled constitution and its laws. It was composed of many little states, but the whole were apparently governed by a priest-caste, and the portraits of priests, frequently repeated upon the monuments, show them as tall and slender, with handsome profile, red-brown in colour, and with hair indifferently straight or curled. The general population are believed to have been of the black and straight-haired Nubian race. Here is the conclusion drawn by a competent German critic, nearly a hundred years ago, from the discoveries made by Gau, Champollion, and others: "In Nubia and Ethiopia stupendous, numerous, and primeval monuments proclaim so loudly a civilisation contemporary to, aye, earlier than that of Egypt, that it may be conjectured with the greatest confidence that the arts, sciences, and religion descended from Nubia to the lower country of Misraim; that civilisation descended the Nile, built Memphis, and finally, something later, wrested by colonisation the Delta from the sea."[1]

The monuments, though eloquent, are not the only grounds upon which this conclusion has been reached. The fame of the Ethiopians was widespread in ancient history. Herodotus describes them as "the tallest, the most beautiful and long-lived of the human race," and before Herodotus, Homer, in even more flattering language, described them as "the most just of men; the favourites of the gods." The annals of all the great early nations of Asia Minor are full of them. The Mosaic records allude to them frequently; but while they are described as the most powerful, the most just, and the most beautiful of the human race, they are constantly spoken of as black, and there seems to be no other conclusion to be drawn, than that at that remote period of history the leading race of the Western world was a black race. When we reflect that this black race flourished within the very latitudes of Africa which European nations are now engaged in opening to modern civilisation, a great interest is added to the study of their possible descendants.

The people of Ethiopia colonised to the north and west. Amongst their colonies to the north, one of the most important was Thebes. Thebes and Meroë together founded the colony of Ammonium in the western desert, and through Thebes the religion of Meroë was carried into Lower Egypt. It was at a much later period, about 1500 B.C., that Egypt returned upon Meroë and conquered it.

In the ancient world, as in ours, commerce and religion were constantly associated. The routes of pilgrimage were also the routes of trade, and with the

[1] Heeren, "Historical Researches: African Nations."

help of the magnificent remains which have from time to time been discovered in the southern regions watered by the Nile and its tributary streams, it has been found possible to re-establish some of the great trade routes which were used by Meroë in the days of her prosperity. In briefly indicating them I follow the account given by Heeren in his "Historical Researches."

There can be no doubt that from a very early period maritime commerce existed between India, Arabia, and the East African coasts. Probably at an even earlier period Chinese navigators frequented the shores of Africa. Marmol, writing of the East Coast of Africa in the sixteenth century, says: "There was a time when the Chinese navigated these shores as freely as the Portuguese now do," and his statement obtains some modern corroboration from the fact that at the excavation, about twenty-five years ago, of Kilwa, once the capital of a native empire, upon the east coast of Africa, where three towns were superimposed upon one another, the lowest town was found to be full of Chinese coins. Commerce between the countries lying on the shores of the Indian Ocean was favoured by the fact, thus recorded by an ancient writer, that for "one half of the year, from spring to autumn, the wind regularly sets in and wafts the vessels from Arabia to India; the other half, from autumn to spring, it as regularly carries them back from India to Arabia." Arrian, in his "Periplus of the Erythrean Sea," written in the first century of our era, speaking of the commerce, which was then, of course, a matter of ancient, though also of contemporary history, says: "Before merchants sailed from Egypt to India, Arabia Felix was the staple (or market) both for Egyptian and Indian goods, just as Alexandria now is for the commodities of Egypt and foreign merchandise." The Indians nowhere appear as navigators; the Arabians always do. It seems to be demonstrated that they possessed the navigation of the Indian Ocean, not only in our own medieval times, but certainly through the period of the Ptolemies, and probably much earlier. That they communicated with Ethiopia in early ages is not a matter of doubt.

Africa contributed largely in gold and probably also in frankincense—which was obtained in the regions now known as Somaliland—to the ancient commerce of the Indian Ocean. Considering the position occupied by Arabia in that commerce, it is not surprising to find that the ports through which the trade entered Ethiopia were Asab and Adule, both situated within the Straits of Bab-el-Mandeb on the western shore of the Red Sea. Roads from these two points led to Axum, in the interior, on the western side of the Abyssinian Mountains, a town of which the colossal remains still testify to its ancient greatness. From Axum, which had its temples and was itself a great centre of trade, the road led north-westward through the State of Meroë to the town of the same name. The town of Meroë was a great centre, whence roads spread in many directions. The principal trade route led from Meroë northwards, either along the Nile or across the Nubian desert to Thebes, thence to the oasis of Siwah in the western desert, thence to Augela, often mentioned as an Egyptian colony, and thence south-westward to the site of the modern Murzuk in the Fezzan, whence communication was direct to Carthage and the Mediterranean coast. These last stations were at the head of the Tripoli-Fezzan route into the southern desert, and marked the junction of that route with the Egyptian route. There was a road from Meroë across the desert which ran due westward into Kordofan. This road still exists, but Burckhardt, who visited Shendy in 1770, says that now, "as in ancient times," the commerce with the west is insignificant. It seems to result from the most careful investigation that the principal commerce of the interior of Africa has always been carried on in two directions: that which has been described from Ethiopia through the Valley of the Nile, and that of the Soudan from the Niger to the Mediterranean coast. The Empire of Bornu, or Kanem, including at one time the present kingdoms of Wadai and Darfour, formed a separation between these two streams which have always run in parallel channels from south to north. This, at least, is the general opinion of explorers and historians, who, it is to be remembered, have necessarily written from the external point of view. What may have been at any given period the lateral branching of local native trade, is difficult for the European writer to determine.

Heeren, in his researches into the trade of the Carthaginians and the Ethiopians, has been able to establish the existence of at least one important cross-road of communication, of which a portion has been already noted in tracing the direction of the main trade route, after it branched from Thebes westward to the oasis of Siwah and the Mediterranean coast. The western end of the road starting from Carthage ran in a south-easterly direction through the Fezzan to the site of the present Murzuk. After making the junction at that point with the Egyptian road, it turned southwards to the Niger, and was the road which has been so often mentioned as the Tripoli-Fezzan road of the present day. Along this road the Carthaginians traded with the Niger for carbuncles, skins, gold, ivory, and other goods.

Thus we get on unquestionable authority evidence of a well-established connection in very early times between Ethiopia and Egypt by the Valley of the Nile; between Egypt and Carthage by a road crossing the desert through Siwah and Augela, and between Carthage and the Niger by the present Tripoli-Fezzan route. If we take Murzuk and Thebes as lying almost on the same parallels of latitude outside the Tropic of Cancer, and Gao and Meroë as having also almost parallel positions on the edge of the summer rains, some eight degrees farther south, we get the four corners of an irregular parallelogram, of which three sides were in permanent communication with each other. The base of this parallelogram rests on the fertile belt, which crosses Africa between the parallels of 10° and 17°; and taking into consideration the fact that Mohammedan states now stretch continuously across it from Bornu to Fashoda, it seems in no way improbable that, at a period when the trade of Ethiopia was important enough to extend down the Valley of the Nile and across the difficult desert road from Thebes to Murzuk in the north, trade may also have found channels of extension along the fertile territories to the west.

In corroboration of the view that the trade and influence of Meroë may have extended farther west than has as yet been ascertained by modern exploration, I may mention a fact told me by Zebehr Pasha, when, during his confinement at Gibraltar in 1886, he related to me the history of the foundation of his ephemeral empire in the Bahr-el-Ghazal. It was that, having occasion to act as the military ally of a certain native king Tekkima, whose territory lay somewhere south and west of the spot marked upon modern maps as Dem Suleiman or Dem Zebehr—that is, presumably about 8° N. and 25° E., he was informed that he had to fight against magicians, who habitually came out of the earth, fought, and then disappeared. A careful system of scouting disclosed to him the fact that they came from under ground, and when, after cutting off their retreat and conquering them, he insisted upon being shown their place of habitation, he found it to be deeply buried in the sand, a wonderful system of temples "far finer," to use the words in which he described it, "than modern eyes have seen in the mosques of Cairo and Constantinople." It was, he said, such work of massive stone as was done only by the great races of old. Through this underground city of stone there ran a stream, and by the stream his native antagonists lived in common straw native huts. "Were your people, then," he asked them, "a nation of stone-cutters?" And they said, "Oh, no! This is not the work of our forefathers, but our forefathers found it here, and we have lived for many generations in these huts."

Whether this accidental discovery of unknown monuments may yet be repeated farther west, and links be established in a continuous chain of ancient civilisation reaching from the Red Sea to the country west of Chad, or whether the civilisations of the western and the eastern ends of the fertile belt of the Soudan were in fact separated from one another by a sea of which the waters of Chad are but the disappearing trace, is, however, a question which, interesting as it is, becomes, in the light of the proved connection by the northern road, a question rather of detail than of principle.

If there was no connection by the south, there certainly was connection by the north, by means of which the early inhabitants of the Haussa States may have been brought under the same influences of civilisation which spread from Ethiopia to ancient Egypt and thence to Europe and Northern Africa.

CHAPTER XXVI

THE PHARAOHS IN HAUSSALAND

The annals of Egyptian history are not without some record of the very early connection which existed between the valleys of the Niger and the Nile. To enter into the spirit of them we must be content to lose ourselves in semi-mythical periods when, according to the records collected and preserved by historic writers, Housâl and his descendants reigned in Egypt. The name of Housâl meant, we are told, "Servant of Venus." We may perhaps, therefore, carry back the date to a period when the Phœnicians dominated Egyptian politics, and the worship of Astarte or Venus Erycina was common in the Valley of the Nile.

Already, before Housâl, Egyptian kings had marched through the west and into the country of the blacks in the south, where they had seen "wonderful things." But it is with his descendant, Nimrod the Powerful, who was also called Nimrod the son of Housâl, that we obtain a direct link with the southern states. Nimrod, we are told, was a king famous for his justice, under whom the people of Egypt lived happily. But his dead brother had been married to a magician from the south. This magician fled with her son, on the accession of Nimrod, towards the south. There, by her charms, she raised a power for her son to claim the throne. Nimrod marched against her and was overthrown, and her son reigned in his stead. This is the Egyptian account. But the people of Yoruba, which is not one of the true Haussa States, but which is a province included within the British Protectorate in the back country of Lagos, claim to descend from Canaanites—that is, Phœnicians—of the tribe of Nimrod. They claim, further, that all the pagan tribes in the mountains of Haussaland descend from them, because in their southward journey they left, in every place they stopped at, a tribe of their own people in the mountains. Sultan Bello, who records this claim of the Yoruba people, was apparently unacquainted with the Egyptian story. But the coincidence between the two accounts is too striking to be ignored. The Nimrod the Powerful of Egyptian history, son of Housâl, who worshipped the Phœnician gods, and Nimrod the Mighty, the first son of Canaan (or Phœnicia) of the Mosaic record, may fairly be taken as identical, and it is easy to comprehend how the dispersion of a large army, of which the component parts would be driven to take refuge where they could, might lead to just such a tradition as that cherished by the Yoruba population of the present day.

It is interesting also to observe in Egyptian records the constant reference to "magicians of the south." The part which magic played in the chronicles of Egypt is of course a matter of common knowledge. The whole north coast of Africa was, we are told, protected by talismans, burning glasses, and other marvels raised on pedestals, which were placed at intervals along the shore. Alexandria could not be built till talismans had been erected which had power to protect it from the monsters of the deep. Macrizi, in his "Historical Description of Egypt," written in the fifteenth century, has preserved for us accounts of some of the most famous talismans constructed by the kings, and quite as often by the queens, who reigned in the Valley of the Nile. We find there the magical bird with outspread wings, raised on a pedestal for protective purposes above towns or graves, which in the seventeenth century had still its prototype in the copper birds, described by Barbot as spreading their wings above all the best houses of Benin. The same idea perhaps inspired the golden bird perched on the cupola of the king's umbrella which Ibn Batuta mentioned in describing the court ceremonies of the court of Melle in the fourteenth century. Marvels of every kind are catalogued among the creations of the wisest of Egyptian sovereigns. Nor need we confine ourselves to the Soudan to find in later times the prototypes of statues which healed, relics which could detect injustice, dirty water which, being washed over sacred stones, had power to impart saving grace. The ideas which underlay the magic of Egypt have been common to all time. They took sometimes, in Egypt as elsewhere, very charming shape. We hear of one benevolent king who constructed a temple in which he placed statues to heal every human infirmity. On the head of each statue was written the name of the evil which it could cure. When he had cured all recognised evils, he made last of all the statue of a smiling woman, "and whoever looked on her, lost his secret sorrow."

In the construction of these talismans the "magicians of the south" played their part. We have seen in the *Tarikh-es-Soudan* that Gao was celebrated in ancient times as a town of magicians, whence the Pharaohs on occasion summoned help. Borgu and its neighbourhood to the south of Gao is to this day celebrated for the pursuit of magic, and the whole coast of West Africa is permeated with a belief in witchcraft and charms. Doubtless when Egyptian records speak of the south, they frequently mean Ethiopia and Meroë. But that the name of Ethiopia was extended in some instances to cover the country as far west as the Atlantic is made quite clear by ancient writers. Strabo expressly says so.

If in the magic practised by the inhabitants of the territories lying between the Niger and Lake Chad, we find one indication of the very early connection of these countries with Egypt, other indications present themselves, as we approach the period of the Pharaohs of the eighteenth and nineteenth dynasties, which appear by comparison to stand on historic ground. I abridge from Macrizi an account of an eleven years' expedition of one of the Pharaohs into the west and south, which seems definitely to confer upon Borgu the honour of connecting the existing territory of British Northern Nigeria with the Egypt known to us in the Old Testament. The expedition took place some 1700 years before Christ. The Pharaoh was king of Egypt when "a young Syrian, of the name of 'Joseph the Truthful,' was sold by his brothers into Egypt." The Pharaoh of Joseph was known by many names. Amongst them the Copts gave him the name of "Barkhou."

After a long struggle with Phœnician forces in the north, this Pharaoh subdued Syria, and then resolved to conquer the world to the south and west. He set out with an army of 700,000 men, marched westward to that point of Africa where the Atlantic meets the Mediterranean, crossed over to Spain, and, having conquered and imposed tribute as he went, he returned and marched eastward through the country of the Berbers. Thence he turned south, fought with various peoples, and sent a general before him to a town situated upon the "black water." The king of this town had never heard of Pharaoh, and being questioned about the water to the south, said that no one had ever navigated it, because of the mists which made it dangerous. When Pharaoh arrived, the native king offered presents, amongst them a mystic black stone, and fruits, chiefly bananas. Pharaoh then "marched into the countries of the Soudan, and came to the country of the Dem-Dem cannibals, who marched against him entirely naked." He conquered them, and took the road to the "dark sea," but as mists arose, he returned northwards as far as a colossal statue of red stone, which bore the inscription, "Beyond me there is nothing." He appears then to have turned eastward. In his march he encountered various marvels which I will not relate, amongst other things a town of hermits or magicians living in the mountains, from whom he received good advice, and by whom he was shown immense stores, worthless to them, of gold and emeralds and sapphires. Finally, after an absence of eleven years, he reached Nubia—showing that, in his day at least, communication was supposed to be possible between the Niger and the Nile along the parallels of the fertile belt—and he re-entered Egypt, having built monuments or otherwise "left traces of himself" in every country through which he passed.

The account, of which I have given the essential geographical points, seems clearly to indicate that this Pharaoh on his return from the west followed the Tripoli-Fezzan route into the desert. The town upon which he marched may have been the town of Kaougha or Kau-Kau, which appears to have existed in ancient times somewhere near to the site of the present town of Kuka on Lake Chad; but remembering that the Arab name of the Niger is the "Huad el Nichar," or Black Water, and that the account of the expedition has been taken by Arab writers from the Coptic, it is equally probable that the town where he got the black stone and the bananas may have been that very town of Gao on the Niger, also called Kaougha, the antiquity of which has been so often alluded to. He marched "thence" into the Soudan and the country of the cannibal Dem-Dems. This at least identifies the locality of a portion of this expedition, for every early Arab writer has located the Dem-Dems in the country to the south and south-east of Gao, spreading down the western side of the river and across the river into the hills to the south of the Haussa States, known later as Bowshy, Bowsher, or Jacoba, and now included in British Northern Nigeria under the name of Bautchi. In these hills the cannibals have survived even to our own day, but on the western side of the river they have long since been driven out, and their place has been taken by the peoples of Gurma and Borgu, or, as this latter province was often called by early Arab writers, Barkou. Here again the coincidence of name is at least striking. A Pharaoh of the name of Barkhou, of whom it is said that he left a trace of himself in every country through which he passed, is stated to have marched victoriously with a large army over a country to the south of the Black Water, which is described as the country of the Dem-Dems. At a very much later period a country bearing his Coptic name, and claiming for its people Coptic descent, is found to be situated between the Black Water and the country of the Dem-Dems. I do not wish to push the argument of names too far, especially when the uncertain nature of the records of those "Traditionists" from whom Macrizi quotes is taken into consideration. Yet in conjunction with the popular belief in Egyptian extraction, this story which I find in the annals of Egypt, where there was no thought of shedding light on questions of the Soudan, seems to me interesting enough to plead its own excuse for insertion.

Whether the "Dark Sea"—rendered in the French translation which I am following by the words "*Mer obscure*"—really meant the sea on the south coast, or whether it was, as I think more probable, some other body of water such as Lake Chad, which must have been passed if the expedition re-entered Egypt by way of Nubia, I leave to the more learned to decide. The direction of his march after achieving the conquest of the Dem-Dems appears to me to have been round the north shores of Lake Chad, and so across the desert into Nubia. If it be true that he built monuments or left traces of himself in every country through which he passed, there is hope that his cartouche may yet be discovered upon some hitherto unexplored rock of Northern Nigeria. The persistent reference in early descriptions to a colossal statue in the neighbourhood of the Almena rocks may have a foundation in interesting fact.

Before and after this Pharaoh, other Pharaohs—including the intrepid Phœnician usurper who, according to Macrizi, was the Pharaoh of Moses—marched at the head of armies into the Soudan and fought and conquered among the blacks and Berbers, forcing the people of the

Soudan to pay tribute. The black nations of Ethiopia were sufficiently vigorous to have at times invaded the southern and western frontiers of Egypt, and to have necessitated the building of a great wall of defence against them. This wall, which extended from the frontiers of Abyssinia to Nubia, and through Nubia to the oases, was built by a queen called Dalouka. It was fortified at intervals throughout its length.

We know from other sources that, about the year 1400 B.C., Rameses the Great, who is usually assumed to have been the Pharaoh of Moses, made extensive conquests to the south. This was the Pharaoh whose conquest of Ethiopia is shown upon the monuments, and on those monuments is also indicated the conquest of tributary nations to the West. In connection with these conquests we must not forget the statement of the *Tarikh-es-Soudan* that it was the Pharaoh of Moses who drew his magicians from Gao. That the nations of the Niger and Lake Chad should have been tributary to Eastern Ethiopia is not surprising, and the inference to be drawn from the monuments and the statements of ancient writers is confirmed by the mere fact that the name of Ethiopia was extended to them. Libyan as well as Ethiopian dynasties are known to have reigned in Egypt after the Pharaohs of the nineetenth dynasty. When, therefore, we read of the re-conquest of Egypt, and a march of Ethiopian armies against the Kings of Israel about 1000 B.C., and of an Ethiopian dynasty established at Memphis under Sabako at a period contemporary with the prophet Isaiah, about 750 B.C., we may assume it to be probable that the peoples in the neighbourhood of Lake Chad contributed their share, if not actually to the armies, at least to the strength of the then conquering empire.

After the Ethiopian dynasty came the Persian conquests, during which, as we have seen, expeditions apparently took place which have left a tradition of ancestry among the black nations of the extreme west of the Soudan. After the Persians came Alexander and the

Ptolemies. The picture given by Egyptian historians of the last of the Ptolemies is very different from that usually received in the West. Cleopatra's vigilance, they tell us, watched over the extreme limits of the kingdom of Egypt, and some historians have attributed to Cleopatra the wall of Dalouka. There was, therefore, we may infer, the same need under the Ptolemies that there had been under earlier dynasties for defence against the peoples of the Soudan.

It is not surprising that Haussaland and Bornu, which lie between the Bend of the Niger and Lake Chad, and of which the territory occupied at the south-westerly end of the great trade routes of the ancient world a position corresponding to that occupied by Ethiopia proper at the south-eastern end, should have received the inspiration of their civilised development rather from Egypt, and at a later period from the Arabs of the Barbary coasts, than from those Arabs who established the civilisation of the Ommeyade dynasty in Spain. As, however, there is no clear distinction to be made between the Arabs of the west and east, so there will be found comparatively little difference between the medieval civilisation of the western and the eastern portions of the West African Soudan. The more remarkable differences were of earlier date, when the influence of ancient Egypt was stronger, and when the schismatic Christians of the Roman Empire found their way, under the pressure of persecution, along the same eastern desert road, to the oblivion and the freedom of the south.

During the second and third centuries of our era, when Christians were liable to spasmodic persecution under the pagan emperors of Rome, the African desert was a favourite refuge of the enthusiast, and the conception of winning heaven by preaching the gospel to the most remote nations of the earth was not daunted by the unknown dangers of the Soudan. In the sixth century, when the Emperor Justinian and the Empress Theodora took opposite sides in the great schism of the Incarnation, the Coptic Church, persecuted in Syria and Egypt, spread its monophysite emissaries far into the heart of Africa, leaving to its Nestorian rivals the open road of Persia, China, and the East. Distinct traces are to be found in the eastern part of the West African Soudan of this Coptic movement. Borgu, already famous for its connection with the Pharaohs, claims to have received in more modern times a form of Christianity from the East, and though the tradition is not general in the country, Borgu natives have recently asserted that their prophet is not Mohammed but Kisra, a Jew who died for the sins of men. In the second half of the fifteenth century the Portuguese had knowledge of a native state in the interior which professed Christianity "after the manner of Egypt." They took that state to be Mossi, but if reliance is to be placed on the very circumstantial account of the *Tarikh-es-Soudan*, they were mistaken in their assumption, and the honour must be attributed to some other people. It may have been Borgu, but it must be admitted that the Christianity of this province, if schismatic to begin with, has wandered now so far from the established path as to be scarcely recognisable.

CHAPTER XXVII

THE HAUSSA STATES

WITH this slight indication that the native traditions of the Soudan are not without some foundation in recorded history, we may return to what should be the surer if narrower ground of local chronicles. Unfortunately, in approaching the history of Haussaland and Bornu, we are met in both cases by the fact that their records were purposely destroyed at the beginning of the nineteenth century by Fulani conquerors in Haussaland, and by the new dynasty of the Kanemyin in Bornu. The new rulers had in both instances the same object, to obliterate as far as possible the trace of their predecessors, and they have been so far successful that the materials of local history which have survived are extremely scanty. A few manuscripts have, however, escaped the general destruction. Dr. Barth found one in Bornu which gives a brief and dry chronicle of the kings of Bornu from a very early, though undated period. There is one containing a chronicle of the history of Katsena. The Niger Company obtained in Kano a manuscript as yet only imperfectly translated, which gives in similar brief fashion a chronicle of the reigns of forty-two kings of Kano. Dr. Robinson found in Zaria another, though more modern manuscript, giving some account of a period of the history of Zaria. We have also, though from a tainted source, native notes on the history of the Haussa States. Sultan Bello, the commander of the victorious Fulani, while he permitted and presumably encouraged the destruction of the Haussa records, so far showed his appreciation of the importance of history as to compile from his own study of documents lost to us, an account of the Haussa States, in which some truth may be assumed to mingle with the presentment of facts coloured to suit the. Fulani point of view. From these and a few other records, combined with oral tradition and the slight notices of contemporary Arabs at different periods of the history of Haussa and Bornu, it is possible to frame a general outline of the history of the two countries. Little trustworthy detail as to the customs, laws, industry, literature, administration, or religion, which would have enabled us to construct a complete picture for ourselves of these long-existing civilisations, has been preserved. More material will, however, doubtless come to light from year to year as the country is opened up, and, in fact, from each province contributions to history are already beginning to be made. This is especially the case in regard to pagan history, which may prove to be scarcely less interesting, in some districts, than Mohammedan history.

Although lying in geographical juxtaposition between the parallels of 9° and 14° N. latitude, and now united within the limits of the British Protectorate, Bornu and Haussaland are two very distinct countries inhabited by people of wholly different race, having their own traditions and their distinct history. Except when, as a consequence of border wars, there has been a temporary overlapping of the frontier, they have always possessed their distinct territories. The Bornuese people are of Berber extraction, and though to European eyes actually black, count themselves among the white or red races of the Soudan. Compared with the history of Haussaland their history is modern. The Haussa is wholly black, but not negroid in type. He has not the smooth hair of the Songhay, but in other respects he has frequently a cast of countenance scarcely less Aryan in type, and in his peculiar and strongly marked characteristics he is universally recognised as ranking among the most interesting of the peoples of the Soudan. His known history, though never brilliant, has been persistent. Many times conquered, he has nevertheless continued to preserve a clearly defined political individuality. He has always been merchant, peasant, soldier, and artisan. Storms have swept over him, to which he has bowed a submissive head. According to circumstances his territory has contracted or expanded, but in the Haussa nation the life of the individual appears to have been so little dependent on the political development of the race, that it has lost no vigour in the incidents of history, and we find him to-day pursuing his avocations as his fathers before him pursued the same avocations when they first emerge to our sight from the dimness of antiquity.

The territory covered by Haussaland to-day stretches roughly from about 9° to 14° N. lat., and from 4° to 11° E. long., and it contains a population estimated at perhaps ten millions of people. No accurate census has as yet been made, and this estimate, lower than that usually given, is only approximate. The Haussa language, which is classed with Coptic amongst the Hamitic languages, is said to be more widely spoken than any other single native language in West Africa. The Haussas have themselves, like most other West African races, a tradition of having come once from the east beyond Mecca, but their presence in the Soudan, somewhat to the north of the territory which they now occupy, is, like that of the Berbers in the Western African desert, of immemorial antiquity. Dr. Barth connects them with the Aterantes of Herodotus. They have also been connected with the Habeches, Habaïs, or Habes, of Strabo. Within historic times they have been known as divided into seven independent Haussa States, upon which certain other states, also largely peopled by Haussas, have been dependent. The seven original states were Biram, Gober, Kano, Rano, Zaria, Katsena, and Daura. Some of these have now sunk into insignificance. Some form still the most important provinces of Northern Nigeria. Though within any period of which we have record—dating for about a thousand years — these states have been independent of and generally hostile to each other, their own traditions point to a more ancient period when they were united in some form of federal bond.

Their mythical history, which presumably reflects some political reality, is that Biram, the father of the states, wedding Diggera—which is the name of a Berber settlement in the desert to the north of Haussaland—had six children, of whom Zaria and Katsena were first born as twins, then Kano and Rano, another pair of twins, and after them Gober and Daura. To each of his children the progenitor of the Haussa States is said to have assigned certain duties. Gober, the most northerly of the states, which in historic times has served as a military rampart between peaceful Haussaland and the warlike tribes of the desert, was appointed war chief, with the special duty of defending his brethren. Kano and Rano, safe behind this rampart, were appointed ministers of industry—dyeing, weaving, &c. Katsena and Daura were ministers of intercourse and trade, and Zaria, which is a province of great extent lying south of the others, and dividing their fruitful plains from the hilly country of Bautchi, was appointed chief of the slaves, with the special duty of providing a supply of labour for the industry of his brothers. Bautchi, the hilly country in question, was for many centuries the home of the cannibal and the hunting-ground for slaves, its name, which is a corruption of Boushy, meaning the country of the Bauwa, or the slaves.

In this myth we get a fairly clear picture of a union of states, of which the northern and southern frontiers were actively defended, and where the Soudanese practice of raiding to the south for a labour supply, by means of which the industry of the Central States was maintained, was in full force. But this condition of things received a still further development before any period of which we have contemporary historic observation, for according to the myth the legitimate children of Biram were presently increased by seven illegitimate children. These are the

States of Zanfara, Kebbi, Nupe, Gwari, Yauri, Yoruba, and Kororofa. In these states the Haussa language, though spoken, is not original, and we have already seen that Yoruba claims for itself a separate descent of more than respectable antiquity. Yoruba, if included, would carry Haussaland practically to the sea at Lagos. Nupe, as we have seen, was considered in the fourteenth century to be one of the most important of the purely native states of the Soudan. In Ibn Batuta's day it still maintained its reputation of being wholly impenetrable to the white man. The period at which these "illegitimate" states became infused with Haussa blood, or were made dependent upon Haussaland, is left, so far as the myth is concerned, indefinite. No part of the account deserves more than such credit as a myth may receive.

When we come to examine the few historical documents which are available, we find no trace of political union between the Haussa States, except when, for certain periods in their history, one among them assumed or acquired a temporary dominance over the others. On the contrary, their history, as embodied in the chronicles to which allusion has been made, and which date back to the eighth or ninth centuries of our era, show them as independent kingdoms in a state of more or less chronic internecine war. Any union which may have given rise to the myth must therefore have existed before the year 800 of our era.

In considering the civil and political conditions of the Haussa States we are necessarily reminded of the organisation of the early states of antiquity. The peoples of Asia Minor, of Arabia, and of Egypt itself, in days before the rise of the Persian, Macedonian, and Roman Empires, were commonly organised in a number of allied but separate cities. Heeren tells us that, amongst the Syrian populations, as far as the light of history carries us back, we find everywhere a number of single cities, with the territory around them, under a monarchical form of government, the sovereign power being placed in the hands of kings or princes. "Examples certainly are," he says, "to be met with where some of these cities and their monarchs obtained a decided preponderance, and assumed to themselves a degree of authority. This, however, was a kind of forced alliance which extended no further than the exaction of tribute and subsidies in times of war, without depriving the subjected cities of their government and rulers." Phœnicia, like Syria, was never one state, but from the earliest period down to the Persian monarchy, was always divided into a number of separate cities, each with its little territory around it. Allied cities in Phœnicia were very numerous, and it is thought probable that there may have been periods when all the cities of Phœnicia formed one confederation, at the head of which at one time stood Sidon, and at a later period Tyre. Necessities of defence led more or less naturally to this system. These confederations, we are told, prevailed in all countries colonised by Phœnicians. Throughout the colonies of Phœnicia, as well as in the mother-country, a common religion formed likewise a bond of union for the cities, and strengthened and preserved the connection between them.

Each city had its own proper government, and in this respect they were perfectly independent of each other. The chief authority was placed in the hands of kings, who in turn were to some extent controlled by high priests. The revenues of the cities depended in large measure on their trade, and the Phœnicians have lived in history as a commercial people.

The parallel between the political organisation of the Phœnician and the Haussa States seems to me to be worth indicating, if only as another trace of the inspiration which Haussaland has unquestionably drawn from the East. There is hardly anything which has been said of Phœnicia which would not be applicable in the present day to the cities of Haussaland. Their independence, their cohesion, their mutual jealousies, their occasional acceptance of a dominant leader, their commercial activity, their common religion, are features of a quite remarkable similarity.

There are, I think, especially interesting conclusions to be drawn from a consideration of the early religion of the Haussa States.

As regards the genealogy of the Haussa people, their Fulani historian, Sultan Bello, not anxious to glorify the race whom he desired his own people to supplant, ascribes their origin to a slave, excepting, however, the people of Gober, whom he admits to have been free-born, and to have descended from the Copts of Egypt. Curiously, the manuscript obtained by the Niger Company in Kano, which professes to carry the history of that town from mythical times to the period of the Fulani conquest in the beginning of the nineteenth century, gives a certain corroboration to this view. "The chief of the people of Kano," it says, "was named Berbushay. He was a black, strong man, and a lover of hunting." Bushay, as has been already said, means the land of slaves. "Ber" is frequently used to signify man. Therefore the name of this first chief of Kano may well be taken to signify "a man from the land of slaves." A man from the land of slaves is far from being necessarily a slave, but the coincidence may be taken to justify, in part at least, the statement of Bello. The story of the founding of Kano town by this hero has a Herculean flavour. He achieved, it is said, many labours, and, having one day killed an elephant with his spear, he carried the animal for a long distance on his head. Where he put it down was the site of Kano town. He himself lived on the Hill Dalla, which is now within the walls of Kano, and he had a family of seven children. He was of course a pagan. It is said of him that "he inherited the customs of Dalla, which were handed down through the pagan families," and this mystic inheritance of Dalla appears to have made of him the high priest, as well as chief, of the pagan tribes who owned his sway. These spread far on all sides of Kano, and they gathered to him for religious festivals. There was a pagan goddess who had many names, amongst them Gonkie and Shemsusu. This goddess lived upon a walled hill which was guarded day and night, and none were allowed to approach her except Berbushay himself. Her religious festivals took place twice a year, and on these occasions the people from north and south and east and west brought black animals for sacrifice. It may be mentioned in connection with this custom that, according to the account given by Captain Clapperton, the pagan natives of Yoruba and Nupe still assemble once a year round a high hill, and sacrifice a black bull and a black sheep and a black dog. The custom was that, when the sacrifices were made, Berbushay went in alone to the enclosure of the goddess, and apparently his intercourse with her conferred some special sanctity upon him, for when he came out, he cried to the people: "I am the heir of Dalla, and whether you will or not you must serve me." And the people replied: "We serve you without fear." There were also in connection with this ceremony mystic rites, during which the people divested themselves of their clothing, but the description given in this very imperfect translation is too vague to be comprehensible. A learned investigator will perhaps some day ascertain whether these primitive customs, dedicated to the worship of a female deity in the Soudan, have any connection with the sanctity of the black stone of the Caaba, and the pagan rites of naked worship with which Astarte, or the Venus Erycina of the Phœnicians, was once honoured within the walls of Mecca. If the paganism of the Soudan were shown to be identical with that superseded by Islam on the shores of the Red Sea during the lifetime of the prophet, it would be a curious and instructive example of the continuity of history that it should be tracked to its last stronghold in equatorial Africa, and abolished to-day, after an interval of more than a thousand years, by a far-off pulsation of the same moral and intellectual forces.

This Berbushay was also a prophet. He foretold the

coming of kings and the building of mosques. "There is one," he said, "coming to this town with his people. He will be our head, and we shall be his servants." And the people cried: "This is a bad saying. Why do you prophesy evil things?" And they wished him to be silent. But he said: "You shall see it by the power of the goddess. If it do not come in your time it will come in the time of your children. He will be lord over all that you possess, and he will forget you, and dwell long with his own people." The people were grieved in their hearts at his saying. But they knew him for a true prophet, and they believed his word. They asked him: "What shall we do to hinder this mighty thing?" And he said, "There is no help but in patience." Therefore they waited in patience till afterwards, in the time of their children, there came Bagoda, also called Daud (or David), who with all his people marched upon the place. Then it was said: "This is the man whose coming Berbushay foretold." And he was the first of the kings of Kano.

I have quoted this narrative at length, partly for the picture that it gives of pagan customs, which vaguely recall those noted by El Bekri as existing in Ghana at the end of the eleventh century, and partly for the sake of the prophecy, so typical of the fate of Haussaland that it can only have been produced by the national character which ensured its fulfilment. "You shall be conquered, and there will be no remedy but in patience." This prophecy alone, accomplished as it has been by history, would seem to confirm the authenticity of that descent from the ever-conquered peoples of Egypt which has been attributed to the Haussa race.

CHAPTER XXVIII

THE DOMINATION OF KANO

I DO not propose, with the very limited material which is available, to attempt to reconstruct any detailed history of the fortunes of the Haussa States. Nor is it likely that such a narrative would be very interesting, even did the material exist for its relation. The daily life of primitive states, and the petty incidents of their public fortune, are no more interesting than the daily life of private individuals. It is with the general movement of civilisation, as it rises or falls in the flood and ebb of national life, that history is concerned; and, in the records of relatively undeveloped peoples, it is only in that portion of their existence which contributes to, or is associated with, the general movement that we are interested.

The scraps of history and legend which have been preserved, and of which some specimens have been offered to the reader, would seem to establish the broad fact that in some period of, to us, remote antiquity, the Haussa people were brought into existence by a union between earlier races inhabiting the Valley of the Nile or the shores of the Red Sea, and the aboriginal pagans whose descendants are now to be found in the hills of Bautchi and Adamawa. At a very early period the simpler arts of domestic and civil life were developed among them, for in the legend of Kano it is related that even before the coming of the founder of that town there were eleven great pagans who were respectively the ancestors and patrons of Love, of War, of Water, of Strong Drink, of Hunting, of Medicine, of Iron-smelting, of Salt-working, and of Blacksmiths, &c. The generally accepted religion was a form of paganism in which a goddess was supreme, and in which the manner of worship would seem to have had something in common with the worship of Venus or Astarte, from which Housâl, one of the earliest recorded kings of Egypt, took his name. It is on the authority of Macrizi that I give this meaning of the name of Housâl, and I am not so rash as to assume from the mere similarity of sound that the same meaning attaches to the name of Haussa, or, as it is sometimes written, Houssaland. I only note the fact that the origin of the name of Haussa is unknown, and that the great common bond of the people who bear it would seem to have been their religion and their language. If this name had its origin in their religion, it would have been the same name wherever their language was spoken. The form of their religion differed from that of the Ju-Ju worship of the coasts, and at the present day the pagans of Yoruba express themselves in terms of horror when speaking of the fetish worship and human sacrifices of Benin.

This universal worship of a supreme goddess appears to have given rise to the tradition that the Haussa States were at one time under the domination of a woman, whose seat of government was said to have been at Zaria. Early tradition attributes to her the founding of the town, and associates a colossal statue of her with some remarkable rocks which bore the name of Almena, to the south-east of the present position of Zaria. But Sultan Bello, who repeats the tradition that the seven provinces of Haussa were at one time under the domination of one queen, says that the name of the queen was Amina, that she was a daughter of the Prince of Zaria, and that she subdued the seven provinces of Haussa by force of arms, making them all tributary to her, and conquering also other native states as far as the navigable reaches of the Lower Niger.

Legend and history seem in this instance to have allied themselves, for, while the worship of the goddess was long anterior to the existence of any lady bearing the suspiciously orthodox name of the Mother of the Prophet, and allusions to the statue are to be found in the very earliest writers, the Kano chronicle places an excellent queen, Amina of Zaria, who reigned for thirty-four years, in just the place in which we might expect to find her—that is, towards the end of the fourteenth century, about a hundred years after Mohammedanism was introduced into the Haussa States. The theory of the domination of Amina over the Haussa States is still further disposed of by the statement that in this reign the long struggle between Kano and Zaria was brought to an end by the final subjugation of Zaria. Queen Amina seems, however, to have been a person whose importance was fully recognised, and after the conquest the King of Kano assigned to her use the whole of the land tax from the southern provinces of Nupe to Kororofa—that is, the country lying on the right bank of the Benué—and also laid on Nupe a special tax of eunuchs and kola nuts to be paid to the queen.

"The country of Haussa," says Sultan Bello, who wrote in the nineteenth century, "consists of seven provinces, to each of which a prince is appointed to superintend its affairs, and the inhabitants of the whole speak one language. The central province of this kingdom is Katsena, the most extensive is Zaria, the most warlike is Gober, and the most fertile is Kano." Sultan Bello thus places Katsena in the centre of the Haussa States, and references to Katsena in the writings of the Arabs imply that it was a place of importance in the later development of Haussaland, famous alike for the industry and the learning of its inhabitants. The myth, to which reference has been made in an earlier chapter, also speaks of it as being, with Zaria, the oldest of the states. But history places its development at a later date than that of Kano. As will be seen, it did not rise to its full power till after the Moorish conquest, when, by the destruction of the eastern capital of the Songhay Empire, a stream of commerce was directed to its gates. The most brilliant period of the history of Kano was already closed before the end of the sixteenth century.

Gober, by its geographical position on the edge of the northern desert, and the necessity which was entailed upon it of constant conflict with the desert tribes, early acquired a more warlike reputation than its sister states; but, perhaps because of the peril to which it was perpetually exposed upon the north, it seems never to have attempted in its earlier period to achieve by force of arms any general conquest in the Haussa States, and its importance in Haussaland, like that of Katsena, is subsequent to the greatest epoch of Kano. At one time it stretched far northward into the desert, and its people inhabited the territories of Ahir or Asben upon the Tripoli-Fezzan route, but it was driven from this position towards the end of the eleventh century by Berber, perhaps Morabite, invaders.

Daura would seem to have been one of the most ancient of the Haussa States, and references to it are frequent in the Kano chronicle; but, like its sister Rano, it does not appear to have played a very important public part in the history that is known to us of Haussaland.

Zaria, the most southerly of the original seven states, distinguished itself from a very early date by the conquest of the southern non-Haussa provinces. It extended its power over the whole of the hilly country to the confluence of the Niger and the Benué, and even beyond it towards the sea.

It will be seen, on glancing at a map of West Africa, that the Niger and the Benué, flowing towards each other from north-west and north-east, and meeting at Lokoja, a little south of the eighth parallel of latitude —whence their combined flood flows under the one name of the Niger very nearly due south for upwards of 250 miles to the Gulf of Guinea—form within the boundary of the British Protectorate of this part of Africa the figure of a large and loosely outlined Y. The connection of the Benué with Lake Chad is a matter of controversy; but the southern portion of this great inland sea, lying north of the sources of the Benué, completes the easterly development of the Y-shaped water-system of the country. It is within the branches of this Y that Bornu and Haussaland proper are contained. One state—Borgu—included now within the limits of Haussaland, though not a Haussa State, lies altogether outside this figure on the west bank of the Niger; but the most southerly extension of Borgu carries it only to the ninth degree. We may say that all the countries with which we are now about to be concerned lie between 8° and 14° north latitude. And the original seven states of Haussa have an even more northerly extension, being all situated to the north of 10°. The southward course of the united rivers runs through pagan countries to the sea.

We are necessarily obliged, in making use of the Kano chronicle, to view the life of the Haussa States through Kano eyes; but for that very reason it is perhaps the more to be trusted when it presents to us a picture of constant strife, with varying fortune, between itself and the other states, leaving us to learn from foreign sources that from time to time a submerging tide of external conquest swept over the country, and reduced all alike to the equality of submission. There can be no doubt that Kano occupied from early times a leading position in Haussaland, but so evenly do the strokes of fate appear to have been distributed, that, notwithstanding the predominant rank of Kano, it is probable that the history of that province offers a fair type of the history of any one of its legitimate or illegitimate sister states. We take it up at a point in the general history of Haussaland, when Daura and Zaria were already fully developed, and the southern country to the confluence of the rivers acknowledged the greatness, if it did not absolutely accept the sway, of Zaria. The non-Haussa States of Borgu, Nupe, Bautchi, and Kororofa, stretched in a belt of formidable pagan strength along the course of the two rivers, and we have already made ourselves acquainted with an outline of the contemporary history of the great non-Haussa nations lying to the west. The pagan belt, stretching from 8° north latitude to the coast, was practically unknown to the early Haussa races.

The first king of Kano, whose second name of Daud, or David, would appear to indicate an Eastern origin, reigned, so far as our uncertain dates may be trusted, towards the end of the tenth century, or about a hundred years before the Morabite invasion from the west, which carried Mohammedanism through the Western Soudan. Opinions differ as to whether the invasion reached as far as the countries lying to the south of the Tripoli-Fezzan route; but if it did, the Mohammedanism of the five tribes was not carried so far south as to enter the Haussa States. The establishment of Islam in Ahir in the desert, is attributed to the eleventh century; but the State of Gober offered an impassable barrier to any more southerly extension of the doctrine of Mohammed by the sword. The Haussa States remained pagan until the emigration of Wankoré or Wangara Mohammedanism from Melle, in the rising epoch of that empire, about the middle of the thirteenth century, brought the new religion peacefully to Kano. It was accepted by a certain King Yahya, who was then reigning, and the story of his conversion is embellished by a graphic account of a miracle worked upon the pagan chief and people of Gazawa, who not only refused to be converted, but purposely defiled the mosque erected by King Yahya. The chief and his people were summoned on a given day, and when they were assembled, "the Mussulmans prayed against the pagans." God answered the Mussulman prayer, and the pagans were all stricken with blindness, "not only the chief and his people who were assembled, but the women in their homes." After this, the chronicle says that the religion of Mohammed was accepted, and that, by the force of the true God, King Yahya conquered his enemies as far as Kororofa and Atagher—that is, practically as far as Lagos. He reigned for thirty-seven years, and was widely feared and respected.

The next reign was a reign of peace, and when the king died he was buried by the imaum. It is recorded of him that he was the first who, when he died, was wrapped in a white cloth and had prayers read over him. But when, in the succeeding reign, the southern provinces refused to pay tribute, and the great war with Zaria began, the king consulted the old pagan priests, and they told him that if he wished to be victorious he must return to the religion of his ancestors. He attended the pagan ceremonies, where the priest "sang the song of Berbushay." After that, when he went against Zaria he was successful. The King of Zaria was killed, and the people were scattered abroad. This king is reported to have introduced the use of iron caps among his soldiers. The shirts of mail in which the warriors of the Haussa States still come out to battle are said to have come to them originally as spoils of the Crusaders, brought down by Arab merchants from Palestine. They may have been in use at an earlier period, but I find no note of any armour until this reign of the early part of the eleventh century.

All the early reigns are filled with the struggle between paganism and Mohammedanism, with miracles duly recorded on either side, and lapses in times of crisis on the part of the kings. Gradually the pagan element drops out, and it becomes evident that all the intelligence and cultivation of the country has become Mohammedan. In the reign of the fifteenth king, another David, Kano enters into closer relations with Bornu, and a king of Bornu, attended by many Mohammedan priests and teachers, spent a period of several months in Kano. The Bornu chronicle quoted by Dr. Barth, says that Kalnama, King of Bornu, took refuge in Kano from his rebellious subjects about the year 1430. The Kano chronicle would seem to date the visit nearly a hundred years earlier, but the agreement between the two chronicles is sufficient to show that, at the end of the fourteenth century, Mohammedanism was generally accepted in the high places of Haussaland. It was in the reign of this David that the conquest of Zaria was completed under orthodox conditions, and Queen Amina ranked among the subject sovereigns of Kano. At this time, according to Kano authority, the whole of the south of what is now Northern Nigeria was subject to Kano. A more malicious interpretation of the facts of the treaty with Zaria would suggest that the generosity of King David in allotting the land tax of the southern provinces, as well as the special taxes of Nupe, to the service of Queen Amina, was not wholly voluntary.

During the next reign a general of the Kano forces remained in the southern provinces for seven years, conquering the pagans, taking many prisoners, and sending every month a thousand slaves from the seat of war to Kano. The King kept the armies well supplied, and after this experience the affairs of the southern portion of Haussaland seem for a time to have given no more cause for preoccupation. Relations with Bornu in the east had in the meantime become pressing. Embassies and the opening of the roads led finally to war, of which the result, towards the beginning of the fifteenth century, is glosed in the single sentence that "many towns were given to Bornu." This king was the first to have camels and to drink wine in Haussaland.

In the reign of the following king, Yakoub, or Jacob —that is, about the year 1402 to 1422—we first hear of the immigration of Fulani, who came from Melle and Masina, to Haussaland, and were given land in Kano,

Zaria, and Gazawa. This was the declining period of the history of Melle, and the emigration seems to have been a movement of considerable magnitude. Some of the Fulani, we are told, passed on eastward to Bornu, some were left on the way with their slaves, and all who were too weak to proceed on their journey remained in Haussaland. At this period, trade seems to have received an active stimulus, and foreign caravans are noticed as coming from various places. Berbers and Arabs came into the country, some of whom settled in Kano and some in Katsena. There was also local trade between Kano and Nupe.

This peaceful reign brings us, in the first half of the fifteenth century (probably 1422–1459), to the reign of a king of Kano, whose name of Mohammed Rimpa has survived in all the chronicles. Under him Mohammedan civilisation spread through the country. Sherifs came to Kano from the East, bringing with them books and learning. Mosques were built, and "religion became strong in Kano." Mohammed Rimpa was the first to observe the fast of Ramadan. He gave titles to his eunuchs, and shut his women up after the fashion of the East. Mohammed Rimpa built the walls of the town of Kano with seven gates. He also built a palace for himself, as did some of his principal officers. He divided the territory of Kano into nine provinces, and appointed to rule over them nine subject kings. "There was no king," says the chronicle, "so great as Rimpa." Of contemporary history during his reign, we are told only that for eleven years Katsena was at war with her neighbour Mastur.

Mohammed Rimpa seems, indeed, to have possessed one of those commanding individualities which, when fortune places it upon a throne, marks an epoch in the country over which it rules. From the reign of Mohammed Rimpa, Kano may be reckoned with the civilised native powers of the Soudan. Yet, as so often happens when the influence of one man has achieved a strong forward movement, the brilliant period of the prosperity of Kano under Rimpa was destined to undergo a speedy reactionary eclipse under weaker successors.

The ten years' reign of the next king was a long series of wars with Katsena in the north-west, with Zaria in the south, finally and disastrously with Bornu in the east. The result of the Bornu campaign is again tersely related in a sentence: "The King of Bornu dethroned the King of Kano, and put his own slave on the throne of Kano."

History does not condescend to record the fate or the doings of the Bornu slave, but after the persistent fashion of Haussaland, we shortly find the son of the defeated king of Kano reigning in his father's stead. This king, Ahmadu Kesoke, had the strong blood of his grandfather Rimpa in his veins. He "conquered the four corners of Haussa, east and west and north and south." Bornu marched against him, but was defeated and driven back with considerable loss. In this reign learning prospered, and various Sheiks and Mallams are mentioned as coming to Kano from other towns.

The reign of Ahmadu Kesoke must have represented the summit of the greatness of Kano, for we know that, in the early years of the sixteenth century, Haussaland was overrun by the armies of Songhay. The dates and account of the campaign given in the *Tarikh-es-Soudan* are too circumstantial to admit of doubt, and Leo Africanus, writing in 1526, speaks of the greatness of Kano as being already in decline. After a description of the state and of its capital, he says: "The inhabitants are rich merchants and most civil people. Their king was in times past of great puissance, and had mighty troops of horsemen at his command, but he hath since been constrained to pay tribute to the Kings of Zaria and Katsena. Afterwards Askia, the King of Timbuctoo, feigning friendship unto the two foresaid kings, treacherously slew them both, and then he waged war against the King of Kano, whom after a long siege he took, and compelled him to marry one of his daughters, restoring him again to his kingdom, conditionally that he should pay to him the third part of all his tribute."

In the storm thus curtly described we may discern the ever recurring conditions of Haussa convulsions. The king, though conquered, was "restored again." The detail of having to add a daughter of the Askia to his harem was not onerous. From the Haussa point of view it would, not unnaturally, be accounted among the customary compliments of an honourable peace. To surrender a third of his tribute was more serious, but to the philosophic Haussa this was but the fortune of war, and the resident officials whom Askia placed at the court of Kano would seem to have incommoded no one.

It is characteristic of the life of Haussaland that the whole of this important and well-attested episode is ignored in a chronicle which professes to give a minute and continuous record of the reigns of the kings. The name of Songhay is never mentioned. Nor can this omission be attributed wholly, as might at first be imagined, to a patriotic desire to ignore an inglorious chapter of local history. In the accounts which are given of contemporary local wars we are told frankly enough when Kano is beaten, and we are allowed to see the disastrous results of the fighting with Zaria and Katsena. I incline to believe, and that is why it may, I think, be properly qualified as characteristic, that the omission of this chapter of foreign conquest from the local annals is based on a real indifference to the event. The net result of the operation was that the King of Kano was restored to his kingdom. The conditions which attached to his restoration were not important in the eyes of a historian who was acquainted with Zaria and Katsena, Gober and Bornu, but who knew practically nothing of the foreign king who reigned at Timbuctoo. Local affairs would seem to have been little affected by the inroad of the Songhay, whose administration of these distinct provinces was never much more than nominal. Therefore, though we know from outside information the epoch at which the Songhay conquest must have taken place, the chronicle pursues its narrative as though Songhay had not existed.

In addition to the disputes with Katsena and Zaria, which, as we know, occasioned the intervention of Askia the Great, we hear from it of civil war in Kano itself. A King Jacob, who was taken off the throne by a local revolution, refused to be reinstated when his generals had subdued the opposing faction, because he preferred to devote his life to study. The fortunes of Kano are very evidently in eclipse. Yet, through several reigns, we are given no hint of what must have been the predominating cause. The conquest by Songhay must apparently have taken place during the last years of the reign of Ahmadu Kesoke, then a very old man. After Kesoke came Jacob, and then others of no importance. During the war with Katsena the condition of the province became so bad that people could no longer farm in the open country. They were obliged to take refuge in the walled towns. The villages were broken up, and the land was left untilled. The King Abu Bekr, who had succeeded to Jacob and another dethroned king, gave himself up to religion. "His throne was uncared for, and so were his people. But the town was crowded with priests and learned men, many of whom came, it is said, from Baghirmi." The next king was more active, but not more fortunate. In his war with Katsena there were two great battles, and being outnumbered, "Kano had to run away, willing or unwilling." The weakness of Kano provoked a revolution of the southern provinces, and in the succeeding reign Kororofa, one of the southern pagan provinces on the right bank of the Benué, invaded the province of Kano, ravaging all the lesser towns and getting actually within the walls of Kano. The Katsena war proceeded at the same time, and the chronicler sorrowfully narrates that the Katsena and Kororofa wars "broke the spirit of Kano." "The people had to sit still and be afraid, and for twenty years they were not able to go to war."

After this, famine, the not unnatural result of a long period of war, during which the agricultural population had been driven from the land, added its desolation to the miseries of the country. It lasted for eleven years, and brought the fortunes of Kano to their lowest ebb, at a moment which must have coincided with the date of the Moorish conquest in the last decade of the sixteenth century.

CHAPTER XXIX

HAUSSALAND TO THE END OF THE EIGHTEENTH CENTURY

THE Moorish conquest, for reasons which will presently be told, affected the Haussa States so much less than it affected the more westerly portions of the Soudan that it will, I think, be excusable to abandon the strictly chronological order of narration, and to say here what remains to be said of the history of Haussaland, even though it carries us somewhat beyond the era of the great convulsion which severed the connection of the Soudan with the civilised world.

I wish that I had the material which will perhaps some day be discovered for a history of the interesting pagan states, especially Nupe and Kororofa, which lay on or to the south of the tenth parallel of latitude, peopling both banks of the Benué, and clustering about the confluence of the Niger with that river. We know of the inhabitants of Kororofa who occupied the eastern end of this belt, that they were long-haired, and apparently of the higher physical type which was brought to perfection in the Songhays. At a very early period we hear of them and of the people of Nupe as practising the arts of smelting, of smith's work, of weaving, dyeing, &c., and as being well clothed in neat cotton robes. Their local civilisation would appear to have preceded the more northern civilisation of the Haussa States proper. Though they were pagan, their paganism was of the order of the goddess-worship of the Haussas, and as far removed from the fetish worship of the coast as their industrial and social habits were removed from those of the Dem-Dem cannibals, whom they partly drove southwards across the river and partly hunted into the mountains which on the north made a defensible barrier between their own and subsequent Haussa settlements. The river, no doubt, at first formed the southern boundary of their territory, and was afterwards peopled by them on both sides.

The northern mountains, constantly visited by all the peoples of Haussaland for the sake of the gold, silver, tin, lead, iron, and antimony, which from the earliest times they were reported to contain, were rendered dangerous by the nature of the rude tribes who inhabited them, and they are to this day the home of lingering tribes of naked cannibals. They were from the earliest period a favourite hunting-ground for slaves, more valuable because more easily obtained than the minerals with which the sometimes inaccessible rocks were reputed to be so richly stored. Landor observed, in travelling south from Zaria to the Benué through this country in 1827, that the people on his route were ready to sell their children for a chicken, and at the moment of the British occupation these districts still formed a slave reserve for the more northern states. Last year, 1904, when the High Commissioner made a tour through these provinces, he found that, notwithstanding the suppression of slave-raiding which has taken place under the British flag, parents were privately selling their children at a price varying from 1s. 6d. to 2s. apiece.

Between these people and the higher-class pagans of Borgu, Nupe, and Kororofa, there has been, for all the time of which we have any record, a very wide gulf fixed. For the most part these lower-class pagans have been driven by the movements of local civilisation far southward towards the coast.

Assuming, as I think we may assume, that the belt of native civilisation which stretched from Borgu on the west bank of the Niger through Nupe to Kororofa, not far from the sources of the Benué on the east, represented the earliest wave and farthest extension of the great movement which at some very distant period pressed upon the Soudan from the north and east, we may observe that the chronological order of civilisation in the Haussa States was almost coincident with the ascending degrees of latitude.

Next after the civilisation of these southern states followed the rise and domination of Zaria, a province which, even in the nineteenth century, the Fulani historian describes as the most extensive of the Haussa States. It is probable that the early prosperity of Zaria may have been contemporary with that of Daura and Biram in the north, but I am obliged reluctantly to abandon the history of these Haussa States for lack of material. References to Daura as an old and still existing state are frequent in the Kano chronicle, and Dr. Barth specially commends Daura, of which the capital is at the present day a town of some importance, to the notice of the antiquarian for the interest of the legends which attach to it. The only legend with which I am acquainted is one resembling that already related in connection with the foundation of Kano, and attributes the foundation of the town to a strong man who killed there the "dodo" or fetish lion. "Dodo," I may say, is a native word signifying the King of Beasts, and may apply equally to rhinoceros, elephant, or any other great wild animal. The myth may, I think, be taken to indicate that, in the time of this hero, the worship of the goddess was substituted for the worship of the fetish, and it is interesting to observe that here, as in the early history of Songhay, the memory of the destruction of the fetish is preserved as an historic era in local tradition. The latitude of Daura is not far from the latitude of Gao, and such facts, collected from wholly different sources, tend to confirm the theory that there was a time when the fetish worship now confined to the belt of the southern coast extended far to the north.

The sign-posts in the almost forgotten ways of ancient local history are few, but they point to the conclusion that at some very early period a general and widespread religious movement, having points of resemblance to the Phœnician worship of Astarte, and assimilated with a superior order of native civilisation, superseded the fetishism which is now to be found among the tribes of the coast, driving it gradually towards the south, and that the difference between the peoples professing this form of paganism and the cannibal fetish worshippers, was scarcely less than the difference which afterwards declared itself between the peoples who accepted Mohammedanism and those who retained the local form of goddess-worship. Interest is added to the subject by the fact that the three types still exist, and can be studied in Nigeria, where it may be said that, at the present day, three distinct historic ages are persisting contemporaneously.

After dominating the southern provinces, Zaria in its turn was dominated, as we have seen, by Kano. With the rise of Kano, and its conversion to Mohammedanism in the thirteenth century, we enter historic times, and the history of Kano involves to some extent the history of the principal provinces of Haussaland. After the period of the Moorish conquest, its arms, which had been directed to the south and east, were turned more continually to the north and west. In its later history Katsena, Zamfara, and Gober, take the place previously occupied by Zaria and the southern provinces, with the difference that, following the mysterious law by which conquest remained ever with the north, Katsena in the first instance established its superiority, and, after Katsena, Gober, a still more northern state, took the leading place, until the Fulani eruption of the nineteenth century, issuing from Gober, subjugated the whole of Haussaland.

Katsena, whose literature, like that of Kano, was purposely destroyed by the Fulani at the beginning of the nineteenth century, but of whose history a chronicle similar to the Kano chronicle has been preserved, would seem to have risen into importance somewhat later than Kano. The dates which have been examined and accepted by

Dr. Barth attribute the foundation of the city to a hero of the name of Komayo as late as the middle of the fourteenth century, while King Ibrahim Maji, who lived about the middle of the sixteenth century, is counted as the first Mussulman king. This must, however, I think, be an error. It seems scarcely probable that Kano, which is at no great distance, should have had Mussulman kings from the end of the thirteenth century, while Katsena, nearer to northern civilisation, and in commercial and intellectual touch with Egypt and the Barbary States, should have waited till 1550 to seat a Mussulman on the throne. A little bit of direct evidence which supports the assumption of Katsena's earlier conversion is contained in the *Tarikh-es-Soudan*, where, in relating the life of one of the distinguished Mussulman scholars of Timbuctoo, Aicha Ahmed, who died in 1529, it is stated that, having spent many years in study in the East, "he returned to the Soudan and took up his residence at Katsena, where the Sultan treated him with much consideration, and conferred on him the function of Cadi." It may, I think, be taken for granted that the appointment of Cadi was not made by a pagan Sultan, nor would a pagan court have offered attractions as a residence to one of the most cultivated traditionists of Timbuctoo. The Kano chronicle mentions Katsena as a place to which many of the Fulani went to settle when they came from Melle in the end of the fourteenth century. It seems probable that Katsena, shortly to be distinguished under a Habe dynasty for superior learning, cultivation, and enlightenment, and gladly sought as a residence by men of letters from all parts of the Soudan, received Mohammedanism very shortly after the foundation of the town.

It is not certain that the present town of Katsena was the first capital of the province, but if it is not certain neither is it material. By the middle of the sixteenth century, that is, after the conquest by Songhay, and the at least nominal incorporation of Katsena with that great empire, the present town had spread to a size of which the circuit was between thirteen and fourteen English miles, and was divided into quarters, of which the names give some indication of its activities. There was the "old quarter," which was believed to have been the site of the original town; there was the Melle, or "strangers' quarters," which would seem by its double name to have been associated with the Fulani immigration from Melle; there were also the quarters for people from Bornu and Gober, and there was an Arab quarter. There were quarters for the different trades and industries, saddlers, shoemakers, dyers, &c. There was, as in all great towns, a students' quarter; there was—not far off—a dancing quarter. There was a government, or official quarter. There were quarters taking their names from the eight gates of the town, and besides these, innumerable others of which, after a list of native names approaching to a hundred, it is said: "These are the names of the larger quarters of the town, but there are still many smaller ones."

The province of Katsena, extending—within probably fluctuating limits—to a considerable distance beyond the town, contained places of importance of which the names compose a long list. The town has now fallen from its former greatness, and has shrunk to a fraction of its dimensions; but the province, like the province of Kano, retains its natural advantages. It is thus described by Dr. Barth, writing about half a century ago: "Altogether the province of Katsena is one of the finest parts of Negroland, and being situated just at the water parting of the Chad and the Niger, at a general elevation of from 1200 to 1500 feet, it enjoys the advantage of being at once well watered and well drained, the chain of hills which diversify its surface sending down numerous rapid streams, so that it is less insalubrious than other regions of this continent. Its productions are varied and rich." In the country lying between Katsena and Kano, though devastated at the time of his passage by civil war, Dr. Barth proceeds to enumerate cotton, corn, yams, sweet potatoes, beans, ground nuts, bananas, papaws, wheat, onions, tobacco, indigo, as forming the ordinary crops. Katsena had also, he tells us, figs, melons, pomegranates, and limes, and, until the destruction of the vines at the period of the Fulani conquest, grapes were plentiful. In addition to these evidences of agriculture, the rich pasturage was dotted with vast herds of cattle and goats, while the park-like scenery, diversified by native woods, formed, he says, one of the finest landscapes he had ever seen in his life. Amongst the woods the shea butter tree of commerce and the tamarind tree were remarkable.

The effect of the Moorish conquest on Katsena was rather to increase than to diminish its importance, for the downfall of Kagho, the Songhay capital, and the disasters which followed under its Moorish conquerors, diverted a stream of commercial activity to Katsena; and the Habe dynasty, whose system of law and administration was so admirable as to command the respect and the still more emphatic tribute of adoption by the Fulani conquerors of the nineteenth century, was founded in Katsena in the beginning of the seventeenth century, shortly after the coming of the Moors. "Habe," which is the name given to this dynasty by the Fulani, would seem to be only a native name for Haussa, but it applies to a special dynasty which at about this period possessed itself of power.

Katsena, like Kano, came early into conflict with Bornu, and would seem to have acknowledged its suzerainty by the payment of a tribute in slaves. No other inconvenience arose from the conquest, and for all practical purposes Katsena not only remained independent, but having come successfully out of the long wars with Kano, filled, during the seventeenth and eighteenth centuries of our era, the position of the leading city of this part of Negroland. In the latter half of the eighteenth century it was said to be at the height of its prosperity. It was important not only in commerce and politics, but also in learning and in literature. It seems to have been regarded as a sort of university town. The Haussa language attained here, it is said, to its greatest richness of form and refinement of pronunciation, while at the same time the manners of Katsena were distinguished by superior politeness over those of the other towns of Haussaland.

During the rise of Katsena in the seventeenth and eighteenth centuries, Kano recovered in part from its prostration. But it was subjected to many indignities, and the end of the seventeenth century was marked by a war with the then rising power of Zamfara on the north-west, in which the troops of Kano were beaten with great slaughter at Argaye, and so utterly dispersed that few were able to find their way home.

The eighteenth century in Haussaland was distinguished especially by the intrusion and rise to power among the more southerly states of Gober — a state which, it will be remembered, occupied a position on the extreme north of Haussaland, and at an earlier period of its history had extended into the desert as far north as Ahir or Asben. At a comparatively early period the more northerly portions of the territory of Gober had been conquered by a Berber combination known as the "five tribes." Whether these were the five tribes of the Morabite invasion led eastward by Abou Bekr at the end of the eleventh century, or five other Berber tribes from the north, is a matter of dispute. The fact alone is undisputed that they established the Mohammedan religion in Asben, and drove the people of Gober, who maintained the higher type of paganism, farther south. Gober was made tributary to them, and the feuds arising between the two races kept the people of Gober constantly occupied upon their northern frontier. In the first half of the eighteenth century the hereditary antagonists of Gober were themselves conquered by the Kellowi, a fine race of North African Berbers. The ultimate consequence was to liberate the attention of Gober, and to change the direction of its military activity. The march of its armies from this date onward was directed to the south instead of the north.

Katsena alone of the Haussa States was able to resist successfully the practised strength of this warlike state. Zamfara was subdued by it about the year 1750, and in Kano the century was chiefly occupied by a long conflict with varying results. Reign after reign has the same record of fighting with Gober, and sometimes success is recorded, sometimes defeat, till at last, about the middle of the century, Gober, under the leadership of the king Babari, who had established himself on the throne of Zamfara, triumphed over Kano. Yet the subjection was not complete. Through this ceaseless wrangle the life of Kano may be seen to be holding on a more or less uninterrupted way. The wealth of the province seems to have helped the town to weather its many storms. A king at the beginning of the seventeenth century is recorded as being the first to take tax in cows from the Fulani who were settled in the province. In the intervals of war we are told that learning prospered and that trade was developed. After the war with Gober had reached its climax, Kano, though conquered, appeared no whit the worse. The king under whom the defeat took place is described as "bad," but of the next we are told that he reigned for fifteen years, and "he was great, kind, and peaceful. The country was prosperous under him, and he was much loved." Three more reigns bring us to the end of the eighteenth century, and under them we hear only of prosperity. One king who reigned for eight years, perhaps about 1770 to 1778, was the first to bring guns into Kano, and is described as being almost like an Arab in everything. The last king mentioned by the Kano chronicler is Al Wali, of whom we are told nothing but that his mother's name was Bawuya, and that he was a very powerful king. Barth mentions that, on the conquest of Kano by the Fulani in the early years of the nineteenth century, Al Wali the king fled to Zaria, and the Zaria chronicle mentions the fact that a king of Kano called Al Wali rebuilt the walls of Kano about the year 1787. We are therefore, I think, justified in supposing that this prince was the last of the line of Haussa kings in Kano. The conquest of Haussaland by the Fulani, which took place in the beginning of the nineteenth century, represented to all the towns alike a catastrophe of the first magnitude, only to be paralleled in the country lying to the east of the Niger by the earlier catastrophe of the Moorish conquest in the countries lying to the west.

CHAPTER XXX

BORNU

To the east of the Haussa States, but lying within the same degrees of latitude—that is, north of 10° and at present south of 14°—though once perhaps extending to the limit of the summer rains, lies the kingdom of Bornu. The history of this country, often closely associated with that of the Haussa States, is, as has been already said, in truth wholly distinct, the people being of Berber descent, and the language quite distinct from that of Haussaland. The difference observable in the national characteristics of the Bornuese and the Haussas is said by travellers amongst them to be marked. The Haussa is by nature lively-spirited and cheerful, the Bornuese melancholic, dejected, and brutal. The Haussas are generally good-looking, with regular and pleasant features and graceful figures. The Bornuese have generally a broad-faced, heavy-boned physiognomy, which, especially in their women, is said to be far from pleasing.

The territory in which the people of Bornu rose to occupy a position of first importance amongst the nations of the Soudan was somewhat to the north and east of the present province of that name. Kanem, a country which now lies in French territory to the north and east of Lake Chad, was their first seat of empire, and the inhabitants of Bornu still take their native name of Kanuri from this circumstance. Under the domination of their early kings the territory of Kanem spread, at one time, on the east to the borders of the Nile, and on the west, Arab historians of the fourteenth and fifteenth centuries, who take no note of the Haussa States, speak of its power as extending to the borders of the Songhay Empire. It has been seen in the history of the Haussa provinces that they were, at different periods of their history, content to pay tribute alternately to Songhay and to Bornu. In the north the authority of Kanem extended to the Fezzan, and its limits must have approached very nearly in its northern, as well as in its western extension, to those of Songhay. The historians of Songhay describe the extent of Songhay as offering a six months' march from frontier to frontier; Macrizi says of Kanem in the fifteenth or early sixteenth century that the breadth of its dominions was a three months' march. It is under the name of Kanem that we get our earliest information about the country, and under that name, though El Bekri speaks of it in the middle of the eleventh century as a land of idolaters, very difficult of access, it seems to have entered at an early period into relations with Europe and North Africa. A pagan dynasty of Dugu, or Duguwa, reigned from about the middle of the ninth century until the end of the eleventh century, and, according to the information of El Bekri in 1067, this dominion extended on the west to the eastern bank of the Niger—that is, over the whole of Haussaland. Whether his information was accurate or not in detail, it tends to show that the kings of the name of Du, to whom he makes allusion, were at the time of more importance than any other rulers in that eastern territory. In the end of the eleventh century a new dynasty of Mohammedan kings was founded, but though Islam was brought to Kanem at about the same period as to the rest of the Soudan, it did not come through the same Morabite agency; it came direct from Egypt.

Under its Moslem kings, Kanem rose rapidly to the rank of one of the first powers of the Soudan. It entered into close relations with Egypt and the Barbary States. We have seen a black poet from Kanem at the court of El Mansour, one of the Almohade sovereigns of Spain, in the end of the twelfth century. In this and the succeeding century the armies of Kanem were very powerful, and the kings of Kanem, who maintained constant intercourse with the Hafside monarchs of the Barbary States, were known as Kings of Kanem and Lords of Bornu.

Ibn Said, who wrote in the thirteenth century, is the first Arab to speak of Bornu by its present name, and to define the country lying on the south-western shore of Chad as forming part of the kingdom of Kanem. Ibn Khaldun, having occasion to notice the embassy which has been already mentioned as having been sent by the King of Bornu to the King of Tunis about the year 1257, adds the information that the capital of Bornu was on the same meridian as Tripoli. This fixes for us the fact that since the middle of the thirteenth century there has been no great change in the position of the Bornuese seat of government. At that time a great and successful invasion was made by Bornu of the southern country, now known to us as Adamawa. The thirteenth century would seem to have been a brilliant period of early Bornuese history. In this century the power of Kanem was extended over the Fezzan, and carried as far north as to a place within eight days' march of Augela, and Islam was widely disseminated in the Soudan. It is probably also to this period that the following passage from Sultan Bello's notice must be referred. Speaking of Bornu he says:—

"Fortune having assisted them, their government flourished for some time, and their dominion extended to the very extremity of this tract of the earth. Wadai and Bagharmi, as well as the country of Haussa, with those parts of the province of Bautchi which belong to it, were in their possession. In the course of time, however, their government became weakened and their power destroyed."

It is no doubt upon this original dominion over Haussaland that certain shadowy claims of sovereignty on the part of Bornu existed. Nevertheless, as we have seen, the Haussa States were at this period rising into individual importance, and Kano did not receive Mohammedanism till it was brought to her from Melle towards the end of the thirteenth century. This information with regard to the source of Mohammedanism in Kano receives interesting confirmation from the history of Bornu, for in the chronicle of the reigns of the kings of Bornu, it is also mentioned that religious teachers came from Melle between the years 1288 and 1306. In the case of Bornu it is added that these teachers were Fulani, but the Fulani immigration did not take place in any force until a century later.

We are told that before the twelfth century the kings of Kanem were light complexioned, proving beyond all doubt their Berber origin, but from the beginning of the twelfth century it is distinctly mentioned that they were black. Presumably there was intermarriage at an early period between Berber rulers and black inhabitants. The original inhabitants of the greater part of the country which we now call Bornu, were a powerful native tribe of the name of Soy or So. No historian, so far as I am aware, has attempted to identify them with the Songhay, and I have no information which permits me to do so. Barth mentions the "So" as the name of one of the four divisions of the Fulani, but he does not appear to regard these people as Fulani. They seem to have been a remarkable and very active people, who towards the end of the thirteenth century rose against their conquerors, and in a long struggle, which lasted for nearly a hundred years, had almost succeeded in breaking the power of Kanem. In the year of Ibn Batuta's visit to Melle, 1352–53, King Edris of Bornu appeared, however, to be holding his own against them. Bornu was doing an active trade in slaves, eunuchs, and yellow cotton cloth, with Tekadda on the north-eastern border of the Mellestine, and from this period the Soy appear gradually to lose their importance, though they remain as a turbulent element in the composition of the Bornu Empire.

Edris would appear to have enjoyed a long and comparatively peaceful reign, but under his immediate successors the eastern neighbours of Kanem, a people called the Bulala, on the other side of Lake Chad, fought against the people of Kanem with such vigour and pertinacity that the power of the Empire of Kanem was broken, and the kings were driven to abandon the old capital Njimye or Jima, and to fix the royal residence in Bornu. This happened about the year 1380, after which time different kingdoms rose to independence in the territory lying between Lake Chad and the Nile, and the Kanuri definitely adopted the present territory of Bornu on the western side of the lake as the seat of their kingdom.

From this date we hear more constantly of Bornu as interfering with the Haussa and southern pagan states of the country lying between the Niger and the Benué. It may be remembered that, towards the end of the fourteenth century, a king of Bornu was driven to remain for several months at Kano. His stay is courteously described as a "long visit." As a matter of fact, it was one of the effects of the Bulala invasion from the east, and represents the final expulsion of the Bornu dynasty from Kanem. The King of Bornu came, it is said, to Kano with a great host, many men with drums on horseback, fifes, flags and guns, and he was accompanied by many Mallams. A usurper who was placed upon his throne was shortly afterwards driven from it and killed by the Bulala.

Thus in the first hours of their adversity the Bornuese kings received shelter and help in Haussaland, but it was not altogether without foresight on the part of Kano of evils to come. When the reigning King David of Kano took counsel with his Galadima, or Prime Minister, as to the manner of entertaining the King of Bornu, the Galadima warned him: "If you allow this man to stay in one of the towns of your territory he will take possession of the whole place." It was therefore determined to make new houses for the Bornu party in an open field shaded by locust trees, between Kano and a frontier town at which they had paused. The King of Kano did all that he could to please his guests, and the next King of Bornu, recovering his throne, was known by the title of the Haussa King, or the King from Haussaland. Fifty years later another King of Bornu was driven to beg for similar hospitality from Kano, and it was not refused. The name of the Bornu king was Othman Kalnama, and he remained in Kano to the time of his death. This was under the great King of Kano, Mohammed Rimpa, and marks perhaps the highest point of the prosperity of Kano, and the lowest point of the fortunes of Bornu before the rise of the Songhay Empire in the West.

All these obligations did not affect the memory of the rulers of Bornu when, after a long succession of civil wars, they at last made good their position on the throne, and, in the person of Ali Ghajideni, who began to reign in 1472, opened a new and glorious epoch of Bornu history. Ali Ghajideni, who built the old capital of Bornu, now known by the name of Birni, three days west of the modern town of Kuka, on Lake Chad, reigned from about 1472 to 1504, and therefore brought the history of Bornu up to the moment of the Songhay conquest of Haussaland. He reformed the government, reorganised the army, and renewed the ancient glory of Bornu. He fought many and successful local wars, and amongst other exploits marched against Kano, where his immediate predecessor had dethroned a weak and incapable ruler.

It will be remembered that the Wankoré, or Wangarawa, were mentioned as having brought Mohammedanism in the thirteenth century to Kano. This people effected a settlement in the Haussa country, and in the fifteenth century the province of Wangara, or Ungara, is described as lying south-easterly of Zamfara and westerly of Bornu. This would seem to place the territory of the Wangarawa between the jurisdiction of Kano and Bornu; so, at least, the rulers of these two places would appear to have considered. Bornu apparently regarded the Wangarawa as in its dependence. The King of Kano, who, in spite of some discrepancy of dates, I take to have been the contemporary of Ali Ghajideni, having a cause of quarrel with them, took their punishment into his own hands. He marched against one of their towns, took it, and, sitting under a bread-fruit tree by the principal gate, ordered that all the roofs should be taken off the houses and burned, but that no prisoners should be made. The King of Bornu, demanding an explanation of the outrage, Kano refused to give it, and war was the result. According to the Kano chronicle the King of Bornu was beaten. According to the Bornu chronicle Bornu had resolved upon the complete conquest of Wangara, when once more the Bulala attacked Bornu upon the east, and diverted its attention from western fields. There is no mention of any conflict with Kano in the Bornu account.

The very brilliant reign of Ali Ghajideni covered the period at which the Portuguese were making settlements upon the Guinea coast, and the intercourse of Bornu with Arab civilisation in the days of its early greatness having caused its territories to be well known, it is not surprising that the fame of Ali Ghajideni should rank with that of his contemporary, Sonni Ali of Timbuctoo. It has already been mentioned that the territories of the Mellestine were shown upon European maps in 1512. The territorial limits of Bornu were known to Europeans at an even earlier date, and Bornu is shown upon Portuguese maps in 1489.

The attack of his eastern neighbours upon Ali Ghajideni prevented him from carrying any further his intended subjugation of the west, and, in the meantime, Songhay, under the great Askia, achieved from the west what Ali Ghajideni had intended to do from the eastern frontier of Haussaland. Askia Mohammed intervened, as has been already related, in the local disputes of the Haussa States, and conquered them all. From this time the central Haussa States lay between Songhay and Bornu, as between the upper and the nether millstones.

It may be remembered that, on the return of the Askia from his second expedition into the Haussa country, in February of 1516, an influential chief, of the name of Kanta, revolted, and that he formed an independent principality, of which Kebbi, on the eastern side of the Niger and to the west of Zamfara and Katsena, became the seat. Sultan Bello, who gives us some further account of him, describes Kebbi as being under his rule a very extensive and fruitful province, which was peopled half by Songhays and half by natives of Katsena. The town of Birni-n-Kebbi, which is to be found now on the north-western frontier of Northern Nigeria, lies almost directly between Katsena and Gao, and it was natural that the at-that-time important province of which it was the capital should be peopled partly from one and partly from the other source. As will presently be seen, this hybrid province played so important a part in defending Haussaland from the inroads of the Moors that its rise to power in the early part of the sixteenth century is worth mentioning. Probably Kanta's court formed a nucleus of meeting for all the more vigorous of the turbulent spirits of Songhay, who for any reason were discontented with the administration of the Askias. The growth of luxury and the love of ease, which gradually undermined the Songhay Empire, left Kebbi perhaps untouched, and thus, at the end of the sixteenth century, there was yet a refuge in the territory lying between Haussa and Songhay, for all that remained of local energy and courage in the empire of the fallen Askias. It was in Kebbi that the Moors met with their first reverse; Borgu and Kontagora sustained the opposition to their rule, and the rocks of Almena, in the province of Zaria, marked the furthest limit of their advance into Haussaland. But these were among the events of a century yet to come. At the beginning of the sixteenth century Kanta had but just established his independence, and the vigour of his arms was yet to prove.

Ali Ghajideni of Bornu lived only through the first twelve years of Askia's reign. But Bornu, like Songhay, was at this epoch of its history fortunate in the succession of two remarkable kings; Edris, who followed his father, Ali Ghajideni, on the throne of Bornu, was scarcely less enlightened than his great neighbour of Songhay. He extended the power of Bornu, and carried still further the administrative reforms initiated by his father. The early part of his reign was distinguished by conquests in the East. He defeated the Bulala, who had interfered with his father's intended conquest of Wangara; but when he in turn directed his arms against Haussaland, he was met and defeated by Kanta. Sultan Bello gives an account of the campaign, attributing it to Ali Ghajideni, but as Kanta did not establish his independence until after the death of Ali, we must take the opposing forces to have been under the command, not of Ali, but of his equally warlike successor, Edris.

Sultan Bello says that at this time Kanta, who had conquered the country, governed it with equity, and had established peace in its very extremities and remotest places. Bello makes no distinction apparently between the conquests of Kanta as a general of Songhay and as an independent prince. He speaks of him as having conquered Katsena, Kano, Zaria, Gober, and the country of Asben or Ahir, all of these being, of course, really the conquests of Songhay and not of Kebbi. It would seem to have been some act of oppression on Kanta's part towards one of these towns, which gave the King of Bornu an excuse to march against him It is evident that the campaign on this occasion was undertaken with the consent of the Haussa States, for the armies of Bornu marched north of Daura and Katsena and to the west of Gober without opposition till they entered the country of Kebbi and reached a fortified place called Surami. Then after a battle, which lasted from the rising to the going down of the sun, Bornu was victorious, and Kanta was forced to fly westward. But the fort held out. The Sultan of Bornu was unable to reduce it, and, finding himself obliged to raise the siege, he marched south to Gando and thence easterly towards Bornu. Kanta reorganised his army, and rapidly, pursuing the Bornu force, he came up with it at a place called Onghoor (presumably Ungar or Wangara) and there inflicted a crushing defeat.

The Sultan of Bornu after this again found himself fully occupied in the East, where, as a result of more than one brilliant campaign, he entirely subdued the old enemies of Bornu and re-established his authority over Kanem. Kanta himself shortly afterwards died, but the successors of Edris of Bornu continued to dispute with the descendants of Kanta the supremacy of Haussaland, while, as we have seen, the life of the individual Haussa States went on without much regard either for Kebbi or for Bornu. The chronicles, though somewhat confused, would seem to assign the final victory to Bornu.

This period of constant war was the period which we have seen to have been one of great adversity in the Haussa provinces. Although we find no mention in their chronicles of the campaigns of their greater neighbours, there can be no doubt that the long struggle between opposing powers for the suzerainty of Haussaland must have contributed much to the conditions of disturbance and unrest which issued for them in local wars. It is only amazing that under the circumstances, every province being at war with each other, and two great powers fighting over their heads, there should have been any possibility of the continuance of trade and the spread of learning, of which the chronicles continue constantly to speak. That trade should have persisted under conditions so adverse says much for the commercial tenacity of the Haussa people. Agriculture probably suffered even more severely than trade, and the great famine with which the century ended was widespread. The famine is mentioned in the chronicles of Bornu as extending to that country, and we find the statement in the Songhay accounts of the Moorish conquest that during the campaigns of the first two years (1591–92) on the eastern side of the Niger, the Moorish soldiers were reduced by famine to eat the pack animals on which the transport of the army depended.

Nevertheless, under a king of the name of Mohammed, Bornu rose about the middle of the sixteenth century to a position of great prosperity and power, and its relations with the outer world were maintained. The causes which operated to cut off the countries of the Western Soudan from their old connection with Spain, and to interrupt their communication with Christian Europe, did not apply to the Mohammedan East, where the Turks were the ruling power. Embassies from Bornu to Tripoli are frequently mentioned, and before the end of the sixteenth century the armies of Bornu, more advanced than the majority of European troops, were armed in great part with muskets. The Spaniards were ahead of the rest of Europe in this respect, but it may be remembered that at the battle of Lepanto, which was fought in 1571, only the crews of the more important ships were armed with muskets. In an engagement which Drake had with the Spaniards off the American coast in 1572, the English crews were armed only with bows and arrows, and when Queen Elizabeth ascended the throne in 1557, the principal weapons in the arsenals of England were bows and arrows. Yet, if the Kano chronicle is to be trusted, the troops of

Bornu had "guns" as early as the beginning of the fifteenth century.

From Ali Ghajideni, who ascended the throne of Bornu in 1472, to Edris Alawoma, who was the contemporary of Queen Elizabeth and died in 1603, the destinies of Bornu were guided by almost uniformly vigorous and enlightened kings. There were a few short reigns of no importance, but for the most part the period was for Bornu, as for Songhay, one of great and prosperous development. The Government of Bornu was, in theory at least, somewhat less despotic than that of Songhay, and was conducted by the medium of a council of twelve, between whom the principal offices of State were divided. According to some authorities the monarchy itself was elective, but with the interruption of certain revolutions it seems to have descended very generally from father to son. The territory of Bornu was divided, like that of Songhay, into districts of which each had its governor, but it does not appear to have had the superior grouping of districts into viceroyalties, which in some degree assimilated the organisation of the Songhay Empire to that of Imperial Rome. In the records of Bornu there is frequent reference to the position and influence of the queen mothers, and women appear to have played a not unimportant part in its history. In the latter half of the sixteenth century, Aicha, the mother of King Edris, herself reigned for a short period before her son's accession. She was a very distinguished woman, to whose advice it is believed that her son owed much of the wisdom of his conduct. Under her influence an important embassy was sent to Tripoli, and the policy of maintaining intercourse and trade with the outer world by the medium of the Turkish Empire, which had always been the policy of prosperous Bornu, was actively developed. In this latter period of Bornuese prosperity, foreign trade and local conquest form the two important notes of its history. We have seen that conquests had been effected on the East, and the domination of Bornu over Kanem had been substituted for the ancient domination of Kanem over Bornu. Campaigns, though not always successful, had been carried out in the West, and the Haussa States at a somewhat later date became one by one tributary, though not in any true sense subject to Bornu.

Ali Ghajideni in the fifteenth century reorganised the Empire of Bornu. His immediate successors enlarged and aggrandised it. Edris Alawoma, at the end of the sixteenth century, undertook the special task of consolidating it and binding its somewhat heterogeneous elements into one political whole. He once more gave attention to the pagan Soy, who continued at that date to defy the power of Bornu in independent fastnesses of their own. Having reduced them with much difficulty to submission in the north-western portions of his territory, he carried away a great number of the people, and the remainder fled eastward to Kanem. He marched then south-westward against other pagan tribes, and it is especially mentioned in recounting his campaigns that he achieved his success mainly by the force of his muskets. He then undertook a great campaign against Kano, which must have occurred during the worst period of the misfortunes of Kano, during that twenty years when, the spirit of the Kano people being broken, they were obliged "to sit at home and be afraid." Nevertheless, though the strong places of the province of Kano fell into the hands of Bornu, the town itself succeeded in maintaining its independence. As this fact is acknowledged by the Bornu chronicle, it may be held to be undoubtedly accurate. After Kano, Edris turned his arms northwards towards the Berbers of the desert, and attacked the "five tribes" or Berbers of Asben, with whom it has been mentioned that Gober during all this period of its history maintained a perpetual war. Here, too, Edris was victorious to the extent of imposing a tributary sort of allegiance. North, south, east, and west he carried his conquering arms. To give a list of the many tribes that he subdued could only weary the reader, but amongst many unfamiliar names that of Katagum, which is of sufficient importance to form now one of seventeen provinces of Northern Nigeria, may be selected for mention as having at this time made its submission to Bornu.

The result of twelve years of fighting is all that the reader can be asked to carry in his mind. This was to weld the Empire of Bornu into one victorious and formidable whole, of which the troops, armed with a weapon superior to any then known in the Soudan, had acquired a military reputation of being practically irresistible as early as the year 1583, that is, eight years before the coming of the Moors. Had Songhay under the later Askias kept pace with her neighbour of Bornu, and introduced as she might have done the musket into the armament of her troops, it is possible that the whole subsequent fate of the Soudan might have been changed. It was the possession of muskets by the Moors which, as will presently be seen, enabled them to make an easy conquest of a once famous empire, while it is probable that the possession of the same weapons by Bornu was among the causes which operated to check the Moorish invasion at the limits which it actually attained.

Edris Alawoma himself was killed in battle in the year 1603 by the rudest of pagan weapons, a hand-bill or hoe, thrown at him by an adversary concealed in a tree, when he was reducing one of the tribes of Southern Bornu to obedience. But at the moment of the Moorish conquest of Songhay he was still upon the throne, and the thirty-three years of his prosperous and enlightened reign had placed Bornu in a strong position to contest the suzerainty of Haussaland with the new-comers.

CHAPTER XXXI

CONDITION OF THE SOUDAN AT THE END OF THE SIXTEENTH CENTURY

THE slight outline which has been given of the course of history in the eastern portion of the West African Soudan, renders it possible to construct some picture of the general condition of the country from the shores of the Atlantic to those of Lake Chad at the moment of the coming of the Moors in 1591.

In the west the Empire of Songhay having risen to the zenith of its prosperity and fame, still enjoyed, according to its own historians, the blessings of peace and order throughout its vast extent. We are expressly told that when the Moorish army arrived in the Soudan, it found the country to be one of the most favoured of the Almighty for wealth and for fertility. Peace reigned in all its provinces, and, thanks to the admirable organisation established by the great Askia in the beginning of the century, the orders of the monarch were obeyed implicitly from the frontiers of the Eastern Viceroyalty of Dandi to the borders of the Atlantic, and from the southern mountains to Touat and Tegazza in the northern desert—as well as in all the dependencies of these Berber towns. The awful misery which followed when the supreme power was suddenly destroyed is laid, without hesitation, to the count of the conquerors, who are held responsible by the local annalists, not only for what they did, but, very properly, for the ravages of the powers of disorder which they let loose. "All was changed in a moment," says the *Tarikh-es-Soudan*. "Danger took the place of security, destitution of opulence, trouble, calamities, and violence succeeded to tranquillity. Everywhere the populations began to destroy each other. In all places and in every direction rapine became the law, war spared neither life nor property, nor the position of the people. Disorder was general, it spread everywhere till it reached at last the highest degree of intensity."

But while the author of the *Tarikh* attributes this condition of things directly to the Moors, we find in his own pages, long before the coming of the conquerors, indications which serve to explain not only how the Moors made of this great and wealthy country such an easy prey, but also to show that in the reigns of the later Askias the strenuous spirit of heroism, which had marked the rise of that dynasty, was dead, and the aspiration to live on a higher plane of civilisation than their predecessors had given place to nothing more noble than a love of luxury. The Songhay Empire at the end of the sixteenth century had become fatally content to exist upon the tradition of its former greatness. One generation had borne the labours of preparing the ground for seed. Another, when the harvest stood ripe, thought only of gorging themselves with the fruit. Thus, when all seemed to be at its best, the empire was in truth nearest to its end. After describing the happiness of the country under the earlier Askias, and the perfect order which prevailed, the *Tarikh* says, in words which might have applied to decadent Rome: "Things continued thus until towards the moment in which the Songhay dynasty approached its end, and its empire ceased to exist. At this moment faith was exchanged for infidelity; there was nothing forbidden by God which was not openly done. Men drank wine, they gave themselves up to vice. . . . As to adultery, it become so frequent that indulgence in it was almost accepted as permissible. Without it there was no elegance and no glory. . . . Because of these abominations," continues the pious annalist, "the Almighty in His vengeance drew down upon the Songhay the victorious army of the Moors. He brought it through terrible suffering from a distant country. Then the roots of this people were separated from the trunk, and the chastisement which they underwent was exemplary."

But, if at the end of the sixteenth century the body of the Songhay Empire stood ready for the axe, there were offshoots to which the felling of the trunk was destined to impart perhaps only the more vigour. In the western province, Masina, already mentioned as having established in the eleventh century, with the help of its Fulani population, an independence which, though it had paid tribute to many rulers, was sacrificed to none, was destined yet to play a part of some importance in the future of the country. In the east the Viceroyalty of Dandi, including the territory of the independent Sultans of Kebbi, the practically independent Haussa States, and the State of Borgu, with its neighbouring territory of Southern Gurma, was the refuge of all that was yet loyal to the old traditions of Songhay. The dynasty of Kebbi, founded in rebellion, was vigorous with the old vigour of conquering Songhay, and it had not cut itself off from the prosperity of the empire to accept a tame share in its defeat. To the Moor who knew no difference between them, Kebbi had a lesson of its own to teach.

Beyond the rampart which was created from Kebbi to Nupe by these states of the Eastern Niger lay Haussaland, a congeries of states, Mohammedan and pagan, of great fertility, of no little local industry, famous from the earliest times for their commercial and agricultural activity, but containing populations composed of such extraordinarily diverse elements that internecine war was their habitual condition. Their lack of internal cohesion deprived them, notwithstanding the many advantages of their position, of external strength. Though one or other in turn assumed a locally dominant position, they can hardly be said either to have made or to have resisted conquest, but under all conquest they preserved their individuality and persisted in their habits. The black traders of the eleventh century, whom we hear of in the pages of El Bekri, did not differ substantially from the black traders whom Idrisi mentions in the twelfth century, and Ibn Batuta speaks of in the fourteenth century. Their trade prospered through the great period of the fifteenth century, and when, in the sixteenth century, Kano fell upon evil days, Katsena rose quickly to take her place. The agricultural population was driven off the land, but misfortune does not seem to have altered the habits of Haussa traders.

When the outposts of Songhay fought with the outposts of Bornu, Haussaland was the battlefield, but the Haussa States took no part in the war. Like a bed of rushes they have ever allowed the storms of encircling forces to beat over their heads. At times they have appeared to be laid low, but when the hurricane has passed they have raised themselves, no worse for the buffeting of fate. Their populations, which have never enjoyed any wide foreign reputation, were perhaps locally, in their modest way, the best known and the best informed of all the peoples of the Soudan. They were very numerous, and in their recognised capacity of travelling traders through all the states, their language was one of the most widely spoken in the Soudan. By the end of the sixteenth century it supplied to the eastern portion of the country a *lingua franca*, which to the present day remains as a means of communication with those "great multitudes of negroes and of other people," of whom Leo Africanus confesses in the beginning of the sixteenth century, that he "could not well note the names." Travelling as they did in small trading caravans through the entire country, they became naturally acquainted with the affairs of every neighbouring kingdom. They were themselves well known from the shores of the Atlantic to the lip of the sacred well of Zem-Zem, where they drank as pilgrims within the precincts of the temple of Mecca and as peace was essential to their trade, they quarrelled only with next-door neighbours and rivals.

Peaceful abroad and quarrelsome at home, they earned the character, which they enjoy to-day, of being at once the best fighters and the most industrious traders of the Soudan.

Eastward again of Haussaland and its multitudes, including the settlements which have been already mentioned of Fulanis, Wangaras, and all the southern pagan states, lay the well-organised Empire of Bornu, occupying on the western side of Lake Chad a territory more extensive, but not widely different from, its present position, as shown upon modern maps, while to the north and east it spread round the shores of the great lake, and extending far into the desert, was almost conterminous with the Egyptian frontiers of the Turkish Empire.

It will be remembered that in the contemporary life of Europe Mohammedanism had been steadily gaining in the East, under the Turks, what it had been losing in the West under the Saracens. The Seljukian Turks had overrun Egypt itself in the middle of the thirteenth century. Their Mamelukes or foreign soldiery elected a Sultan for themselves in Cairo in the year 1260, and though the Abbasside Caliphs preserved a nominal supremacy, which was chiefly religious, Egypt was, in fact, governed by the Mameluke Sultans, until they in turn were overthrown by the Ottoman Turks. The Ottoman Turks were established in Europe, in the Balkan Peninsula, in 1353, exactly one hundred years before their final conquest of Constantinople. About the year 1389 their famous leader, Bajazet, accepted the title of Sultan from the Abbasside Caliph of Egypt, who still kept the name of Head of the Moslem Church. Shortly after accepting the title of Sultan he defeated the confederate army of the Christian powers at Nicropolis, and while an attack of the gout prevented him from fulfilling a vow to stable his horse in St. Peter's at Rome, he was able so closely to besiege Constantinople that it must have fallen in 1402 but for the intervention of Tamerlane.

Tamerlane, chief of that other branch of the Tartars which is best known to history as the Moguls, was the representative, though not the legitimate descendant, of the heirs of Genghis Khan. He frankly aspired to conquer the world, and he had conquered Persia, Tartary, and India, when, hearing on the banks of the Ganges of the conquests of Bajazet in Europe, he resolved to march against the rival of his military glory. The Mogul and Ottoman conquests already touched each other in the neighbourhood of Erzeroum and the Euphrates. Tamerlane's first move was to attack Syria, which was still subject to Egypt. Aleppo, Damascus, and Bagdad fell to his arms amid awful massacres. Ibn Khaldun relates the interview he had with him outside the walls of Damascus, in 1401.

But the Mamelukes defended their territory with vigour, and the losses and fatigues of the campaign caused Tamerlane to turn from Egypt and Palestine, and concentrate his forces upon the Ottoman Empire. At the battle of Ancyra, in Anatolia, Bajazet was overthrown and taken prisoner, in 1402, and while the Mogul armies advanced to the Asiatic shores of the Sea of Marmora, Bajazet himself died in captivity. Thus, in 1403, Tamerlane held Asia from the Ganges to the Mediterranean. But the Ottoman Turks held one passage into Europe at the Hellespont, and the Christians of Constantinople held the other at the Bosphorus. Bajazet's successor, Suleiman, and the Greek Emperor, both agreed to pay tribute to Tamerlane on the condition that his armies did not pass the Straits. Egypt also agreed to pay him tribute, with a similar condition that he should not pass into Africa. How long these compositions with superior force, on the part of rich, weak nations, would have held good, cannot be known. Tamerlane died in 1405. After his death the Mogul Empire gradually sank beneath the processes of time and war, till it lost itself in the sham splendour of the throne of Delhi.

The empire of the Turks, on the contrary, recovered

from the short and sharp attack of Tamerlane. In 1421 a grandson of Bajazet succeded to his five uncles as Amurath II., and during his capable reign of thirty years, the Turkish Empire reconstituted itself alike in Europe and in Asia Minor. The capture of Constantinople, though attempted by Amurath in 1422, was reserved for his successor, Mohammed II. The town was taken by the Turks on the 29th of May 1453, and with it fell the Christian Empire of the East. St. Sophia became a Turkish mosque. The throne of Constantine and his successors became the seat of Islam. There was at that time no power in Christendom which could dislodge the Turk from the almost impregnable position of Constantinople. It was in vain that the feeble heirs of the family of Paleologus sold their imperial rights to European sovereigns. Before the end of the fifteenth century the Greek Empire in Europe and Asia had passed into Turkish hands, and the sack of Otranto by the Turks in 1481 convulsed the Christian world with fear that the conquest of Rome might be added to that of Constantinople.

But Mohammed died in 1481, and his successors turned their attention rather to the east and south. The Turkish fleets which had been created during the reigns of Amurath and Mohammed, and numbered no less than 250 galleys, under the command of the famous Barbarossa scoured the African coasts. Algiers and Tripoli became Turkish strongholds in the opening years of the sixteenth century. Egypt and Syria, which had continued to exist under the Mamelukes during the period of European conquest, were taken by Selim I. in the year 1517. The Knights Templars were driven out of the island of Rhodes on Christmas Day of 1522. Tunis was captured in 1534, Gibraltar was sacked in 1539, and though the fortress was held for Spain, the Turkish fleet sailed round the coast, pillaging the Spanish towns as they went. Thus, from one end of the Mediterranean to the other, Turkish corsairs became the terror of the sea. The greater part of the North African coast passed into Turkish hands, a position which was not conquered without much fighting, taking and re-taking of towns. Tunis and Tripoli changed hands more than once.

Italy itself was not spared. A separate squadron, under Dragout, another famous Turkish sailor, ravaged its coasts. In 1569, in a great naval campaign, the Turks attacked and pillaged the coasts and islands belonging to Venice. They took parts of Crete and Cyprus. Finally, on the 1st of August 1571, Famagosta capitulated to the Turks, after a long and arduous siege, and the island of Cyprus was theirs. This was the last Turkish triumph of the century. The Christian Powers were at last able to combine effectively under the leadership of Don John of Austria against the common enemy, and the battle of Lepanto, which was fought on October 7th of the same year, destroyed the Turkish sea-power in the Mediterranean.

I owe an apology to the reader for this crude list of dates, but the rapid rise of a relatively new Mohammedan power on the eastern shores of the Mediterranean must be borne in mind in order to understand with what a different world the commercial and intellectual intercourse of Bornu was carried on, to that known and frequented in the West by the caravans of Melle, and of Songhay in its earlier days, and also to explain the fury of hatred and persecution by which the Moorish citizens of Spain were, in the fifteenth century, attacked, conquered, and driven out of the country which they had once civilised and still enriched. As the crescent waxed stronger in the East it waned in the West, and the decline of those nations of the Western Soudan which were dependent on their touch with Western markets and Western sources of civilisation, is proportionately observable.

It was not to be supposed that Christian Powers, however indifferent individually to each other's fate, could collectively regard with indifference the rise of a force which threatened to destroy them all. Had they not been enfeebled by jealousies, corruption, and superstition, they must have learned long before the end of the sixteenth century to combine in such force as to prohibit the further advance of Islam. But in the fifteenth century the darkness of the Middle Ages was still upon them. Gibbon, in relating the fall of Constantinople, quotes from Æneas Silvius, afterwards Pope Pius II., who thus describes the state of Christendom: "It is a body," he says, "without a head; a republic without laws or magistrates. The Pope and the Emperor may shine as lofty titles, as splendid images; but *they* are unable to command, and none are willing to obey; every state has a separate prince, and every prince has a separate interest. What eloquence could unite so many discordant and hostile powers under the same standard? Could they be assembled in arms, who would dare to assume the office of general? What order could be maintained? What military discipline? Who would undertake to feed such an enormous multitude? Who would understand their various languages, or direct their stranger and incompatible manners? What mortal could reconcile the English with the French, Genoa with Arragon, the Germans with the natives of Hungary and Bohemia? If a small number enlisted in the Holy War, they must be overthrown by the infidels; if many, by their own weight and confusion."

This picture of the weakness of Europe in the fifteenth century needs no amplifying touches. It may, however, be recalled that at the very moment that Mohammed II. was engaged in besieging and sacking Constantinople, a private German citizen of the name of John Gutenberg was no less absorbed in the work of perfecting at Mentz an invention of cut metal types from which he printed, in the years between 1450 and 1455, the first typed copy of the Latin Bible. If the work of Mohammed tended to consolidate Christendom by the blows which were struck against its distracted kingdoms from outside, the work of Gutenburg was perhaps even more effectual in rendering the angular forces malleable by mutual comprehension from within. It took more than a hundred years for the use of printing to spread to some of the remoter parts of Europe. There need be no surprise that it took more than a hundred years for Europe to emerge sufficiently from the disunited state described by Æneas Silvius, to present a united front to the Turk, and it is a curious but not inappropriate coincidence that we find the use of printing extended to the farthest western shore of Europe by its first adaptation to Irish characters in 1571, the very year of the battle of Lepanto. There is no need to dwell on the part that must have been played by the discovery of this art alone in the movement which drew the warring nations of Christendom together. Similarity of thought is the great unifier of peoples, and from the middle of the fifteenth century the learned in all the nations of Europe had the means of communicating their thoughts not only to each other, but to the body of their respective nations.

But if in 1453 Europe was unfit, as a whole, to oppose the progress of the Turk, there were individuals who burned with a holy zeal. The sack of Otranto, which, in 1481, had almost driven the Pope to abandon Italy, found Isabella and Ferdinand on the throne of Spain, and it is hardly to be wondered at that these Catholic sovereigns, sharing to the full in the grief and terror which Turkish triumphs were spreading through Christendom, were inclined to act with something of the harshness of panic towards the Mohammedan peoples who filled the southern towns of Spain, and still held within the precincts of Granada an independent kingdom upon Spanish soil. The policy pursued against the Moors, the ruin of the industries of Spain by the expulsion, under circumstances of the utmost rigour, of immense multitudes of its most skilful artisans and most valuable citizens, stands out in such striking contrast to the general wisdom and benevolence of Isabella's mild and enlightened reign, that it can only be understood by reference to a state of feeling which was stirring the orthodox Catholics of every court of Europe to preach the duty of a new crusade against the infidel. The natural sagacity of Isabella would lead her to deal directly with the infidel upon her own borders, rather than to waste her energy and resources in the endeavour to unite Europe in a common movement. The Spanish sovereigns were besieging Granada when Columbus obtained from them, in camp, in April of 1492, the long-desired permission to start on his voyage of discovery to the West, and it is indicative of the general tone of feeling in Europe, that he vowed to provide out of the proceeds of his enterprise, if it should prove as successful as he hoped, funds for the prosecution of a crusade to deliver Palestine from the Turks. From Gibraltar to Constantinople a dread of victorious Islam inspired the policy of every court.

The result was the expulsion of Mohammedanism from Western Europe. When Granada submitted to Ferdinand and Isabella in 1492, the Moors were not at first driven out of Spain. They remained as subjects of the Catholic kings. But Cardinal Ximenes Isabella's great adviser, did not long remain content with this measure of moderation. In 1502 they were expelled. The contents of their famous libraries were collected and destroyed, with the exception, as has been already mentioned, of some 300 books of medical science. Their property, offered in nominal sales, for which gold and silver were not allowed to be used in payment, was, in fact, subjected to wholesale pillage. All that they took with them to enrich the cities of Africa to which they went, was the skill, the taste, the learning, the industry, the habits of good citizenship, which each man carried in his breast, and by the loss of which Spain was for ever impoverished. Spain has never recovered from the blow dealt against its public life by the wisest of its sovereigns.

Africa, which for a time seemed to receive all that Spain had lost, suffered on her part by the severance which took place between her own life and the progressive life just then opening upon new possibilities of the West. Isabella died in 1504. She was succeeded by her daughter, Joanna, the mad queen, and after her by Charles V., who ascended the throne in 1516, just one year before the Turks took Egypt from the Mamelukes. Charles V., Emperor of Germany as well as King of Spain, and champion of Catholicism against the tendencies of the Reformation in Europe, reigned for forty years, and during the whole of that time showed himself the determined enemy of Islam. He pursued the Moors to the shores of Africa. He took their coast towns. He engaged the European Powers to help him in closing the ports of the Mediterranean to their ships. He fought indiscriminately against Moors and Turks, and in beating the Moors, prepared the way for the triumph of the Turks, who proved themselves a harder enemy for him to overthrow. Tripoli had been already taken by Spain in 1510. When the Turks took the island of Rhodes in 1522, Charles V. gave Malta to the Knights Templars, and five years later established them in the very camp of Islam by giving them Tripoli, which they held till the Turks took it again in 1551.

Orán, which had also become Spanish in the early part of the century, was gallantly defended against successive attempts, alike on the part of Moors and Turks, to repossess themselves of it. In the siege of 1563, in the succeeding reign, the Turks used muskets, heavy artillery, and mines, but without avail, for the place, on the eve of surrender, was relieved by the fleet of Andrea Doria. In 1535 Charles led in person the attack on Tunis, which the Turks had taken in 1534, and he succeeded in capturing the town, which was held by a Spanish garrison till the Turks, under Barbarossa, retook it in 1550. But though the Christians were able to take certain seaports, and eventually, after the battle of Lepanto, to hold the sea, the Turks gradually possessed themselves of the coast of Northern Africa. The provinces which surrounded the seaports were in their hands. "Where the Turks have once taken foot," says Marmol, who wrote about the year 1573, "they can never again be dislodged."

Charles V. abdicated in 1556. His son Philip abated nothing of his policy, and while he persecuted Protestants in Flanders, he found time to pursue with equal zeal Turks, Jews, and heretics in the Mediterranean. This reign saw the battle of Lepanto. The fleets of Spain and Italy could close the Mediterranean to the Turks, but the Italians and Spaniards could never penetrate into Africa. All that happened was that the Turks—banned as militant infidels by the nations of Europe—possessed themselves of the fruitful provinces stretching from Egypt to Morocco, that harbours once crowded with the merchant shipping of the world became mere nests of corsairs, sallying out to prey upon a trade that passed them by, and that between the interior of Africa and the civilised world a barrier was erected which, as years went by, became impassable—Africa was cut off from Europe.

The Moors, suffering equally beneath the blows of Turks and Christians, withdrew into the north-western corner of the continent. Unable to maintain external relations with any equal power, they lost the finer elements of national life, and rapidly became a decadent people. During the long struggle of the sixteenth century we hear of them as taking part, under their chiefs, from time to time in the sieges and battles of the coast. At the end of that century they made one effort, which was as the last flicker of their expiring glory, to obtain for themselves in some other direction the outlet which had been closed upon the Mediterranean and Atlantic coasts. The North was held against them by superior force. Before they submitted to the living death which isolation marked for them in the heart of Africa, they endeavoured to break through to the South. The outcome of their endeavour was the Moorish conquest of the Soudan.

CHAPTER XXXII

THE MOORISH CONQUEST

"DJOUDER PASHA was a little man with blue eyes." Thus begins the chapter in the *Tarikh* which recounts the coming of the Moors. Another account says that he had a light complexion of the colour of steel. Djouder Pasha was the commander-in-chief of the Moorish army. He had at his disposal for the purposes of an expedition to the Soudan only a small force of something under 4000 men, but they were well armed with muskets—which were apparently unknown to the western armies of the Soudan—they were well mounted, well disciplined, well equipped with tents and medical stores, and, for the purposes of an army which meant to live upon the country through which they passed, they were sufficiently well provisioned. Their organisation had been reformed on the model of the Turks, with whom the armies of Morocco had had more than one occasion to measure their strength.

A little steel-coloured man with blue eyes, at the head of such a force, was in a position to play, if he chose, amid the rich and supine populations of the Soudan, a part not unlike that of the leader of a pack of wolves among flocks of sheep. The disproportionate numbers of the sheep were only so much the more to the advantage of the wolves. Djouder Pasha was an accomplished soldier. He had gained experience in the wars of the coast with Turks and Spaniards. The results to be obtained with modern weapons were well known to him, and it is probable that he fully appreciated the importance of moving with a small, rather than with a large unwieldy force, across the difficult and waterless deserts which had hitherto served as the best military defence of the Soudan.

When a military nation wishes to fight with one which it has reason to believe to be unprepared, a cause of quarrel is never far to seek. Morocco found its cause of quarrel with Songhay in the possession of the salt mines of Tegazza. It will be remembered that these mines lay upon the western road leading from Tafilet, or Sidjilmessa, to Ghana and Timbuctoo. Their position upon modern maps is about 8° W. by 26° N. They were within the limits of the Mellestine, and when the power of Songhay had succeeded to that of Melle, they were included in the territories of the Songhay Empire. They furnished the principal salt supply of the Soudan, and their possession was therefore a matter of supreme importance to Songhay. We have seen that during the sixteenth century the Sultans of Morocco had from time to time made efforts to dispute the supremacy of Songhay over this valuable border district, and that their claims had been vigorously rejected by the earlier Askias. It happened, in the year 1590, when the second Askia Ishak was on the throne of Songhay, and that of Morocco was occupied by Muley Hamed, that a certain Songhay official, who had been interned at Tegazza as a punishment for malpractices by a previous Askia, succeeded in effecting his escape, and fled across the northern border to the court of Morocco. He there represented to Muley Hamed the ease with which the conquest of Songhay, in the present condition of the country, could be effected, and he treacherously placed all his knowledge at the disposal of the enemy. As a consequence of these representations, Muley Hamed wrote to Askia Ishak, and announced that he proposed to invade his country, unless he were willing to transfer to Morocco the salt mines of Tegazza. The sovereign of Morocco urged that he had a right to possess the mines, since it was only thanks to his exertions that the country was defended and protected against the incursions of the Christians. Askia Ishak rejected the claim as indignantly as the Ishak of a previous generation had rejected a similar proposition, and, by way of defiance, accompanied his answer with the significant present of spears and iron shackles.

Muley Hamed accepted the defiance, and in November of 1590 Djouder Pasha, with a staff of ten picked generals and a very carefully selected body of officers, crossed the border at the head of his already well-prepared little force. Military expeditions had been attempted before against Songhay by Morocco. They had always failed in consequence of the difficulty of moving large bodies of men through the desert, and their record had been records of disaster. Djouder Pasha knew his business better. The march, which is supposed to be one of from fifty to sixty days for an ordinary caravan, seems to have doubled itself for his army, which, with carriers, hospital corps, &c., amounted to about 10,000 men; but on March 30, 1591, he encamped safely on the Niger. It was a river which had never before been seen by Moorish troops, and the general celebrated the event by a great banquet. The force appears from the account to have passed in the desert to the east of Timbuctoo, and to have then descended upon the river at a point still east of Timbuctoo, leaving the town entirely untouched.

After recruiting his forces with food and drink in the fertile country which they had entered, Djouder marched without delay towards Kagho.

In the meantime Askia Ishak, having information of the approach of the Moors, called his generals and the principal personages of the kingdom together, in order, it is said, to ask for their opinion, and to consult them on the measures to be taken. But nothing can more graphically represent the fallen condition of the country than the description which is given in two lines of the debates of this council: "Whenever judicious advice was given it was hastily rejected." To the last moment the officials of Songhay refused to believe that the Moorish army would succeed in reaching the river. Finally, however, an army of 12,000 horse and 30,000 foot was put in motion.

On the 12th of April, 1591, the forces met at a place called Tenkoudibo, which I have not been able to identify, but which would appear by the context to be in the valley of the Niger, on the northern side of the river, perhaps something more than half-way between Timbuctoo and Kagho. The battle resulted in the absolute defeat of the Songhay army. The cavalry was routed, the chivalry of Songhay fled. But among the rank and file of the foot-soldiers a touching incident is reported. Seeing that the battle was lost, and being pledged by their oath as soldiers not to fly in case of defeat, the infantry, we are told, kept their oath by throwing their bucklers upon the ground and sitting upon them to await the onset of Djouder's troops, and were all massacred in that attitude. Askia Ishak fled with the rest of the army, sending word to the populations of Kagho and Timbuctoo to evacuate these towns, and to join him on the other side of the river in the province of Gurma. He himself, without passing through Kagho, fled to Korai Gurma. He camped there with the remnant of his army, surrounded by lamentations. Next day, "with cries and vociferations," the passage of the Niger was commenced in little boats. The boats appear to have been insufficient. In the confusion which resulted great numbers perished, and wealth, "of which God only knows the amount," was lost. Djouder marched on Kagho, but in that town there remained no one except a few aged persons, teachers, students, and merchants, who had not been able to leave in a hurry with the rest of the population.

A certain Khatib Mahmoud Darami, an old man held in high esteem amongst the people, received Djouder Pasha and his staff, and entertained them "with magnificent hospitality." He was treated by them in return with every consideration. He had long discussions with Djouder, and became the negotiator of the terms of peace which were offered by Askia Ishak. The account which has reached us of these appears to be very incomplete. All we are told is of one condition—that Songhay should pay an indemnity of 100,000 pieces of gold and 1000 slaves, and that the Moorish army should return to Morocco. To these advances Djouder—who seems to have been very little impressed with the riches of Kagho—was content to reply that he was not a principal: he was the servant of the Sultan, and could only refer the question to Morocco.

After consulting with the Arab merchants of the town, he drew up proposals which he despatched by a sure messenger to Muley Hamed, and leaving Kagho, after having been only seventeen days in the town, he withdrew his troops to Timbuctoo, where he resolved to await the answer of the Sultan. The people of Timbuctoo, in view of the difficulty of transporting themselves and their property with safety into the province of Gurma, had not obeyed the summons of Askia, but preferred the chances of negotiation with the Moors to the certainty of destruction among their own countrymen. They only profited so far by the order to evacuate the town as to hold themselves dispensed from any duty to defend it. They received Djouder coldly, but without opposition, and he, who during the whole of this early period appears to have kept his troops in admirable control, selected the quarter of the town which he preferred, and proceeded to build a fortress in it, while he kept the greater part of his army encamped outside the town. Cold civilities were exchanged on both sides between him and the authorities. People augured, it is said, nothing good from the position of affairs; but a sort of thunderous truce was maintained until the messenger should have time to return from Morocco with the signification of the Sultan's will. The messenger left Kagho in April. The Moorish troops entered Timbuctoo on the 30th of May. It was not until August that the answer of the Sultan was received.

In the meantime, though Djouder held his troops sternly in leash, Askia Ishak remained in the far eastern provinces, and the Songhay Empire became aware that one form of central authority had been destroyed, and that no other had been substituted. Subversive forces began to work on all its borders. The antagonistic tribes which had been held in peace by the strength of supreme authority broke into war. The first to rise were tribes in the neighbourhood of Timbuctoo itself, who plundered the rich territory on the banks of the river which is known as the Ras-el-ma, or Head of the Waters, and carried off the inhabitants as slaves. Then the people of Zaghawa, a particularly wealthy district to the south-west, which was mentioned, it may be remembered, by Ibn Batuta, did the same thing in territories lying within the Viceroyalty of Kormina. The territory of Jenné was ravaged in the most horrible manner by pagan barbarians from the south who had long been a terror to its inhabitants. Throughout the west there was an outbreak of brigandage, and among the tribes who profited by this period of licence to enrich themselves at their neighbours' expense are to be found more than one under the leadership of Fulani chiefs. In the eastern portion of the empire the disaffected populations tended to gather round the defeated Askia in the territory of Borgu to which he had fled.

Upon all this Djouder's blue eyes appear to have looked with steely indifference while he waited for the orders of the Sultan. They came in a form which was not expected. The receipt of the proposal for peace aroused nothing but fury in Muley Hamed's mind. That such a victory as had been achieved should lead to so small a result appeared to him to be the evidence only of treachery. Advisers were not wanting who whispered that the general had been bribed, and in a transport of rage the Sultan deposed Djouder Pasha from his command. A personal enemy, Mohammed ben Zergoun, was made commander-in-chief in his place.

Djouder's first intimation of the storm was the arrival of Mohammed ben Zergoun at Timbuctoo, accompanied by a new staff and invested with full powers by the Sultan.

Mohammed immediately deposed Djouder and assumed the supreme command, at the same time indulging his personal enmity by the bitterness of a military cross-examination, in which he taunted Djouder with his inactivity, and asked what had prevented him from pursuing the Askia across the river. Djouder answered that it was the lack of boats, which had all been removed by the enemy. Mohammed ordered boats to be constructed, for which purpose the plantations of trees which had been made within the walls to beautify the town of Timbuctoo were cut down, and the panels of the doors were torn from the houses. It was the beginning of the destruction which was soon to fall upon the country. From this time Songhay was allowed no pause upon the downward path.

The orders of Muley Hamed to his new commander-in-chief were that Askia Ishak was to be driven from the Soudan, and Mohammed lost no time in proceeding to carry his instructions into effect. Djouder Pasha had reached the country in April, at the beginning of the rains, and his period of inactivity corresponded to the season of highest flood, when in many districts the Niger, overflowing its shores, spreads like a lake over wide tracts of country. Mohammed arrived at Timbuctoo on the 17th of August. In the last week of September, when the rains are drawing towards their close, the army, having with it Djouder Pasha and all the revoked generals who had composed Djouder Pasha's staff, marched south-eastward towards Kuka in Borgu, where Askia Ishak was established. In a battle which was fought on October 14th Ishak was completely defeated, and fled within the confines of the Viceroyalty of Dandi to the same spot, Korai Gurma, at which the remains of his army had crossed the river when fleeing southwards from Djouder Pasha. They now recrossed in the opposite sense, and from this time the river in its eastern course formed the defensible frontier which was maintained between the lingering remains of Songhay authority and the country which was soon to be known as the Moorish Soudan. Mohammed occupied the position evacuated by Ishak in Borgu, and we are able to form an estimate of the fighting strength of his columns by the fact that the camp included 174 tents, each tent containing, in accordance with the Turkish model followed by the Moors, twenty fusiliers. He had, therefore, at his command a force of 3480 men armed with muskets in a country in which the native army had fallen into a disorganised rabble, badly led, and armed only with bows and arrows. There was no unreasonable arrogance in the supposition that he would be able to do what he pleased.

I will not attempt to follow this or succeeding campaigns in detail. I will only indicate the essential points.

Askia Ishak, intending to fly for safety into the territory of Kebbi, was murdered by pagans in Gurma, and was succeeded in April of 1592 by a supine brother, Mohammed Kagho, who, shortly after his succession, offered to take the oath of fidelity to the Sultan of Morocco. The famine, which has already been mentioned in connection with the history of Kano, was making itself felt, and the Moorish army was reduced during its campaign in the eastern provinces to eat its pack animals. Mahmoud therefore called upon Mohammed Kagho to prove the sincerity of his proposals by coming to the assistance of the troops and providing them with food. Mohammed Kagho ordered all the crops which were ripe in Haussaland to be reaped for the benefit of the enemy, and this was appropriately enough the last exercise ever made of Songhay authority in Haussaland. Mohammed Kagho was required to come in person to the camp of the Moors to make his submission to the Sultan. He did so, and by order of Mahmoud he was treacherously murdered. Of the eighty-three notables who accompanied him the majority were massacred, but a few of the ablest escaped to group themselves round the new Askia, a younger brother of Kagho, who succeeded under the name of Askia Nouh. One of the eighty-three, Suleiman, a cousin of Nouh, was selected by Mahmoud and proclaimed as a rival Askia at the camp near Kuka in Borgu.

From this time until the authority of the Askias altogether disappeared there were always two Askias—one at Timbuctoo, appointed and maintained by the Moors, and used as a puppet when convenient to give a semblance of legitimacy to their acts; the other, representing the wishes of the Songhay people and claiming legitimate descent, maintained himself in some degree of independence in the Viceroyalty of Dandi, which, though it included Kebbi and the practically independent Haussa States, still constituted nominally a portion of the Songhay Empire that never submitted to the Moors.

Askia Nouh formed a seat of government in 1592 near the southern border of the province of Kebbi. During some of his earlier battles Kanta's people, it is said, could hear the sound of the firing. Nouh was of a different temperament from the later Askias, and all the efforts of Mahmoud Zergoun were insufficient to overthrow the resistance which he organised to the advance of the Moors. War continued for two years, during which time the Songhay forces, notwithstanding their inferior arms, obtained many successes. "Numerous and terrible," says the *Tarikh*, "were the combats which took place in this region." On one occasion, at the battle of Birni, Mahmoud lost eighty of his best fusiliers. Famine and climate worked on the side of Askia Nouh. The Moorish army suffered severely. Mahmoud wrote to the Sultan that the whole of his cavalry was destroyed. Six army corps were sent successively in reinforcement, but at the end of two years Mahmoud, still unsuccessful, was forced to withdraw, and to turn his attention to Timbuctoo and the Western Provinces. He left Djouder Pasha at Kagho in the capacity of lieutenant-governor, with the river, along which a chain of fortresses had been constructed, to serve as an eastern boundary. We can imagine the deposed commander-in-chief smiling grimly at the failure of his rival to achieve that which he himself had judged it best not to attempt.

CHAPTER XXXIII

THE SOUDAN UNDER THE MOORS

THE events which recalled Mahmoud Zergoun to the west were of a serious character. The whole country was in disorder. Shortly after the army had marched eastward, in September of 1591, riots had broken out at Timbuctoo, and had continued until the last days of December. The Moors, having some difficulty in holding their own, had called in the help of the Tuaregs of the desert, already employed in ravaging the fertile territory of the Ras-el-Ma, and, with the help of these allies, had put the town to fire and sword. Nevertheless, on the withdrawal of the Tuaregs, the Moors were again driven to take refuge in the fortress which had been built for them by Djouder Pasha. They succeeded in conveying intelligence to Mahmoud of their position, and he detached from his army a force of 324 soldiers under one of his best young generals, who, marching to the relief of the imprisoned garrison, struck terror into Timbuctoo. The town submitted, and took an oath of fidelity to the Sultan of Morocco. After this, peace was for a short time established in Timbuctoo. The roads were opened, and the military forces of the Moors were directed against the Zaghrani and other rebels who were pillaging the surrounding country. Jenné also made its submission, and took the oath of allegiance to the Sultan of Morocco. But the riots were hardly at an end in Timbuctoo before similar disturbances broke out in Jenné. The Moorish Cadi of the town was taken prisoner, and sent in chains to a distant stronghold in the pagan country to the south. The rioters, whose forces were largely composed of pagans, ruled Jenné for a time, and committed many atrocities. They wished to .elect an Askia for themselves, but were dissuaded from that design by the representations of the principal Songhay officials that nobody as yet knew what would be the issue of the fighting between Mahmoud and Askia Nouh. Finally, order was restored in Jenné by the same young general whom Mahmoud had despatched to Timbuctoo, and the heads of the principal rioters, sent as proofs of the success of his operations to the political governor of Timbuctoo, decorated the market-place of that town. Throughout these operations, the native forces do not appear to have been uniformly opposed to the Moors. On the contrary, the officials, at least, appear to have in many instances endeavoured to support their authority. There was no well-organised movement of revolt, but the general condition of the country was fast resolving itself into chaos.

No sooner was Jenné reduced to order, than the Tuaregs, once the allies of the Moors, possessed themselves of a Moorish fortress established in the Ras-el-Ma, and threatened to attack Timbuctoo. The numbers of the Moorish garrison were much reduced, but hearing that an army corps sent from Morocco for the reinforcement of Mahmoud Zergoun was on the way, messengers were sent into the desert to hurry its arrival, and with its timely assistance the Tuaregs were overthrown. The reinforcements were then passed on to Mahmoud Zergoun in the east, and reported to him fully the state of affairs.

Mahmoud Zergoun returned to Timbuctoo in the autumn of 1593. He first occupied himself with an expedition against the Tuaregs, who were again ravaging the Ras-el-Ma, and then turned his attention to the internal affairs of Timbuctoo. He had probably good reason to doubt the sincerity of the official attitude of submission, and so long as riots continued in this and the neighbouring towns he suspected some understanding between the leading citizens and the rioters.

The first requirement which he made, therefore, was that all arms which were in the town should be given up. To ensure a complete surrender, an announcement was made that on a certain day the houses in the town would be searched, with the exception of the houses of the jurisconsults and certain privileged persons. The natural result of such an announcement was that the populace, fearing lest much besides arms would be taken by the soldiery in their search, deposited everything that they had of value with the owners of the exempted houses.

But the measures of Mahmoud ben Zergoun were thorough. The jurisconsults — a term which seems in the narratives of the Soudan to cover all the educated portion of the population—were precisely the class at whom he proposed to strike. When the search for arms in the houses of the populace had been effected, he caused a further announcement to be made that an oath of allegiance to the Sultan of Morocco would be publicly administered in the Sankoré Mosque. The taking of the oath was to be accompanied with all due ceremonial, and three days were allotted for its completion, October the 18th, the 19th, and 20th of 1593.

The two first days of the ceremony are interesting, as showing incidentally to what distance the authority of Songhay at that time extended in the north and west. The first day was entirely occupied by the swearing of the people from Touat, Fezzan, Augila, and the northern regions of the desert; on the second day the oath was taken by people from Walata, Wadan, and the western regions; on the third day none were left to take the oath but the jurisconsults and distinguished residents of Timbuctoo, who were to swear in presence of the assembled people. On that day, when the mosque was full, the doors were suddenly closed. Every one was told to leave the mosque, with the exception of jurisconsults, their friends, and their followers. When none but these remained in the building, Mahmoud

Zergoun ordered the whole of them to be arrested. He then divided them into two groups, and sent them by different roads to the fortress in which they were to be confined.

Whether by accident or by design, one group was massacred. Amongst the victims were representatives of some of the greatest families of the town. The houses of the jurisconsults were then pillaged. Their wives and daughters were subjected to every indignity, and the whole of their wealth, including that deposited with them by the less influential persons of the town, was appropriated by Mahmoud Zergoun to himself. The families of the jurisconsults, after suffering these injuries, were imprisoned, and were kept in confinement for about six months. During this interval the Fulani ruler of the semi-independent province of Masina made the most urgent representations in their favour. Mahmoud, however, rejected his advice, and resolved to deport them to Morocco. This resolution involved the deportation of the whole body of the best society of Timbuctoo. All that was cultivated, all that was enlightened, all that was rich, refined, and influential, was driven out, and the greater number, men, women, and children, were taken in chains across the desert.

The caravan which conveyed them left Timbuctoo on 18th March 1594. The scenes which were witnessed were, we are told, very terrible. Fathers, children, grandchildren, men and women, were made to march together, "pressed close as arrows in a quiver." They were exposed to all the brutality of the Moorish soldiery, and they had a journey of upwards of two months through the desert. Amongst the exiles were the most distinguished men of letters of the Soudan, and the most delicately nurtured women and children of the town. Ahmed Baba, the biographer and historian, who has already been mentioned more than once, and to whom we are indebted for many of the most interesting pages of the *Tarikh*, was among them. Fortunately for him, his fame was so widespread as to command respect in all centres of learning. When he arrived in Morocco he was treated with the respect due to his great reputation, and, though he was not permitted to return to Timbuctoo for many years, he was given practical freedom in Morocco, and allowed to form a school, where he continued the life of study and of teaching which he had led in the Soudan. Many others were less fortunate, and the note is to be found in more than one biography of his distinguished contemporaries: "He died a martyr in Morocco."

It is interesting, in the midst of all that the exiles had lost, to find them chiefly concerned for the destruction of their libraries. "I," said Ahmed Baba afterwards to the Sultan of Morocco, "had the smallest library of any of my friends, and your soldiers took from me 1600 volumes." Others, those who in the happier days had so generously lent their books to all who needed them, lost every volume that they possessed. Unfortunately, while other forms of wealth were greedily appropriated, the contents of the libraries were destroyed.

The sack of Timbuctoo was the signal for the letting loose of all the evils of lawless tyranny upon the country. From this time the history of the Soudan becomes a mere record of riot, robbery, and decadence. The appropriation to himself of the immense wealth of Timbuctoo did not redound to the ultimate advantage of Mahmoud ben Zergoun. The caravan deporting all the distinguished exiles of Timbuctoo arrived in Morocco on the 1st of June 1594. With it arrived information which led the Sultan to understand the extent of the wealth which had been confiscated, in comparison to which the 100,000 gold pieces sent to him as the royal share was as nothing. Informers further carried to him reports of the independent arrogance of Mahmoud ben Zergoun, from which it was not difficult to draw the deduction that he aimed at nothing less than the independent sovereignty of the Soudan. "When any one speaks to him of the Sultan," said one report, "he draws his sword half out of the scabbard, and says, 'Here is the Sultan!'" The indignation of Muley Hamed knew no bounds, and he despatched a new Pasha, Mansour Abdurrahman, to the Soudan with orders to arrest Mahmoud ben Zergoun and put him to an ignominious death.

With this sentence, of which he was of course quickly informed, hanging over his head, Mahmoud determined to make what he could of his position. By the cruel licence of his rule, the western part of the Soudan had become too hot to hold him. The Fulani ruler of the province of Masina, who had interceded urgently, but vainly, in favour of the noble families of Timbuctoo, had revolted against the Moors. The once prosperous territory of Jenné was also in perpetual disorder. After a short campaign against Masina, of which, though it was accompanied by widespread massacre of the peaceful population and destruction of the crops, the result was practically nil, Mahmoud resolved to rally all his forces for a campaign against the still independent Askia of Songhay in the east, and to put the greatest possible distance between himself and the avenging emissary of the Sultan.

Askia Nouh, having in the meantime strengthened his own position in the province of Dandi, and entered into close alliance with Kebbi on his northern frontier, had succeeded in forcing the chain of Moorish fortresses at a place called Kolen on the Niger, and advanced into the Bend of the Niger, where he awaited the coming of Mahmoud. Mahmoud called upon Djouder to join him with all available forces from Kagho. But Djouder finding a suitable excuse, Mahmoud, who seems in the first instance to have been successful and to have possessed himself again of the territory of Gurma and Borgu, pressed on in an easterly direction, taking with him the dummy Askia Suleiman as far as the rocks of Almena. Unless there exist some other rocks of Almena not mentioned, so far as I have been able to ascertain, by any other writer, these must have been the rocks already alluded to once or twice, in the province of Zaria, where in very ancient days a colossal statue is said to have been carved. The spot is interesting, because it marks the farthest extension of the conquest of the Moors in Haussaland.

Mahmoud camped at the foot of the rocks, which were strongly held by pagan troops. He determined, much against the advice of Askia Suleiman, to whom the country was well known, to endeavour to storm the position by a night attack. Suleiman represented that nothing short of certain death could result. Mahmoud listened to no advice. Death lay behind him as well as in front. He selected a storming party of his best men, and in the early hours of the morning made the attempt. The result was as Askia Suleiman had predicted—Mahmoud himself was among the first to fall, pierced by many arrows. In the attempt to rescue his body his men were put to flight. The pagans cut off his head and sent it to Askia Nouh, who in his turn sent it to Kanta, the King of Kebbi, and it was exposed on the end of a stake in the market-place of Lika for a very long time. Suleiman the Askia rallied the Moorish troops and effected a hurried retreat, ultimately succeeding in joining Djouder, under whose orders the troops remained until the arrival of Mansour from Morocco.

In 1595 the combined Moorish troops, under the command of Djouder Pasha, made one final and successful attempt to deal with what remained of the Songhay Empire, and in a great battle which took place between them and Askia Nouh in the Bend of the Niger in June of that year, the Songhay army was hopelessly defeated and put to flight, leaving the population at the mercy of the Moors. The people were carried into captivity, and placed by the Moors under the jurisdiction of Askia Suleiman.

Djouder now became the ruling power of the Soudan. The new Pasha Mansour died, poisoned, it is said, by Djouder's orders, when he was on the eve of a further expedition against Dandi. His successor, Mohammed Taba, also about to march into the eastern province, died, poisoned, again it is said by orders of Djouder. The next general, Mostafa, died, strangled by orders of Djouder. There would be no interest in following further the details of the history of the Moorish conquest of the Soudan. It is enough to say that nominal Askias continued to succeed each other on the south-eastern district, which for a long time kept the name of Dandi, while attempts to invade Haussaland by a more northern route were vigorously and successfully opposed by the independent Sultans of Kebbi. The domination of the Moors may therefore be said to have never spread more than nominally beyond the south-eastern Bend of the River Niger.

In the west the history of the Moorish dominions presents a record of ceaseless fighting, accompanied by the destruction of all that was civilised and admirable in the Soudan. Djouder, the best of the Pashas, who knew his own mind and could keep his rude soldiery in order, even though his methods were somewhat trenchant, returned to Morocco in 1599. He was a loyal soldier and servant of his sovereign. He was also an able administrator, and had he been properly supported he would have converted the Soudan into a rich dependency of Morocco. As it was, he was made the object during his stay in the Soudan of ceaseless cabals. In 1599 his counsels were, however, needed nearer to the throne. He was recalled with honour, and he returned no more to Timbuctoo.

After him Pasha succeeded Pasha, each to be the victim of military revolt and civil misrepresentation, while misrule prevailed in the Soudan until, in 1612, the last Pasha appointed by Morocco was deposed by the troops, who put their general in his place. After 1612 the army in the Soudan elected its own rulers. The tribute to the Sultan was not paid, the country conquered at so much cost became independent of Morocco, and the native populations of the Western Soudan, barred from all access to civilisation, fell under the despotism of a purely military tyranny. From this date their descent in the scale of nations was rapid and inevitable. By the end of the seventeenth century they had become practically what they now are.

CHAPTER XXXIV

THE SOUDAN CLOSED TO THE WESTERN WORLD

AHMED BABA records that the Sultan Muley Zidan, son and successor to Muley Hamed, told him at a later period that, from the time of Pasha Djouder to that of Pasha Suleiman, his father, Muley Hamed, had sent in different army corps 23,000 of his best soldiers into the Soudan, and added: "All this was a pure loss. The whole of the men perished in the Soudan, with the exception of 500 who returned to Morocco and died in that town." As a matter of fact, the Sultan was ill-informed. His armies, as we have seen, had not perished in the Soudan, but had simply cut themselves off from their allegiance, and had formed in the southern countries an independent system of military brigandage of which the remains exist to the present day.

But for all practical purposes the Soudan itself was from this date lost to the world. Its military tyrants had their own reasons for breaking off relations with Morocco. Morocco in turn was cut off by the religious sentiment of the Western world from all connection with Southern Europe, and the political rivalry of the Turks deprived her at the same time of the position which she might otherwise have occupied upon the Barbary coast. The Saracens, whose rule had once extended from the borders of China to the western coast of Spain, had become an outcast race, the seat of whose dwindling monarchy was to be looked for, if anywhere, in Morocco, and whose representatives, wandering at hazard through the desert wastes of Africa and Arabia, hardly knew to which of the cardinal points to set their faces when they desired to turn themselves towards home.

While access to the civilised world was barred to the western portion of the Soudan, the most easterly states, Bornu and Haussaland, still kept their touch through the Tripoli-Fezzan route with the old markets of Egypt and Arabia. Whatever they had of external civilisation still came to them by that route from the north-east, and the influence permeated through them to the rest of the Soudan. But the influence was the influence of Turkey, and it is unnecessary to dwell on the difference between the Ottoman Empire from the sixteenth century onwards, and the civilisation of the Egyptian and the Arab which it had overthrown. Rome in the great days of the republic might as fitly be compared with Italy after the conquest by the Huns.

Nevertheless, though cut off in the sixteenth century, alike by the triumph of Mohammedanism in the east, and by the downfall of Mohammedanism in the west of Europe, from all true touch with northern centres of civilisation, the Soudan could not unlearn the lesson of centuries. It continued to keep its face turned blankly to the north. I have endeavoured to show that throughout its history the touch of the Soudan with the world had been maintained ever through the desert to the north. Everything that was interesting, its new races, its religions, its science, its literature, its commerce, its wars, had come to it from the north. It faced north to civilisation. And behind it to the south there had always been the unknown, the barbaric, the uninhabitable. It is no doubt this last qualification which maintained the character of the equatorial region in regard to the other two. From about the latitude of 7° southwards the climate of the Western Soudan became practically uninhabitable for those finer races which, whether they derived their origin from Egypt or elsewhere, required a good climate in which to attain to their natural limits of perfection. The Copts have a saying that "in the beginning when God created things he added to everything its second." "'I go to Syria,' said Reason; 'I go with you,' said Rebellion. 'I go to Egypt,' said Abundance; 'I accompany you,' said Submission. 'I go to the desert,' said Poverty; 'I will go with you,' said Health." Barren though it was, the reputation of the desert which lay to the north had been a reputation of health from time immemorial. It had its dangers, but all that escaped from them alive was the better for the experience. For those who knew how to traverse it, its sands were but as the sea, and its edges were the most favoured portions of the Soudan. In proportion as the fertile belt receded from the desert it became unhealthy and unsuitable to the habitation of the higher races.

I have tried to show that, through the whole of the history of these higher races, their tendency had been to drive southwards before them everything that was weak or degraded or outworn. All the lower human types to be met with in the country went southwards into the equatorial belt, where frequent rain and the swampy overflow of rivers running to the coast develops a malarial climate unsuitable to higher activities. In the early tradition, quoted by Herodotus, pigmy races seem to have inhabited the country of the Middle Niger. At the present day they are to be found in the regions of the Congo. In the twelfth and thirteenth centuries the cannibal belt extended along the northern slopes of the Kong Mountains to about 12° north latitude. Now, though there are some exceptions, it is rare to find cannibals north of 7°, and the southern base of the Kong Mountains may be taken as the limit of habitation of the pure negro.

The movements of religion will, I think, be proved, when research has obtained clearer results than can now be securely claimed, to have corresponded to the movements of race. Fetishism, which is now to be met with chiefly in the strip lying between the Kong Mountains and the coast, extended at one period to the north of Songhay and Haussaland. It has been related in the early myths of Gao, of Kano, of Daura, that the killing of the fetish and the substitution of a higher form of religion was the beginning of their recorded history. This higher form of paganism, which would appear to have been derived from sources similar to those that furnished the religions of Phœnicia, Egypt, and Arabia, seems gradually, at some very early period, to have pushed fetishism southward before it, and to have held the ground to the north until, in the four hundred years between the tenth and the fourteenth centuries, Mohammedanism was generally accepted along the northern border. The higher form of paganism then suffered the fate which it had itself inflicted upon fetishism. It was driven south, and in turn drove fetishism farther before it, until, as in the present day, the religions of West Africa could almost be defined by latitudinal lines. If, following the opinion quoted in the earlier portion of this book from a distinguished French authority, we take 10° as the most southerly limit of Mohammedanism, and give 7°, as I think we may be justified in doing, as the farthest extension northwards of fetishism, we get three degrees, from 7° to 10°, in which the higher forms of paganism may be held still to prevail. As a matter of fact, these latitudinal divisions will be proved to be too arbitrary. M. de Lauture wrote upwards of half a century ago, and Mohammedan influence has since his day extended farther south. On the other hand, the higher paganism also extends in places farther north than the limit which he assigned. In the Nigerian Provinces of Zaria, Bautchi, and Yola, through which the tenth parallel extremity passes, but which extend to and even beyond 11°, many tribes of pagans still exist. And I have little doubt that the same observation would hold good in French territory farther west, with which I am unacquainted.

The general drift, however, of the observation is, I think, sound, and it is with this that we are for the moment concerned. There have been evidently three stages in the history of West Africa, to which three great religious movements have corresponded. There was a first and very early period of what I may call pure negroidism, to which the religion of the fetish corresponded. During this period pigmy races occupied the Middle Niger, and fetish worship prevailed upon its banks. There was a second period, still very early, of occupation by peoples whose origin is variously stated to have been from India, Babylon, Persia, ancient Egypt, and Phœnicia, and with this occupation came a form of paganism of which the rites, still practised, have points of similarity with what we know of the worship of Astarte, Jupiter-Ammon, and Isis. There was a third period of Arab influence and subsequent conquest, of which the beginning may be placed in the ninth or tenth century of our era, that was accompanied by the spread of the Mohammedan religion. The Soudan, under the higher form of paganism, attained, as its parent nations in the north and east had attained, to a relatively high stage of civilisation. Indeed, the Fulani conquerors of Haussaland in the nineteenth century put forward the unfounded claim that, up to the period of their conquest, Mohammedanism was scarcely known in the great cities of the Haussa States. This, as has been shown in the chapters upon Haussaland, was not the case, but undoubtedly paganism of the finer type continued to flourish for a long period, and is now, after a thousand years of Mohammedanism, still to be met with side by side with the faith of Islam. The difference between these two was not so great as the difference between paganism and fetishism. It was fetishism, and fetishism only, which was banished with the lower negroid races to the jungle belt of the coast.

These considerations of the general movement of civilisation in West Africa bring us to an important development in its history. The first chapter of European settlement in the country was opened at a critical moment. During the latter half of the fifteenth century, while the

Turks were pressing upon Eastern Europe and interfering with all the old routes of the Indian and Chinese trade, the Portuguese, in their capacity of an Atlantic people, were making courageous efforts to find another and a safer road by sea to the Eastern markets. Already, as has been seen, they had crept round the shoulder of the African coast, and had made a few cautious settlements upon its shores. In 1497 they attained the object of their desire, and Vasco da Gama doubled the Cape of Good Hope. The date of the expulsion of the Moors from Spain was 1502. Thus, within five years of each other, there happened two events which profoundly influenced the history of the Soudan. The expulsion of the Moors, followed during the sixteenth century by the wars of Charles V. and his successors against Mohammedanism upon the Mediterranean coasts, closed the old means of approach by land to the territories of the finer races of the Soudan. The discovery of the passage of the Cape of Good Hope opened at the same moment new means of approach by sea. It diverted the whole stream of European intercourse with the far East, and as the caravan trade of Egypt, Persia, and Arabia sank into insignificance, the maritime trade of the Atlantic rose in importance. The Atlantic Ocean became a highway of the world, and while, all unaware of the change, the peoples of the interior continued to look vainly towards the closed avenues of the north—the west coast of Africa fronting on the Atlantic began to face no longer north but south to civilisation. The sea was open to all who had ships to sail upon it. Thus, when Europe approached West Africa, it was upon the coast that her adventurers landed. It was with coast natives that she had to deal—natives who had from time immemorial been enslaved—and it was in the coast climate that her settlements were made. The coast belt was too broad for her to traverse. Its inhabitants were savage, its climate was deadly, its jungle impenetrable without the auxiliary force of steam. For upwards of 400 years

Europe held the coast. Slaves were hunted for her in the far interior. Ivory was shot for her, gold was washed for her; but Europe herself, the civilisation, the order, the justice for which her name now stands, penetrated no farther than perhaps twenty miles inland.

Thus not only did the finer races of the Soudan lose touch with the civilised world, but the civilised world lost also touch with them. Their records were preserved by Arab writers, and modern Europe, in its religious fervour, had banished Arabic from its literature. The traditions of intercourse with the Soudan had been all traditions of Saracen Egypt and of Moorish Spain. Turks had destroyed the one, Ferdinand the Catholic had obliterated the other. By the end of the sixteenth century the mystery of Africa had closed round these ancient races, and they were lost to history for a period that was to last three hundred years.

CHAPTER XXXV

EUROPE IN WEST AFRICA

THE first chapters of European intercourse with the West Coast of Africa are not chapters of which we have any reason to be proud. I do not propose to relate in detail the history of early European settlement upon the coast, but the relations of civilisation with the natives had certain general characteristics which it is necessary very briefly to indicate. They cannot, however, be fairly indicated without a constant recollection of the fact that the races with whom Europe had now to deal were not those fine races of the northern territories known to ancient historians as Nigritia, but the generally negroid inhabitants of that strip which was for a long time included under the appellation of the Guinea Coast. Barbot, a Frenchman, who traded with West Africa in various capacities for upwards of twenty years towards the end of the seventeenth century, and who, writing both in French and English, is perhaps to be counted as the best and most voluminous historian of the coast, defines Nigritia as extending northward from 8° to 23°, and Guinea as extending southwards from 8° to the coast. The history of European settlement deals exclusively with the southern strip.

The progress of the Reformation in Europe throughout the sixteenth century tended to deprive Papal decrees of the authority which once attached to them, and throughout that and the succeeding century the nations of the Atlantic coast competed eagerly with each other for a share of the newly-opened African trade. With the exception of France, where, however, a great industrial population professed the Protestant faith, the countries which contested with Portugal the validity of the papal gift to her of all countries which she might discover to the east of the Azores, were of the Reformed religion. France justified herself, perhaps, by the argument that she had prior claims, for it is stoutly asserted on her behalf, and the claim is admitted by some foreign writers, that during the fourteenth century, and before the approach of the Portuguese, French adventurers had discovered and French companies had traded with the West Coast of Africa. Such trade had not, however, according to the accounts which are given of it, proved successful, and all traces of French occupation had disappeared before the Portuguese discoverers of the middle of the fifteenth century made Europe acquainted with the coast.

Whatever may be the truth of this story, France was among the earliest and the most successful of the competitors of the Portuguese upon the coast. She was very shortly followed by the English, Dutch, Danes, and Prussians. The first Portuguese company was formed in 1444 for the purpose of exploring the coast, and it initiated the European trade in slaves by sea. Both Spain and Portugal had long been supplied with slaves from the Soudan by land.

Spain, having its hands full elsewhere, willingly entered into an agreement with Portugal not to interfere with its possessions in Africa. Towards the end of the fifteenth century the King of Portugal formed a Guinea Company, and caused forts to be built at Accra, Axim, Elmina, and at other places up and down the coast. The Governor-General of these forts resided at Elmina. No attempt was made or could be made to penetrate inland, the natives being barbarous, and most of the way being, as Barbot tells us, "through vast, thick forests, swarming with robbers and wild beasts." This part of the coast, now known as the Gold Coast, was the best part of the coast for gold, and though inland wars often spoilt the trade, the position of Governor at Elmina was regarded as one in which a European could speedily accumulate vast wealth. It was as a rule bestowed upon some king's favourite, and by the gradual operation of this system the garrison, we are told, came to be commonly comprised of "lewd and debauched persons," intent on making speedy fortunes. The Portuguese Government also used the West Coast from a very early period as a place of deportation for convicts. No wonder, therefore, says Barbot, "that the histories of those times give an account of unparalleled violences and inhumanities committed there by those insatiable Portuguese."

Barbot does not over-estimate the character of the blacks with whom the Portuguese had to deal. "They are," he says, "generally extremely sensual, knavish, revengeful, impudent liars, impertinent, gluttonous, extravagant in their expressions, and giving ill language, luxurious beyond expression, and so intemperate that they drink brandy as if it were water, deceitful in their dealings with Europeans and no less with their own neighbours, even to the selling of one another for slaves if they have an opportunity, and, as has been hinted before, so very lazy that rather than work for their living they will rob and commit murders on the highways and in the woods and deserts. . . . It is very dangerous travelling in that country. . . . They are so very dexterous and expert at stealing that the ancient Lacedæmonians might have learnt from them the art." Nevertheless this certainly open-minded judge thought that the Portuguese treated them too badly for human nature of any sort to endure.

In 1587 the blacks rose against the barbarities of the Portuguese, surprised the fort of Accra, and razed it to the ground. The French, who had as yet only a very slight footing upon the Guinea Coast, seized the occasion for intervention, made the most of their opportunities, and from that date the power of the Portuguese declined. The French Senegal Company established itself successfully upon the Senegal, and became in the course of the following century the principal French company in West Africa. A French West India Company also traded to the Slave and Ivory Coast, and the French company on the Senegal established the tradition, well maintained by Frenchmen in later years, of pressing further than other Europeans into the interior. They did not, however, accomplish anything which amounted to real communication with Nigritia. All that was known of the inland country were vague rumours of Arabs and white people riding upon mules and asses, and living in great state at Timbuctoo and the richer of its sister cities. The accounts of Leo Africanus and of Marmol were both, we must remember, published during the sixteenth century. Imperfect as they are, they represent a certain amount of information about the interior which, though it was not gained from the coast, must have been presumably in the possession of all persons interested in the coast. Some knowledge of the internal country was, of course, felt to be very desirable, but writing at the end of the seventeenth century, a hundred years or more after the appearance of the latest of these publications, Barbot explicitly states that "none of the Europeans living along the coast have ever ventured far up the land, it being extraordinarily difficult and dangerous, if not altogether impossible, for Europeans to venture so far into such wild and savage countries."

The Dutch very rapidly followed in the footsteps of the French. The first Dutch venture was conducted by a man of the name of Ericks in 1595. The natives, liking his goods, became more and more restive under Portuguese exactions, and another rising in the year 1600 practically confined Portuguese authority within the walls of their forts. The native chiefs entered into treaties with the Dutch, and in 1624 allowed them to build forts at Moree and Cape Coast. This transaction was made with the Dutch Government, but the forts afterwards passed into the possession of the Dutch West India Company. The Portuguese bitterly accused the Dutch of obtaining their influence over the nations "more by wine and strong liquors than by force of arms," and even here, on the West Coast of Africa, we get the echo of the religious controversies which were raging so furiously in the countries at that time engaged in the Thirty Years' War. The Portuguese had consistently sent many Catholic missionaries among the natives of the coast, and then, as now, commerce and conversion went hand in hand. But the blacks, we are told by Portuguese writers, "being a barbarous people, readily enough swallowed Calvin's poison spread among them, intermixed with merchandise."

It was not long before this attitude of mutual detestation broke out into open war, and on August 29, 1637, the Dutch possessed themselves of the fort of Elmina. From this period the Portuguese were gradually driven from the trade. The Dutch took Axim from them in 1642, and by the end of the century there was only one Portuguese fort left upon the coast. In 1664, on the outbreak of the Dutch war, the English took from the Dutch the fort known now as Cape Coast Castle, with many others. But during the continuation of hostilities, the Dutch under De Ruyter fully revenged themselves, and took all the principal English stations upon the coast, besides recovering their own, with the single exception of Cape Coast Castle. The peace which shortly followed left the Dutch in a very strong position on the coast, where they erected a chain of forts, and, as was the uniform outcome of all operations, "used the natives with great severity." The influence of every European war was, of course, felt upon the coast. As the successes of the Dutch under De Ruyter threatened in 1665 to destroy the English settlements, so in 1677 the French were for a time predominant, and captured all the more important Dutch settlements. Under the Treaty of Nimeguen in 1678 these were, however, given back to Holland.

Denmark and the Electorate of Brandenburgh, two small but also Protestant powers, had their share in the coast trade, and, making friends with the blacks at two or three points of the coast, built forts from which they traded. These were commercial settlements of no great importance, whose local representatives won small respect for themselves upon the coast, and they were at a later period bought out by the English.

The rise of English trade followed close upon the heels of the Dutch. It may perhaps be said to have begun with the famous slave-raiding expeditions of which Hawkins relates the details without any shame, and of which Queen Elizabeth was not too proud to share the profit.

Hakluyt, in describing the initiation of the English trade, shows clearly enough in what good esteem it was held. "Master John Hawkins," he tells us, "having made divers voyages to the Isles of the Canaries, and there by his good and upright dealing being grown in love and favour with the people, informed himself . . . that negroes were very good merchandise in Hispaniola, and that store of negroes might easily be had upon the coast of Guinea." He accordingly "resolved with himself to make trial thereof, and communicated that devise with his worshipful friends of London, namely, with Sir Lionel Ducket, Sir Thomas Lodge, Mr. Gunson, his father-in-law, Sir William Winter, Mr. Bromfield, and others. All which persons liked so well of his intention that they became liberal contributors and adventurers in the action. For which purpose there were three good ships immediately provided." These good ships sailed under Hawkins' command in October of 1562, touching at Sierra Leone, where Hawkins "stayed some good time, and got into his possession, partly by the sword and partly by other means, to the number of 300 negroes at the least. With this praye he sailed over the ocean sea to the island of Hispaniola." His venture proved so profitable that, in addition to lading his own ships, he laded two other hulks with hides, sugars, ginger, pearls, and other commodities of the islands. "So with prosperous success, and much gayne to himself and the aforesaid adventurers, he came home, and arrived in the month of September 1563."

The names quoted by Hakluyt are evidently names to be respected, yet the account given by Hawkins himself of his methods in a subsequent expedition of 1567 differs in nothing from the accounts given by eye-witnesses of Arab slave-raids of the present day. He not only traded, he raided. "There came to us," he says, "a negro sent from a king oppressed by other kings, his neighbours, desiring our aide, with promise that as many negroes as by these warres might be obtained, as well of his part as of ours, should be at our pleasure." As a result, "I went myselfe, and with the helpe of the king of our side assaulted the towne both by land and sea, and very hardly with fire (their houses being covered with dry palm leaves) obtained the towne and put the inhabitants to flight, where we took 250 persons, men, women, and children; and by our friend, the king of our side, there were taken 600 prisoners, whereof we hoped to have had our choise, but the negro (in which nation is seldom or never found truth) meant nothing lesse." The negro king decamped in the night with his prisoners, and Hawkins was left with the "few which we had gotten ourselves." It is interesting to observe, in Hawkins' letters describing these and other expeditions, the perfect reliance of the mariners upon the Almighty to be on their side, and to bring them out of all their dangers with "good store of negroes" for sale. On one occasion they were becalmed for eighteen days, and in great danger of death from starvation, having so great a company of negroes on board; but "Almighty God, who never suffereth His elect to perish," sent, we are told, a special wind to carry the slave-raiders safe to their destination, and when they reached it they obtained licence to sell their cargo on the ground that their vessel was "a shippe of the Queen's Majestie of England," and that the cargo "pertained to our Queen's Highnesse." Church and State watched over their operations, and they worked in an odour of the highest sanctity.

Another famous English sailor, Drake, who as a young man accompanied Hawkins on one of his earlier expeditions to the coast, was more humane or more fastidious in his tastes than his great leader, for after one experience he never again went slave-raiding.

Except for a patent granted in 1588 to Exeter merchants, the English trade was left during the reign of Queen Elizabeth in the hands of individuals. The first charter to an English company for the purpose of trading to the coast was granted by King James in 1619. The charter was supposed to convey exclusive rights, but the private merchants who were already interested continued, in spite of regulations, to trade on their own account, and with many complaints of the "interlopers" who robbed them of their profits, the Chartered Company acknowledged its failure and withdrew. The Dutch West India Company, being either better organised or more vigorous in holding its own against "interlopers," from whom it also suffered, in the meantime pursued with success its design of supplementing the Portuguese, and became a very important power upon the coast. Charles I. granted a fresh charter to another English company. But England was shortly afterwards distracted with civil and foreign war, and this company had no better fortune. The Dutch and the Danes profited by the opportunity to push their West African trade. They not only increased the number of their forts and settlements, but being well supported by their respective Governments, and protected by what was then the best navy in the world, they seized English merchant ships, and inflicted damage to an extent afterwards estimated at £300,000.

The Chartered Company being of course ruined, a petition was presented to Parliament shortly after the restoration of Charles II., which stated the condition of affairs. At the same time it was represented by Ministers to the King that his American Colonies were languishing for want of labour. The King himself, therefore, "for the purpose," as a contemporary account informs us, "of supplying those plantations with blacks," publicly invited subscriptions for the formation of a joint-stock company, of which the object was to be the recovery and carrying on of the trade to Africa. The new company was formed under the title of "the Royal Adventurers of England," and received a charter in 1662. But it had no better luck than its predecessors. War broke out with Holland in 1664. It was during this war that the Dutch Admiral de Ruyter swept the African coast, ravaged the English settlements, destroyed their factories, containing goods valued at £200,000, and took their ships. The fort known now as Cape Coast Castle, taken by the English from the Dutch, was alone, as has been said, successfully held, and remained in English hands on the conclusion of the peace. This was the third Chartered Company ruined in the West African trade.

On the conclusion of the war, King Charles again invited subscriptions for the formation of a new company. His appeal was responded to, and in 1672 a company, of which the name and fame have lingered in the history of English trade, was formed under the title of "the Royal African Company."

Where so many others had been foiled this company at last succeeded, and the permanent establishment of English influence on the West African coast was effected by it in the latter part of the seventeenth century. The new company opened and developed a valuable export trade of English goods to the West Coast of Africa. It also, according to its own statement, presented at a later date to Parliament, "furnished the new American Colonies with frequent supplies of considerable numbers of slaves at very moderate rates, and that in so encouraging a manner that it sometimes trusted the planters to the value of £100,000 and upward till they could conveniently pay the same." Besides this three-cornered trade of goods to Africa and slaves to America, the company also brought home "ivory, red-wood, and gold dust in such quantity that it frequently coined 40,000 to 50,000 guineas at a time, with the elephant on them for a mark of distinction." In fine, its trade not only produced a dividend, but also "gave many other public and national advantages to the whole kingdom, and the British plantations in general."

This flourishing state of things of course attracted "interlopers," who, without regard for the company's charter, carried on trade. The usual course followed. Protests were made on the one side against interference, on the other side against privilege. Every opportunity was taken by outsiders to find fault with the company, and by the company to prove that, in the best interests of the public, they should be allowed to keep their monopoly. Finally, public opinion proved too strong, and that happened which must always happen to the best of chartered companies, when the field which it exploits is widely profitable. The general trading community insisted upon having its share, and in 1697 permission was granted to the "interlopers" by vote of Parliament to trade to the West Coast, on payment of a percentage to the Royal African Company for the maintenance of its forts and castles for defensive purposes. One of the principal arguments used in support of the adoption of this policy was that the plantations would be supplied with slaves in greater numbers and at cheaper rates than could be expected from the company alone.

Many traders profited by this permission. The result, according to a somewhat rueful report of the company, was that the natives advanced the price of slaves and beat down the price of English manufactures, while the American planters, having to pay a higher price for their labour, advanced the price of sugar. The Royal African Company had to raise £180,000 of fresh capital, and in 1707 we find the company petitioning Queen Anne to recommend their case to the consideration of the Lords Commissioners for Trade and Plantations. Nevertheless trade flourished, and notwithstanding the strong presentation of their case by the company, and the many evils which unquestionably attended the throwing open of the coast, we may be permitted to doubt whether West African trade would to-day be valued in the substantial millions which its total has reached, if the monopoly of the Royal African Company had been sustained.

CHAPTER XXXVI

THE EUROPEAN SLAVE TRADE

THE West African coast history of the eighteenth century is mainly a history of trade, and as the most profitable trade was done in slaves, it is hardly an over statement to say that it is a history of the slave trade. It may be remembered that one of the most valued privileges conceded to Great Britain at the Peace of Utrecht in 1712 was the Assiento contract, or the right to supply the Spanish colonies on the American coast with slaves. In that treaty, which may be said to have laid the foundation of the British Colonial Empire, other British colonies and settlements obtained other advantages. The concession of a monopoly in the Spanish slave trade was the special advantage pressed for by the section of the country which was interested in the West African trade, and was obtained for them by British diplomacy in satisfaction of what was felt to be their legitimate claim. Other European nations were no less active in the same traffic, and thus it came about that whereas in the interior the influence of ancient and medieval civilisation, operating from the north, had been an influence tending to the development of all that is admirable in the history of nations, in the south the modern relation of Europeans to the natives of the coast was simply as the relation of beasts of prey to their victims.

The victims were generally of a very low order of humanity. Europe made its settlements at the extreme southern edge of what may be called the equatorial slums of Western Africa. Europeans seldom lost sight of the sea, and European influence scarcely extended beyond the forts which protected it. The nearer to the coast the worse was the native type. Barbot, who was of course himself a slave-dealer, tells his readers pathetically that "'Tis hard to conceive what patience is required to deal with these brutes." They were all gross pagans, worshipping snakes, consecrated trees, the sea, and many lesser objects. This was the fetishism which had been driven southwards at an early period from Gao, Daura, Kano, and other towns in the northern territories. We find here also in the seventeenth century—as at the present day—traces of the paganism which was expelled by the Mohammedans from Ghana in the eleventh century. "Almost every town or village has near to it a small consecrated grove to which the governors and people frequently resort to make their offerings." And here too we find, in the so-called monumental stones carved to represent half a human figure, which are revered to the present day, a reminiscence of the Teraphim of ancient Egypt. The people of Benin were in the seventeenth century "the most genteel and polite of the coast." Barbot gives a very interesting account of their capital town. But on festive occasions human sacrifices were made on a vast scale.

At the back of Cape Verde, between the Senegal and the Gambia, the Fulani had a "little empire" inland, and the natives reckoned their king to be the "most potent prince in all those countries." It was said that he could put from 40,000 to 50,000 men into the field. The coast was, however, densely wooded, and swarmed with wild beasts. The character given by Barbot of the coast natives at this district has been already quoted. Sorcerers, idolaters, robbers, and drunkards, they were indeed "no better than their country." At the back of the Gambia the natives were "very savage, cruel, and treacherous;" they were "gross pagans, said to worship demons more than any other blacks;" and a cannibal people, driven southwards about the year 1505—which we may remember was the date of some of the great Askia's conquests—perpetually warred upon the older inhabitants. "On the Ivory Coast the natives," says Barbot, "are very savage cannibals who file their teeth. The place might yield a good trade," he adds, "but for the savagery of the natives, who have massacred at different times English, Dutch, and Portuguese." Though for the sake of the ivory all European nations traded at this coast, no settlements were made and the ships' crews "dared not land." On the Gold Coast, where the natives were among the most civilised with whom the Europeans dealt, few or none were to be trusted. They were gross pagans, and, like the people of Benin, made human sacrifices. They were generally "of a turbulent temper, very deceitful and crafty, and so continually at war with one another that this was the best part of all the coast for slaves as well as gold," the prisoners being sold immediately on their capture. After some of their quarrels with their neighbours a trader might "ship prisoners as fast as they could be fetched from the shore in a boat." The natives of the Slave Coast were the greatest and most cunning thieves that can be imagined, "therein far exceeding our European pick-pockets, and on the least outrage received would poison the offender." The inhabitants of Biafra farther east were "very gross pagans of a wild temper," and made human sacrifices to the devil. Inland from New Calabar and the Cross River the natives were cannibals, and southwards from this district the country was inhabited by "very low class naked natives" to Gaboon, where the inhabitants, "very savage and animal in their habits," were "barbarous, wild, bloody, and treacherous." These were the most wretchedly poor and miserable of any in Guinea. They were excessively fond of brandy, and "married indifferently any female member of their family, including their mothers."

These wretched beings were worth £40 apiece in the market of Jamaica, and with the ideas that then prevailed it is hardly perhaps surprising that they were regarded as fair prey. Synods of the Churches—Protestant as well as Catholic—countenanced the trade. Two Synods of the Protestant Churches held in France, at Rouen and Alencon in 1637, to consider a question raised by certain "over-scrupulous persons" who "thought it unlawful that many Protestant merchants who had long traded in slaves from Guinea to America should continue that traffic, as inconsistent with Christian charity," decreed after long discussion that slavery, always acknowledged to be of the right of nations, "is not condemned in the Word of God." Therefore they contented themselves with exhorting merchants who had liberty to trade not to abuse that liberty contrary to Christian charity, and not to dispose of those poor infidels except to such Christians as will use them with humanity, and above all will take care to instruct them in the true religion. The "inestimable advantage which the slaves may reap by becoming Christians and saving their souls," was put forward by the righteous of that day as one of the strongest arguments in favour of continuing a traffic which was so profitable as to enlist very powerful support.

How far this reason and the mild advice offered by the Synods of the Churches was likely to influence the Europeans of different nationalities who were locally engaged in the coast trade, may be gathered from the descriptions which are given by Barbot and other contemporaries. The conduct of the Portuguese has already been described. Of the English, Barbot says that the trade of the Royal African Company "daily decays through the ill management of their servants in Guinea, who, to their own vices, add those of the people among whom they live and converse. . . . The fondness of the English for their beloved liquor, punch, is so great, even among the officers and factors, that whatever comes of it, there must be a bowl upon all occasions, which causes the death of many of them. Consequently the garrison (of Cape Coast Castle) becomes very weak, the survivors looking poor and thin, not only the soldiers, but the officers and factors, whose countenances are shrivelled and dismal through ill diet and worse government." The conduct of all Europeans towards the black women was as discreditable as it was injurious to themselves. Rum and spirits were sold in great quantities by the English and Dutch. The Prussians and Danes were even fonder of strong liquor than the English, and their conduct generally was equally bad. The governors of the Danish stations were often men of the meanest extraction, a gunner from the fort being sometimes raised to that position. The unfaithfulness to the Danish Company of their servants was such that "scarce any one of integrity" sent out from Denmark was allowed to live. The Dutch treated the natives with arbitrary cruelty. In return the blacks were often uncivil to strangers, and this "put Europeans upon ravaging the country, destroying their canoes, and carrying off some of their people into captivity." "If," says Barbot, "the negroes be generally crafty and treacherous, it may well be said the Europeans have not dealt with them as becomes Christians, for it is too well known that many of the European nations trading amongst these people have very unjustly and inhumanly, without any provocation, stolen away from time to time abundance of the people, not only in this (the Sierra Leone) coast, but all over Guinea, and when they came on board their ships in a harmless and confiding manner, carried great numbers away to the plantations, and there sold them with the other slaves they had purchased for their goods. . . ." "Certain it is," he says in another place, "that few who can live well at home will venture to repair to the Guinea Coast to mend their circumstances, unless encouraged by large salaries. . . . This must be said, once for all, that the generality of those who look for such employments are necessitous persons who cannot live at home, and are, perhaps, most of them of a temper to improve all opportunities of mending their worldly circumstances without much regard to the principles of Christianity. For without reflecting on particular persons, it may be said that what I have here asserted is sufficiently made out by the irregularity of their lives in those parts, and particularly as to lewdness and excess of drinking. It is almost incredible how many shorten their days by such debauchery."

Agents of this character were not likely to deal over tenderly with their human merchandise. Ships of 300 and 400 tons burden usually took cargoes of from 500 to 800 slaves. A ship carrying 500 slaves needed to take in 100,000 yams, the slaves generally sickening and dying upon any other food. The space which was left for the slaves when such provision was made for feeding them, and for storing a proportionate amount of water, was not great. Here is Bosman's description of the manner in which slaves were shipped at Whydah. After explaining that they were usually prisoners of war, he says: "When these slaves come to Whydah they are put in prison all together, and when we treat concerning buying them, they are all brought out together in a large plain, where, by our surgeons, whose province it is, they are thoroughly examined, and that naked, too, both men and women, without the least distinction or modesty. Those which are approved as good are set on one side. . . . The invalids and the maimed being thrown out, as I have told you, the remainder are numbered, and it is entered who delivered them. In the meanwhile a burning iron, with the arms or name of the companies, lies in the fire, with which ours are marked on the breast. This is done that we may distinguish them from the slaves of the English, French, or others, which are also marked with their mark. . . . They come on board stark naked, as well women as men." Bosman, proud of the superior organisation of the Dutch ships, which he described as being "for the most part clean and neat," while the ships of the English, French, and Portuguese are always "foul and stinking," explains that on these better-class Dutch ships the lodging-place of the slaves is divided into two parts, one for the women and one for the men, and that "here they lie as close together as it is possible for them to be crowded." Barbot, who traded for himself, chiefly in the neighbourhood of New Calabar, says nothing about cleanliness nor separate compartments. He tells us that in that neighbourhood the slaves were "a strange sort of brutish creatures, very weak and slothful, but cruel and bloody in their temper, always quarrelling, biting, and fighting, and sometimes choking and murdering one another without any mercy." Both traders were much disturbed by a widespread belief among the natives that "we buy them only to fatten and afterwards eat them as a delicacy." Barbot tells us that "natives infected with this belief will fall into a deep melancholy and despair, and refuse all sustenance, though never so much compelled and even beaten to oblige them to take some nourishment, notwithstanding all which they will starve to death. . . . And, though I must say I am naturally compassionate, yet have I been necessitated sometimes to cause the teeth of those wretches to be broken, because they would not open their mouths or be prevailed upon by any entreaties to feed themselves, and thus have forced some sustenance into their throats." Many of the slaves came from the back country, and had never even seen the sea.

Those of us who have crossed the Bay of Biscay in bad weather on a return journey from the Tropics, with all the alleviations that can be given by swift transit, comfort, and warm clothing, are in a position to imagine what some of those naked shiploads must have suffered. The death-rate amounted to two, three, and even four hundred out of every five hundred shipped in Guinea. Yet so profitable was the trade that ten ships might often be seen loading slaves in the same port.

The slaves being commonly prisoners of war, the trade had of course the indirect effect of putting a premium upon intertribal fighting. There was indeed scarcely a vice which it did not encourage alike in slaves and slavers. It is interesting to observe, from the records of European intercourse with the coast, that the evil of trading in arms and spirits was very early apparent to the intelligent. Barbot and Bosman both deplore the trade in arms, but the one speaking for the French and English and the other for the Dutch agree in regarding it as inevitable, "since should one nation abstain from the profit of the trade, other nations would only sell the more." "Abundance of firearms, gunpowder, and ball," says Barbot, "are sold by all the trading Europeans, and are a very profitable commodity when the blacks of the coast are at war, yet were it to be wished they had never been carried thither, considering how fatal they have been and will still be upon occasion in the hands of the blacks to Europeans who, for a little gain, furnish them with knives to cut their own throats; of which each nation is sensible enough, and yet none will forbear to carry that commodity which proves so dangerous in the hands of those blacks. The best excuse we have for this ill-practice is that if one does not sell the other will sell them, if the French do not the Dutch will, and if they should forbear it the English or others would do it." The idea of the delegates of seventeen European nations assembled for the purpose of agreeing to limitations to be placed upon the trade of their respective countries was one which had not presented itself to the eyes of the seventeenth century. The International Conferences of Berlin and Brussels belonged to another age.

The effect of the slave trade upon the coast was felt into the far interior, and in the later records of the Haussa States we hear of slaves being hunted for purposes of sale to the black traders from the south, who in turn sold them to Europeans on the coast. Mungo Park's account of his travels in passing from the Gambia to the Niger at the end of the eighteenth century gives a sufficiently sorrowful picture of the condition of populations which had then been ground for two hundred years between the oppression of the European slave trade on the south and the Moorish conquest on the north.

It was only very gradually that the conscience of humanity revolted against a means of making profit so opposed to every conception of freedom and justice. But the movements of thought of the eighteenth century, which emancipated Europe, had also their result upon the West Coast of Africa. There wanted still a few years to the centenary of the Treaty of Utrecht, when the slave trade was abolished, at least in name, in 1807. It was unfortunately far from being abolished in fact, and the greater part of the nineteenth century saw unavailing efforts made by European governments to put an end to the exportation of slaves from Africa by sea.

The early part of the nineteenth century witnessed also determined efforts made by European exploration to penetrate the mystery of Central Africa. England took a brilliant part in this movement on the West Coast, and, in the early part of the century, the principal exploring parties were led by Englishmen. Mungo Park, sent out by the Royal Geographical Society, made his first journey, travelling in from the Gambia, in 1796, and struck the Niger at Segou. His second journey ended fatally at Boussa in 1805. Between 1810 and 1825 English expeditions made many attempts to reach the interior from the coast. When René Caillié, the French explorer, who eventually reached Timbuctoo in 1828, disembarked at St. Louis in 1816, with the intention of penetrating, if possible, to the Niger, he found that "nothing was talked of there but the English expeditions into the interior." It was with the expedition of Major Grey in 1818 that he first started for the interior. I find it stated in a French account that England spent upwards of £760,000 at this time upon exploration.

Efforts to reach the interior were made from the north coast as well as from the south. Hornemann attempted in 1810 to cross the continent from Tripoli to Ashantee, and reached the Haussa States, travelling by the Tripoli-Fezzan route, but died of dysentery in Nupe. A little later Lyon and Ritchie went in from Tripoli, and in the years 1818–20 explored the Fezzan as far south as lat. 23°. Ritchie died at Murzuk, but Lyon brought back a good deal of information about the Fezzan and the country to the south, including Bornu and the Haussa States. Their work was carried further by Major Denham, Captain Clapperton, and Dr. Oudney, who went in together by the Tripoli-Fezzan road, and succeeded in the years 1822–23 and 1824 in reaching Bornu and the Haussa States, travelling as far west as Sokoto, and as far south as the tenth parallel of latitude. The others returned safely—Oudney died in Bornu. Captain Clapperton, making a second journey by way of the West Coast in 1826, died at Sokoto. Major Laing, going in also from the north, reached Timbuctoo, and was murdered in the desert a little way from the town in 1828. The most famous of the expeditions from the north was that carried out by Dr. Barth and Mr. Richardson at the instance of Lord Palmerston between the years 1850–55, in which, though Mr. Richardson died, Dr. Barth was able to collect a mass of valuable information, afterwards published in five bulky volumes, which form the standard work upon the interior of the West African Soudan.

It was reserved for Clapperton's faithful servant, Richard Landor, to navigate the Lower Niger from the Boussa Rapids to its mouth in 1832. From this time onwards, expeditions were renewed upon the coast. The French took an active part in exploring the territory in which they were politically interested, and a certain amount of information with regard to the interior was acquired.

The change of civilised opinion with regard to the slave trade led in the meantime to corresponding changes in the administration of European settlements on the West Coast. Already in 1783 the trading rights of France in the Gambia had been made the subject of exchange for the trading rights of England in the Senegal, thus preparing the way for the modern system of "spheres of influence." Shortly after the conclusion of the war with France in 1815, the British Government took over from the merchant companies the various forts and stations established by British enterprise, and created a colony of "West Africa Settlements" that included the whole of the coast in which English trade was interested. This initiated the system, which, however, was not for some time fully carried into effect, of Crown Colonies upon the coast.

In 1843 the colonies of Gambia and the Gold Coast were erected by letters-patent into separate colonies, having each their executive and judicial establishments. In 1850 the Danish forts on the Gold Coast were purchased by Great Britain from the King of Denmark, and with the forts the Danish Protectorate was transferred to England. In 1861 Lagos became British by cession from the natives. In 1871 the Dutch finally abandoned to Great Britain the whole of their rights upon the coast. With various changes in the administration of the settlements themselves the existing colonies of Gambia, Sierra Leone, Gold Coast, and Lagos, came into being, and trade with the West Coast in more legitimate products than human flesh was carried on under the local protection of an Imperial flag.

Unfortunately, the long-indulged taste for spirits, and the natural desire of the natives to possess firearms, gave a predominance to these two articles of European export, which up to the end of the nineteenth century continued to produce deplorable results, and to lower alike the utility and the value of European dealings with the coast. It was not until the conscience of Europe, revolting at last against this evil as against the slave trade, made itself heard in the international agreements signed at Berlin and Brussels in 1885 and 1890, that any determined effort was made to restrict by legislation the limits of this injurious traffic. The result of this movement of opinion may already be very plainly traced in the different character which trade with West Africa has assumed within the last twenty or five-and-twenty years. In the earlier part of the century, when the British Government assumed the duty of watching over the suppression of the slave trade, other trade fell to an almost nominal figure. A return presented to the House of Commons in 1865 shows the total value of exports from the West African settlements to amount to £650,000, while the total value of imports into the settlements amounted to £533,000. The cost of the very elementary government which was maintained in the four settlements for the purpose of promoting this trade and suppressing the slave trade, inclusive of the squadron maintained in West African waters, amounted to a charge on the Treasury of about £320,000.

The later history of these colonies is sufficiently well known to render it unnecessary for me to deal with it here. I must only guard myself from seeming to attach to modern traders with West Africa the slur which undoubtedly did attach to their predecessors of an earlier period. The trade of the coast of late years has been placed upon a much wider, and I think it may be said without fear of contradiction by events, an ever-widening basis. It is associated with some of the most respectable names in commerce, and under enlightened and beneficent direction may not improbably become one of the most valuable fields of British industrial development. Since the period of which I write, a body of educated coast natives has also been developed which would have a just right to be profoundly wounded were they to be confused with the cannibal savage who lives not far from them in the interior. In this connection, the names of Bishop Crowther and Dr. Blyden will occur to every mind, and if among the coloured officials and professional men of the coast colonies all have not attained to the same reputation, there are no doubt many who merit the same distinction. But these are to be met with only within the limits of the European settlements. What I have said in regard to the earlier trade is, I think, sufficient to prove the statement with which I set out, that if the original native of the coast is inferior to the native of the interior, the influence exercised by Europe on the coast has been very different from that exercised by Europe in the interior in days when black poets were welcomed at the court of Cordova, and the University of Timbuctoo exchanged knowledge with the universities of Spain.

There is one other point to which I am anxious to draw attention. It is that, with the exception of Mr. Maclean's temporary extension of British influence on the Gold Coast as Governor for the Merchant Government, between 1838 and 1842, no colony up to the last decade of the nineteenth century extended beyond the immediate seaboard. From the date of the abolition of the slave trade the constant policy of the British Government was to withdraw as far as possible from any intermeddling with native affairs, and from any attempt to establish British influence, or to incur political responsibilities, upon the coast. It was as a matter of duty, and mainly for the purpose of enforcing the abolition of the over-sea slave trade, that Great Britain in 1808 assumed the government of Sierra Leone, and in 1821, after the abolition of the existing Chartered Company, annexed to it the settlements of the Gambia and the Gold Coast. The greatest care was taken to repudiate responsibility for native affairs outside the limits of the small English settlements. As late as 1865, it was stated before a Committee of the House of Commons that British territory on the Gambia was so small, that when the native tribes fought with each other, "all their bullets, without meaning us any harm, came into the British barracks." In the Gold Coast Colony, Fantees and Ashantees fought with each other on the sea coast, and an English victory obtained over them in 1827 took place, not in the interior, but at Accra.

The settlement of the country and the policy of the

Government with regard to the West Coast were fully expressed in the finding of a strong representative Committee of the House of Commons which sat for several months in the early part of 1865, and, after a careful examination of witnesses and consideration of reports specially prepared and submitted to it by commissioners charged with the investigation of the affairs of the West African colonies on the spot, reported to the House certain resolutions at which it had arrived.

In reporting these resolutions, the Committee stated first that the chief object of all undertakings on the coast, since the passing of the Act for the abolition of the slave trade, had been the suppression of the trade; secondly, that "if the promotion first, and afterwards the suppression, of the slave trade had not been the object of British West African establishments, commercial enterprise would never have selected the Gold Coast for its locality, nor would the British probably have undertaken any settlement whatever in West Africa; still less would the Crown have implicated itself in government there or in treaties of protection." The Committee found that the slave trade, "the suppression of which is now the chief object of the British establishments in West Africa, was rapidly diminishing, that the only demand remaining in 1865 was from Cuba, while there was a good hope of its speedy and total extinction. They also found, as regards the encouragement and protection of other trade, that "in the sole interests of trade the evidence of merchants is that it is better that their agents should feel the necessity of keeping on good terms with native powers than that they should be backed by English governments, or even by consuls, more than is necessary for a reference of disputes to constituted authorities."

For these and for other reasons which are fully set forward in the report, the Committee submitted as a resolution to the House: "That all further extension of territory or assumption of government, or new treaties offering any protection to native tribes, would be inexpedient, and that the object of our policy should be to encourage in the natives the exercise of those qualities which may render it possible for us more and more to transfer to them the administration of all the governments, with a view to our ultimate withdrawal from all, except, probably, Sierra Leone." This resolution, with six others arrived at by the Committee, was adopted and reported to the House on June 26, 1865.

CHAPTER XXXVII

ENGLAND AND FRANCE ON THE LOWER NIGER

THE Committee of 1865 may be taken to represent the lowest ebb of British sentiment with regard to the West African colonies. The evidence which was given before it forms a bulky volume, and, in reading through its pages, there is no escape from the conclusion that the result of three hundred years of occupation and of trade with the West Coast was to leave us with no interest there which could appeal to the British public as justifying the expenditure of British money, and the employment of British officials to defend. Upwards of two centuries had been spent in developing the West African slave trade, the better part of one century had been spent in suppressing it, and when, in 1865, it became possible to report that the over-sea slave trade was practically abolished, the only proposal that appeared to be warranted by the existing condition of affairs in West Africa was that, with the exception of a coaling station to be retained at Sierra Leone, Great Britain should abandon a position of which the advantages seemed to be purely nominal upon the coast. The principal evidence which was given before the Committee went to show that British settlement had no extension, that British administration claimed no authority, and that British trade had no interests which the increase of political influence could assist. The private trade which remained outside the slave trade was small, and was reported in two out of the four settlements to be rapidly declining.

But though this is the position which is emphatically

presented by the findings of the Committee of 1865, there is to be traced, even in the evidence which was taken before the Committee, a faint indication of the coming change which was soon to reverse the direction of public opinion. In the examination of an important witness, Colonel Ord, the Special Commissioner employed by the Government to visit the four settlements and to prepare a report from information collected on the spot, a question was put as to the probable reasons for the maintenance by France of the large military garrisons which he reported as existing at Senegal and Goree. In reply, Colonel Ord said that the only surmise which he had heard expressed upon the subject was that "they" (the French) "desire eventually to connect their Algerian and their African possessions, and to become possessors of the whole of the north of Africa."

Thus, in 1865, outside the circles of philanthropy and philosophic Radicalism which still retained a predominating influence over British colonial policy, the first notes had been already sounded of that international conflict of diplomacy which was soon to be known under the name of the "Scramble for Africa."

The Franco-German war of 1870 intervened, and delayed for a few years the development of ideas which were already germinating in 1865, but, the war once over, its effect was, perhaps, rather to stimulate than to crush the ambitions of France and Germany to sustain their position as colonial powers. Among non-political influences which also tended to give an impetus to continental exploration, no single element was perhaps more potent than the application of steam to land and river transport. The development of railways, which took place during the middle of the century, had for the first time in history rendered possible the commercial exploitation of the centres of great continents. The discoveries of gold which had been made in America and Australia, and of diamonds and gold at a somewhat later period in South Africa, revolutionised trading operations and raised expectancy to the highest point. Capital became available for every enterprise, and in the last quarter of the nineteenth century colonial apathy on the part of the western nations gave place to a keen competition for the acquisition of fields of commercial operation—which were known by the political name of "spheres of influence"—in hitherto undeveloped portions of the world.

Africa became the scene of an international race for territory and power. In the heart of the continent the Congo Free State was brought into existence by mutual agreement of the European Powers in 1885, and was placed, with what were held to be due guarantees for freedom of trade, under the direction of the King of the Belgians. The position of England was unchallenged in the south. Portugal retained, and Germany made good claims upon the east and west coasts. England too secured from the east coast a position, which at a later period was extended to the interior, and gave her the command of the great waterways and the Valley of the Nile. France held an undisputed position of predominant influence in the north, as well as important centres of trade and of military influence on the west coast.

That under these circumstances the directors of French colonial policy should have cherished the ambition ascribed to them of joining their possessions on the coast of the Mediterranean to their possessions in the west, and thus becoming the possessors of the whole of North-West Africa, was in no sense to be wondered at. The introduction of railways had abolished distance, and there was no apparent obstacle to obstruct the spread of French influence from the Mediterranean seaboard to the equator. A map showing the limits of the West African colonies of Great Britain, which was prepared and submitted to the Committee of 1865, gave practically no dimensions to the British settlements. They are indicated simply as pink lines upon the sea coast, with here and there a dot, of which it appeared in evidence that one mile might be taken as the greatest extent inland. Only on the Gold Coast there was an indication of protected territory lying inland from the pink line, and there had been a public declaration of the intention to withdraw from that territory. In the interior there was therefore no bar whatever to the continuous extension of French influence.

When, after the conclusion of the Franco-German war, French policy began to declare itself in West Africa, the movement, co-ordinated with traditional intelligence, and supported by brilliant personal initiative on the part of individuals entrusted with its execution, would appear to have included a design of steady extension from the north towards the south, accompanied by supplementary expeditions of penetration to be directed inland from all portions of the western coast which were not held by any other foreign power.

The English settlements of the Gambia, Sierra Leone, the Gold Coast, and Lagos, covered certain strips upon the seaboard. Between these were found points of penetration in some instances for official military expeditions, in others for expeditions of trade and exploration. To the south-east of the English colonies, and lying between them and the French colony of the Gaboon, there was situated the very important highway which British exploration of the early part of the century had shown to exist in the course of the Lower Niger. It will be remembered that Mungo Park lost his life at Boussa in the attempt to follow the course of the river from the interior in the year 1805, and that Clapperton's servant, Richard Landor, finally established the connection of the Niger with the Atlantic in 1832. From that date onward a certain amount of British trade had existed upon the river, and notwithstanding disastrous experiences of climate, the courses of the Lower Niger and the Benué had been explored, and a small trade settlement maintained at the native town of Lokoja at the confluence of the two rivers.

The Niger, of which the many mouths flowed to the sea through a politically unprotected coast, and of which the upper courses in the back country of Sierra Leone were already the object of French exploration, was naturally selected as one of the lines to which the French policy of penetration was to be applied. In this instance the policy took a commercial form. A French company was started upon the lower river, and the commercial attack was met quite simply by British commercial opposition. English traders had no friendly feelings towards foreign competition, and in mere self-defence were well inclined to oppose French intrusion, but in the earlier years of the movement there was a lack of leadership, and no very definite intention animated the action which was taken.

As the struggle for Africa waxed hotter, and all parties to it became more clearly aware of the objects at which they were aiming, the value of the Niger as a commercial highway, and of the territories included in the watershed of the Niger and the Benué, became more apparent. There was still no opposition to French activity in Western Africa, except that which was privately sustained by British trade, but the opposition took a more active form. The British companies trading on the river began to feel that it was becoming a matter of life and death to them to overcome the foreign competition, which threatened them with extinction, and under the pressure of their struggle for self-preservation they found a leader and evolved a policy which had for its result to revolutionise the entire position of Great Britain in West Africa.

In 1879, under the inspiration of a young engineer officer, Mr. Taubman Goldie, whose tastes for travel had led him to acquire some personal knowledge of the interior of the Soudan, and whose interests, owing to family circumstances, had become involved in West African enterprise, the British companies trading upon the Niger were induced to amalgamate, and took the name of the National African Company. The effect of amalgamation was to abolish personal rivalries between them, and to enable them to present a united front to the advances of French enterprise upon the river. In the sharp round of commercial war which ensued, Mr. Goldie, afterwards Sir George, became the acknowledged leader on the British side of a movement which, under his guidance, rapidly assumed an overtly political character.

It was essential to the existence of British trade that French competition should be driven from the native markets on the banks of the river; but the immediate French reply to the amalgamation of the British companies was the formation on the river of another and more powerful French company, which was known to have the support and encouragement of the French Foreign Office. For two or three years the National African Company sustained the brunt of an international duel, of which the end was clearly seen to be the withdrawal of one or other of the combatants from the scene. The French company yielded. They were finally bought out by the National African Company in 1884, and the British representative at the conference opened in Berlin in that year was able to announce that no other Power but Great Britain owned any trading establishments on the Lower Niger. The result was that the conference adjudged to Great Britain the duty of watching over the application of regulations laid down for the navigation of the Niger, and in the same year Great Britain notified to the Powers her assumption of a Protectorate, under the name of the Oil Rivers, over that portion of the African coast which lay between the British colony of Lagos and the territory now known as the German Cameroons.

The first round was won, but the conflict, which had hitherto been waged upon the coast, was now carried into the interior. Throughout the period of its existence the National African Company had found it necessary to secure its commercial position by the negotiation of treaties with native chiefs. Upon the lower river, where the political organisation of the natives was of a primitive character, the number of petty independent chiefs was very great, and the treaties negotiated by the Company were counted by hundreds. It was known that in the interior chiefs of more importance commanded the submission of wide areas of territory, and the value of obtaining treaties of amity and trade with these potentates was obvious. But if obvious to the British company, it was of course equally obvious to French and German competitors; and from 1884 onward the influence of Germany, which in that year established itself in the Cameroon territory, to the east of the British Protectorate, became no less active in the back country than that of France. The position of the British company, in presence of this double rivalry, is described in a speech made by the Governor at a much later date. "We knew," he said, "that the Haussa States were by far the most valuable region of equatorial Africa. We were aware that Germany was organising an expedition to deprive us of them, and we knew that the acquisition by any other European Power of political influence over this empire would before long entail our complete retirement from our position on the Middle Niger and the river Benué to the district south of Lokoja, and probably even to Asaba, only 150 miles from the sea." It was constantly pointed out by the Governor of the Company, in his speeches to his shareholders, that the prosperity and success of trading operations upon the coast depended on the maintenance of British influence, with its accompaniments of peace and security, in the interior. Animated by this view of their own higher interest, the Company adopted and maintained, in the first instance at their private cost, the policy of sending missions into the interior to negotiate treaties with distant Mohammedan states. But it had early become evident that British interests could not be maintained unless the commercial position of the British company were strengthened by some sort of political sanction. So long as their treaties were made only by a private company, they were of the nature of private and individual agreements, which carried no weight as against the official treaties of foreign Powers.

In 1886 the political sanction, of which the need had made itself more urgently felt with every extension of competing foreign influence towards the interior, was accorded by the grant of a Royal Charter. By the charter the Company acquired, under the new name of the Royal Niger Company, the international position of a recognised government, whose treaties with native chiefs were protected by Great Britain, and from this date the flag of the Company became for international purposes the equivalent of the British flag. Where it flew, the authority of Great Britain was held to be established, and where the company negotiated a treaty of protection with a native power, such treaties were held to exclude any political treaties from being made in the territories of the same potentate by other European nations. The charter also conferred upon the Company the power to levy taxes to a limited extent for the purpose of meeting the expenses entailed upon it by its political expenditure. Chief among the items of this expenditure was the raising of a small native military force.

CHAPTER XXXVIII

THE ROYAL NIGER COMPANY

THUS from 1886 the Royal Niger Company took the position, familiar in the annals of British history, of a commercial body endowed with political powers, extending over a territory of which the limits were undefined, and in which the character, the numbers, and the history of the native populations were unknown. England, in general, knew as little of Nigeria and its possibilities at the end of the nineteenth century as it knew of India in the sixteenth century. The territories over which these powers were granted were at first known by the name of the "Territories of the Royal Niger Company." A little later this title was changed for the more convenient name of Nigeria.

Sir George Goldie, acting first as Vice-President and afterwards as President of the Chartered Company, continued to direct a policy, in which the legitimate and commercial interests of the Company in the lower reaches of the river were safeguarded and developed by a system of political missions, extending inland for 500 miles, to the Emirates of Sokoto and Gando in the north, to Yola and Adamawa in the east, and finally to Borgu, lying in the back country of Lagos, in the west. As a result of these political missions, treaties were negotiated, and in many instances subsidies were given to native chiefs. The disturbed condition of the territories and the hostile attitude of native chiefs, combined with the difficulties of penetrating to the interior, through unknown tropical country, laid waste in many districts by centuries of slave-raiding and inter-tribal war, rendered these missions in most cases expeditions of no little danger, which had to be conducted at the personal risk of the leaders whose services were secured to command them.

It was in 1884 that Mr. Joseph Thomson was commissioned to negotiate the first treaty of the Company with Sokoto. In 1894 my husband, then Captain Lugard, made his first experience of West Africa by conducting an expedition into Borgu, and negotiated the last treaties of the Company upon that frontier.

In the ten years which elapsed between these two expeditions, the action of the Company in the interior led to the further declaration of a British Protectorate over territories lying on the Middle Niger, and to the definition by successive international agreements of British frontiers round a territory covering an area of about 500,000 square miles, of which a considerable part was situated in some of the richest, most healthy, and most thickly populated regions of Western Africa.

The most important of these agreements were those with Germany of 1886 and 1893, and that of 1890 with France, to be followed a few years later by the agreement of 1898.

By the German agreements the eastern frontier of the territory was defined from the coast to the borders of Lake Chad. By the first of the French agreements the northern frontier, separating British territory from the southern extension of the French hinterland of Algeria, was fixed at a line of some 800 miles in length, to be drawn, with the necessary deviations for local political boundaries, near to the fourteenth parallel of latitude, and continued from a point upon the western shore of Chad to another selected point upon the Niger. The points chosen were Barrua upon Lake Chad, and Say upon the Niger, but these were altered by subsequent modifications. This line, when the details of its delimitation are finally fixed, will form the northern frontier of Nigeria. It runs now from Ilo on the Niger, and making a curve northward to include the territories of Sokoto, is deflected to the western shore of Chad. With the frontiers fixed by the Anglo-German agreement of 1893 it determined in principle the boundaries of British territories to the north and east. In addition to the agreements referring to these frontiers, there were some other minor agreements with France and Germany, by which various details relating chiefly to the inland development of other West Coast colonies were determined.

The five years from 1893 to 1898 were marked by a tension on both sides of the then undetermined frontier on the west, which threatened at times to break out into open hostility. National interests, as well as personal honour, were held by local representatives to be involved in the maintenance of a forward movement which was, perhaps, to be excused if it sometimes disregarded lines of latitude and longitude too pedantically laid down by the distant Foreign Offices of London, Paris, and Berlin. In 1893 France formally assumed the Protectorate of Dahomey, a native kingdom bordering upon the English colony of Lagos upon the coast, and carried her inland frontier to the parallel of 9° N. latitude. Numerous French expeditions were then pushed into the territory extending towards the Niger, directly south of the point which had been chosen at Say for the terminus of the northern frontier line of British Nigeria.

The contention of the Royal Niger Company was that the effect of the Anglo-French agreement of 1890, which drew the Say-Barrua line, was to give to France everything which lay north of that line, and to give to Great Britain everything which lay south of it, with the exception of the French territory of Dahomey, for which special arrangement had been made. Under this contention the meridian of Say became automatically the western frontier of British Nigeria, and gave the native kingdom of Borgu and part of Gurma, lying on the western bank of the river Niger, to Great Britain. It was of great importance to British trade that both banks of the river should be British, and the Niger Company had not neglected to affirm the position assigned to it under the agreement by negotiating treaties of commerce and protection with the trans-riverine potentates. French diplomacy denied the British contention, and French officers on the spot, gallantly acting upon, or exceeding, their instructions, endeavoured to create an argument of the *fait accompli* by the negotiation of treaties with native chiefs, whose powers they asserted to be greater than those of the chiefs with whom the British treaties had been signed.

The Borgu chief, with whom the Niger Company negotiated the principal treaty on the western side of the river, had his headquarters at Boussa. French authorities asserted that he was the vassal of another and more important chief, who had his residence at Nikki, a town lying in the back country of Dahomey, farther west. By the middle of 1894 it came to be generally understood that the possession of the provinces lying on the western bank of the river was to be determined by the negotiation of a treaty with Nikki. On the 24th of July a strong French expedition under Captain Decoeur suddenly left France for Dahomey. Dahomey was favourably situated for penetrating into the territory in dispute. M. Ballot, the Governor, had already pushed a friendly reconnaissance to the borders of Borgu, only fifty miles from Nikki. The Niger Company could not mistake the intention of Captain Decoeur's mission. Four days later, on July 28, Captain Lugard, fresh from a long struggle to assert British supremacy in East Africa, left London, having accepted a mission on behalf of the Company to reach Nikki, if possible, before Captain Decoeur, and to negotiate a treaty.

Throughout the progress of these discussions, Germany, who held the territory of Togoland, adjoining the French colony of Dahomey upon the coast, had not been indifferent to the extension of its own back country, and the condition of affairs in Borgu was described at the time in the French press as a "veritable steeple-chase, to which France, England, and Germany are devoting themselves, in order to gain that part of the 'Bend of the Niger' which impinges on the lower river." In this steeplechase the, till then, unknown town of Nikki had become the winning-post. The odds were against Captain Lugard. He had started later than Captain Decoeur. He had to go round through the Niger Company's territories, which involved ascending the river to Jebba, situated in latitude 9.10°, and marching thence some 200 miles westwards through the unsettled territory of Borgu, whence it was the boast of the natives that no white man had ever come out alive. It was essential also that the expedition should be proceeded with at once in the season of the rains, when every natural difficulty was increased. This is not the place in which to recount the adventures of the expedition. African experience served its leader in good stead. He reached Nikki with his little escort of forty men, and successfully negotiated the required treaty, which was signed on November 10th. Five days later, Captain Decoeur arrived with a force of 500 Senegalese, only to hear that Captain Lugard had already left the town, taking with him the British treaty duly signed. Other treaties, securing the northern territory behind Lagos, had been negotiated for Great Britain on the way to Nikki, and passing southwards, the British expedition on the return journey concluded treaties with the frontier chiefs of Northern Yoruba. The British position was thus secured upon the western bank of the Middle Niger.

Captain Decoeur loyally acknowledged his defeat. It was not accepted in the same spirit by other representatives of French interests, and during the two following years there was a further development of semi-responsible expeditionary activity, of which the manifest dangers could not be ignored.

The hazardous nature of the position thus created led, in the year 1897, to a decision on the part of the British Government to raise a local military force, of which the primary duty should be the defence, under proper control, of the inland frontiers of the British settlements. It was decided to raise this regiment, which was to be known as the West African Frontier Force, from native Haussa material, to be officered by picked white officers selected from the regular army for the purpose. In addition to the duty of defending the frontier, the force was to be available for all local military service in West Africa.

The duty of raising and organising this frontier force was entrusted to Captain, or, as he shortly became, Lieut.-Colonel Lugard, who was recalled from private work in South Africa for the purpose. Among the officers selected by Colonel Lugard to help him in the work, was Major, now Sir James Willcocks, by whom, as well as by other members of the first English staff, he was most loyally assisted.

It was thought desirable, chiefly for military reasons, to fix the headquarters of the force at Jebba, a point upon the Niger nearly 500 miles inland. The regiment, of which the formation was successfully accomplished, under conditions not likely to be forgotten by any of the officers who were engaged in it, has since then done conspicuous honour to its founders in the Ashantee War of 1900, as well as in many local campaigns. Its strength, first fixed at two battalions of infantry, each 1200 strong, and three batteries of artillery, has since been increased by the addition of a battalion of mounted infantry 700 strong.

The strained situation was fortunately not prolonged. In June of the following year the Anglo-French agreement of 1898, perhaps the most important of all the international agreements by which the position taken for Great Britain by the Niger Company was affirmed, happily brought to an end the ambiguities of the political situation. By this agreement, which gave to France the back country of the colony of Dahomey, and accepted a point near Ilo instead of Say as the point of separation between French and English spheres upon the Middle Niger, the western frontier of Nigeria was fixed at its present limits. These include, on the western bank of the Niger, the eastern half of Borgu, and carry the British frontier from the junction between Lagos and Dahomey to join the northern line at its terminus upon the Middle Niger.

The formation of a new military force at public expense, designed chiefly for local service in the interior, was not only an indication of the very remarkable change in public opinion, which, contemporaneously with the movements in Nigeria, operated to bring about a gradual enlargement and expansion towards the interior of the territories of the other West Coast colonies; it also indicated approaching change in the government of the territories of the Niger Company.

During the whole of the period which elapsed between the grant of the charter of the Royal Niger Company and the formation of the West African Frontier Force, the Company had carried on the fight for British extension in the interior on the gallant but unequal terms of a private corporation contending with two foreign Governments. In the events which preceded the agreement of 1898, when officially organised French expeditions were directed against the territories secured by treaty to the Company, and a French gunboat did not scruple, in the excitement of local rivalry, to enter the waters of the river which were open by international agreement to merchant vessels alone, it became evident that a stage had been reached in which the adventurous energy of a trading company, however well directed, could no longer suffice for the efficient protection and necessary development of the territories which had been brought under British rule.

Obviously it was undesirable that territories, of which

the defence was provided at public expense, should be administered at private discretion. The Company had not, of course, attained the accomplishment of its ambitions without exciting many jealousies, and giving rise to widespread criticism at home and abroad. By foreign Powers its too successful methods were made the object of vituperative campaigns in the press, and of more discreet but not less urgent diplomatic remonstrance in the Cabinet. At home complaints were frequent that the concentration of administrative and commercial powers in the same hands gave advantages to the Niger Company over its commercial rivals which amounted to a virtual monopoly of trade which was nominally free. An internal campaign against the Mohammedan chiefs of Nupe and Ilorin, which was forced upon the Company in the opening months of 1897, successfully executed as it was, had also served to give some indication in responsible quarters of the probable development of administrative difficulties on an increasing scale, as soon as any serious attempt should be made to establish white authority, for practical purposes, over vast territories where the thorny questions which mark the difference between civilised and semi-civilised administration were as yet untouched.

For these and other reasons it was recognised that the pioneer work of acquisition had been accomplished, and that the time had come, more swiftly than in the case of other great British companies, on whose precedent the Niger Company had been founded, to abolish a charter which had served its purpose, and to incorporate the territories acquired by the Company with the other colonies and dependencies of the Empire. The charter of the Company was surrendered to the Crown. Its territories were divided: the lower reaches of the river south of Ida being included, under the name of Southern Nigeria, with the Protectorate of the Oil Rivers, extending from the colony of Lagos to the German frontier; while the interior cut off from the sea was erected, under the name of Northern Nigeria, into a separate Protectorate. The transfer of authority from the Company to the Imperial Government took place on January 1st, 1900, on which day Colonel Lugard assumed office as the first High Commissioner of Northern Nigeria.

In summing up the service rendered to the Empire by the Company, it will hardly be disputed that by the ability, the foresight, and the activity of a single man, who in the first instance united, and subsequently for twenty years directed with laborious care, the principal British interests upon the Niger, a territory was added to the British Empire, and a field secured for all time to British trade, which, without his personal exertions, would assuredly have passed into the possession of France and Germany. In the execution of his work Sir George Goldie was very loyally supported by the shareholders of the Royal Niger Company; but it was by his personal qualities that he won and retained the confidence of those whose interests he took into his charge, and it was by his personal perception of the opportunities inherent to the situation that he was able to use the force acquired by that confidence for great purposes of public utility.

The commercial success of the Company is sometimes quoted in disparagement of the merit of its public service; but that its Governor was able, without injustice to private interests, to carry out the important scheme of policy in which they were involved, gave, in fact, a substantial value to his work, which no mere recklessness of political annexation, however generous, would have possessed. When the relative positions of France and England were finally adjusted in 1898, British interests had been created in the interior, which it was impossible for either government to ignore. The enlightened view that the prosperity of coast trade depended on the extension of civilised relations to the interior, which led to the expansion of the sphere of operations of the Niger Company, has been illustrated, not only by the commercial success of that Company, but by the remarkable development in the prosperity of all the coast colonies which has followed upon the extension of their protected areas towards the interior, and the greater security which the establishment of British administration has carried with it.

In acting as the pioneer of this policy for Great Britain, Sir George Goldie was in part the originator, in part the interpreter, of the great change which had come over modern sentiment. He was not alone in desiring to reverse the policy of abandonment dictated by a sentiment of distaste and discouragement, which amounted almost to public remorse. Other nations, as we have seen, were quicker than Great Britain to perceive that the true solution of the problem of European relations with uncivilised Africa lay in accepting, not in abandoning, the responsibilities of civilised administration. Many influences were at work to foster and to direct the forward movement, which, not in West Africa alone, but on every frontier of the Empire, took the place, during the last quarter of the nineteenth century, of the concentrating and restrictive tendencies of an earlier period. What Sir George Goldie did was that which has been done by all original and successful workers. He gave personality to a great idea, and by the exercise of qualities which belonged to himself alone he was able to bring his interpretation of the idea to a distinguished practical success. In doing so he added to the Empire a territory of which the area is no less than half the size of British India, and for this service his name will deservedly be ranked among the unforgotten names of English history.

CHAPTER XXXIX

TRANSFER OF NIGER COMPANY'S TERRITORIES TO THE CROWN

It was a necessity of commercial success, and therefore of existence to the Company, that the greater part of its practical work should be done upon the lower reaches of the river. The waterways of this part of Africa, as they approach the coast, pass through a forest belt rich in valuable forms of sylvan produce. Palm oil and palm kernels, which form one of the most important staples of West African trade, are obtained in such quantities from the palm trees of this belt that the strip of coast through which the rivers of the district flow to the sea was for a long time known by the name of the "Oil Rivers" Protectorate. Little industry or ingenuity is required on the part of the natives in order to collect the wild products of the forest, which they are willing to exchange for European goods, and the mere numbers of the population, in conjunction with the fertility of the soil, constitute the elements of a valuable export trade. The primitive nature of the needs of the natives unfortunately gave to the return trade from Europe the low character which it has always borne.

The Niger Company was so situated as to have no coast area beyond the main mouth of the Niger, and a small portion of the delta which attached to it. Its sphere of commercial activity lay in the valley of the river. Here, for upwards of 150 miles, the banks on both sides served as frontage to numerous tribes whose back country extended into the network of lesser waterways which irrigate the forest area of the coast. It was with these tribes that the main trade of the Company was done, and for the protection of this trade that its treaties were in the first instance negotiated.

Coincidently with the growth of trade it was found necessary to establish some form of political control, and as the operations of Mohammedan slave-raiders from the north, year by year, extended the circle of their devastation, and destroyed flourishing markets by the wholesale depopulation of areas in which they were situated, the further necessity was forced upon the Company of giving some form of military protection to threatened districts. For this purpose a constabulary was formed, and military outposts were advanced to Lokoja, at the confluence of the Niger and the Benué. Trading stations under the protection of Lokoja were subsequently established upon the Lower Benué and upon the Niger between the Boussa Rapids and Lokoja.

The ninth parallel of latitude may be taken as the farthest northerly extension reached by the outposts of the Company, and the Company's stations upon the rivers east and west from the confluence marked the meeting ground of the pagan states they desired to protect, and the militant Mohammedan civilisation of the north.

The great difference which existed between this civilisation and the primitive condition of the peoples of the lower river will have been gathered from what has been already written in the earlier sections of this book. The difference from the point of view of European trade was no less marked than from the more general point of view of political history. The Governors of the Company had always expressed the opinion that ultimately their most valuable trade would be done with the northern territories. In a speech made by the Governor at the annual meeting of 1889 he informed the shareholders that, after long and persistent research, palm oil and kernels appeared to form the only considerable resources of the maritime districts, and that the Directors felt that the "ultimate and permanent prosperity of the territories must depend still more on a widely spread and properly directed culture of indigo, tobacco, cotton, and other products," which were grown in the interior. The trade with the south was prosperous; but, while the Company did its principal work on the coast, it looked forward to opening the northern territories.

"We can hardly impress too strongly on our shareholders," the Governor said in the same speech of 1889, "the fact that our hopes of future prosperity rest far less on the lower regions of the Niger . . . than upon the higher and inner and recently explored regions acquired at great expense of money and of energy." Throughout the political life of the Company this view was constantly impressed upon the shareholders, and at a very early period the Company marked, in a manner which did credit alike to its foresight and its enlightenment, its perception of the difference between the two divisions of its territories. The consumption of liquor by the pagan natives of the coast has been, through the whole period of European intercourse with them, a hardly less prolific source of demoralisation than the slave trade itself. In the lower river the Company yielded to circumstances, and cheap European spirits formed one of the principal articles of importation for purposes of the barter trade. But among the Mohammedan peoples of the north the use of alcoholic liquor is forbidden by their religion, and in 1887, before prohibition within certain latitudes became general under the rules agreed to by the Brussels Conference, the Niger Company, desirous of defending the markets of the interior from the invasion of this curse, fixed a line at the back of its coast territories beyond which it absolutely forbade the importation of liquor.

But though the trade of the northern territories was regarded from the beginning as likely to prove beyond all comparison more valuable than that of the lower river, it was, from artificial as well as from natural causes, more difficult to attract into British channels. It was, of course, of a very different order from that of the south. Indigo, cotton, and tobacco, as well as other exports of the northern territories, are products of organised industry which, unlike the native products of the palm-oil belt, demand the employment of regular labour. Conditions of peace and security are as necessary for their production as for the development of sustained trade relations. The slave-raiding operations of the Mohammedan rulers were undertaken for the purpose of obtaining labour. But, while the industrial system was based on slavery, the ceaseless disturbance to which slave-raiding gave rise, coupled with political conditions of civil war and the exactions of a practically uncurbed foreign tyranny, of which some account has yet to be given, operated to prevent the prosperous development of all industry. In addition to these disturbed conditions, there was also, in the Mohammedan states, long-established tradition to contend with. If the wants of the people were more elaborate than those of the southern population, they had better means of satisfying them. What trade there was was done either locally, between state and state, or across the desert, by the old routes, with the north of Africa. Tea and sugar, commonly sold in the market of Kano, were brought with other commodities by Arab caravans from the Mediterranean coast.

This was also the case with many other necessities of life. Beyond the valley of the Niger and the Benué no administrative influence had been exercised by the Company. Its intercourse with the Mohammedan emirs had been confined to political missions, of which the direct object was to obtain promises of future trade and to exclude antagonistic foreign influence from their territories. By these treaties prospective markets were secured, but the condition of the country was such that trade was not open to the north.

Under the division which was made of the Company's territories on the surrender of the charter, the principal centres of its commercial and administrative activity passed, with the river valley south of Ida, to Southern Nigeria. In Northern Nigeria its occupation was represented only by the outposts which have been named upon the river, and by an agency established in Ilorin.

In 1897, practically, though not actually, the last year of the Company's administration, a campaign against the Mohammedan state of Nupe, which at that time held both banks of the Niger above Lokoja, was forced upon the Company by the persistent slave-raiding of the Mohammedans in trade areas farther south.

The campaign gave occasion for the most careful organisation of the military forces of the Company. It was recognised as involving perhaps the existence of British authority in the country. An additional number of officers from the regular army were lent specially to the Company by the War Office, and the campaign was conducted at very considerable expense upon the lines of European war. The military operations were directed against Bida, the capital of Nupe, situated on the northern side of the river, and were completely successful in their immediate results. The town was captured, the emir was deposed, a portion of his territory which lay upon the southern bank of the river was declared independent of the suzerainty of Nupe, and a new emir was placed upon the throne.

But in accentuating, by the precautions which it rendered necessary, the difference between Mohammedan civilisation to the north of the confluence and pagan barbarism to the south, this war gave, as has been already said, a very serious indication of the enlargement of the proportions which the problem of British occupation was likely to assume when any attempt should be made to establish white authority in the Northern Territories. The Company did not feel itself to be in a position to make a permanent occupation of Bida. As soon as its troops were withdrawn the deposed emir rallied his defeated followers, assumed again the supreme authority of which he had been deprived, and maintained his province in a state of revolt against British authority north of the river. It became clear that conquest without occupation, or the establishment of some form of British authority in the conquered provinces, would result only in the creation of a line of impenetrably hostile border states, with which neither trade nor any peaceful relations could be maintained.

Troubles on the western border, resulting in the agreement of 1898, and the consequent surrender of the charter, gave the Company no opportunity of dealing with the situation which was thus created. The authority which had been successfully asserted over the pagan tribes of the lower river, and which had not shrunk from the first shock of conflict with the forces of Mohammedanism, was withdrawn at this critical and interesting moment.

Thus it came about that when British administration was officially established in the interior, it found itself limited in fact to territory of which the northern line was fixed by the Company's stations upon the river, and to the western province of Borgu, which, subsequently to the formation of the West African Frontier Force, had been organised as a military province outside the territories of the company.

The duty which lay before the first British High Commissioner was to organise the territorities of Northern Nigeria for administration. The whole of these territories had placed themselves nominally under the protection of Great Britain. They extended roughly, as will be remembered, from 7° to 14° north latitude, and, including Borgu, from 3° to 14° east longitude. They covered an area of 350,000 square miles, or about one-third of the size of British India, and they lay almost wholly in the area occupied by those finer races of the Soudan whose touch with civilisation had from time immemorial been from the north. Never before in the history of this part of the Soudan had any civilising influence come from the south.

Two new and interesting chapters of history were therefore initiated on the same day. For the first time in the history of the Mohammedan states a superior and civilising influence was established in an administrative capacity upon their southern borders, and by its mere presence began the process of drawing as a magnet towards the south all the thoughts, the activities, the fears and hopes, which the tradition of intelligence had directed, through their entire previous existence, towards the north.

On the other hand, for the first time in British history colonial government was established in the interior of West Africa. In determining to extend our influence to the relatively healthy uplands bordering upon the desert, to enter into friendly relations with the fine races which inhabit them, and to open new fields to commercial enterprise in regions famous through all antiquity for their wealth, a wholly new departure was made from the traditions which had limited us for three hundred years to a coast occupation of the malarial regions fringing the Gulf of Guinea, and had confined our relations to the type of negro who inhabits its shores. The history of British West Africa entered upon a new phase, and if, as we may venture to hope, British influence upon the races of the interior may be of such a nature as to revive in them the old traditions associated with the civilisation of Europe in their best days, the influence of the Mohammedan races upon British West African policy may be not less important. They offer us a field for the foundation of a West African Empire, of which neither they nor we need be ashamed.

CHAPTER XL

ORIGIN OF THE FULANI

BEFORE attempting to give any account of the establishment of British administration in Northern Nigeria, there is still a chapter of native history to be told.

We left the Mohammedan states of the Soudan in the seventeenth century, when after the conquest of the Moors they became isolated in the heart of Africa, and fell into the decadence in which we know them. The *Tarikh-es-Soudan*, of which the chronicle continued to the middle of the seventeenth century, informs us that after the Moors of the Soudan had cut themselves off from Morocco, the government of the Pashas rapidly degenerated. In 1623 it is stated that "excesses of every kind are now committed unchecked by the soldiery, and that the country is profoundly convulsed and oppressed." About the middle of the eighteenth century the Tuaregs, pressing down from the desert upon the Moors, deprived them of the principal towns of Songhay, and established a kingdom of their own upon the Niger. What the Moors had become at the end of the eighteenth century, some thirty years after they had been driven from Gago and Timbuctoo, may be gathered from Mungo Park, who had experience of them in his journey from the coast to the Niger in 1795.

The Moors, he says, are divided into many tribes, each more entirely barbarous and cruel than the other. Each tribe is governed by a separate king, who owns no allegiance to a common sovereign. They pay but little attention to agriculture, purchasing their corn, cotton cloth, and other necessaries from the negroes in exchange for salt, which they dig from the pits in the great desert. Describing them as a whole, "They are," he says, "at once the vainest, the proudest, and perhaps the most bigoted, ferocious, and intolerant of all the nations of the earth." They had a very primitive system of justice and taxation, but they had "neither dignity nor order." They lived in a condition of constantly plundering the negroes around them, and, like the nomad Berbers, they frequently roamed from place to place.

But the Moors did not fall from their high position in the Soudan without the interposition of another power. This time the dominating people, although not black, were, like the conquering races of Melle and of Songhay, of local origin. As the Moors declined, the Fulani rose.

This remarkable people, of whom mention is made in the earliest records which have been preserved of the history of the Soudan, have given rise to much learned controversy in the endeavours to determine to what branch of the human race they properly belong.

In the sixteenth century of our era, they may fairly be spoken of as being of local origin in the Soudan. At that time they knew of no other home, and there was record of their presence in the country for upwards of 1000 years. But they were of a race wholly different from that of the other races of the Soudan. Though profoundly modified by intermarriage, they counted themselves as a white people, and even when the mixed blood gave to their skin the prevailing colour of black or red, their features, their hair, their carriage, and their distinctive characteristics, proclaimed them of other than negro race.

The variations in their appearance are at the present day so marked—ranging from the jet black of the Joloffs of the western coast through "tawny," "white," and even "Syrian red" skins, to the blue-eyed individuals mentioned by Baikie as having been met by him upon the Benué—as to present arguments in support of the most opposite theories regarding the birthplace of their race.

We have already seen in the *Tarikh-es-Soudan* a description of the black Joloffs, which counted this people among the "best of men," and very superior to "all other Fulani." Marmol, in describing a chief of this race who visited Portugal at the end of the fifteenth century, tells us, it will be remembered, that he had a fine figure and was generally well made, also that he had a long and well-trimmed beard, and "did not appear to be a negro, but a prince to whom all honour and respect were due." In Mungo Park's day the distinction of the *Tarikh* between the Joloffs and "the other Fulani" had grown into a permanent distinction of race, and Mungo Park speaks of them as two peoples. He says, however, of the Joloffs, whom he praises as an active, powerful, and warlike race, that "their noses are not so much depressed nor the lips so protuberant as among the generality of Africans, although their skin is of the deepest black." In the case of this people, intermarriage upon the coast with purely negroid types had no doubt brought them to a near resemblance with negro peoples, but the Foulah strain was still of effect enough to make of them a people who were highly thought of by the white traders of the coast.

The Foulahs proper, whom Mungo Park distinguishes from the Joloffs, are, he says, "chiefly of a tawny complexion, with soft, silky hair and pleasing features." These Foulahs, like others scattered through the entire length of the fertile belt, were "much attached to a pastoral life," and had, he tells us, by the end of the eighteenth century "introduced themselves into all the kingdoms on the windward coast as herdsmen and husbandmen, paying a tribute to the sovereign of the country for the lands which they held." The same pastoral Fulani migrated, as we have seen, in the thirteenth and fourteenth centuries to the Haussa States and Bornu, and paid tribute to the reigning kings of Kano and other towns.

They are known to this day in Northern Nigeria under the name of Cow Fulani. Mungo Park also says of the Foulahs, "They are naturally mild and gentle. . . . They evidently consider all the negro nations as their inferiors, and when talking of different nations always rank themselves among white peoples. . . . They are Mussulmans, and the authority and laws of the prophet are everywhere looked upon as sacred and decisive." He tells us that, in his day, they possessed in the Soudan many kingdoms at great distances from each other, and he notices the diversity of their appearance. "Their complexion, however, is not quite the same in the different districts. In kingdoms which are situated in the vicinity of the Moorish territories (meaning to the north), they are of a more yellow complexion than in the southern states." He mentions the fact that they have a separate language, and gives specimens of its vocabulary. Francis Moore, speaking of the Fulani of the Gambia in 1734, gives them much the same character as that given them by Mungo Park. "They have chiefs of their own," he says, "who rule with so much moderation, that every act of government seems rather an act of the people than of one man." He also speaks of their charitable and humane qualities. Dr. Blyden, writing of them in the present day, tells us that every man and woman among them can at least read Arabic.

Denham, writing a little later than Mungo Park, gives us a description of another class of Foulah or Fulani as he met them on the shores of Lake Chad. "They are," he says, "a very handsome race of people, of a deep copper colour, who seldom mix their blood with that of the negroes, have a peculiar language of their own, and are Moslem." These were the conquerors of Bornu, aristocrats and military rulers. He says of them in another place that they resembled the inhabitants of Tetuan in Morocco. He also finds in them a resemblance to the gypsies in England. But a Foulah whom he met in one of the border towns of Bornu told him, he says, that he had been to Mecca, and that there he had met Wahabis, who "were the same people and spoke the same language as the Fulani."

Barth speaks of the Fulani as a race distinguished by its absorbent powers, and now comprising many other races, of which there are four main divisions. He gives the names as the "Jel," the "Baa," the "So," and the "Beri," but these again are subdivided. Both Barth and Denham speak of the great capacity of the aristocratic Fulani for ruling other races. Denham says of them on the western border of Bornu, "They are here much esteemed by the people whom they rule for their impartial administration of justice." In all this, we are reminded of Bacon's axiom, that "States that are liberal of naturalisation towards strangers are fit for empire." Throughout the entire history of the Soudan, members of the Fulani race are to be found in positions of importance and responsibility. There were in every successive civilisation Fulani judges, Fulani imaums of the mosques, Fulani men of letters, Fulani advisers to the kings, and frequent mention is made of the Fulani wives of persons in high position. This influence was not confined exclusively to the Soudan. It spread even to Morocco. More than one Moorish sovereign had a Fulani counsellor, and it is mentioned that Muley Hamed, the reigning sovereign of Morocco, at the moment of the Moorish conquest had a favourite Fulani wife, Lella Aouada by name.

It is not surprising that a race of such varying activities, lending itself to such different developments, should give rise to widely-varying scientific theories of its origin.

The one point upon which all scientific investigation is agreed is that the language of the Fulani is not African, and that this people, which has maintained in the Soudan an individuality no less marked and persistent than that maintained by the Jews in Europe, was originally wholly foreign to the environment in which we find it.

Its first home in Africa would seem to have been the south-western corner between the Senegal and the Atlantic, in which, according to Herodotus and Strabo, the Phœnicians made their early settlements. As this was the remotest extremity of the western world known to the ancients, it follows as a matter of course that the original home of the Fulani is supposed to have been further east. It is indeed a disputed point whether their first movements in Africa were from west to east, or gradually in the first instance from east to west, and only later, within our own times, from west to east. One theory of their origin is that they are of the same Malayan or Polynesian stock as that which is believed to have colonised Madagascar. Another is that they came originally from Egypt, and this involves the assumption that their movement in Africa was a gradual advance from east to west. This theory would seem to be disproved by the fact that their language has no affinity to the languages of the Nile. It has also been sought to associate them with the Jews, but it has been shown that their language is still further removed from languages of Semitic origin than it is from the idiom of the Soudan. I do not know whether this objection would apply to the language of the Phœnicians, nor have I anywhere seen the theory of Phœnician descent scientifically examined. The theory which seems to be most generally received and most logically supported is that the fount of origin of the Fulani people must be sought in India. This is the opinion of M. de Lauture, who relates the legend of their origin, as he learned it in Darfur, to be that they sprang from the marriage of a Hindu, who entered the Soudan by way of Egypt, with the female of a chameleon. He takes the legend to mean that the Fulani were the outcome of a union of Hindu stock with different tribes of the Soudan, in this way accounting for the great diversity of their characteristics.

Dr. Thaly supports the Indian theory. He connects the Fulani with the gypsies of Europe, and traces both gypsies and Fulani to an Indian origin. There are legends quoted by Barth and by M. Berenger Feraud to the effect that the Fulani entered the Soudan originally by way of Morocco, and these, though offered in opposition to the Indian theory, might, with very little straining, be made to support it, for Strabo, after describing a populous and flourishing African nation dwelling to the far west of Africa in the country opposite to Spain, adds the remark, "Some say that they are Indians who accompanied Hercules hither." The legend of Strabo, added to those quoted by modern writers, might therefore account for an Indian origin, even in Fulani who had entered the Soudan by way of Southern Morocco. It has also been sought to connect the Fulani with the Berbers, but this theory is rejected by philologists. It will, however, be remembered that among the nomad tribes of the desert, mentioned in an earlier chapter, allusion was made to one tribe not to be confused with those of Berber race. These were the Zingari or gypsies, who were believed to be of Indian descent. In assuming a Berber origin for the Fulani, it is again not improbable that the opponents of the Indian theory may unconsciously be supporting it by a confusion between one nomadic race of the desert and another.

That the Fulani may have owed their origin to the downfall of the dynasty of the Hyksos, or Shepherd Kings, who were driven from Egypt about the year 1630 B.C., is finally a theory which would seem to reconcile many conflicting arguments. M. Delafosse, whose studies in West African languages give special weight to his opinions, and who is one of the latest writers upon the subject, is inclined to espouse this view. He thus countenances the opinion of those who contend that the Fulani entered the Soudan by way of Egypt, but at the same time he emphatically rejects the theory of Egyptian origin, and carries the question of origin one step further back to that of the origin and race of the Hyksos themselves. This he would find in India, "probably on the southern slopes of the Himalayan Mountains." He puts forward as a suggestion that the same migrations of Hindu origin may have given us the Hyksos and the gypsies and the Fulani. He does not regard the question as having been yet decisively examined, and he appeals to anthropologists and philologists to assist in its scientific elucidation by comparison between the racial characteristics and the dialects of the Fulani, the gypsies, and certain existing pastoral tribes in India. As a result of some slight study of his own of gypsy language he adds, "I think I may say that of all African, Asiatic, Oceanian, and European tongues which I have compared with the language of the Fulani, the language of the gypsies is that which appears to me to possess the greatest point of resemblance."

In connection with the theory of the descent of the Fulani from the Hyksos, I would quote the great similarity observed by my husband to exist between the Wahuma of Eastern Africa and the Fulani of the Western Soudan. The Wahuma, like the Fulani, were pastoral nomads who, in the endeavour to secure fresh grazing ground, became invaders and conquerors. In Uganda, Unyoro, Karagwe, and other eastern states the Wahuma founded the royal dynasties, while their tribesmen, corresponding in position to the Cow Fulani, tended the cattle of the negroids. The Wahuma, who have a great physical likeness to the Fulani, are often strikingly handsome and extremely intelligent. That the Wahuma should have descended upon East Africa from the valley of the Nile is not surprising. Of both races, Fulani and Wahuma alike, it can at least be said that they so far support the theory of a common origin in the Hyksos, as to have maintained through all their history, in the diverse countries in which they are to be found, the ancient position of Shepherd Kings.

CHAPTER XLI

RISE OF THE FULANI IN THE SOUDAN

ASSUMING the Fulani and the gypsy to be of similar Indian race and to have entered the Soudan by way of Egypt, perhaps nearly two thousand years before Christ, we have still the fact that within historic times the movement of the Fulani in the Western Soudan has been from west to east, not from east to west.

The earliest definite mention which we get of them is the rumour mentioned by the author of the *Tarikh-es-Soudan*, that the first white king of Ghana, who reigned presumably in the third century of the Christian era, was reputed to have had a Fulani name—Quaia Magha, which in Fulani means Quaia the Great. Whether Phœnician or Fulani, the first white rulers of Ghana continued to reign for twenty-two generations, and were then superseded by a black dynasty.

In the ninth century we hear of Fulani occupying the town of Masina, situated on the Niger between Jenné and Timbuctoo, and the following story is told of the origin of their kings.

Maghan, a fugitive prince from his own country of Koma, in the territory of Quaiaka, came driving a few oxen before him to a hill called Masina, in the territory of Baghena. He and his followers made friends with the Senajah (Berbers), who occupied the territory, and after a time, Maghan having been joined by more followers, the King of Baghena named him king of those who had followed him. All the Fulani then joined themselves to Maghan, some being of his own tribe and some of Sankora. From this time (to which no date is affixed),

Masina drew its kings from four tribes, of which one inhabited Quaiaka and one Borgu. We are also told that, by an agreement between themselves, the people of Masina had for their kings alternately a Berber and a Fulani. Presumably, therefore, the tribes of Quaiaka and Borgu were Fulani, and the other two of the four were Berbers. This arrangement, mentioned at so early a period, is illustrative of the adaptable nature of Fulani institutions.

Masina was independent enough at the end of the ninth century to solicit help from the Berber kings of the Desert Empire against black neighbours who pressed upon it inconveniently, and to carry through a victorious campaign. It held its own against Ghana in the great days of that pagan empire, and maintained itself as a centre of Fulani rule through the administrations alike of Melle and of Songhay.

It is in the early period of the rise of Melle—that is, in the thirteenth century—that we have the first record of Fulani immigration from Melle into the Haussa States and Bornu. From this we may infer a certain pressure by the rising power upon the Fulani of the west, but those who migrated to Haussaland at this period were apparently purely pastoral nomads, who took their place humbly in their new home as Cow Fulani, and were content to pay tax to the local kings. During the military campaigns which preceded the rise of the Songhay dynasty in the fifteenth century, we hear constantly of expeditions undertaken against the Fulani, who would seem to have resisted stoutly all encroachments upon their liberty. Sonni Ali in 1492 conquered the Fulani of Gurma in the eastern portion of the Bend of the Niger. Sonni Ali also apparently conquered Masina so far as to induce it to pay tribute and to accept the investiture of its rulers from the hands of Timbuctoo, but it jealously guarded its administrative independence, and throughout the records of the Songhay dynasty wars with Masina were of frequent recurrence. Differences of religion were often apparently involved, and at least one false prophet who arose amongst the Fulani was driven before the conquering arms of Songhay to found a new kingdom for himself in the south-western corner of the Soudan, close to the kingdom of the Joloffs. Independence of action, independence of religion, independence of administration, would seem to have been the sturdy characteristic of Fulani social life.

Opinion is divided as to the period at which the Fulani generally accepted Mohammedanism, but the fact mentioned in the chronicles of Bornu that Fulani teachers from Melle were among the first to preach the doctrines of Mohammed in Bornu in the early part of the thirteenth century, combined with the high position constantly taken by Fulani individuals throughout the history of the Soudan as teachers, men of letters, &c., would seem to indicate that the conversion of the upper class of Fulani was of comparatively early date. There seems to have been always a distinction between the purely pastoral shepherd, or Cow Fulani, who occupied the position of a nomad peasant, caring for nothing but his cattle, and the aristocratic or ruling Fulani, from whose numbers some of the most distinguished individuals of Soudanese history were drawn. The Cow Fulani are to the present day believed to be pagan in many districts.

The connection with the Fulani of Borgu on the eastern edge of the Bend of the Niger that was mentioned in relation to the founding of Masina on the western edge, is indicative of a somewhat wide distribution of Fulani tribes, and of an alliance, or at least friendship, between the Fulani of the east and west, which appears to have existed from very early times, and was often made use of by them when there was occasion to rise against the Songhay kings.

Some writers assert that Kanta, the rebellious general of Songhay who founded the kingdom of Kebbi, was himself of Fulani origin. This is uncertain, but in the next generation to Kanta the Fulani of the eastern portion of the Bend of the Niger joined the banners of his son. It was as a partly Fulani kingdom that Kebbi became great, and the Fulani may perhaps be said to have first taken a position as rulers on the eastern side of the Niger when they helped Tomo, the son of Kanta, to fight Bornu, and to found the even now celebrated town of Birni-n-Kebbi within the borders of Haussaland in 1544. They had also, in the sixteenth century, spread into Baghirmi on the eastern side of Chad. In the west they gradually absorbed the province of Wangara, and greatly aggrandised their ancient territory of Masina.

It is clear that, throughout the whole period of the domination of the Songhay, the Fulani in their different centres of occupation increased in importance and in military strength, and were beginning to assert themselves definitely as a cultivated people with a capacity for rule. The Askias, by the many expeditions which are recorded against Fulani tribes, display a certain uneasiness at the growing independence of this people. In the year 1591, the very year of the coming of the Moors, Fulani chiefs took a leading part in the sack of the territory of Jenné, and more than one punitive expedition was rendered necessary by their turbulence.

Thus, at the end of the sixteenth century, the Fulani had already extended themselves through the Western Soudan as pastoral nomads, independent, though paying a grazing-tax, in all the countries which they occupied from the sources of the Senegal to Lake Chad. At more than one point on this extended line centres of government had been founded, and Fulani troops had established for themselves a reputation as military conquerors.

At the moment of the coming of the Moors they were the rising power of the Soudan, and during the Moorish troubles at the end of the sixteenth and the beginning of the seventeenth centuries, they used their opportunity to assert their independence of Songhay. The resistance offered by the half Fulani state of Kebbi to the eastward advance of the Moors has been mentioned in an earlier chapter. In 1599 Masina opened a campaign against the Moors, and though defeated in the first instance, the reverse would only seem to have consolidated Fulani resistance to the foreign rule. In 1629, the kings of Masina refused any longer to accept investiture from the decadent government of Timbuctoo, and during the seventeenth century the Fulani fought for their independence in the eastern as well as in the western districts of the Bend of the Niger. The Moors, harried upon the north by the Tuaregs of the desert, and on the south by the Fulani, abandoned the vain attempt to maintain their supremacy in the Soudan. They were driven out of Gago, as has been already mentioned, in 1770. They continued to hold the town of Timbuctoo, but during the eighteenth century, when the Moors had fallen to the condition described by Mungo Park, the contest for the sovereignty of the Soudan would seem to have been between the Fulani and the Tuaregs. It was the Tuaregs who finally drove the Moors from Timbuctoo in the year 1800, and within a generation the Tuaregs themselves were driven out by the Fulani.

During this whole period of tumult the Soudan was closed to Europe, and we have no accurate account of the series of local wars by which it would seem to have been distracted. At the beginning of the nineteenth century, when, after an eclipse of two hundred years, its history once more emerges to our view, the situation is so far clear that the Fulani had become the dominating people, alike in the west and in the east.

In the west, where the Tuaregs were their opponents, they were a little later in attaining to supreme power than in the eastern states, but in 1813 Masina became the seat of a powerful Fulani Empire, ruled by a Sheikh of the name of Ahmadou. Under the leadership of Ahmadou, Masina conquered Timbuctoo in 1833. On the death of Ahmadou in 1844, Timbuctoo was once more taken by the Tuaregs, but it was reconquered by the Fulani in 1855, and, with the exception of three years, from 1860 to 1863, when it was taken and held by the Toucouleurs, a half-breed Fulani people, the true Fulani continued to hold it up to the moment of its conquest by the French in 1893. The Toucouleurs, who remained masters of a portion of the Niger Valley, and who also submitted to France in 1893, were a people in whose veins Fulani blood predominated to so great an extent that their ascendancy on the upper river may be accepted as representing for that part of the country the general ascendancy of the Fulani races.

The history of the Fulani conquest of the Haussa States, where another Sheikh, as famous as Ahmadou, founded a Fulani Empire, is comparatively well known. The country was, we have seen, permeated with Fulani influence. Cow Fulani fed their cattle in every province. The principal towns had their Fulani quarters; Fulani teachers had for six hundred years spread the doctrines of Mohammed; distinguished members of the Fulani race occupied high places as councillors, judges, high priests, and men of war. Zaria had had, according to one account, a Fulani king from the year 1780. The western provinces of Bornu were also full of Fulani. The conquest of Haussaland by the Fulani may therefore be said to have been half achieved in the seventeenth and eighteenth centuries, at the same time that the Fulani were rising in power throughout the whole Soudan.

It was not, however, till the opening years of the nineteenth century that the military and political conquest was completed.

It will be remembered that, at the end of the eighteenth century, the still pagan state of Gober had established a military ascendancy over the more northerly Mohammedan states of Haussaland. It had conquered Zanfara and subdued Kano. Katsena alone had been able successfully to resist its power. Throughout this period the Fulani would seem to have greatly increased in numbers in Gober, and under their own chiefs and religious teachers they began to form a community of which the independent doctrines gave offence to the pagan authorities.

In the year 1802, the King Bawa sent for their Imaum, Othman dan Fodio, and all the principal Fulani chiefs, and administered a severe public reprimand on account of the religious and political pretensions that they were beginning to put forward. This was but a spark to the tinder. Indignation spread through the Fulani community at the insult which had been offered to their chiefs. Othman dan Fodio inflamed the general sentiment by his preaching, in which he urged the Fulani to submit no longer to the yoke of a pagan people. The Fulani chiefs raised the standard of revolt; Othman was elected Sheikh, and under his leadership a Holy War was declared which was to counterbalance, by the successes which it gave to the Fulani on the eastern side of the Niger, any temporary loss which this people had suffered in the west. The date of the opening of the Holy War is given differently by different authors, who vary between 1800 and 1804, but it evidently broke out immediately after the taking of Timbuctoo by the Tuaregs in 1800, and Othman dan Fodio gave the lead in Haussaland, which was shortly followed by Ahmadou in the west. Between them these two Fulani Sheikhs conquered the Western Soudan from Masina to Bornu.

The first efforts of the Fulani in Haussaland were stoutly resisted by Gober, and, though the province was subdued, the capital, Alkalawa, was not taken during the lifetime of Dan Fodio. But through the rest of Haussaland, where the towns were already half in Fulani hands, the conquest of the Fulani spread rapidly. Zanfara was conquered in the first year of the war; Zaria was either conquered, or allied itself with the conquerors, within a month of the submission of Zanfara. The conquest of Kano shortly followed; Katsena was taken in 1807; and in 1808 the victorious arms of the Fulani were carried into Bornu.

Here, however, after a short period of triumph, they

were met and successfully resisted by another Sheikh, Mohammed el Kanemi, who arose in Kanem, and took the reins of power from the effete sovereigns of Bornu. This man, who founded the existing dynasty of Bornu, was visited by Major Denham in 1823, and is described by him as "a most extraordinary instance in the Eastern world of fearless bravery, virtue, and simplicity." His career was remarkable enough to deserve something more than a passing mention. He was born in Fezzan, though of Kanem parents, having, it is said, on his father's side, some Moorish blood. He appears to have been, at least partly, educated in Egypt, and to have been already in the position of a Sheikh before he first visited the home of his parents in Kanem. Here he lived for some years, greatly beloved and respected for the extreme uprightness and benevolence of his life.

It was the conquest of Bornu by the Fulani which brought him into public life. Believing, or causing his Kanemi followers to believe, that he was inspired by a vision of the Almighty to undertake the liberation of the country, he collected a little body of the faithful, only 400 strong, and with them marched to a first encounter with the Fulani. He is said to have overthrown an army 8000 strong. The result was, of course, to bring more soldiers to his standard, and in ten months he was victorious in forty battles. It is said that he had all the qualifications of a great commander, but so little of personal ambition that when, after he had driven the Fulani out of Bornu, the people desired to make him Sultan, he refused the offer, and placed Mohammed, the brother of the deposed Sultan Achmet, on the throne. He refused all titles for himself, except that of "Servant of God," but he kept the practical powers of a dictator, and, while he lived without ostentation, he was the head of the army, and the real ruler of the kingdom. He completely overthrew the Fulani, and defended the Empire of Bornu in many desperate campaigns against the attacks of Baghirmi. On the death of Sultan Mohammed he still refused to be made Sultan, and again put a dummy Sultan on the throne, reserving for himself the responsibility of power without any of its outward display. His campaigns were usually successful, and it is said of him that he "turned all victories to the advantage of those whom he overthrew." By the purity of his administration and the reforms which he introduced, the kingdom grew in enlightenment as well as power. Nowhere were the laws of Islam more strictly observed than in Bornu under his administration. The wider education of his youth had given him a knowledge of other countries, which he used for the benefit of his own. Foreigners were well received, trade prospered, and the roads, through the Sheikh's government, were, according to Major Denham, "as safe as any, even in happy England itself."

After the overthrow of Baghirmi, which was achieved with the co-operation of the ruler of the Fezzan about the year 1824, the ruler of Bornu turned his arms against South-western Haussaland, where he was at first successful, and took from the Fulani the province of Bautchi, which they had conquered shortly after the taking of Zaria; but here, in the year 1826, he was destined to meet with a reverse. His armies were defeated by the Fulani, and he himself narrowly escaped with his life. Shortly after this he came to terms of agreement with the Fulani.

He died in 1835, when his son, who succeeded, abolished the dummy Sultans, and established the dynasty of the Kanemi openly on the throne of Bornu.

CHAPTER XLII

SULTAN BELLO

THE whole of Haussaland up to the borders of Bornu had before this become subject to the conquering Fulani. Othman dan Fodio himself died in 1816, and divided his newly conquered empire between his son, Mohammed Bello, and a brother, Abdallai. He gave to Mohammed Bello, who, during his father's lifetime, had founded for himself the new town of Sokoto, the sovereignty of the Eastern Provinces, while to his brother, whose headquarters were at Gando, south and slightly west of Sokoto, he gave the provinces of the West. Sultan Bello, a man no less remarkable than his great rival, Mohammed el Kanemi, of Bornu, continued to reign until 1837, and this period, almost coinciding with the great period of Bornu under its new ruler, must be regarded as forming also the great period of Fulani rule in Haussaland.

Sultan Bello ascended to the throne at a very difficult moment. His father's arms, largely under Bello's direction, had completed the conquest of the principal states of Kano, Katsena, and Zaria, in the centre of Haussaland, and had spread to the south-east over the Bautchi Hills, and into the provinces bordering upon the Benué. The Fulani had also, as we have seen, fought successfully with Zanfara and Gando. But the western group of provinces, including Zanfara, Gober, and Gando, had been very imperfectly subdued. These provinces, of which the governments would seem to have been pagan, were filled with stubborn fighters. It suited the Fulani to proclaim a holy war, and to inflame the courage of their armies by treating their enemies as infidels, but, as a matter of fact, there were many Mohammedans amongst their opponents, for Islam had long been the religion of the upper classes of all the principal towns of Haussaland. In the central provinces of Katsena, Kano, and Zaria, the government and the whole organisation of society was Mohammedan, a fact admitted by the Fulani when they adopted, as they subsequently did, the existing Haussa, or, as the conquerors preferred to call them, "Habe," systems of law, justice, and taxation. All these were based upon the Koran. In Zaria the reigning dynasty was actually Fulani; in Katsena and Kano the reigning sovereigns were of Haussa dynasties, but for many generations they had been Mohammedan. Kebbi, one of the most stubborn opponents of Fulani domination, was itself, as we have seen, at one time partly populated by Fulani. There existed, therefore, in all these provinces large bodies of Mohammedans, who were driven out before the conquerors, and in many cases we hear of Mohammedan Haussas obliged to take refuge, like the pagan population, in the hills. This is to say, that everywhere there existed large sections of the cultivated upper classes profoundly antagonistic to Fulani rule. Shortly after 1808 the defeats of the Fulani by Mohammed el Kanemi in Bornu began to inspire new courage into the disaffected, and about the year 1816, the very year of the accession of Mohammed Bello, a confederation was formed of Haussa States determined to fight for their independence with the Fulani.

According to a Mohammedan account written by a certain Hadj Said, and translated as a fragment of the history of Sokoto by M. Houdas, Sultan Bello had hardly received the oath of allegiance when all the provinces neighbouring upon Sokoto abjured Islam and rose in revolt against the Mohammedan rulers, who were apparently supported, perhaps nominated, by Bello. The native chiefs of Gober, Zanfara, and Nupe, were the first to form the confederation. They were shortly joined by Northern Katsena, Yauri, Kebbi, Kano, Kontagora, Daura, and Southern Zaria. It would seem that all the lesser states of Haussaland at one time joined this "Tawias" or revolt against the Fulani. That it was not a religious but a political revolt is made fairly clear by the names of Kebbi, Kano, and Katsena, who were distinctly Mohammedan, and by the fact that the confederation entered into alliance with the Moors.

One native chief led the revolt in Zanfara, and established himself in a stronghold almost within sight of Sokoto. Another led the revolt in the province of Gando. The early years of Bello's reign were occupied by constant expeditions against the revolted provinces. After fighting the pagan leaders in Gando, Gober, Zanfara, and Kebbi, he encountered the Moors and was himself defeated. It is to be noted that in these campaigns Bello's successes are always attributed to the exertions of his cavalry.

At a date which is not specified by Hadj Said, but which must probably have been about the year 1820, the confederated states made a determined effort to overthrow their Fulani conqueror. They renewed their alliance with the Moors, and having assured themselves of the sympathy of Mohammed el Kanemi of Bornu, their combined forces marched upon the territory of Sokoto. Bello collected an immense army at Wurnu, and Omar, the head of the Fulani Church, a very holy man living in high repute at Sokoto, addressed the soldiers. The Fulani professed to regard the war as a struggle for life and death between Islam and paganism. The soldiers of Bello's army were enjoined to keep their hearts pure, and to commit no atrocities. With these injunctions the army marched to the encounter of the federated forces. The attack appears to have been made from the north, and in the dry season of the year. The sufferings of the army from thirst were terrible. Bello, in person, encouraged the troops by reminding them constantly of the sacred cause for which they fought, but at last the position grew so desperate that the army was halted, and Bello called upon the Sheikh Omar, who had, of course, accompanied the troops, to pray for guidance as to whether it was the will of the Almighty that they should return without encountering the enemy.

It is rather interesting to find among the religious enthusiasts of the Fulani of Sokoto in the early part of the century the same ideas of spiritualism, higher thought, and second-sight, which are to-day animating the modern religious sects of England and America. Omar, it is said, having spent the night in prayer, at sunrise heard a voice which cried three times, "Victory has come!" The Sultan at this moment sent to inquire of the holy man what was the will of God. Was the army to advance or to retreat? "To advance!" replied the Sheikh. The troops accordingly marched and encamped one station farther in the thirsty land. Here, by the holiness of the Sheikh, a wonder was achieved. For Omar, having prostrated himself in prayer and remained long upon the earth, saw as in second-sight water coming underground. Only when he saw this did he raise his head from the ground. The Sultan then took a spear, and plunging it into the earth, gave the order, "Dig here!" Hardly had they begun to dig when water rose. Every man then received orders to dig in the place on which he stood, and everywhere that the soldiers dug water was found.

This incident is quite in the spirit of the religious life of Sokoto. One of the principal generals of the army, Abd el Kader, who was also famed for the holiness of his life, used to have visions in which he had intercourse with the dead, and at the house of one of the noble ladies of Sokoto spiritualistic séances used to be held, in which the spirits of the great dead showed themselves, we are told, to those who were worthy to perceive them.

The army remained on this spot for two days. On the following Monday they prayed, and on the Tuesday the "army of the infidels" arrived. With them was Aber,

King of the Moors. Certain Moors who were with Bello pointed this out to him, and the unwelcome evidence that the opposing army was not composed entirely of infidels made Bello so angry that he ordered the Moors who were with him to quit the ranks.

The battle began. "God gave the victory to the Moslems, and 25,000 of the enemy were killed." The number of confederated states engaged may be partly estimated by the havoc made among their rulers. Al, King of Gober, was taken prisoner; Roud, King of Katsena, was killed; Aber, King of the Moors, fled. Bello kept his soldiers in strict order, and allowed no slaves to be made. He assembled the notables of Gober, and bade them choose a king in place of the king whom he had taken prisoner. They chose Bello's own son, Fodi. We are not told whether the votes were free. But even the complaisant chronicler of the Fulani records that Fodi's conduct in his new kingdom was "scandalous." He was "tyrannical, dissolute, impious, and occupied himself solely with games and pleasure." The appointment is worth noting, as Fodi furnishes in the lifetime of Sultan Bello an example of the bad Fulani of whom, in the universal praise of the Fulani race, there is a tendency to lose sight. If it may be said of Sultan Bello that he was himself an embodiment of the very best qualities of his race, this favoured son may no less justly be taken as a prototype of the cruel and self-indulgent despots, under whose rule at a later period Haussaland fell into the state of ruin and decadence in which we found it.

The battle in which this victory of Islam was achieved was called the battle of Dagh. Disastrous as it was to the interests of the confederation, the states did not accept the result as a final and decisive defeat. They continued their resistance to Fulani rule, and Bello addressed himself to the task of reducing each singly to submission. Zanfara was conquered, and he placed his brother Atiku upon that throne. Gando then raised a revolt against Abdallai, Bello's uncle. Bello marched against the revolted province, and the campaign is interesting for the illustration which it gives of Bello's respect for his father's division of the territory of Haussaland, and also for the growing evidence—which even the Fulani generals could not ignore—that the opponents of Bello were not entirely pagans. Throughout the campaign Bello forbade his troops to enter the town of Gando, which was under his uncle's rule, and we are allowed to know that warm discussions arose between the generals as to whether their enemies were infidels or not. When at last the battle which put an end to the revolt was fought, it was found necessary, in observance of Koranic law, to apply some religious test to the prisoners. They were called upon to recite the *fatiha*, and to make their ablutions. Those who passed the test satisfactorily were set at liberty. Those who did not were sold as slaves. The refusal to permit slaves to be made after the battle of Dagh already indicated some scruple of conscience on Bello's part.

It was at about this period that Mohammed el Kanemi of Bornu, having completed the subjection of Baghirmi, turned his attention to Haussaland. All the vanquished Sultans of Western Haussaland, says the chronicler, grouped themselves round him, and he promised to restore them all to their thrones should he prove victorious in the struggle with the Sultan Bello.

The encounter between the two forces took place, as we have seen, in the south-eastern provinces, and was unfavourable to the hopes of the Haussa kings. The army of Bornu, bearing a letter of defiance to Sultan Bello, marched in the first instance upon Kano. Bello, who appears to have fully recognised the magnitude of the danger which threatened him in now, for the first time, frankly facing a Mohammedan foe, rallied all his forces from the south, and called upon the Fulani sovereigns of Zaria and Bautchi to put their armies in the field. A general advance was made against El Kanemi, who appears to have turned and marched southwards. The exact spot in which the first battle took place is not indicated; but the fight raged long and fiercely, and it was the troops of Yakoub, the Sultan of Bautchi, who at last decided the action against Bornu. This battle, which, as we learn from the history of Bornu, took place in 1826, appears to have been the last important battle of Sultan Bello's reign. After it a lasting peace was concluded between Sokoto and Bornu, and the principal Haussa dynasties appear to have acquiesced in their final deposition from the thrones of Haussaland.

The western states of the Haussa confederation, according to the account given by Clapperton, finally made peace on the understanding that they were to continue to be ruled by their hereditary native princes, and that the Fulani were not to interfere with them. It is not definitely stated that these were the states subject to Gando, but the general course of events would lead to this inference. The ruler of Gando had from the beginning leaned upon Sokoto, in order to obtain the submission of his subject provinces. Thus Sokoto apparently gained a vague overlordship of Gando, while the states of which Gando was suzerain existed on somewhat different terms from those acknowledging direct allegiance to Sokoto. Sokoto became the universally accepted suzerain of the entire territory, and Fulani rule was established more or less completely from the capital of that province to the farthest limit enclosed between the Middle Niger and the Benué.

According to the Fulani chronicles, while Bello lived, Haussaland enjoyed a period of great prosperity. Clapperton, who travelled through the country during the lifetime of Sultan Bello, tells us that under Fulani rule trade was discouraged by heavy duties, but that agriculture flourished. The country round Zaria, when he first saw it, was "like the finest in England." There were quantities of rice and corn, and the land everywhere "looked beautiful." He notes fine cattle and horses, and heavy crops of grain "just high enough to wave with the wind." Wheat began north of Zaria. Zaria was then largely populated by Fulani and Arabs, who had flocked to Dan Fodio's standard, and to whom he had given the lands of the former inhabitants, who had fled to the mountains in the southern part of the province. These Mohammedan inhabitants maintained, like the pagans, a chronic state of war against the Fulani. The general form of residence of the Fulani rulers in Haussaland seems to have been adapted to this condition of affairs, and was, Clapperton tells us, "like the old keeps or castles in Scotland, near the borders."

Throughout the whole of his active life Bello found time to devote to literature. He was extremely fond of study, and wrote many books. His numerous works were, it is said, usually written in the form of dissertations, or replies to questions which raised doubtful points of law. But he also wrote some purely literary essays, amongst them one upon the poems of his father, which were "composed in the Soudanese language." Some short notes of his upon the geography and history of the Soudan, compiled by him from Haussa manuscripts, have been preserved. He is said to have encouraged science and learning, and at his court distinguished men from all countries were well received. It must, however, be counted as a serious blot upon his literary reputation that he everywhere permitted Haussa manuscripts to be destroyed, in order to efface the records of the conquered people.

He encouraged the members of his own family to acquire learning, and protested warmly against the form of Haussa superstition, which would have accredited them, by the mere fact of their birth, with inherited wisdom. "That," he constantly told them, "is pure illusion; knowledge can be maintained only by instruction."

In his public dealings he was equitable and modest. He maintained himself in early life entirely by his own exertions, refusing to live upon the public treasury. He had entered into this compact when he and his father opened their first holy campaign. "For you," he said to his father, "it is unavoidable that you should use the public money; but I am young: I can learn a trade and support myself." This, according to one of his historians, he continued to do all his life; but it is more probable that after his accession he yielded, like his father, to the pressure of necessity, and made use of the public funds.

He was, we are told, very good to the people, full of indulgence, calm and patient. He was an able administrator. When he wrote the treatises upon points of law, to which he devoted much of his time, the first thing that he did with them was to make them known to all his people, in order that the law might be generally observed. He inspected the Cadis, kept them in check, and annulled any unjust judgment. When, after his death, he was succeeded by his brother Atiku, the judges begged Atiku not to reverse their judgments as Bello had done; but Atiku was of the same breed, and only replied: "Judge with equity, and I will not reverse your judgments. Be on the side of right wherever you find it." The system of justice adopted by the Fulani was that already instituted by the Haussas. In their system of taxation the Fulani would seem, however, to have introduced innovations which must have been in many instances grievous to the Haussa people.

In appearance Bello was "red, tall, and bald, with a tufted beard." He wore the veil. His final illness lasted for some months. When it became grave, he sent for his son Ali, and warned him against trying to become Sultan after him. He refused to name a successor; but desired that his successor should be elected according to the custom of the people. He died at fifty-eight years of age, and left many sons and daughters.

CHAPTER XLIII

NORTHERN NIGERIA UNDER FULANI RULE

Bello of Sokoto and Kanemi of Bornu, who died within two years of each other, were the two great native sovereigns of the nineteenth century in the country now known as Northern Nigeria.

They had established their dynasties securely on their respective thrones, but the impression of their greatness did not long survive them. It would but weary the reader if I were to attempt to relate the little wars and counter wars which filled the second half of the nineteenth century, and immediately preceded the introduction of British administration. What has been told of the establishment of the Bornuese and Fulani powers is enough to show that in both cases very strong elements of disruption were waiting only for the removal of the hand which had welded the state together to break into active discord. There has remained the difference between the two empires, that in Bornu the power established was to a great extent a native power, which had to war against foreign invading elements, while in the rest of Haussaland the power established was a foreign power which fastened itself upon the necks of already existing and well-established native rulers. The wars, which in the latter half of the century decimated both empires, kept the different character imposed by this circumstance.

In the case of Bornu, the attacks of old enemies and foreign invaders from the east tended to minimise the native power, while pagan states previously held subject in the south profited by every opportunity to assert their independence.

On the western border of Bornu some Fulani states also made good an independent position; desert tribes raided from the north, and Bornu proper became, in the course of fifty years, a mere section of the Bornu Empire as it was ruled by Mohammed el Kanemi. Barth, who entered Haussaland from Tripoli in 1850, and travelled through Bornu, gives some account of troubles already tending to overthrow the power and dignity of Bornu. By various causes, of which perpetual slave-raiding was not the least active, the country was gradually desolated. Its trade was almost destroyed, its agriculture ruined, and towards the end of the century it fell an easy prey to a native military adventurer known as Rabbeh Zubeir, who, marching with a large army from Darfur, subdued for a time the whole Mohammedan belt to the east of Chad. In 1893 Rabbeh overthrew the existing dynasty of Bornu, and continued to rule the country under a military tyranny till in April of 1900 he in turn was overthrown, not by the British, but by the French. French troops encountered his forces upon the border of what is now German territory, and having placed their own nominee on the throne of Bornu, their commanders were actually levying tribute in British territory at the moment when British administration was established in Northern Nigeria. The fortunes of Bornu had never in all its history been so low; the pride of its rulers, represented by an unhappy puppet held captive in foreign territory, was in the dust.

In the remainder of Haussaland a no less disastrous condition of affairs had been produced by the convulsive efforts of some of the Haussa States to cast off the rule of the Fulani, of others to aggrandise themselves at the expense of weaker neighbours, and of the pagans to maintain their cherished independence against all Mohammedan and slave-raiding powers alike; while above the seething mass of discontent, rebellion, and civil war, the Fulani power tightened its hold only the more despotically upon such portions of the country as it could keep. A domination, which was established in the name of religion and justice, had fallen into tyranny, tempered only by the weakness or the moderation of personal rulers. Under Dan Fodio and Bello the conquering armies of the Fulani were enjoined to spread the true faith and to convert the pagans to Islamism. At a later period it was found more profitable to leave the pagans in a condition in which it was lawful to make slaves and to exact tribute, and Fulani wars degenerated into little more than slave-raiding expeditions.

The judicial system of the Haussas, already founded on Mohammedan institutions, and adopted in the first instance by the conquerors, was allowed to fall into disuse. Courts continued to exist, but the Alkalis who should have presided over them and dispensed justice according to Koranic law, irremovable from their positions as the judges of Great Britain, were either disregarded, as in some cases by the great chiefs who held their own courts and gave decisions at their own will, or over-ruled by the emir, or worse still, subjected to the authority of the emir's favourite slaves, who decreed to their enemies inhuman punishments of their own invention. For the nails to be torn out with red-hot pincers, for the limbs to be pounded one by one in a mortar while the victims were still alive, for important people who had offended to be built up alive gradually in the town walls, till, after a period of agony, the head of the dying man was finally walled up, were among the punishments well attested to have been inflicted in the decadence of Fulani power. It is said that a considerable number of the walls of Haussa towns are known by the people to have been so built up, and are even now called by the name of the most distinguished victims whose corpses they contain. Impalement and mutilation were among the penalties of lesser offences. Some of the Fulani emirs would themselves appear to have been monsters of inhumanity, who rejoiced, like the depraved emperors of Rome, in witnessing the mortal agonies of their victims. The public prisons became places of public torture, from which few who were confined in them could escape alive. Here is the description of the prison of Kano, as it was in existence up to the moment of the British occupation of the province. I quote the High Commissioner's account, given in the Colonial Report for Northern Nigeria, 1902 :—

"I visited the dungeon myself. A small doorway, 2 feet 6 inches by 1 foot 6 inches, gives access to it. The interior is divided, by a thick, mud wall, with a similar hole through it, into two compartments, each 17 feet by 7, and 11 feet high. This wall was pierced with holes at its base, through which the legs of those sentenced to death were thrust up to the thigh, and the condemned men were left to be trodden on by the mass of other prisoners till they died of thirst or starvation. The place is entirely air-tight and unventilated, except for the one small doorway, or rather hole in the wall, through which you creep. The total space inside is 2618 cubic feet, and at the time we took Kano, 135 human beings were confined here each night, being let out during the day to cook their food, &c., in a small adjoining area. Recently as many as 200 have been interned at one time. As the superficial area was only 238 square feet, there was not, of course, even standing room. Victims were crushed to death every night, and their corpses were hauled out each morning. The stench, I am told, inside the place when Colonel Morland visited it was intolerable, though it was empty, and when I myself went inside, more than three weeks later, the effluvia was unbearable for more than a few seconds."

These were the forms and these the instruments to the use of which Fulani justice had degenerated, and in the midst of them the only chance of obtaining favourable consideration of a given case lay in heavy bribery. The powers and constitution of the courts varied in every Fulani province, but in all the tendency was to inflict heavy fines for the benefit of the emir and the court. In all, without exception, such justice as there was, was bought and sold.

The system of taxation, like the system of justice, originally based in the Haussa States upon Koranic law, and in the first instance adopted by the conquerors, was similarly debased. The legitimate taxation established under the Haussa dynasties divides itself roughly into the four classes of taxes on land and crops; taxes on cattle; taxes on handicrafts and trades; customs, tolls, and death duties. To these there was added, in the first instance, a tax payable from all the conquered states to Sokoto and Gando, which, though payable from Moslem to Moslem, and called by a different name to distinguish it from the tribute only lawfully to be taken from pagans, was, in fact, the equivalent of a tribute, and by its payment conveyed the recognition of sovereignty. Had this been all, the conquered states might reasonably have accepted the inevitable. But if the abuse of justice is one of the means by which arbitrary authority can assert its power, the abuse of taxation is an even more fruitful and more tempting method. Taxes multiplied in the Fulani states. Under the four legitimate headings, now increased by the institution of the Sokoto and Gando tribute to five, each ruler invented at his will new imposts. Even in Bello's lifetime, Haussa trade was, according to the contemporary observation of Clapperton, hampered under Fulani rule by heavy dues. In the degradation of Fulani rule in the latter half of the century, trade was practically destroyed, and agriculture rendered almost impossible by the ceaseless creation of new taxes. Not only were new taxes imposed at the will of each new ruler, but the collection of existing taxes was made the subject of such abuse as the collection of taxes has been ever subject to in countries where personal authority has supported law. A body of alien tax-gatherers fastened like parasites upon the country. Fulani tax-collectors oppressed the native peasantry of every village. To show any sign of wealth was to invite the rapacity of those higher in the social scale. The Fulani conquerors claimed sovereign rights in land. Whole districts were given as feoffs to favourite retainers, who, living about the court in the enjoyments of office, collected taxes for the emir and for themselves from their feoffs through the agency of certain officials. These officials became practically their private servants, and of course shared the spoil. Agriculture groaned under the exactions that were laid upon it.

In nearly all the country districts the peasantry had remained pagan. To raid pagan countries for slaves was lawful according to the Koran. In the earlier years of their rule the Fulani used this permission to carry out raids against the pagan centres of the southern districts. Gradually, however, rebellion had its effect. As their power weakened, and was confined within narrower limits in the southern emirates, they were forced to abandon the process of distant raiding. They began to raid and sell their own peasantry, and thus completed the desolation of the country by a process which resembled the fabulous devouring of its own body by a snake.

It is not to be wondered at that revolt succeeded to revolt, and that Fulani power was more and more confined in the southern states to the limits of its own walled towns. Mutually defiant strongholds arose over the country. In the mountainous districts the wilder tribes of the pagans, including still some who preserve the habits of cannibals, found for themselves natural fortresses, in which they defended as they could the liberty which was their sole possession.

Yet through all the degradation of earlier Fulani ideals it is to be understood that in the Fulani emirates there was still to be found something of the nobler traditions of ancient thought. Individual rulers were still merciful and just. Abuse of power had not wholly destroyed its dignity. Though nominally the rulers of the whole of Haussaland, the principal seats of Fulani power were to be found in the north. Here Sokoto still commanded, as the suzerain of Haussaland, a something more than nominal allegiance; Kano sustained its ancient reputation as a trade centre, of which the relations extended to the Atlantic, to the Red Sea, and to the Mediterranean; Katsena and Zaria, notwithstanding many abuses, maintained themselves as administrative centres of importance.

The resemblance between the feudal system of the Fulani and the system established by the conquests of northern nations in Europe in the early portion of the Middle Ages, will not have escaped the reader. The parallel is remarkable with the system established in England by the Saxons, but in Haussaland it was perhaps closer to that which was developed in Italy under the Lombards. There is also this point of difference, that whereas the Haussas were an agricultural people, the Fulani were in their origin pastoral, and it is a recognised law of historic evolution that the rule of pastoral races has a stronger tendency to despotism than the rule of agricultural races. Underneath all the abuses which have established themselves in the Fulani administration of Haussaland there is said to exist, by those who have had the opportunity of studying the state systems of the different emirates, evidence of a deep-rooted desire for self-government. Presumably the conquered states endeavoured to retain as many as possible of the existing safeguards of their constitutions. The emirs are elected by a council of elders, and this council is not an empty name. It has a right to be consulted by the emirs in relation to all their important acts. The emir who ignores it is regarded as a tyrant, and runs great risk of losing his throne.

The constitution of Bida, by which the Fulani emirate of Nupe is now ruled, is one in which the principle of constitutional government was carried under the

Fulani to its most complete expression. Here, in addition to the emir and a council of princes composed only of descendants of the founder of the dynasty, which, though not entirely hereditary, bore some resemblance to a House of Lords, there was also a council corresponding in some degree to our own House of Commons. This was a council of notables, not of royal blood, but holding important state offices, and including the waziri or prime minister, the chief justice, the chief preacher, the commander-in-chief of the army, and the principal officers of the emir's household. The head of this council was the prime minister, and it was the prime minister, not one of the members of the council of princes, who was regarded as second in the state to the emir. Neither council was in a literal sense elective, the appointment to both being in the hands of the emir. But by native custom no appointment was made to either council without giving time for an expression of public opinion, and there were certain recognised methods by which the emir took the advice of his people in the matter both of appointments to council and to all the principal offices of state. Important matters of public policy were referred to the consideration of the two councils sitting together, but the ordinary business of the state was carried on by a privy council composed of two officers taken from each council, who were in constant consultation with the emir. This constitution is believed to have been adopted from the original Nupe state system. The constitutions of Sokoto and Gando, both of them new states created by the Fulani, are less elaborate.

By the end of the nineteenth century, that is, at the moment of the introduction of British authority, the territory of Haussaland may be said to have divided itself into three classes of states. There were states under Fulani rule such as those just named, where Fulani institutions were in active existence; other states conquered by the Fulani and nominally under Fulani rule, where taxes and Mohammedan institutions were imposed in different degree according to the amount of real authority exercised by the conqueror; and states which, from varying causes, were wholly independent. These last were either states which had succeeded in always defending their independence, and were ruled over by responsible native rulers of their own race, such as Boussa, Kiama, Argungu, &c., or Haussa and pagan communities which, having been once under Fulani rule, had succeeded in throwing it off, and were generally known by the name of Tawai, or "Revolted Peoples." Finally, there were independent pagan tribes, mostly in a low stage of development — sometimes even cannibals — and owning allegiance to no single authority. These resembled the pagans of the coast, among whom the authority of an individual chief is sometimes limited to the ramifications of his own family. As the higher development of Mohammedan institutions was to be found in the northern states, so this lowest type of pagan was most numerous in the southern districts lying upon both sides of the Benué. And, correspondingly, while the low class of pagan still held occasional fastnesses in the hills of the Fulani states, Fulani conquerors had imposed themselves upon the southern districts and held certain walled towns in the pagan areas.

Through the chaos of these conflicting interests, the practice of slave-raiding, carried on alike by the highest and the lowest, ran like the poison of a destructive sore, destroying every possibility of peaceful and prosperous development.

CHAPTER XLIV

SLAVE-RAIDING

FROM time immemorial the slave trade of the ancient world had its markets of supply in the Soudan. The earliest Greek historians speak of slaves captured by the native tribes of North Africa, and the monuments of Persia and Ethiopia show that the enslavement of the negro was a custom more ancient than any written record. In modern times the horrors of the African slave trade have been fully exposed by the great army of explorers who have penetrated into the interior of the continent. Livingstone, Baker, Stanley, Cameron, and many others, have given the testimony of eye-witnesses to the sufferings of the natives, whom the demand for slaves caused to be hunted like wild beasts in their homes. My husband, when he fought against the slave-raiders of Nyassaland, was himself a witness of the brutalities of the Mohammedan slave-hunters in East Africa. The curse of the slave-hunt in the equatorial regions of the continent has known no limit of time or place. It has spread broadly from sea to sea. To abolish it has been one of the aims which has most strongly enlisted the sympathy of the public in the modern movement of carrying civilisation into Africa.

During the whole period of which the principal historic movements of the Western Soudan have been so scantily outlined in this book, the trade in slaves was one of the most important elements of local industry and of foreign commerce. Spain and Portugal, North Africa and Egypt, drew their supply of slaves through the Middle Ages from the Soudan. We have seen at a later period how the slave trade of Europe was conducted on the coast.

Slave trade carried on upon an extensive scale involved the practice of slave-raiding as necessarily as the export of gold involved in West Africa the practice of alluvial gold-mining. From the earliest times it had been the custom, as we have seen, not only of Haussaland, but of all the countries of the Western Soudan, to raid the territories of the cannibal pagans to the south regularly once a year for slaves, and when war offered occasion for further profitable captures, whole armies were sometimes enslaved.

To the cannibal, whose practice it was to kill and eat his prisoners, slavery presented itself in the light of a merciful fate, and it was so considered by the conqueror. The view of the Mohammedan or of the higher class pagan with regard to the practice of raiding for slaves, would seem to have been almost identical with that of the Spaniards and Portuguese at the time of the discovery of the East and West Indies. Inferior races of a different faith did not count in the ranks of free human beings. They were little better than cattle, and as such might be hunted and taken without any derogation from the laws of humanity. The difference between the humane man and the cruel man lay not in the practice of or the abstinence from slaving, but in the manner in which slaves were treated; and in general the slaves of Negroland would seem to have been governed with tolerant good-humour. Their sufferings were not directly intentional, but were incidental to the barbarities of the slave-raid, by which whole villages were destroyed, and to the horrors of transit on foot across the desert.

Were it not that human remains are destructible, the caravan route from Tripoli to Haussaland would be paved deep with human bones. Here is a description, given by Major Denham in 1822, of the condition of that road less than a hundred years ago. He mentions a well within half a mile of Mesbroo. "Round this spot," he says, "were lying more than a hundred skeletons, some of them with the skin still remaining attached to the bone. The Arabs laughed heartily at my expression of horror, and said they were only blacks, *nam boo* (damn their father), and began knocking their limbs about with the butt end of their firelocks, saying: 'This was a woman! This was a youngster!'" As the road wound southwards skeletons were passed at the rate of eighty and ninety a day, and at the wells of El Hammar, three days farther on, the numbers of skeletons that lay about were countless. "Those of two women, whose perfect and regular teeth bespoke them young, were particularly shocking; their arms still remained clasped round each other as they had expired, although the flesh had long since perished by being exposed to the burning rays of the sun." On the following day, as Major Denham dozed on his horse about noon, overcome by the heat of the sun, he was suddenly awakened by "a crashing under my feet, which startled me excessively. I found that my steed had, without any sensation of shame or alarm, stepped upon the perfect skeletons of two human beings, cracking their brittle bones under his feet, and by one trip of his foot separating from the trunk a skull which rolled on before him." Along the greater part of the way, Major Denham says that every few miles a skeleton was seen through the whole day. "Some were partially covered with sand, others with only a small mound formed by the wind; one hand often lay under the head, and frequently both, as if in the act of compressing the head. The skin and membranous substance all shrivel up and dry from the state of the air: the thick muscular and external parts only decay." When it is remembered that this description applies in the beginning of the nineteenth century after Christ to a road which has been used for the same purpose of slave transit for perhaps as many as nineteen centuries before Christ, the imagination quails before the total of grief and suffering which must lie embedded in its dust.

The raids by means of which slaves are obtained in the hunting grounds of the interior to be despatched upon this journey across the desert, are even more productive of human suffering, more desolating to all that makes up the most primitive conceptions of human happiness. Apart from the enslavement of prisoners of war, which constitutes a separate branch of the same custom, and occurs whenever a successful war gives the opportunity for it, the slave-raid, as a national habit, is still usually directed against natives of a different religion, who are assumed to be of a lower order of humanity. Throughout the West of Africa, at the beginning of the present century, the custom remained among the races bordering northwards upon the desert to raid southwards among the pagans and cannibals for the purpose of filling their slave-rooms, stocking their farms, and increasing their revenues by the surplus which could be disposed of in the market. It was a relatively small surplus only which experienced the pains of the desert journey for purposes of exportation, but though relatively small it was numerically great, and the sum of misery inflicted by the slave-hunts of countless generations defies all computation. It is not to be supposed that it was the Christian nor even the Mohammedan who first invented the theory that there is no moral obligation to respect the rights of infidels. Indeed, if modern experience may be trusted, it would seem rather that the less is the grade of difference the more is the sense of distance between the despiser and the despised. The contempt of the superior pagan for the inferior fetish worshipper is just as keen as that of the Christian for the pagan, and from race to race in a descending scale the theory of inferiority has been acted on as a justification of the practice of enslavement.

In West Africa, where the superior race preyed directly upon the inferior, the practice has probably been peculiarly demoralising, for there the brutality of the slave-raider was added to the despotism of the slave-owner. The right of slave-raiding, like that of making war, would seem to have been originally a royal prerogative, and it was apparently maintained as an annual practice, to which no sense whatever of immorality was attached. It was simply, like elephant hunting, one of the means by which the royal coffers were replenished, and those who took part in the raid received their share of spoil. Leo Africanus complains, in relation to Bornu, in the beginning of the sixteenth century, that merchants who took horses there for sale were sometimes delayed a whole year because the horses were paid for in slaves, and the king raided only once a year.

Dr. Barth, who accompanied a slave-raid, made by the forces of Bornu against the pagan natives of Musgu in the winter of 1851–52, has left an account of the operation, which is interesting as applying to districts with which the British Government has now to deal, and may serve to show how such practices must affect the private and public life of peoples amongst whom they are tolerated.

His account is too long to quote in full, but some of the principal points may be briefly given. The ruler of Bornu, finding his treasury and his slave-rooms empty, determined upon a slave-raiding expedition. There was at first some doubt as to the exact direction in which it should be sent. Finally, it was determined to attack the pagans of Musgu in a territory south of Bornu, and not far from the present German frontier in the east. Towards the end of November a host numbering over 20,000 cavalry and a larger number on foot, including many women, and a proportionate amount of tents and baggage, marched southwards. So long as this force was within the limits of friendly territory they were supposed to be under discipline, and to take nothing from the villages but corn and rice. As a matter of fact, discipline was impossible to maintain, and not only were the crops forcibly reaped, but as the army marched towards the frontier the friendly villages which lay upon its road were looted. As soon as the frontier of the pagan country was reached, a general licence was, of course, given, and Dr. Barth describes day by day the progress of this vast band of robbers, who spread like a swarm of locusts over the fertile country.

The pagans were apparently in this instance of the higher type. They were no homeless savages. On the contrary, they were better agriculturists than the Bornu people themselves. The whole country was rich, and village after village of neatly built huts, having their pagan cemeteries and rude monuments to the dead, stood among fields of corn, tobacco, indigo, cotton, sorghum, and rice. In one place Dr. Barth says: "The landscape was exceedingly beautiful, richly irrigated and finely wooded, while to our great astonishment the ground was so carefully cultivated that even manure had been put upon the fields in a regular manner, being spread over the ground to a great extent, the first example of such careful tillage that I had as yet observed in Central Africa, either among Mohammedans or pagans."

Throughout this district the army marched, murdering, burning, destroying as they went. The inhabitants, knowing the object of their march, usually fled before them to the forest, abandoning their property that they might save their persons. This manœuvre was frequently successful, and slaves were not always obtained. The villages were none the less burnt, and the surrounding crops destroyed. When prisoners were captured, only women and the young were kept. Full-grown men were massacred. On one day Dr. Barth reports: "A large number of slaves had been caught this day. Altogether they were said to have taken a thousand, and there were certainly not less than five hundred. To our utmost horror not less than one hundred and seventy full-grown men were mercilessly slaughtered in cold blood, the greater part of them being allowed to bleed to death, a leg having been severed from the body." On other occasions the whole day's spoil was limited to a handful of slaves, "unfortunate creatures whom sickness or ill-advised courage prevented from leaving their native villages." The pagans made occasionally a desperate and sometimes even an heroic defence, but the superior arms, and still more the numbers of the Bornuese troops, invariably secured the victory. The country which was the scene of these operations is described, not only as well cultivated, but as densely inhabited. The villages themselves afforded everywhere the same appearance of comfort and cheerfulness, and in their wholesale destruction by fire, the destruction of the granaries which they contained was of even more importance than the destruction of the huts themselves, for as the grain was already harvested, this must have meant, not only starvation during the winter, but the loss of seed corn for the ensuing season.

Scenes of fire and sword during the active days of the expedition were succeeded at intervals by the partition of the prisoners. This proceeding was accompanied, says Dr. Barth, by the "most heartrending scenes caused by the numbers of young children, and even infants, who were to be distributed, many of those poor creatures being mercilessly torn away from their mothers, never to see them again." This comment indicates also that the raid was carried on over the country of higher-class pagans. The lower types part in many instances with perfect indifference from their young. Cattle was, of course, carried off, as well as slaves, wherever it was met with.

The expedition returned on this occasion, after two months, to Bornu, and when the total gains were reckoned up, they were found to amount to something over 3000 slaves and 10,000 head of cattle. The slaves consisted almost entirely of women and young persons, mostly children, and the slaughter of full-grown males was said to have amounted to no more than 300, or one in ten. The great majority of full-grown males had therefore escaped, as had the more active of the full-grown young women. Of the 3000 taken, the commander-in-chief claimed one-third. There remained 2000 slaves and about 7000 head of cattle to divide between the 20,000 persons who had composed the expedition. That is to say, that if the spoil was evenly divided, each man would receive the tenth part of a slave and the third part of a bullock as his individual share. That such waste of life, destruction of property, and loss of time could be considered, even from the purely practical point of view, to be compensated by such poor results, is indication enough of how little all these things are valued among races where practices of this kind are countenanced.

I have quoted the account of this raid at some length, for, as it happened to be accompanied by two trustworthy Europeans, the details may be accepted as correct, and the incidents, though varying, no doubt, on every occasion, are typical enough to illustrate vividly the absolute incompatibility of slave-raiding with the maintenance of civilised government in the country raided. The more cultivated nations of West Africa, though tolerant of the practice of slave-raiding in the territory of their pagan neighbours, never, of course, permitted such a practice in what may be called the home territories. It was only in the decadence and feebleness of a multiplication of petty monarchs that the custom of raiding within the narrow limits of individual provinces became general, and it is hardly necessary to say that where it prevails neither order, security, nor prosperity are in an even moderate degree attainable.

Between the date of 1851 and the year of the introduction of British authority into Northern Nigeria, the practice of slave-raiding as described by Dr. Barth had become general throughout the Protectorate. It has already been said that the feoff-holders of the Fulani emirates resorted at times to the expedient of selling their own peasantry, and there was no province of which the entire territory could be said to be free from the curse of the slave-raid.

It will be easily understood that, however broken

might be the spirit of the raided populations, such aggression did not pass without leading to some form of retaliation. Roads were closed in every direction, and the approach of the Mohammedan was resented in arms by a peasantry who always cultivated their fields with weapons slung upon their backs. The bow and arrow—often the poisoned arrow—of the pagan is in dexterous hands a more effective weapon than the clumsy and old-fashioned musket of the local Mohammedan, and it was by force of numbers rather than by superior weapons or military skill that the Fulani armies overpowered the pagan populations in their raids. It lay with the pagans in return to close their roads to the passage of all individual traders who might prove to be but spies upon fertile or thickly populated lands. Nor is it to be understood that the pagans themselves were wholly free from the vice of slave-raiding. They paid their tribute usually in slaves. They raided their enemies for slaves, and, as one of the incidental results of this preying of man on man, the roads through the country became generally so unsafe that travelling was only possible in well-defended caravans.

It is also to be noted, as the result of half a century of anarchy, that the population of the Haussa States and Bornu, described by Dr. Barth in 1854 as dense, and estimated at about fifty millions, had, at the period of the British occupation, entirely deserted some of the most naturally fertile areas, and had fallen to a total which is now believed to equal only one-fifth of the estimated amount, or about ten to twelve millions.

CHAPTER XLV

THE ESTABLISHMENT OF BRITISH ADMINISTRATION

It will be understood that in attempting, as I am now about to do, to give some account of the establishment of British administration in the midst of the conditions which have been described, I enter upon a difficult portion of my task. The British High Commissioner is my husband. Many members of his staff have become my personal friends. It is impossible for me altogether to clear my mind of favourable prejudice, and I am forced to realise that the detachment which gives the proportion of history is no longer at my command. I can only therefore ask beforehand for indulgence if in this last section of my book personal sentiment tends to warp my judgment of the relative importance of events.

The rulers of the Nigerian territories had placed themselves nominally, for reasons which rendered a choice of European protectors essential to them, under the protection of Great Britain. By their treaties with the Royal Niger Company some of them had nominally surrendered their territory with all sovereign rights. Others, and these the most important, including the emirates of Sokoto and Gando, had agreed to enter into treaty with no other white nation but the British; to give to Great Britain jurisdiction over all foreigners and non-natives in their dominions, with right to tax them; to transfer to Great Britain sovereign rights in the riverine territories of the Niger and the Benué for a distance of ten hours' journey inland from the banks of the two rivers; to confer also rights of mining and trading; and generally, while reserving their own powers of internal rule, to subordinate themselves in external matters to the protecting power. They had, in fact, by treaty, accepted the recognised position of protected native states. The equivalent which was to be given by Great Britain was protection against external powers and respect for internal law and custom. On one side, as on the other, the maintenance of communication and friendly relations was provided for.

Bornu had made no treaty with the Company, but by virtue of international agreement it fell within the territory allotted to the influence of Great Britain.

The relations of protecting powers to protected states are always a question of discussion until they have been placed by the logic of accomplished facts outside the limits of theory. The exact measure of responsibility accepted by Great Britain in Northern Nigeria, at the moment of the establishment of British administration there, would have been difficult to define. The vague title of suzerain covered the position, and, beyond a general desire that slave-raiding should be suppressed and trade routes thrown open, there was probably no wish in any quarter in England to see a rapid advance towards the assumption of more defined duties, or of responsibilities which would involve expense. The public generally knew nothing of the country. Political necessities had imposed the creation of a military force for the defence, not only of the Nigerian, but of all West African frontiers. A small grant in aid to meet other administrative expenses was reluctantly added by the Treasury to the sum required for the maintenance of the West African Frontier Force. These concessions were made rather by respect for the judgment and the wishes of Mr. Chamberlain, then occupying the position of Secretary of State for the Colonies, than by any strong conviction on the part of the British Government that Northern Nigeria was likely to prove a very valuable acquisition to the Crown; and in the absence of a clearly expressed interest on the part of the House of Commons, in the adoption of a new West African policy, it seemed improbable that funds would be willingly voted for any full development of the Nigerian Protectorate. In these circumstances the wishes of the Government and of the country, if they had to be condensed into one phrase of instruction to the High Commissioner, would perhaps best have been rendered by the words, "Go slow!"

But events upon the spot refused to wait. From the moment in which the British flag ran up at Lokoja on the 1st of January 1900, the High Commissioner and his staff found themselves taxed to the utmost limits of their capacity in the effort to keep pace with the developments which hurried them along.

The first desire of the High Commissioner upon taking up the duties of his position would naturally have been to give effect to British treaty obligations by establishing residents at the native courts, and proceeding to open friendly relations throughout the Protectorate. He found himself face to face with a chaos of civil and inter-tribal war, in which his immediate duty was to endeavour to ascertain the disposition towards the Government which he represented of the dominant powers. He had also everything to learn about the actual condition of the northern country.

The civil staff allotted for the purpose of founding an administration was very small, and its numbers were liable to be reduced by illness and leave. The Ashantee War, which had broken out in another portion of West Africa, shortly claimed all the troops of the West African Frontier Force that could be spared, and the South African War drawing to itself all the best military activity of the nation, rendered it difficult to obtain efficient officers for the remainder of the regiment. Almost single-handed in every administrative department, the little group who formed the government at Lokoja felt that they had every reason during the first year of the administration to wish for their own sakes to "go slow."

There was the machinery of administration to establish, of which the seat was temporarily fixed at Jebba, where the military headquarters had been formed. There was the transfer from the Royal Niger Company, the taking over of their assets, and the work of assigning to them their trading stations, to be attended to. There was the neighbouring country to survey, in the hopes of finding, within friendly territory, a more suitable and central position in which the permanent seat of government could be established, under healthier conditions than those offered by either Lokoja or Jebba, in the malarial valley of the Niger, and there were relations to establish with such chiefs as might prove friendly in the neighbourhood. While the High Commissioner and the civil staff undertook the formation of Administrative Departments, the duty of surveying the country was committed to military expeditions, which, moving in strength sufficient to protect themselves against disaster, were strictly enjoined to avoid all occasion of conflict with the natives, to endeavour as far as possible to win the confidence of the people, and to submit reports on the economic and geographical conditions of the country. Three such parties were sent out to examine the country lying to the north of the confluence of the Niger and the Benué between the river Kaduna and the eastern highlands of Bautchi.

Though Fulani emirs were at the time slave-raiding in these districts, it was believed from information received that the native tribes were friendly and would be willing to welcome Europeans, and here it was thought likely that a permanent administrative centre might be formed in the southern part of the province of Zaria, bordering upon the Kaduna river. In the absence of railroads, necessities of transport rendered it impossible for any position to be taken far from a navigable river. Some little opposition was met by two of the survey parties, who were obliged to reduce some intractable pagan tribes, but no serious fighting occurred; and from the geographical and topographical reports of the surveys, it was, after some discussion, decided that the site for the new seat of government would be most favourably placed in the neighbourhood of the native town of Wushishi, on the river Kaduna. This river, often mentioned in the ancient geography of the country, is one of the important rivers of the Protectorate, and drains the south-western watershed to the Niger. It is navigable for a large portion of the year by steamers, and during the dry season by steel canoes. A small garrison was accordingly left at Wushishi, and relations were in the meantime cultivated with the southern states. The disturbed condition of the country was such that, pending the establishment of the new headquarters, no attempt was made to open relations with the Fulani emirates of the north, otherwise than by the despatch of conciliatory letters informing the Sultans of Gando and Sokoto of the assumption of administration by the British Government, and of the desire of Great Britain to maintain friendly relations.

The southern provinces of Northern Nigeria, as they spread on the south bank of the rivers from west to east, are Ilorin, Kabba, Bassa, part of Muri, and part of Yola. Immediately to the north of these, and with the exception of Borgu, all on the northern side of the rivers, are—taking them again from west to east—Borgu, Kontagora, Southern Zaria, Nupe, Nassarawa, Bautchi, and the northern half of Muri and Yola; in all, eleven provinces out of the seventeen of which Northern Nigeria is composed. Of these provinces three only, Borgu, Ilorin, and Kabba, were, in the first instance, effectively occupied by the British. Jebba, situated on an island in the Niger between the mainland of Ilorin and Kontagora, commanded the southern province.

On the northern banks the pagan populations welcomed the advent of the British, but the Fulani emirs of Kontagora and Nupe soon removed all doubt as to their hostile attitude. The British occupation was scarcely effected before they were openly slave-raiding to the banks of the river. Their combined armies laid waste their own country from the Niger banks on the west and south to the eastern highlands, and to the north as far as the frontiers of Sokoto and Zaria. The Emir of Zaria, in whose territory the site chosen for the future seat of

British government, near Wushishi, was situated, was nominally friendly to Great Britain, but in the beginning of July 1900 information reached the High Commissioner at Jebba that Kontagora and Nupe had planned a combined attack upon the little British garrison at Wushishi, and he hurried there in person with reinforcements under Major O'Neill. The situation became so acute that the population began to desert Wushishi, and in order to obtain supplies for the British troops and to protect the villages which had been friendly, it became necessary to erect some small forts in the neighbourhood, and to order Major O'Neill to patrol the country. This task being admirably performed, and the cavalry of Nupe and Kontagora defeated in a series of brilliant skirmishes, the country was occupied by British troops for some twenty miles south and east of Wushishi. Great loss was inflicted on the slave-raiders in the encounters by which the occupation was effected, and the people, siding as always with the party of success, crowded in thousands to the protected villages for safety. A situation was created in which the British Government already represented in the eyes of the natives a power strong enough to protect them against the scourge of the slave-raider.

But, as a matter of fact, with the body of the troops still absent in Ashantee, the local administration did not feel itself to be in a position to sustain suspended hostilities. A British Resident had been placed at the friendly court of Ilorin, where, while he worked hard at the introduction of domestic reforms, he was made aware that emissaries from Nupe and Kontagora were endeavouring to induce the Emir of Ilorin to join with them in an attempt to overpower the British and drive the white anti-slaver out of the country. The position was dangerous as well as delicate, and while the small force of soldiers at Wushishi held their own, and even on one occasion, somewhat rashly, drove the enemy before them to the walls of the Nupe capital at Bida, the desire of the High Commissioner was to avoid all but strictly necessary fighting. The Resident at Ilorin, Mr. Carnegie, by whose subsequent death the administration lost a most valuable officer, exerted all the tact and the pluck at his command to keep things quiet in Ilorin.

During these months the High Commissioner at head-quarters was pressing forward the organisation of the administrative departments, creating a system for dealing with the freed slaves, especially the slave children who were liberated in the encounters with the slave-raiders, endeavouring to get into touch with other provinces who gave friendly indications along the river banks, and evolving the first framework of local legislation.

The creation of a judicial system was among the early necessities of the administration, and in these first few turbulent months the seeds of future order were sown. By legislative proclamation, British Supreme and Provincial Courts were established, and the jurisdiction of each defined. Two Cantonment or Magistrates' Courts were also established in Lokoja and Jebba, and by a Native Courts' proclamation the establishment of Native Courts by British warrant was provided for in all provinces under British jurisdiction. This measure, necessary for the province of Ilorin, was as yet hardly applicable to pagan provinces, where native institutions had not attained to the level of a judicial organisation. A slavery proclamation forbade the enslaving of any person within the Protectorate, and without directly touching the institution of domestic slavery, reaffirmed, under the new administration, the abolition of the legal status of slavery, which had been proclaimed by the Niger Company after their Bida campaign. All children born within the Protectorate after April 1, 1901, were declared free. Laws were also issued against the importation of liquor and firearms.

The busy days as they passed pressed their own conclusions upon the minds of the High Commissioner and his staff, and the theory of a future policy was formed under the light of daily practice. The High Commissioner had the advantage of including in his staff one or two of the servants of the Niger Company, whose knowledge of local conditions was invaluable. The Accounting Department, which he had used in connection with the organisation of the West African Frontier Force, became, with a little reorganisation, the Treasury of the new administration. The vessels which formed the material of a Marine Department were taken over from the Niger Company. The staff included the necessary doctors and legal officers for the formation of Medical and Legal Departments. The Public Works Department, after an unfortunate preliminary delay, during which the European staff was left almost without houses, was formed, under the direction of Mr. Eaglesome, an engineer of Indian experience, into a body of which the efficiency and economy soon became a subject of considerable local pride. The rest of the staff, loyally supported by a few white non-commissioned officers and civil subordinates, was chiefly composed of that fine type of young Englishmen who, whether as soldiers or civilians, have it in their minds to serve their country, to the best of their ability, in some adventurous capacity which will take them out of the common round of comfortable life. Their experience of Africa was mostly nil, but they had the training of the public school, the army, and the university, which fits men equally for the assumption of responsibility and for loyal subordination to authority. They were ready to go anywhere and to do anything, and with the few inevitable exceptions, who were rapidly weeded out, represented, in the eyes of the High Commissioner, the very best stuff of which the English nation is made.

He had in them the instruments that he wanted, and he worked them without mercy, as hard as he worked himself. The staff was short-handed. There was three men's work for every man to do, and during the initial stage of the establishment of British authority in the country, it is not too much to say that the whole of the staff, civil as well as military, gave themselves with entire devotion to their task. There was little of alleviation or of pleasure in the early conditions. Miserable houses, bad food, a malarial climate, and ceaseless responsibility, formed the accompaniment of their daily existence. With the inveterate determination of Englishmen to have some form of sport, a polo ground was among the earliest of the public institutions established by the soldiers at headquarters. But it was the work itself which furnished the real attraction of the life, and had the small body of Europeans who formed the first British staff been polled for their opinions, there would not probably have been found one who wished to turn back from the task which grew day by day under their hands.

In view of the pessimism which appears in some quarters to be gaining ground with regard to the capacities of the English race, I may perhaps without indiscretion quote a passage from one of the latest of my husband's despatches, which shows at least how in his opinion the staff working under him have sustained the promise of the first year's performance. "There are no words of praise," he writes under date of August 1905, "that I can find too strong to describe the indefatigable efforts and the enthusiasm for their task which has been shown by the Political Staff. By their ceaseless devotion to duty they have not only increased the revenue in the way that I have shown, but have brought order, peace, and security out of chaos, have established an effective judicial system, and have substituted progress and development for misrule and stagnation." This is satisfactory reading for those who doubt whether the Englishmen of to-day are capable of the same achievements as their fathers, and it must be counted as not the least among the advantages of the colonial development of the Empire that by its very roughness it gives opportunity for the exercise in individuals of qualities which under less stimulating circumstances might perhaps lie dormant through the whole course of a too easy life. The names, alas, of more than one of the first small Nigerian group are engraved now upon tombstones on that border of the Empire which they helped to make. They live in the memory of good service done, and their work accomplished is, as they would have wished it to be, their monument.

CHAPTER XLVI

MILITARY OCCUPATION OF THE SOUTHERN EMIRATES AND BORNU

At the end of December 1900 the return of the troops from Ashantee relieved the position of some of its acuteness.

The first thing to be done was evidently to bring hostilities with Kontagora and Nupe to an end. An expedition in force was immediately organised, which marched against the combined armies of the emirs, and was entirely successful. The town of Kontagora was captured, and the emir barely effected his escape, flying with a few followers to the north. It was observed that on their march to Kontagora the troops passed through an absolutely depopulated country. The Emir of Kontagora was one of the worst examples of Fulani chiefs who raided the peasantry of their own provinces for slaves. This emir, at a later period, was captured by the British, and when remonstrated with by the High Commissioner, and urged to abjure slave-raiding and to accept British protection, he replied with graphic force: "Can you stop a cat from mousing? When I die I shall be found with a slave in my mouth." His downfall was received by the population of the province with great joy, and the event was made the occasion of a public conciliatory move towards the Emir of Sokoto, who, as suzerain of Kontagora, was invited by the High Commissioner to nominate a successor to the deposed Ibrahim. Sokoto did not respond, and for some time the throne of Kontagora remained empty.

In Nupe, where the result of British victories was equally complete, the High Commissioner took his stand upon the condition of affairs created by the previous victory of the Company. The emir driven out by them had returned, as has been already mentioned, and ousting the heir placed upon the throne by the Company, had ever since maintained a condition of hostility to the British. This emir, Abu Bekri, now fled, like his colleague of Kontagora, to the north. The High Commissioner did not call upon Gando, to whom Nupe was tributary, to nominate his successor, but himself took the initiative and reinstated the emir selected by the Company upon the throne.

But if the High Commissioner was desirous that the lesson of the previous war should not be lost upon the native dynasty of Nupe, he drew also his own moral from the experience. On this occasion there was to be no more of conquest without permanent assertion of British influence.

The reinstatement of the ousted Emir of Nupe was made the opportunity of a preliminary declaration of British policy. It was pointed out to the people of Nupe and Kontagora that two of the most powerful Fulani emirs had been deposed, because, after repeated warnings, they would not desist from laying waste the whole country and carrying off the people as slaves. At the same time no looting and no destruction of the country had been permitted by British troops. Both the cities which were the Fulani capitals had been preserved, and the loss of life had been confined entirely to the Fulani cavalry employed as slave-raiders. The peaceful populations had in no case suffered from British arms. Nevertheless, though individual emirs had been deposed, it was not the intention of the Government to overthrow Fulani rule as such, and to substitute rulers of another race. On the contrary, it was the intention of the British Government to maintain existing institutions, including the rule of the Fulani, established now for a hundred years, but to insist on such reforms as should restore the administration of the country to its ancient purity, and bring its customs into conformity with the principles of justice and humanity.

The emir-elect of Nupe, upon the suitability of whose appointment the opinion of the native council was previously taken, having accepted British conditions, was formally installed at Bida, before a full parade of British troops and a great assemblage of his own people, in February of 1901. He has since—under the guidance at first of Major Burdon, one of the officers transferred from the service of the Niger Company, and specially selected for the duties of first Resident of Nupe, because of his known sympathies with the Fulani people—acted with the utmost loyalty towards the British Government. Nupe has prospered exceedingly under the new system, and the emir's sons are now being educated at a school established in Bida by the Church Missionary Society, where they are learning, at their father's keenly expressed desire, to speak English.

As a result of the subjugation of Kontagora and Bida their great organised slave-raids were brought to an end, the friendship of Zaria was confirmed, and there was a pacification of the neighbouring pagan tribes. Other provinces along the river bank indicated their readiness to open trade routes, and to accept British Residents, with the garrison which the presence of a Resident implied; and though the limited numbers of the British staff rendered it impossible immediately to take full advantage of these favourable dispositions, the High Commissioner was able to report by the end of the financial year 1900–1901 that the British Government was in effective possession of the eight provinces of Borgu, Ilorin, Kabba, Kontagora, Nupe, Zaria, Nassarawa, and Muri.

Throughout these provinces the Government endeavoured as far as possible to bring into operation the policy which it had declared of utilising and working through the native chiefs, while it insisted upon their observance of the fundamental laws of humanity and justice. Residents were appointed whose primary duty it was to promote this policy by the establishment of native courts administering restored native laws, but in which bribery and extortion and inhuman punishment were to be abolished. Provincial courts, in which the British Resident acted as magistrate, were instituted in each province to deal with non-natives and to enforce the laws of the Protectorate, especially those dealing with slave-raiding, slave-trading, importation of liquor and firearms, and extortion from the people by terrorism and a false use of the name of the Government, which was among natives one of the most frequent and at the same time mischievous offences with which the British administration had to deal. The authority of the emir was supported by an insistence on the part of the British administration that lawful tribute, with the exception of that taken in slaves, should be paid.

Thus, by the beginning of 1901, the south-western portion of the Protectorate had frankly accepted British rule. The turbulent Fulani emirates, which had been disposed to challenge it in that district, had been conquered, and while the sovereign rights of Great Britain had in this way been placed on a basis which every native could understand, the occasion had been made to serve as a great public illustration of the intended policy of the British Government to disturb as little as possible the existing institutions of the country. The pacification of the belt of country between the Niger and the eastern highlands had been effected, and the only difference which had become markedly apparent to native eyes from the change of administration, was that henceforward pagans as well as Mohammedans were to live in the enjoyment of human rights. As a sign of this, slave-raiding had already been brought to an end in the territory under British rule.

Correspondingly with the cessation of slave-raiding trade routes had begun to open themselves through the country. While the operations of the slave-raiding

Emirs of Kontagora and Nupe remained unrestricted, trade was of course impossible in the districts over which their armies ranged, for it was the practice of the pagans to retaliate upon the slave-raiders by attacking all small caravans. After the emirs had been brought into obedience and slave-raiding stopped, it became the duty of the British administration to put down with an equally firm hand the habits of brigandage of the pagan tribes. For this purpose it was occasionally necessary to apply force, but even in the early stages of the administration it was found that capable officers did more towards effecting the pacification of the country by getting into touch with the people, than could be effected by many punitive expeditions, and the High Commissioner looked forward to superseding military occupation at an early date by an efficient system of civil police. Not only had the trade routes to the south from Kano and Zaria been rendered unsafe by the slave-raiding of Nupe and Kontagora and the retaliation of the pagan tribes; it was also found that the caravan tolls extorted by the southern emirs had been of the most excessive and onerous description. By stopping the slave-raiding of the Fulani, keeping the pagans in order, and lessening the tolls, the roads on the western side of the Protectorate were rendered safer and more attractive, and trade began to improve. New stations for European trade were opened by the Niger Company on the Kaduna, and from Borgu to Bautchi the increase in local trade was even in the first year remarkable.

But while this condition of things in the eight provinces which had been occupied was satisfactory, the inadequacy of the numbers of the British staff to deal with the rising tide of work thrown upon the administration became ever more apparent. With the removal in some districts of Fulani rule each petty village began to claim its ancient land, and to show disposition to raid its neighbours in support of its claim. The need of a survey and land settlement was urgent. More Residents were wanted to maintain the moral influence acquired in the provinces. Police and revenue officers were also needed. The housing of Europeans and the erection of public offices in the new settlement, of which the site was selected at a spot called Zungeru, within ten miles of Wushishi, on open ground rising from the Kaduna, had become a matter of some importance, and for the opening year of 1901–1902 the necessity of some increase in the estimates to provide for these pressing requirements was apparent.

The continuance of the South African War still gave no relief to the exchequer at home. The inclination of the public was still such as could only be interpreted by the Government as a desire to "go slow" in West Africa, and still affairs upon the spot continued to urge the necessity for the assertion of British rule.

Five more provinces were in a condition in which the danger of abstaining from interference was greater than the inconvenience of interfering.

British Residents had been accepted—though not enthusiastically—by the governing power in Nassarawa, the province bordering eastward upon Nupe, which was a sub-emirate of the nominally friendly Zaria, and was very largely occupied by pagan tribes. In Muri too, a little farther along the Benué, where pagans were glad to be protected, British stations had been formed. But the Fulani Emirs of Bautchi and Yola in the east, believing themselves strong enough to defy the power of Great Britain, and rendered only more antagonistic by the fate of Kontagora and Nupe, and by the effectual British protection given to the pagans of Muri and Nassarawa, were creating a situation which became every day more difficult.

The Emir of Yola, a well-educated Fulani and religious fanatic, ordered the representatives of the Niger Company, notwithstanding treaty rights to the contrary, to haul down their flag and close their trading station on the river. In Bautchi the important town of Guarram was destroyed, and the population carried into slavery by slave-raiders acting under the instructions of the emir. Both emirs traded openly in slaves, which they imported from German territory and sent through the Haussa States, while trade routes for legitimate commerce were closed. The pagans of the river looked from its eastern to its western end, waiting to see whether the protection of the British Government was strong enough to be effective in these circumstances. It was essential, if we were to retain the respect of the pagan peoples, to check the wholesale depopulation of their territory. It was also necessary to protect the legitimate rights of British traders at Yola.

A military expedition was therefore decided upon, and was sent against Yola in September of 1901, under the command of Colonel Morland. It was successful, and though some obstinate resistance was encountered, the capital was taken. The emir, who preferred exile to capitulation, took refuge in flight. The province was brought under British administration, and an emir appointed on conditions similar to those of Nupe.

In the two provinces of Bornu the situation which called for British intervention was of a wholly different order, but the claims for attention which it put forward were perhaps even more imperative than those of the southern states, for they involved difficulties with a European neighbour, which were, of all others, those which it was desirable to avoid.

It has been mentioned that in Bornu the conqueror Rabbeh was overthrown and killed by the French in 1900, and a puppet sovereign of Bornu appointed. Rabbeh's son and successor, Fad-el-Allah, appealed to the British for redress and protection, and offered to obey the orders of the British Government. The question arose whether he, who was a usurper, should be recognised and supported in Bornu, or whether the lawful sovereign overthrown by his father should be restored.

While the question was under consideration in 1901, the French took the matter into their own hands, and, marching into British territory, defeated and killed Fad-el-Allah at Gujba, 150 miles inside the British border.

Such a violation of territory accentuated the necessity of asserting effective control of the border province, and a small expedition was accordingly sent into Bornu at the end of 1901 to make full inquiry into the events which had taken place, and to ascertain whether there was truth in the report that the French had carried natives of the British Protectorate into captivity across the frontier, and were levying tribute in British protected villages. On further information received it was decided to occupy Bornu.

The route to Bornu lies through Bautchi, where the massacre of Guarram by the emir was still unpunished. Bautchi was at this time the centre of the slave trade, and slaves were openly sold in the market of its principal town. The emir had shown himself antagonistic to British government, and it was considered probable that he might oppose the troops of the Protectorate. The expedition destined ultimately for the occupation of Bornu was sent in force under the personal command of Colonel Morland in February of 1902. Preparations which had been made in Bautchi to oppose its advance were abandoned when its strength was known.

The Emir of Bautchi proving quite intractable, was, however, deposed. The council of notables, in whom, according to native custom, the election of emirs is vested, was summoned, and elected his heir. The emir took the usual refuge in flight, and his heir was duly appointed under the same conditions as the Emirs of Nupe, Yola, and Kontagora, to which last-named emirate the British Government had, on the continued refusal of Sokoto to respond to the invitation to exercise his function as suzerain, nominated a temporary chief.

Thus Bautchi also was brought under British administration, and as, in every letter of appointment, the sovereignty of the British Crown was asserted, and in every installation oath was accepted by the appointed emir, British sovereignty was accepted from Borgu to Yola.

A British Resident and a garrison were placed in the capital of Bautchi, and it may be said here that the newly appointed emir proving loyal to his engagements, the Resident was able by June of 1902 to report that the slave trade was practically abolished in Bautchi as a recognised practice. Underhand slave dealing still continues to some slight extent, and constitutes one of the principal offences with which the provincial courts have to deal.

As was usual after the suppression of the slave-raider, the retaliation of the raided had to be dealt with, and there was some fighting with turbulent pagan tribes who rendered the road unsafe. They were successfully subdued, and the expedition continued its march towards Bornu. A little later the ex-Emir of Bautchi, becoming a centre of intrigue and trouble, was caught and sent into honourable exile in Ilorin, where he lived under the charge of the Emir and Resident.

Between Bautchi and Gujba there lay the territory of Gombe, which had been for some years in the possession of a brave fanatic of the name of Jibrella, who declared himself to be the Mahdi, and who had for some years maintained himself victoriously against all neighbours. On the news of the approach of the British expedition he took the initiative and attacked. His troops charged the British force most gallantly, but they were defeated and pursued for two days, when Lieutenant Dyer effected the capture of the Mahdi himself. Jibrella, who was a white-haired old man already feeble with age, was sent as a prisoner to Lokoja, where he was treated with the consideration due to his distinction as a soldier and a priest. The Gombe country, which had once formed a portion of the Bautchi province, was, like Bautchi, brought under British administration, and the expedition pressed on to Gujba in Bornu, leaving the road all British behind it.

No further opposition was encountered in Bornu. A company was left at Gujba, and Colonel Morland, with the rest of his force, proceeded to Maidugeri. Here it was found that the report of a French expedition into British territory was correct. On the death of Rabbeh in 1900 Fad-el-Allah, his son, had defied the French, who, after some fighting, had retired across the boundary to their headquarters at Dikwa, in what is now German territory. They were again attacked by Fad-el-Allah, and they had then pursued him as far as Gujba in British territory, defeated, and killed him. They had raised levies and caravans for this raid in British territory. A great number of prisoners and much loot were taken at Gujba, and the prisoners were made to carry the loot and baggage. In return for delivering the lawful Sultan of Bornu from Fad-el-Allah the French imposed upon the Sultan a war indemnity of $71,000, in addition to $9000 already paid by his elder brother, who had been deported to the east side of Chad. The sum was to be collected by tribute from the villages, and till it could be collected the Sultan was kept prisoner by the French at Dikwa. The already impoverished country, desolated by war and counter-war, was ground to the lowest depths by this imposition.

The Sultan of Bornu was informed in his internment at Dikwa that the British Government would recognise him as sovereign if he liked to return, and in the meantime the collection of French tribute was stopped. The Sultan, or Shehu (as the Sultans of Bornu are called), readily accepted British proposals, and returned to occupy his throne under British protection, accepting the usual conditions. A garrison was placed at Maidugeri, and Residents appointed to Bornu. By this action an area of some 60,000 square miles was brought under administrative control.

On the return of the expedition some unruly pagan tribes of the Yola province were subdued, and prevented from harassing peaceful traders upon the trade routes.

In the province of Nassarawa, which lies upon the north bank of the Benué between Nupe and Bautchi, a great deal of trouble had been caused by Fulani raiders, of whom the headquarters were at a town called Abuja. The trade routes in the western part of the province were much interrupted by the lawless brigandage of Abuja, and in the summer of 1902 an expedition was sent which reduced Abuja to obedience. A new king was placed upon the throne, who agreed to observe British laws, and the expedition marched back through the disturbed belt, reducing such lawlessness as it encountered. But at Keffi, the headquarters of the province, where a British Resident was already established, slave-raiding was being openly carried on by the Magaji or native commander-in-chief, who had been appointed by the Emir of Zaria. This officer, much stronger than the local emir, defied authority and refused to submit to the representations of the British Resident. There came a day when the Resident, Captain Maloney, called upon the Magaji to appear and answer for his conduct before the emir. The Magaji refused to come. The British Resident, after an unavailing attempt had been made by the Assistant Resident to bring the Magaji to reason, issued an order for the troops to be called out, and the Magaji, rushing from his house, murdered the British Resident with his own hand before troops could reach the spot.

The Magaji was, of course, the leader of a rebellious party in Keffi. After the murder of Captain Maloney he and his followers immediately fled. They were pursued by British troops to the northern borders of the province, where, taking refuge in Zaria, they were presently passed on in safety to Kano, still outside the limit of British administration. At Kano the Magaji was received with much honour by the emir, who gave him presents and assigned him a house, placing him always on his right hand when he rode.

In March 1902 a Resident had been placed with Zaria, which was nominally friendly. But the Emir of Zaria was very unsatisfactory. Not only did he continue slave-raiding and other lawless proceedings, but he continued them in the name of the British Government, wishing at the same time to profit by the strength of that Government, and to make it detested. More than once, in his armed forays, his people came into contact with British patrols. He was known to be intriguing with Kano. It had even been debated between them whether he should surprise and overpower the British garrison. He was suspected of having attempted to poison the Resident. Under these circumstances the Resident determined to arrest him and bring him to Zungeru. It was done, the council of chiefs willingly surrendering him, for he was much detested in Zaria. He was kept in nominal confinement at Wushishi, and one of his principal officers administered the Government in his absence. This man, the Galadima, worked loyally with the British Government.

CHAPTER XLVII

CONQUEST OF SOKOTO AND KANO

THE situation was such that all eyes were now turned to the north. Sokoto was the recognised religious and political head of Haussaland. All the Fulani emirates which were not subject to Gando took their investiture from him. The British High Commissioner, anxious to interfere, according to the terms of the British treaties, as little as possible with Mussulman law and custom, had done what he could in the circumstances to conciliate Sokoto and Gando. But the British treaties did not cover a position in which the leading emirates of the south should initiate an attack upon the British Administration, as in the case of Kontagora and Nupe, or should repudiate their agreements, raid British protected natives for slaves, and drive British traders out of their dominions, as in the case of Yola and Bautchi. These acts on the part of the southern emirates had created a new position. From the Niger to Bornu British sovereignty had been imposed by right, not of treaty, but of conquest, and in consequence of the refusal of Sokoto to exercise the functions of immediate suzerainty, in which Great Britain would willingly have maintained him, by nominating successors to the deposed emirs, all the emirs of the southern emirates now held their investiture from Great Britain. But the force of tradition dies hard, and so long as Sokoto existed, and had not signified his assent to the appointment of the Fulani rulers, there was for them an uncomfortable sense of irregularity in their position. The more loyally they worked with the British Government the less were they likely to please Sokoto, and in the lower ranks the offence of working loyally with a British-appointed emir was scarcely likely to be less fatal, in the event of Sokoto ever regaining the upper hand, than to have worked with the British themselves.

The question of the future turned upon whether Great Britain or Sokoto were to be the permanent head of Haussaland. The Haussas have a proverb, "Only by fighting can the better man be found out"; and the feeling was universal that a trial of strength would have to take place between the new power of the white man and the old power of the Fulani. Until it was decided which of the two was the stronger, no waverer knew on which side to cast in his lot. The result of conciliation on the part of the British had been vain. A letter, couched in friendly terms, which was sent to Sokoto in 1900 to announce the establishment of the British Administration on the river, was not answered, and the messenger who bore it was treated with indignity. The request made in 1901 that Sokoto would nominate the successor to the deposed Emir of Kontagora, was not complied with, and in May of 1902 a letter was addressed by Sokoto to the British High Commissioner, couched in the following terms: "I do not consent that any one from you should ever dwell with us. I will never agree with you; I will have nothing ever to do with you. Between us and you there are no dealings, except as between Mussulmans and Unbelievers—war as God Almighty has enjoined upon us. There is no power or strength save in God on high."

Kano, which was the strong place of Haussaland, possessing an organised army and a well-fortified town, gave evidence of its hearty support of the antagonistic attitude of Sokoto. While it was known throughout the Protectorate that the less important emirates of the south had been wholly unable to stand before British power, it was very generally believed by the natives that Kano would prove impregnable, and that Fulani rule would be victoriously maintained.

This being the condition of affairs, it became evident that, the sooner the issue was decided, the sooner would peace and progress become possible in the Nigerian territories. It was not without a profound sense of the responsibility attaching to British action at a juncture when all eyes, pagan and Mohammedan alike, through the vast congeries of native states, were turned upon the little knot of white men, by this time permanently established in the British headquarters at Zungeru, that the High Commissioner determined to urge upon the authorities at home the necessity for striking one clear and decided blow before the resistance to British authority had had time to gain weight and force by preparation and a sustained belief in its own chances of conquest.

The highest authority of Haussaland had repudiated the position nominally established by treaty. He had declared that between him and Great Britain there could be nothing but war. The alternative for the British Administration was either to take up the challenge thrown, or to abandon the work of pacification and civilisation upon which it had entered in Haussaland. The treaty ground of the British position having been cut from under our feet, it was necessary either to leave the country, to abandon those who had already trusted to our protection, and to throw away in the eyes of Europe all the ground taken by successive international agreements, or to face the position frankly, and base our future supremacy in the Protectorate upon the indisputable argument of conquest.

In the case of the southern emirates this had already been done. In Kontagora, Nupe, Bautchi, Yola, and Nassawara, we had already been welcomed by the subject populations as the conquerors of their conqueror. In every emirate the new ruler had been appointed by the British Government, and had accepted office on British conditions. In the Empire of Bornu the position was even more strongly emphasised. There, in fulfilling the obligations of an international agreement, British arms had restored the ancient dynasty of the country, and the Sultan had accepted his throne as a gift from the sovereign of Great Britain. The emirs of the southern emirates were, in spite of their doubts as to the future, working loyally with the British Government. British Residents were established at their courts, a British garrison in the capital of every emirate acted as an efficient body of police, not to overawe the local ruler, but to give effect to edicts issued by him in the interests of civilisation. Slave-raiding, forbidden in the territories of every ruler placed on the throne under British protection, was becoming a practice of the past; taxes were being peaceably and regularly collected. Trade routes, as has been seen, were daily opening. But the whole foundation of this progress was the belief of the native in British strength. The position remained uncertain till this was placed beyond a doubt.

So fully was this situation appreciated that symptoms of unrest and expectancy were making themselves generally felt when the incident occurred in the middle of 1902 of the murder of the British Resident at Keffi, and the escape of his murderer to the court of Kano. Kano represented the principal military power of the northern states, and it was well understood that Kano was the power with which the British strength would be first seriously measured. The comment of the Emir of Kano upon the murder of the British Resident represented a very general feeling. "If the little town of Keffi could do so much," he is reported to have said, "what could not Kano do?"

Towards the end of November 1902, the Emir of Kano went so far as to march, without any declaration of war, against the British garrison of Zaria. His armies turned back on the news reaching them of the death of the Sultan of Sokoto, and also, as was subsequently ascertained, on the refusal of the Emir of Katsena to join in the policy of war. It became necessary to strengthen the garrison of Zaria, of which province the emir remained a prisoner in British hands. From this moment it was known that war between Kano and the white men was inevitable.

In all these circumstances there was one consideration which was of first importance in the minds of the British authorities. It was that, in fighting the Fulani, we were fighting not with the people of Haussaland, but with rulers whose misconduct, notwithstanding certain splendid aptitudes for rule, had rendered them hateful to the bulk of the population. In imposing conditions upon their administration, and in transferring to ourselves the suzerainty which they had acquired only by right of comparatively recent conquest, we believed ourselves to carry with us the wishes of the numerous Haussa and pagan peoples who make up the body of the inhabitants of the Protectorate. The strength of the northern states was not to be despised, for should their arms obtain a first success, the surrounding populations would of necessity declare in favour of those who appeared likely to affirm themselves in the position of supremacy. But it was a strength which, notwithstanding its armed appearance, had none of that permanent resisting power which is drawn from the love of a people for its liberty, its territory, and its institutions. What strength there was in such patriotic sentiment was upon the British side.

The expeditionary force which was at the disposal of the High Commissioner consisted of about 1000 rank and file and 50 Europeans, including the garrison of Zaria. It appeared to be sufficient for the purpose, and after very careful preparation the bulk of it was concentrated at Zaria in January of 1903. On January 29th the order to advance was given, and a force consisting of 24 officers, 2 medical officers, 12 British non-commissioned officers, and 722 rank and file, with 4 guns and 4 Maxims, left Zaria under the command of Colonel Morland. Captain Abadie, the Resident of Zaria, another of those members of the early staff whom, to the sorrow of all his comrades, death has since claimed, accompanied the force as Political Officer.

The first opposition was encountered at a walled town eight miles within the Kano frontier, where the inhabitants, after a parley with the Political Officer, said that they were obliged to resist, under a threat of death from the Emir of Kano to any one who should open the gates. A British shell blew in the gate, and the question of resistance was determined. The town was not looted or injured, and non-combatants were unharmed. A series of newly fortified towns, all instructed by the emir to fight, were expected to hold the approaches to Kano. After this first experience the garrisons abandoned them, and fled without fighting to Kano. The inhabitants remained quietly in the towns, and brought ample supplies for the British troops, which were paid for as in time of peace. The troops were kept within strict discipline. No looting and no disorder was allowed. The populace, knowing already by report the practice of the British on similar occasions, showed no alarm.

The force, therefore, reached Kano unopposed. The wall of the town, of which the circumference was eleven miles, was forty feet thick at the base, and from thirty to fifty feet high. It was loopholed, and strengthened in front by a double ditch. Its thirteen gates had been lately rebuilt, and some of them were designed in a re-entrant angle, so that access to them was enfiladed by fire from the walls on either side, while the ditch was full of live thorns, and very deep. The fortifications were such that, had there been any determined resistance on the part of the defenders, the town might have stood an almost interminable siege.

The event justified the British belief that in fighting the Fulani they had the wishes of the people of Haussaland on their side. The town made practically no defence. There was some fairly well-directed firing from behind the walls, but, a small breach having been effected, an assault was ordered, and the defenders fled as soon as the heads of the storming party appeared in the gap. A considerable loss was inflicted upon the enemy outside the walls when the British force endeavoured to cut off their retreat. As they fled they suffered severely. The town itself, which occupied only a small part of the great area enclosed by the walls, was entered unopposed. The inhabitants exhibited no concern. No disorder on the part of the soldiers was permitted. Captain Abadie immediately summoned the fourteen headmen of the principal quarters of the town, and made them responsible for the maintenance of order in their districts. A rate of exchange was fixed between the local cowries and British silver, with which the troops paid for all they purchased. The slave-market closed itself. Otherwise the life of the town pursued its usual course. Within three days the great market showed its usual activity, and fully equipped caravans started for the south and arrived from the north and east as though the country were in perfect peace.

The capture of Kano took place on February 3. The High Commissioner, travelling up from Zungeru to Kano for the purpose of dealing at once with this new development of the political situation, traversed a few days later the country over which the troops had marched, and was able to write under date of February 8: "It is a striking comment on the situation here that, although fighting is going on between the British and the Fulani rulers of a district close by, the road I am traversing is as safe as Piccadilly. I met to-day caravans which must have numbered scores of loaded donkeys, ponies, and oxen, and flocks of sheep for sale down south which must have numbered many hundreds. These are being taken from Kano itself, and the traders I met saluted with smiles and unmistakable goodwill.

Women travel alone along the road, and men are all unarmed, except a few nomad herdsmen who carry the inevitable spear. The headmen of the villages bring presents of food."

It was soon ascertained that the emir had not himself directed the defence and surrender of Kano. He had removed a month previously to Sokoto, taking with him a considerable force of soldiery and all members of the ruling dynasty who could by any possibility be chosen to supersede him. The defence of the town had been left to two trusted slaves.

He now returned towards Kano with the whole body of his army, but there was a fatal division in his councils. One of his brothers, known as the Wombai, disapproved of the new policy and refused to fight. The Wombai influenced a large part of the army, which he separated from the body of the troops, and drew off upon a different road. In presence of the difference of opinion between his chiefs, the emir adopted a course of conduct which ensured defeat. He placed the loyal portion of the army under the command of his Vizier or Waziri, and himself fled northwards in disguise towards the French frontier. On the following day his army was encountered by British troops marching out to meet it, about 100 miles from Kano, and, after a resistance which did honour to the courage of its leaders in the circumstances in which they fought, and gave occasion for the display of distinguished gallantry on the part of three young British officers—Captains Wright and Wells and Captain Porter; the first two in sustaining the shock of attack by an overwhelming force of the Kano army, and the third in leading a decisive charge—the native forces were completely defeated.

The deciding actions took place on February 25th and 26th. On the 4th of March the Wombai, with that portion of the army which he commanded, and many others who had joined themselves to him, signified to the High Commissioner, who had now taken up his quarters in Kano, their desire of surrendering to the British. Having been told that they would be honourably received, they accepted the condition of returning to Kano and delivering all firearms, bows and arrows, into British hands. They were required to enter by one gate, where a guard was stationed to take the arms, and it was estimated that about 2500 horsemen and a total of at least 10,000 persons entered by the gate on this occasion. The Wombai, having expressed his desire to work loyally with the British Government, was provisionally placed in charge of the town, with a prospect of being appointed emir after trial, under conditions which he showed himself cordially willing to accept.

Immediately on the fall of Kano the surrounding towns had sent in to submit to the British, and to express their wish for friendship, and it was significant that this had been done even while their Fulani chiefs with an armed Fulani following were absent in the army of the emir. The defeat of the emir's forces and the submission of the Wombai confirmed these towns in their acceptance of British rule, and it was explained to all that it formed no part of British policy to upset or to interfere with existing institutions in so far as they conformed to laws of justice and humanity. Conciliatory letters also were sent to the Sultans of Katsena and Sokoto, explaining that Great Britain had no quarrel with them, nor any desire to fight, provided they would receive the British in peace and carry out the conditions under which Great Britain was prepared to confirm them in their positions. The letters conveyed emphatic assurance that their religion would not be interfered with. Katsena immediately replied that he had no desire for war, and would willingly accept the British conditions.

No reply being received to the letter which was sent to Sokoto, the British force advanced westward. It was the season of the Harmatan wind; the heat in the middle of the day was terrific, rendering the stones so hot that the horses could hardly tread upon them, and the dry wind blew like the breath of a furnace, parching the throats of the men. The water of the country during the greater part of the march was impregnated with salts of soda and potash, and increased, instead of allaying thirst. At night the temperature suddenly fell, and the cold became so sharp that the native troops suffered severely from pneumonia and lung diseases. At a place called Shagali the force turned southwards to effect a junction with some British troops which had been employed on escort duty for French convoys, and for the Boundary Commission near Argungu. Here a letter was received from the Emir of Gando, to whom also conciliatory messages had been sent, making his submission. Sokoto alone remained obdurate, and the column, somewhat depleted by the hardships of the march, but reinforced by the troops from Argungu, marched upon the town. On the 15th of March a battle took place, in which the Sokoto troops were defeated and put to flight.

In the meantime the High Commissioner, anxious as before to be on the spot for the purpose of arranging political conditions as soon as the military blow should have been delivered, left Kano on March 7, accompanied by Captain Abadie as Political Officer, and an escort of seventy Yorubas under a white subaltern, with the intention of making his way by forced marches in the rear of the troops towards Sokoto. The British force had about twelve days' start of him; but, in consequence of a misunderstanding when it turned southward on its approach to Sokoto, the road was left undefended. The High Commissioner's party had therefore the interesting experience of marching six Europeans strong, without any mounted men to act as scouts, through an enemy's country full of populous walled towns, owning allegiance to the sovereign upon whose capital the body of the British force was advancing. The distance from Kano to Sokoto was about 250 miles. The road for the greater part of the way lay along the twelfth parallel of latitude, and the party moved on at the rate of about twenty-eight miles a day. As they drew near to Sokoto as many as four and five walled towns were passed on each day. They were generally moated, and the walls were sometimes a mile long on each face. Fortunately the inhabitants showed themselves quite friendly, and, with no worse adventure than tolerably severe discomfort, the High Commissioner arrived at Sokoto on the 19th of March in time to see, as he came over some rising ground, a dark crowd streaming towards the British camp, composed, he was informed, of the principal notables of the town coming to make their formal submission to the British. He received in person the submission of the Waziri and principal chiefs of Sokoto. The emir, like the Emir of Kano, had fled.

The trial of strength had come and gone. The Fulani emirates were in our hands, and Great Britain was the acknowledged sovereign of Northern Nigeria.

CHAPTER XLVIII

BRITISH POLICY IN NORTHERN NIGERIA

THE first feeling of the territories appeared to be one of profound relief, and the High Commissioner hastened to take advantage of the favourable movement by a speedy declaration of British policy. In Kano, as has been seen, he had left the Wombai as provisional chief, with the intention of appointing him to the emirate if he should prove satisfactory; in Katsena and Gando the reigning emirs had made submission; in Sokoto, as in Kano, the emir had fled, leaving the throne vacant.

The work of reconstruction began with Sokoto. It has been seen in the case of the southern emirates how useful the old Councils of Notables had proved in enabling the British Administration to appoint in every case emirs chosen according to the law and custom of the land. The same principle was adopted at the heart of the Fulani empire. The Sarikin Muslimin, or Commander of the Faithful, as the Sultan of Sokoto was called, was the chief who of old gave investiture to the lesser emirs chosen by their own Council of Notables. But to the Sarikin Muslimin himself no investiture was given. He was elected by the Council of Notables drawn from certain tribes. Immediately on the fall of Sokoto, and the submission of the headmen, the High Commissioner, having been informed of the flight of the emir, called the Council together and asked them to consider whether the emir, who had very lately succeeded to the throne, should be recalled and reinstated, or whether a new emir should be appointed. Time was taken to consider the matter. The decision of the

Council was in favour of the appointment of a new emir, and the favoured candidate—Atahiru—was, after some hesitation, selected. The High Commissioner agreed to nominate him, and appointed the following day for a formal meeting to explain to him, and to the Council of Notables, the future system upon which the government of the country would be carried on.

Accordingly, on the 21st of March, the Council, headed by the Waziri, and having with them the Sultan elect, assembled in the British camp, and the High Commissioner read to them a statement which was very carefully translated phrase by phrase by a competent interpreter, checked by the same Resident, Major Burdon, whose name has been already mentioned in connection with Nupe, and whose knowledge of the Haussa language enabled him to guard against misrepresentation of the meaning of the document. As the speech laid down the policy to be pursued by the British Administration, I give the essential passages of it in the words used by the High Commissioner. After a preamble alluding to the treaties of alliance made between Sokoto and Great Britain, and recording the circumstances which had led to war, much against the desire of the British Government, the High Commissioner continued:—

"The old treaties are dead—you have killed them. Now these are the words which I, the High Commissioner, have to say for the future. The Fulani in old times, under Dan Fodio, conquered this country. They took the right to rule over it, to levy taxes, to depose kings, and to create kings. They in turn have by defeat lost their rule, which has come into the hands of the British. All these things which I have said the Fulani by conquest took the right to do now pass to the British. Every sultan and emir, and the principal officers of State, will be appointed by the High Commissioner throughout all this country. The High Commissioner will be guided by the usual laws of succession, and the wishes of the people and chiefs; but will set them aside, if he desires, for good cause, to do so. The emirs and chiefs who are appointed will rule over the people as of old time, and take such taxes as are approved by the High Commissioner; but they will obey the laws of the Governor, and will act in accordance with the advice of the Resident. Buying and selling slaves, and enslaving people, are forbidden. It is forbidden to import firearms (except flint-locks), and there are other minor matters which the Resident will explain. The alkalis and the emirs will hold the law courts as of old; but bribes are forbidden, and mutilation and confinement of men in inhuman prisons are not lawful. The powers of each court will be contained in a warrant appointing it. Sentences of death will not be carried out without the consent of the Resident.

"The Government will, in future, hold the rights in land which the Fulani took by conquest from the people, and if Government requires land, it will take it for any purpose. The Government hold the right of taxation, and will tell the emirs and chiefs what taxes they may levy, and what part of them must be paid to Government. The Government will have the right to all minerals, but the people may dig for iron and work in it subject to the approval of the High Commissioner, and may take salt and other minerals subject to any excise imposed by law. Traders will not be taxed by chiefs, but only by Government. The coinage of the British will be accepted as legal tender, and a rate of exchange for cowries fixed in consultation with chiefs, and they will enforce it.

"When an emirate, or an office of state, becomes vacant, it will only be filled with the consent of the High Commissioner; and the person chosen by the Council of Chiefs, and approved by the High Commissioner, will hold his place only on condition that he obeys the laws of the Protectorate and the conditions of his appointment. Government will in no way interfere with the Mohammedan religion. All men are free to worship God as they please. Mosques and prayer-places will be treated with respect by us. Every person, including slaves, has the right to appeal to the Resident, who will, however, endeavour to uphold the power of the native courts to deal with native cases according to the law and custom of the country. If slaves are ill-treated, they will be set free as your Koran orders, otherwise Government does not desire to interfere with existing domestic relations. But slaves set free must be willing to work, and not to remain idle or become thieves. . . .

"It is the earnest desire of the King of England that this country shall prosper and grow rich in peace and in contentment; that the population shall increase, and the ruined towns which abound everywhere shall be built up; and that war and trouble shall cease. Henceforth no emir or chief shall levy war or fight; but his case will be settled by law, and if force is necessary, Government will employ it. I earnestly hope to give effect in these matters to the wishes of my king.

"In conclusion, I hope that you will find our rule sympathetic, and that the country will prosper and be contented. You need have no fear regarding British rule; it is our wish to learn your customs and fashion, just as you must learn ours. I have little fear but that we shall agree, for you have always heard that British rule is just and fair, and people under our King are satisfied. You must not fear to tell the Resident everything, and he will help and advise you."

The speech was amplified and fully explained in the sitting which took place after it was read. The messenger who had been ill-treated at Sokoto on the reception of a first letter from the British High Commissioner was present and gave his evidence, the original letter from the late Sultan declaring war was shown. The existing position having been fully discussed and appreciated by the Council, and the conditions of installation agreed to by the Sultan elect, the following day, the 22nd of March, was appointed for the installation.

The details of the ceremony were determined in consultation with the proper Mohammedan authorities, and it was arranged that, in sign of the acceptance of the sovereignty of Great Britain by Sokoto, the Sultan, who had never hitherto received a gift of investiture, should, like the lesser emirs, receive a gown and turban from the hands of the representative of the King of England. These were to represent the insignia of office, which up to the present day it had been the custom for Sokoto alone to present on installation to his subordinate emirs.

The installation ceremony was performed with some pomp. The troops, with guns and Maxims mounted, were drawn up on three sides of a hollow square. An immense crowd of natives was assembled. On the arrival of the High Commissioner on the spot he was received with a royal salute. A carpet was spread for the emir and for his principal officers of state. The High Commissioner then made a speech in the same sense as that of the document which has been quoted. When he came to the statement that the British Government would in no way interfere with the exercise of the Mohammedan religion, that all men were free to worship God as they pleased, a deep and most impressive murmur of satisfaction broke from the crowd. On the conclusion of the speech the High Commissioner called upon the Sultan to say if he fully understood and accepted the conditions of his installation. The Sultan replied that he understood and that he accepted them. The High Commissioner then proclaimed him Sarikin Muslimin and Sultan of Sokoto, and the gown and turban were presented to him as the insignia of office. The High Commissioner shook hands publicly with the Sultan, and gave permission for the royal trumpets, which can only be sounded for a duly appointed and accepted emir, to be blown. A prayer was recited aloud by the criers, and the crowd dispersed amid discordant sounds of rejoicing and expressions of mutual goodwill.

The High Commissioner was very favourably impressed with this Sultan, as with the Wombai of Kano, and with many of the leading men of their councils. Amongst the upper class Fulani of the northern states he met men deserving in every way of the name of cultivated gentlemen. He found them able in argument, cultivated in discussion, open to the conclusions of reason. In manner they were dignified, courteous, and sympathetic. Nor did they seem to him to lack the essential qualities of frankness and humanity. There could be no question to his mind, nor to those of the officers who accompanied him, that among the educated classes of the northern state they were in the presence of a wholly different standard of civilisation to that generally accepted in the southern emirates. A similar experience was made at a later period in Bornu, and the recognition of this fact naturally went to strengthen the conviction of the wisdom of the policy which proposed to rule, as far as possible, through the existing Fulani and Bornuese machinery of the greater part of the Protectorate, modified and controlled by the advice of British Residents.

Leaving a Resident and a small garrison at Sokoto, the High Commissioner, on the day following the installation, took the road towards Katsena, escorted by the new Sultan and throngs of chiefs and horsemen for a portion of the way. On parting, the Fulani chiefs thanked him profusely for all that had been done, displayed great pleasure at his praise of the plucky stand which they had made in opposition to the British troops before the capture of the town, and gave signs of much relief that the fighting was over, and that events had taken so favourable a turn. He and his staff gained the impression, which subsequent events have done much to confirm, that the majority were genuinely surprised and pleased at the treatment which had been accorded to them. The Sultan of Sokoto has up to the present time continued to work in the utmost cordiality with the British Resident.

Katsena, which had not yet been visited by troops, was reached on March 28. On the following day, an explanation of the British position and policy, similar to that made at Sokoto, was made to the emir and chiefs, and the emir was installed under conditions similar to those of Sokoto. As Katsena had a special reputation as a centre of learning, assurances were added in the High Commissioner's speech of the willingness of the British Government to give such assistance as it could to education. Here, as in the other towns, the value of a staple currency was discussed, and a rate of exchange fixed between British silver and cowries. Other lesser chiefs of the northern neighbourhood made their submission, and were interviewed and dealt with.

From Katsena the High Commissioner marched back to Kano, and on April 2nd, after explanations similar to those of Sokoto and Katsena, the Wombai was installed as emir, with observance of some special ceremonies in historical use at Kano. With Kano, Katagum was brought under British administration. On April 7 the High Commissioner reached Zaria; there he also installed, after the usual explanations, a new emir, Dan Sidi, who, in consultation with the Sultan and Waziri of Sokoto, had been indicated as the best successor to the emir deposed at Zungeru, and who was willingly accepted by the Zaria Council.

It may be incidentally mentioned, as an illustration of the pace at which work was done in a Protectorate where the loyal desire of every one was to "go slow," that, from the date of leaving Kano on the westward march, to the moment of arrival at Zaria on the return journey, thirty-eight days had elapsed. In that period eight hundred miles of enemy's country had been traversed on foot or horseback, the political situation of Sokoto,

Katsena, and Kano had been investigated, three emirs had been installed, many minor chiefs of importance had been interviewed, and the principles of British policy had been personally explained by the High Commissioner to the leading representatives of all the native states through which the British troops had marched.

The province of Kontagora had remained without an emir for two years. The population had been much dispersed, and no suitable heir to the throne had presented himself. At Sokoto, when the advice of the emir and Council was asked, a unanimous desire had been expressed that the recalcitrant chief Ibrahim, who was first cousin to the ex-Emir of Sokoto, and a man connected with the best families of the northern states, might be reinstated. Ibrahim, after experience of exile and confinement, had become a profoundly altered man. The vehemence of his abjuration of all slave dealing, when the question of his restoration was discussed, was in somewhat comic contrast to his previous utterances on the same subject, and though the experiment seemed doubtful, it was decided to replace him, under conditions similar to the other emirs, upon the throne. The installation of Gando was provided for to take place at a later period.

Every important emir of the Protectorate now held his throne under a letter of appointment from Great Britain, and to many of the lesser pagan chiefs a no less formal "staff of office" had been given. The pledges given by emirs and chiefs in return had been made in their own forms, but with full pomp of unmistakable public ceremony. By the end of April 1903 there was no population in the Protectorate that did not understand the transfer of sovereignty which had taken place from their ancient Fulani rulers to the British Government. This was strikingly illustrated by the action of the Munshis, an extremely ignorant and truculent native tribe occupying the northern bank of the Benué, nearly opposite to Bassa, one of the five provinces which at the beginning of the year 1901–2 had been mentioned by the High Commissioner as calling for attention. These pagans, who had entirely refused to have any dealings with the British, on hearing of the fall of Kano, came at once in a strong deputation to the Resident, and brought presents, saying that the white man was now stronger than Sokoto.

At a later period it was thought well to assimilate the system of appointment, and the emirs and chiefs of the Protectorate have been divided into chiefs of the first and second grade, and minor chiefs of the third and fourth grades. The rank of a chief of the first grade is reserved for the Shehu of Bornu and the great Fulani emirs, such as Sokoto, Kano, Gando, &c.; the rank of chief of the second grade is for the lesser emirs, such as Katagum, Hadeija, Lapai, &c., and the chiefs of the principal pagan communities, such as Argungu, Kiama, Boussa, &c. The ranks of third and fourth grade are for district headmen and pagan chiefs of less importance, but having executive authority. The formal recognition of all chiefs, whatever their grade, is accompanied by the presentation of a "staff of office," and the staff varies according to the importance of the office conferred. Chiefs of the first grade have a long staff surmounted by a silver headpiece, chiefs of the second grade have also a long staff, but it is surmounted by a brass headpiece. In the case of the third and fourth grades the staves are short and of plainer design. For the Shehu of Bornu and the Emir of Sokoto special staves have been designed as a mark of honour in recognition of their ancient positions of supreme importance. There are only these four symbols of executive authority. Below the rank of fourth grade chief, certificates of office are given, but without a staff, to certain graded headmen, &c.

The oath of allegiance, which is taken on receiving the staff of office, has also been brought into regular form, and for Moslems is as follows:—"I swear, in the name of Allah and of Mohammed his prophet, to serve well and truly his Majesty King Edward VII., and his representative, the High Commissioner of Northern Nigeria, to obey the laws of the Protectorate and the lawful commands of the High Commissioner, and of the Resident, provided that they are not contrary to my religion. And if they are so contrary I will at once inform the Resident for the information of the High Commissioner. I will cherish in my heart no treachery or disloyalty, and I will rule my people with justice, and without partiality. And as I carry out this oath, so may Allah judge me." To pagans, the substance of the same oath is administered in whatever form is most binding on their conscience.

To all the chiefs it is explained that it is no part of the British policy to lessen their influence or authority—that, on the contrary, it is the desire of the British Government to rule with them, and through them.

Residents are instructed strictly to observe the etiquette of proper ceremonial in their dealings with the chiefs. It is recognised that, the Fulani chiefs being aliens who have won their position by conquest, it would not be surprising if the bulk of the people, seeing that the Fulani power has been broken by the British, were no longer to accord to the chiefs their accustomed obedience and respect. The desire of the British Government is to counteract this tendency in every possible way, and Residents are instructed that "the privileges and influence of the chiefs can best be upheld by letting the peasantry see that Government itself treats them as an integral part of the machinery of the administration—that there are not two sets of rulers, one British and one native, working either separately or in co-operation, but a single Government, in which the native chiefs have clearly defined duties, and an acknowledged status equally with British officials." It is, however, considered necessary at present, and probably for some time to come, to retain the means of enforcing order—namely, the military and police force—solely under the British Government. The emir's orders must be enforced by the native courts. In the last resort it may, of course, become necessary for the British Government to compel obedience, but this emergency is as far as possible to be avoided.

The powers of native chiefs are defined, as are the powers of the native courts, for which warrants are now issued in all the Mohammedan emirates, and it is interesting to observe that in the elaboration of the details of this system the opinions and advice of the emirs and their leading native counsellors have been sought and willingly given. In many discussions British officers have been struck by the acuteness and ability with which the weak or distasteful point of a proposal is discerned, and arguments in favour of a preferred alternative sustained. The readiness of the emirs to co-operate in the construction of a new system of government has been extremely helpful, and where it has been possible their wishes have been gladly deferred to.

CHAPTER XLIX

NIGERIA UNDER BRITISH RULE: SLAVERY

THE position of the Fulani chiefs was, however, in the first instance, profoundly modified by a condition which was of the very essence of British administration. A large part of their revenue had consisted of tribute paid in slaves, and, in some cases, of the tithe levied on the produce of slave-raids, which they conducted either in person or by the medium of the commander of their troops. But under British government, the slave-raid and the slave-trade were abolished, and all dealing in slaves became illegal. It was not made illegal for a native to own slaves, but by the abolition of the legal status of slavery, every slave who chose to do so could assert his freedom, while the decree making all children free who were born in the Protectorate after April 1, 1901, was a decree of general emancipation of the coming generation.

The fact has to be faced by the administrator in Mohammedan Africa, that the abolition of slavery is not a straightforward task of beneficence. It carries with it grave and undeniable disadvantages to the slaves as well as to their owners, and the objections urged against it by the local rulers and employers are not by any means without foundation.

Property in slaves, whatever may be thought of it by the enlightened conscience of Europe, is as real to the Mohammedan as any other form of property. Slavery is an institution sanctioned by the law of Islam, and to abolish it without compensation to the Mohammedan slave-owners would be an act of injustice amounting to nothing less than wholesale confiscation.

It has to be remembered, also, that in countries

where all industries are based on slave labour, slave power takes the place which steam and electric power take in the West. It cannot be suddenly abolished without a universal dislocation of industrial life. Slavery is at present the only form of labour contract known in many districts of Northern Nigeria, and before it can be done away with, time is needed for other forms of labour contract to be substituted. My husband, whose opinions I am quoting in regard to the whole of this important subject, and who, as his early career has publicly proclaimed, is among the most convinced opponents of slavery, has pointed out, in memoranda intended for the instruction of the Residents, that a substantial return is given by the master for the work of the slave. The slave is protected, housed, clothed, and fed. In many cases he is allowed to employ a portion of his time for his own exclusive benefit, and his rights are carefully protected by Koranic law. It is not wise to encourage a reckless rejection of these present advantages without full consideration of his possible future position.

The slaves of Northern Nigeria may be divided into two classes, household slaves, and farm slaves.[1] The household slaves are domestic slaves in the sense usually understood, though they frequently rise to positions of great responsibility and independence. The status of farm slaves differs from that of household slaves, and is rather that of serfs attached to the soil, than of slaves in the common sense of the term. They are inalienable from the land. They cannot legally be sold. They have certain rights as regards produce, the houses they live in, the land which they are allowed to cultivate for themselves, and the time which is allotted to them for their own use. They form, in fact, the body of the agricultural population, and any sudden change which should lead these people to abandon the land and flock into the towns would manifestly be disastrous. The slaves of

[1] See the description given by Hume of the slaves of England under the Saxons.

Northern Nigeria, by the universal testimony of the British Residents now stationed in every province, are generally happy and contented.

This condition of affairs is sometimes made the basis of an argument in favour of the permanent toleration of domestic slavery, which, under proper supervision, is thought by some people to be an institution suited to the present condition of Africa. In opposition to such a view there is the simple logic of the fact that slavery cannot be maintained without a supply of slaves acquired under all the horrors of slave-raids, and transported with great suffering and loss of life from their original homes. The evils of this system, whether they are considered from a humane, or simply from an economic and administrative point of view, do not need to be insisted on. For this reason alone slavery must stand condemned in any society which aspires to civilisation. But there is also a second aspect in which slavery as an institution is opposed to the march of progress. It keeps a very large portion of the population in a state of tutelage, in which the individual is not held responsible for his acts. This, in my husband's opinion, is the reason why Mohammedan Africa, which readily reaches a higher stage of civilisation than the black pagan territories, does not progress beyond a certain point. It is too heavily weighted by the irresponsible multitudes who are not concerned with, and do not directly contribute towards public life. This from the administrative point of view is very undesirable.

It is the British tradition that slavery is not tolerated in any country which has been annexed to the Crown, and has become a colony under the British flag, but that in countries which are only in that partially dependent condition which is known by the name of a Protectorate, and are still governed by their own laws, it is not possible to forbid the institution of domestic slavery where it exists. In all British Protectorates the step is now taken to abolish the legal status of slavery.

In Northern Nigeria the value of the immediate

abolition of slave-raiding and slave-trading need not be discussed. There is no voice that would be raised in humane society in favour of the maintenance of these institutions. The abolition of the legal status of slavery has an effect in two ways. It is different from the abolition of slavery. It means only that the law as administered in British courts does not recognise the existence of slaves, and that property in persons as slaves is not admitted. It is not forbidden to a native to hold slaves so long as the master and slave are mutually satisfied, but the slave can at any time assert his freedom if he wishes to do so. Under this system emancipation is gradual, and the value of it is that, without dislocating the whole machinery of labour in the Protectorate, it gives to the individual slave the power to change his condition if he pleases. This is the first and obvious use. The second effect is no less useful. It tends to lessen the value of property in slaves by the fact that no one is a slave any longer than he chooses to remain one, and that property in slaves is not property in the eyes of British law. This, combined with the increasing difficulty and expense of obtaining slaves in consequence of the abolition of the slave-trade and slave-raid, will have the natural economic effect of preventing the investment of money in slave property. Thus, by pressure of circumstance, without abolition, and without compensation, the slave-owner will gradually cease to exist.

Having set the machinery of freedom in motion towards an inevitable end, it is not to the interest of the administration to hasten its operation. On the contrary, it is evidently to be desired in the interests of the country that it should work slowly.

While the stream of investment is being diverted from its old employment, and a free generation of children born after the advent of British administration is growing up, a process of education is going on of both classes, upper and servile, to the conception of a free labour contract and the respective responsibilities under it of master and servant. To this end Residents are instructed to direct the attention of chiefs and employers of labour to the inevitable nature of the approaching change, and in order to encourage a gradual adaptation of the social system to the new conditions, they are specially to point out the practical advantages of the employment of free labour under the British administration. These are, in fact, very real, since, if an employer's slaves choose to desert him, the British courts cannot force them to return, while, if he employs free labour, he has the full assistance of the administration in enforcing his contract. It is hoped that the example of Government, in employing gangs of free labour for public works, may serve to illustrate the nature of a free contract, and be gradually adopted by the native chiefs. The more intelligent among them have shown a great willingness to accept the necessary transition, recognising themselves that, since their raiding grounds are closed, the present system must come to an end. Already, from different parts of the Protectorate, interesting accounts have been received of experiments which have been tried by native employers in free labour. They have generally taken the form of piecework—plots of land being divided into the equivalent of pennyworths of cultivation, which are paid for in cowries. The experiments reported upon have been successful, and accentuate the value which will attach in this connection to the introduction of a cash currency in which labour can be paid. The development of a system of direct individual taxation will also tend to teach the peasant his responsibilty to the State, and his personal interest in and obligation to it. The conception of individual responsibility has to be taught to the slave, and respect for this individuality has to be learned by the master, in the transition period through which both are passing.

The transition period has its own difficulties. One of these consists in the numbers of runaway and freed slaves, for whom, though the practice of running away is as far as possible discouraged, some provision has to be made. This difficulty is met in part by the establishment of freed slave homes for the women and children, the larger number of runaways being women whose cases are more properly cases of divorce. Men are expected to support themselves. Another difficulty of the transition period which has to be taken notice of, is the master's difficulty of obtaining labour for necessary industries as the bond of the existing labour contract is loosened. This would certainly become grave were runaway slaves provided for on any large scale in a condition of idleness. In tropical Africa the ground is so fertile, and the wants of the primitive native so few, that a family may be easily supported for a year on the produce of a few weeks' work. Dr. Barth says that, in Northern Nigeria, a family could live comfortably for a year on produce of which the equivalent value in English money would be £5. Beyond the satisfaction of these simple requirements there is no need for the native to work. As a free agent he may therefore prefer to be idle. But he has, in slavery, the habit of work, the country can only be developed and made prosperous by labour, and it would be retrogression, not progress, if a race now fairly laborious were, by a too sudden alteration of the social system, to be rendered idle and vagrant.

There is no need that this should happen in Nigeria, where, as we have seen from Dr. Barth's description, the pagans whom the Bornuese raided for slaves were in their free state extremely industrious. Two conditions appear to be of value in preventing such an unsatisfactory result. One, which is the first essential of all social progress, is that each man should feel himself secure in the possession of the fruits of his labour; the other, which seems at first sight like a contradiction in terms, is that he should be obliged to contribute his share towards the expenses of the State. The apparent contradiction is accepted by all civilised societies, and takes the form of security from confiscation accompanied by regular taxation.

CHAPTER L

NIGERIA UNDER BRITISH RULE: TAXATION

The necessity to contribute to the maintenance of the state is no more a new proposition to the African who has lived under Mohammedan rule, than is the habit of labour. He has been accustomed to arbitrary levies for the purpose. What the British Administration hopes to effect is the introduction of order and moderation in the claims which are made upon him in regard both to labour and to taxes. It is right that, as a free man, he should work for the maintenance of the State as well as for the maintenance of his own family, and it becomes essential that, contemporaneously with the introduction of liberty, there should be established a regular and equitable system of direct taxation.

This brings us to the subject from which we started: of compensation to the emirs and fief-holders of the Protectorate for the loss of revenue which they were likely to suffer as a consequence of British intervention in the slavery question, and also of the abolition of excessive tolls on trade.

On the assumption of sovereignty in the southern emirates it became immediately necessary to secure to the emirs some revenue which would enable them to meet the expenses of their position, and this was done by allowing them to collect their taxes under the protection of the British Government. But in the quick succession of events it was understood that all arrangements were temporary. It was not until after the fall of Sokoto that full attention could be given to the subject. When the submission of the northern emirates had placed the permanence of British rule beyond a doubt, the natives of the Protectorate, well aware that no government could be carried on without a revenue, looked for an early declaration on a subject which was to them of supreme importance.

Northern Nigeria, it has been said, has no seaboard. Internal fiscal frontiers were abolished when its territories were transferred to the Crown. The fruitful source of customs is, therefore, under present arrangements, cut off from its fiscal possibilities. It must look to direct taxation for its resources. Direct taxation is also that to which the natives have been accustomed. The broad system on which the country was taxed under native administration has been already alluded to, and it has been seen that the burden was heavy. Under it the revenue of the emirs and the principal fief-holders from the quite legitimate sources of land, cattle, duties on crops, trades, &c., should have been considerable. But in the decadence of Fulani rule, the disorders which prevailed, the chronic rebellion of tributary states, and the abuses of tax-gatherers, prevented these revenues from flowing as they should have done to the public treasury. While the dynasties were detested for their arbitrary exactions, the emirs were generally poor.

The advent of the British and the overthrow of Fulani rule were at first hailed by the peasantry as an excuse to repudiate all obligations to pay taxes, and even in the well-organised province of Kano the revenue could not be collected. It was evident that, if the policy of ruling through the Fulani was to be maintained, the first duty of the British Administration was to provide for the peaceable collection of the taxes; and since the conquered emirs had been deprived of the power to raise troops or police in their territories, it was necessary that British force should even be applied in case of need to compel payment.

The recognition of this obligation had the good effect of enlisting the sympathy and goodwill of the ruling classes, and of carrying to their minds some conviction of the truth of the assurances contained in the British declaration that the native chiefs were themselves henceforward to form an integral part of the administration. But it followed that, unless the British Administration were to allow itself to be made the instrument of misrule, it had to assure itself that the taxes were fair, and that the method of collection did not involve oppression and cruelty.

From this situation a result was evolved so important to the future administration of the country, that I will ask the reader to take patience if I describe it at what may seem to be undue length.

The emirs and councillors of the different states placed their knowledge heartily at the disposal of the British Administration. In many cases it was found that their experience was *nil*, and that abuses which the name of their government had covered were wholly unknown to them, having been perpetrated by the often worthless favourites who had been allowed to over-ride the proper officials. But they had intelligence and knowledge of native custom, and by the cordial working together of the Native and British Administrations, a system of reformed taxation was elaborated, of which the Imperial Government has in principle signified its approval.

Under this system the aim in the Mohammedan states has been to retain the ancient and legitimate taxes based upon Koranic law, while relief has been given to the peasantry by the abolition of those modern impositions which had been multiplied by the caprice of successive tyrants.

The principal taxes recognised by the law were, first, the "Zakka," or tithe in corn, which was limited to the two staple crops of the country, dhourra and gero. In theory it was due from Moslems and not from pagans, and should have been devoted to purposes of charity and religion. In practice it had lost its special character, and in all the provinces except Sokoto it was levied on Moslems and pagans alike. Second, the "Kurdin Kasa," a land tax, which, in exact opposition to the Zakka, was in theory levied only upon conquered pagans. In practice it was arbitrarily levied, and was subject to purely capricious increase. Third, the plantation tax was a tax levied upon all crops other than the two which paid Zakka. Fourth, there was the "Jangali" or cattle tax: it was originally a tithe, and was levied only on cattle, and not on flocks. Fifth, the Sokoto Gaisua was a varying sum paid by all subordinate emirates to Sokoto and Gando: in theory it was a tax upon the rich, and represented an acknowledgment of suzerainty, having its counterpart in the present usually made upon appointment by lesser chiefs to their superiors. In practice it became a levy made by emirs upon all their subordinate chiefs, and consequently through them upon the peasantry. The emirs retained a portion of it for their own benefit, and sent a portion to Sokoto. Before the British occupation many emirates had ceased to send their contribution to Sokoto, and when British suzerainty was substituted for that of Sokoto they took the opportunity to discontinue it. In Sokoto, which was a Moslem province, no taxes were levied except the Zakka. Consequently Sokoto was at first deprived of revenue. Sixth, the "Kurdin Sarauta" was an accession duty paid by every chief or holder of office on appointment. The abuse of this tax had led to the sale of offices to the highest bidder, and put a premium on the dispossession of holders of office in order that vacancies might be created. Seventh, there was a tax on handicrafts, under which head fresh impositions were perpetually devised. Eighth, there was a tax on traders, under which head merchants, brokers, shop-keepers or common vendors in the market, all paid their contributions to the revenue. Caravan tolls were apart from these, and ought perhaps to constitute a separate heading. Ninth, there was Gado or death duties, complete enough to satisfy the most Radical of European reformers, under which, when there was no direct heir, whole estates lapsed to the emirs. Tenth, there were fines, court bribes, presents, arbitrary collections made on special occasions, and forced labour, of which slavery was, of course, the base. In addition to these there were almost countless special taxes, such as those on date palms, honey, dancing girls, prostitutes, gamblers, &c., which can only be classed as various, and were imposed almost at will. In Bornu the traditional taxes, of which a careful separate study was made by the Resident, Mr. Hewby, were found to be the orthodox Zakka, Jangali, and Gado, with another called the "Haku Binirum," which was of the nature of a graduated tax on property, whether represented by land or other forms of wealth.

Upon the assumption of British rule the Residents of every province were instructed to study and report upon the existing system, its uses and abuses. As a result of their reports, combined with the advice and help given by the native administrations, the following reformed system has been compiled.

All agricultural taxes, with the exception of the Sokoto Gaisua, and its provincial counterpart, the Kurdin Sarauta, are to be merged in a general assessment which will be paid as heretofore, but under a reformed system of collection, to the Native Administration, and of which it is proposed to allot a definite proportion to the uses of the Native and the British Governments. It will be a matter of arrangement what expenses shall be borne by each.

The Sokoto Gaisua and the Kurdin Sarauta will be retained as a traditional recognition of suzerainty, but will be much reduced in amount. The reduced Sokoto tribute will henceforth be paid to the British Government, from whom investiture is now received, but it will be in every case deducted from the amount due on other counts to the British Government, and a portion of it will be given by the British Government to Sokoto to be used for charitable and religious purposes, in acknowledgment of the special position of the Emir of Sokoto as religious head of the church of the Soudan. The Kurdin Sarauta, or appointment tax, will be paid as before to the local chiefs, but it will be nominal in amount, and the chief who receives it will pay half to the British Government in acknowledgment of the authority under which he makes the appointment. As no appointment will be made in future without the concurrence of the Resident, the old abuse of perpetual re-appointments for the sake of collecting more tax will be abolished. Gado, or death duties, will not be interfered with, and will be paid as before to the Native Administration. Legitimate industrial taxes will be maintained as before, but their proceeds will be merged in the general assessment. Caravan tolls, which are being used as a road tax, at present form a monopoly of the British Government, but it is proposed to merge them also before long in the general assessment. All other forms of taxation—forced labour, fines, bribes, arbitrary impositions upon industry, &c.—are to be abolished.

Thus we get in the Mohammedan areas a general assessment covering all the old legitimate taxes upon agriculture and industry, an accession duty, nominal in amount, paid in accordance with traditional custom as a recognition of suzerainty, and the old Gado, or death duties, left undisturbed. The old system of tax-gatherers will be abolished, and the general assessment tax will be collected by the reformed Native Administration under British supervision. A proper proportion of the proceeds of this tax will then be paid by the Native Administration to the British Government, and will constitute the revenue drawn for Imperial purposes from the country.

In working out the details of the reformed scheme it is felt that a certain safeguard has been secured by the co-operation of the emirs and native authorities; but it is not to be expected that a long-established system of taxation can be suddenly reformed without friction, or even entirely without unintentional injustice, which may be found in practice to press unfairly upon some special section of the people. The new system must, in its nature, be regarded as tentative for some time to come. If the reports of the provincial Residents are to be trusted, it promises to meet with cordial acceptance from the emirs and chiefs, who fully understand and appreciate the dignity and security of the position which it proposes to confer upon them, while it is in accordance with native tradition to pay taxes in the form of tribute to a superior government. The obvious difficulty of the scheme lies, first, in a just assessment of the people, and, secondly, in a regulation of the amount paid to the British Government.

The assessment has been the principal work carried out under the supervision of the British political staff of each province during the past year. To indicate the manner in which it has been done, and the effect which it is likely to have upon that amalgamation of the Native and British Administration which it is the desire of the Government to effect, I would like to quote from the report of Dr. Cargill, the Resident of Kano.

It was his duty to make the assessment of the district of Gaiya, of which the Waziri of Kano, son of the emir, had, under the old system, been the fief-holder. He accordingly went to Gaiya, accompanied by the Waziri. On arrival at Gaiya, the Seriki, or local chief, was interviewed in the presence of the Waziri, and the business of assessment and reform of the system of collection explained. The local chief proved intelligent, and rendered all the assistance in his power. The local tax-collectors, or Mayungwas, twelve in number, who collect the taxes from the people in the town, were summoned, and each brought with him the farmers of his quarter. Each Mayungwa was asked how much he collected from his district under each head of taxation. Each individual farmer was then separately summoned, and was asked what he had paid, and what was his trade, and the number of people in his house. "In this way," says Dr. Cargill, "I completed the assessment and census of Gaiya town within two days. I then turned the work over to two of my own clerks and to two mallams (native scribes) brought by the Waziri, and told the chief of the town to call in all the tax-collectors from the district outside the town to inform the clerks of the amounts they collected from their respective quarters." While this was being done, the Resident and Waziri travelled through eight more towns. On their return to Gaiya at the end of three days the clerks were found to have finished their work. One of the Waziri's scribes, assisted by one of the chief of Gaiya's scribes, were then left to go round the district, making a complete list of the names of the farmers, the amounts they paid, their trade, and the numbers of their households, as had been done by the Resident in Gaiya. The Resident returned with his own clerks and the Waziri to Kano. "The time actually occupied by myself and staff," writes the Resident, "was seven days at Gaiya and four days' travelling. The result is map, census, and assessment of one district completed, and one jakada (chief tax-gatherer) abolished. I calculate that it will take me some months to complete the map and the assessment of the whole of the Kano district. In the same time I hope that the junior Residents may be able to accomplish the same work in the other emirates of this province. . . . The Waziri took a very intelligent interest in this tour." He was present at every interview, and he is soon "to try his own hand at assessment." It is also the British Resident's opinion that the more important fief-holders may turn out, after some instruction and supervision, to be of real use to the Government. "As a class," he says, "they are men of refinement and understanding, and existing abuses can hardly be laid to their charge, as their offices have hitherto been merely nominal, and their functions usurped by the big slaves."

The process thus described is at work over the entire area of the Mohammedan states, and under it the difficulties attaching to assessment and the reform of the system of collection, both of which are, of course, being carried out upon one design throughout the whole of the states, are rapidly disappearing.

The second difficulty of the new system—the decision

of the amount of the general assessment tax which is to be apportioned to the Native Administration and to the British Government—has, as a matter of fact, given no trouble. The proportion which it has been proposed to take for British purposes has so far been willingly accepted by the emirs, and it has been found in those provinces where the system has been put in operation, that, though the burden upon the peasantry has been greatly reduced, the reformed system of collection, by its regularity, and by the abolition which has been effected of the army of tax-gathering middlemen, promises to place the emirs in a secure financial position, which will amply compensate for the loss of slave tribute and of the excessive tolls on trade which were previously imposed.

In connection with the payment of a share of the assessment to the British Administration, the extended use of cash currency is urgently desirable. The assessment will be subject to periodical revision, and it should, as the country develops, show a steady increase. Sums now small may become considerable, and even now the difficulty of payment in kind is obvious.

The satisfactory promise of the new system has of course helped substantially towards the amalgamation of the native with the British rule, and tends happily to remove a cause of discontent which might have placed difficulties in the way of the enforcement of the laws against slave-dealing and slave-raiding. These, under present circumstances, have been loyally accepted by the emirs, and are now in practical application in every province. The slave-trade has been abolished, and the rulers and fief-holders who profited most by it have a fair prospect of enjoying, under the system which has abolished it, more regular incomes than they possessed under the old system. It is proposed that a portion of the general assessment retained by the Native Administration shall be assigned to the fief-holders, and their advantage, like that of the emirs, will be intimately associated with the prosperity of the country. There will remain, of course, a body of slave-traders who, until their commercial capital has been diverted to more legitimate trade, will be discontented, and will naturally be disposed to foment any ill-feeling to which the new distribution of taxes may unwittingly give rise. There is always the danger, in writing of a generally popular reform, of describing it too confidently as a universal cure for evils which are inherent to society. Reform is not usually an unmixed benefit, but unfortunately brings with it its own drawbacks. Experience will discern these in the new scheme of taxation, and their appearance may be the cause of troubles which will have to be dealt with as they arise.

For the moment, however, the reorganisation of native finance would seem to have been satisfactory, and it has been so important a factor in promoting the speedy and peaceable settlement of the Protectorate that, after the abolition of slavery, it must be held to take the first place. It is easy to imagine how the relief of the peasantry on the one side, and the satisfaction of the rulers on the other, affect the whole relations of government.

CHAPTER LI

NIGERIA UNDER BRITISH RULE: JUSTICE AND GENERAL REORGANISATION

BUT if conquest is best when it is speedy, the work of reorganisation must in its nature be always slow. The campaign of 1903 placed Northern Nigeria definitely under the British Crown. It will tax the energies of many generations of Englishmen to develop the territories thus acquired, and to bring them, with the widely varying populations which they carry, to the full realisation of their own best possibilities. In the meantime the work of the existing administration is to carry forward to the best of its ability the extraordinarily interesting work of organising the new fabric of government, of which the elements have been placed in its hands.

I have spoken only of the taxation of Mohammedan areas. These include, of course, the pagan peasantry of those areas, and they also include pagan communities under Mohammedan rule. There remain independent pagan communities, and these are of two classes. States which have histories as old and as respectable as those of the Mohammedan states themselves, though they have never attained to quite the same high stage of civilisation, and which are governed by one chief. Among these may be named Argungu and Jegga, within the geographical limits of the province of Sokoto; Gorgoram in Western Bornu, possibly a modern development of the old province of Gwangara, Wangara, or Ungara, whose population migrated to this neighbourhood from Ghana; Kiama in Borgu; and some of the Jukum cities in Muri. These independent states will be treated, according to their degree, more or less in the same way as the Mohammedan states, their taxes being assessed on the basis of tradition, and the result shared with the British Government. The second class of independent pagans are of very low type, and have hardly yet so far advanced in civilisation as to have an organised state, owing allegiance to a recognised chief. Their chiefs are little more than elders or heads of families. Upon these communities it is proposed to levy a very light tax, payable direct to the British Government as an acknowledgment of its suzerainty. The tax is to be a communal tax, payable through the village elders, and it will be the object of the administration gradually to group these villages together under a central chief, in the hope of raising them to the higher social plane of more civilised races. The obligation to pay tribute to the power whose laws they recognise is well understood by these tribes. It constitutes an acknowledgment on their part of authority and submission to a superior power which forbids brigandage on the roads, &c. As they are often industrious, and rich in flocks and herds, the burden is nominal, while the moral to be enforced is of importance.

But though reform of taxation is as the bed-rock of other reform, it is but a foundation upon which much else must be raised before the substitution of a reign of law for a reign of force can become permanently effective.

To give law a proper place in its literal sense, it was necessary partly to create, and partly to restore and reform the means of dispensing justice through the Protectorate. The principle by which the Native Administration has been incorporated as an integral part of one executive with the British has been applied as far as possible to the judicial system. This has as its machinery three principal engines. There is first a Supreme Court, which is the highest judicial tribunal in the country, and is presided over by the Chief-Justice. To this court there are affiliated local cantonment courts, presided over by British cantonment magistrates, who are Commissioners of the Supreme Court. There are also British provincial courts, presided over by the Resident in charge, of which one is situated in every province. All sentences of death and punishments for serious offences awarded in these courts must await confirmation by the High Commissioner, who, of course, acts with the advice of his law officers. A Resident has no judicial power outside his own province. All other officers exercising civil judicial powers in the province are Commissioners of the provincial court, and may hold courts in any district of the province. Native courts, of which there may be an unlimited number in every province, complete the judicial system. They are constituted by warrant, and the extent of their powers is laid down in the warrant appointing them. No native court, except those of Kano and Sokoto, to which the concession has lately been made, has had power given to it to pass sentence of death, and in these two courts the death sentence is subject to the concurrence of the Resident. The Resident of the province has access at all times to the native court, and may transfer any case from it to the provincial court. He thus exercises supervision over the native court.

In the native courts justice is administered by a native judge called the Alkali or El Kadi. Under the old native system he usually sat alone as judge, and the emir or head chief also usually held a court dealing chiefly with political cases. There was also usually a Limam, who dealt with cases of probate and divorce.

As found at the time when British administration was introduced, the powers and constitution of native courts varied with every province, and, as has been mentioned in a previous chapter, the system of justice had from different causes greatly deteriorated.

The policy of the British Government is to interfere as little as possible with these courts, but merely to restore them to the original purity of their jurisdiction, subject to the abolition of punishments which modern civilisation regards as inhuman, and to make them effective instruments of justice. They are to be so far supervised as to put an end to flagrant abuse. The Alkalis are to be taught the principles of British justice, and the elementary rules of evidence. The number of the courts is to be increased so that justice may be brought within easier reach of complainants.

In order to constitute a native court, a warrant is issued which defines its powers, and confers legality on its sentences. In practice, the jurisdiction of the native courts is usually confined to civil actions. The number of these courts is now rapidly increasing through all the provinces. In the pagan districts, where courts consist only of a council with judicial powers composed of the chiefs or elders of contiguous villages, their action is still uncertain and elementary, but in Mohammedan centres they are in full activity, and the number of cases brought to them for settlement is steadily increasing.

This peaceful development has not been wholly without disturbance since the fall of Sokoto. Difficulties have arisen, caused by the efforts of deposed emirs to make good their pretensions to the thrones from which they have been deposed, or from the recalcitrancy of smaller independent chieftains who did not, in the first instance, accept the submission of the northern states as universal and complete. In some instances these difficulties have been settled without fighting; in others, there has been occasion for the display of military force; but the conquest and death of the ex-Sultan of Sokoto, and of the rebellious Magaji of Keffi, which took place in an engagement near Burmi, on the western frontier of Bornu, in July of 1903, practically put an end to any further question of opposition to the supremacy of British rule. This has been the only fighting of importance since the fall of Sokoto.

It is, of course, to be expected that from time to time disturbances will arise which will have to be repressed by force. But for ordinary purposes of law and order, a native police force has been organised under white officers, of which detachments are stationed in every province, thus liberating the troops of the West African Frontier Force for more purely military duties. The troops are now stationed in certain capitals, and chiefly at the headquarters of Zungeru, Kano, and Lokoja. There are also garrisons at Maifoni and Dumjeri, the respective British capitals of Western and Eastern Bornu, and in order to preserve the northern states from the incursions of desert tribes, a chain of frontier forts has been established and garrisoned by mounted infantry, who have 170 miles to patrol between each fort.

It has been essential that the organisation of the British Administration, both central and provincial, should as far as possible keep pace with the rapid development of the Protectorate. There are now four classes of Residents, as well as police officers, charged with political duties in the provinces. The rank of the Residents is divided into first class, second class, third class, and assistant, and though the roll is not yet complete, four Residents have been generally allotted to each province. Six out of the seventeen provinces into which the Protectorate is divided have been formed into double provinces, and placed under the charge of a first-class Resident. The six which have been selected for the first experiment are Sokoto and Gando, Kano and Katagum, Eastern and Western Bornu, and the Residents placed in charge as first-class Residents have, of course, been chosen for their special ability and experience. It is proposed to devolve upon these officers a large measure of administrative control, and gradually to extend the system of grouped provinces with a view to relieving the central administration of the direct supervision of separate provincial units. Within each province the same system of devolution will be adopted as a larger body of officers having experience of the special kind of work is formed.

The duties of Residents are extraordinarily diversified, ranging from those of political adviser to the native sovereign, and head of the Provincial Court, to surveying, map-making, and reporting on the economic, commercial, and social conditions of the province. Each Resident writes for the information of the High Commissioner a report upon his province, which has hitherto been monthly, but which will, as conditions become more normal, be submitted at longer intervals. Thus at headquarters a body of information respecting the entire Protectorate is being gradually accumulated, while the maps and descriptions of routes also sent in regularly by the Residents form material for filling up the outline of the Nigerian map. The prototype of the Resident of Nigeria is probably to be found in the Deputy Commissioner of India, but the circumstances, though parallel, are of course far from similar. Assistant Residents are placed in charge of specified districts under the Resident, and in consequence of the cordial co-operation and remarkable administrative aptitudes of the Fulani, when they once understand that oppression and tyranny are forbidden, the work of the provinces is being carried on with a smaller number of white men than might have been imagined possible.

There are now in all, counting non-commissioned officers and civil subordinates, about 400 white men in the Northern Nigerian service, which, allowing for one-third absent on leave, as under the rules of West African service they have a right to be, leaves about 270 on duty. With this number the whole service of the Protectorate—military, legal, medical, and administrative—is performed over an area which successive boundary concessions have reduced to about 300,000 square miles.

The organisation of the Medical Service, with a system of hospitals and white nurses at headquarters, doctors at out-stations, and sanitary regulations, which are now being carried generally into effect, has greatly reduced the number of casualties from sickness, which at first subtracted substantially from the list of white men available for service, and often threw the machinery of work into confusion by the absolute necessity which it created of providing, from an already short-handed staff, for the performance of the duties of the invalided. The climate of the Protectorate, as a whole, is found also to be much better than that of the valleys of the Niger and the Benué, in which at first the only centres of British occupation were situated. The climate of Zaria is indeed so good as to be exhilarating to Europeans, who, during a portion of the year, can enjoy the pleasure of frosty nights, and as the territories approach the desert in the north they become generally more suitable for white occupation. Native towns are frequently insanitary, but it is believed that, with the exercise of due care in the selection of sites for white settlements, these may in the northern states be rendered perfectly healthy.

The position nevertheless is one which throws into relief the very great importance of the question of communications. There are at present telegraph lines between some of the more important centres, and it is hoped soon to connect them all with the administrative capital at Zungeru. It is even now possible, by a system of runners to Kano, to communicate by cable between the shores of Lake Chad and London in ten days. But there are as yet no railroads in the Protectorate, except about twenty-two miles, which have been constructed from a port on the Kaduna to communicate with Zungeru, and the distances to be traversed are very great. For the Residents of Bornu to reach their stations from the administrative capital at Zungeru, takes longer than it takes them to travel from London to Zungeru, and thus causes a very serious loss of official time in proceeding to and from their work. Between station and station, in the event of promotion from one part of the Protectorate to another, or if the need arises for two Residents to meet in order to discuss the affairs of their provinces, the same loss of time has to be reckoned with. Through the southern states the travelling roads were originally little more than tracks, and at the moment of the introduction of British Administration, the navigability of the minor rivers for any craft larger than canoes was untested.

Under British Administration something has been done to improve the state of the communications. Tracks have been widened into roads; districts rendered unsafe for travelling by the brigandage of pagan tribes have been policed, and waterways have been opened to navigation. By the opening of the river Gongola, an important tributary of the Benué, last year, an addition was made to the navigable course of the Niger and the Benué, which gives at certain periods of the year 1100 miles of continuous waterway without a rapid from the Niger mouth, and the time and expense of getting stores into Bornu have been greatly diminished. In the northern states there are broad caravan roads neatly bordered with hedges as in England, and it has, of course, become part of the work of the Native Administration to maintain and to develop these roads. Roadmaking is one of the subjects to which the attention of the chiefs is being directed in every province.

In the present state of the communications the High Commissioner was able last year, accompanied by his secretarial staff and a small military escort, to visit every capital of the Protectorate, with the exception of Sokoto. The tour, which included Yola, Bautchi, Bornu, Kano, Katsena, and Katagum, occupied him about four months, marching at a rate scarcely less rapid than that of his march to Kano and Sokoto in 1903. Sites were selected during this tour for all the new British stations. Oaths of allegiance were taken from the Emirs of Bautchi and Yola. The Shehu of Bornu, one of the most cultivated and intelligent of the native chiefs of the Protectorate, was installed with much ceremony, and many interesting discussions were held with him upon the principles and application of British policy A somewhat sullen and recalcitrant chief, who claimed independence in the border town of Hadeija, was also interviewed, and brought to submission and to the acceptance of a British garrison, which will occupy Hadeija as one of the chain of frontier forts already mentioned. The Emir of Katsena, whose conduct since the occupation of Katsena by the British had been radically unsatisfactory, was deposed, and his heir, selected by the Council of Notables, was installed in his place. This new emir, and the Shehu of Bornu, both took the oath of allegiance to King Edward on the Koran in public, with the knowledge of all their people, as a part of the installation ceremony.

In Kano and Katsena, as at Bornu, much interesting conversation upon the subject of the new system of administration was held with the emirs, and the knowledge that the High Commissioner in person, the representative of the British sovereign, had travelled within a few months through every capital of the Protectorate, had its visible effect in helping forward the realisation of the fact that the Protectorate has been consolidated into a unity administered in the name of the King of England.

The capitals of the other provinces—Kontagora, Ilorin, Nupe, &c.—were visited in a separate short tour. Thus a personal supervision of the provinces has already, to a certain extent, become possible, and, notwithstanding the obstacles of space and time, free communication between them may be said to have been established. But for the purposes of that further communication, which is essential to the opening of trade and the development of their commercial resources, the crying need of the Protectorate is, of course, for a railway through the heart of its most populous districts, which should connect the commercial centres of Kano and Zaria with an all-the-year-round navigable port upon the Niger.

CHAPTER LII

ECONOMIC RESOURCES OF NORTHERN NIGERIA

WHAT are we to do with it? is perhaps the question which will arise in many minds as they think of the vastness of the territory which has thus been brought under British rule. To this question the growing recognition of the value of the tropics, to which allusion was made in the first chapter of this book, will gradually bring the full answer. No one can so foretell the course of history as to know yet all that may be done with it.

To those to whom the liberation of many millions from the curse of slavery, and the introduction of the elements of a finer civilisation into the local life of the interior of Africa, do not in the meantime give a sufficiently satisfactory reply, it may be briefly said that we shall presumably do with it as we have done with India. We shall administer it, trade with it, and help both directly and indirectly in the development of those natural resources which form at present, as Sir Robert Schomberg said more than fifty years ago of British Guiana, the "buried treasures" of its soil.

When it was decided, towards the middle of the last century, to withdraw from the West Coast of Africa, the commercial use of many valuable commodities of the tropics was unknown, the existence of others was ignored; but science and experiment are every day demonstrating the value of new products. The forest areas of the tropics are rapidly proving to be reserves of wealth no less real than that which has for centuries lain hidden in the mineral beds of Australia, California, and the Transvaal. Rubber, shea butter, palm oil, wood oil, gums, and many other articles of modern trade, exist in the forests in quantities which represent an almost limitless addition to the circulating wealth of the world—if labour can be found to harvest them, and transport facilities can be given to carry them to the markets of civilisation. That these sylvan products require enterprise for their development, and for the conversion of their potential resources into realised wealth, is all the better. They offer a fresh field to the activity of new generations.

In Northern Nigeria an important forest belt spreads across the southern states and up the valleys of the principal rivers.

In Ilorin and Kabba, the two most westerly provinces south of the Niger, the forests contain much valuable timber, in which mahogany is especially noticeable. There are also in these provinces extensive plantations of kola trees, bearing the nut most valued in the markets of the Protectorate. In Ilorin there is little rubber, but in Kabba there is a great deal, *Funtumia elastica* and several Landolphias being common. The forests are known also to contain many commercial products which further exploration would bring to light. Bassa, on the southern side of the Benué, is practically a rubber reserve. Here there exist stretches of what may be called "rubber forest," in which thick masses of Landolphia vines scramble over the trees. Nassarawa, both north and south of the Benué, contains great quantities of rubber. On the banks of the Lower Benué, and also on the banks of the Gurara River, flowing through the western part of Nassarawa into the Niger, there are splendid forest areas, in which mahogany and ebony predominate. These woods, being situated on the banks of navigable rivers, could be easily worked. The same observation applies to the rubber forests of Bassa, a province which occupies the angle formed by the meeting of the Benué and the Niger. In the western part of Nupe, between the Kaduna and the Niger, there are extensive plantations of the *Kola acuminata*, esteemed through the whole of North Africa: these might become the basis of an important export trade. Shea butter trees abound in most parts of the Protectorate, and oil palms in the river valleys. The larger rivers of the Protectorate possess the usual characteristic of African rivers, and in time of flood overflow their normal borders, leaving every year a deposit of rich alluvial mud, which renders the soil of the valleys not only extremely rich, but practically inexhaustible. Heavy crops of rice, tobacco, cotton, &c., are cultivated as in Egypt on the land thus left exposed. This fertility is particularly observable in the valleys of the rivers which drain the highlands of Nassarawa and Bautchi to the Niger and the Benué.

In the Gongola Valley the soil is described as "ideal black cotton soil," and existing native cotton crops are specially good. Fine fields of dhourra, gero, tobacco, &c., spread round all the villages; two crops of dhourra and tobacco being obtained in the year. On the exposed banks of the Lower Benué after flood, rice enough could, it is believed, be grown to supply the whole Protectorate, and to leave a considerable surplus for export.

All these areas are inhabited by naturally industrious agricultural tribes, who have for centuries been the prey of slave-raiders. It is evident that a very large population has at one time existed here, and now that slave-raiding has been stopped, the country should once more provide all the labour that can be required for its extensive development.

Farther east, the territories of Southern Bornu carry forests of gum-bearing acacias, breaking towards the north into mahogany tamarinds and dum palms.

In the open northern portions of the Protectorate the products are more purely agricultural. They are under present conditions grown mainly—though not entirely—for local consumption, and consist commonly of various kinds of corn and beans, cassava, rice, ground nuts, yams, sweet potatoes, tomatoes, sorrel, onions, taniers, ochres, gourds of many kinds, and peppers. In addition to these, wheat and sugar-cane are grown as a special form of cultivation in some districts; wheat rather extensively in the Wobe Valley, in North Bornu, where the same conditions of rich soil repeat themselves, as in the valleys of the south. For industrial purposes the most widely grown crops are cotton, tobacco, indigo, and beniseed.

Of these cotton is the crop which will at first most naturally attract European attention. It has from time immemorial been a crop native to the soil. It is grown in large quantities and of good quality all over the Protectorate.

It has been already seen that the soil of the Gongola valley, repeating the conditions of the valley of the Nile, is particularly favourable to the growth of heavy cotton crops, and, owing to the cheap water-transport available, its harvest could be easily exported. The greater part of Southern Bornu consists of cotton soil. On the edge of Lake Chad a specially fine quality of cotton, locally known as "Ballum," grows with extraordinary luxuriance. At the time that the High Commissioner's party passed in December last, the cotton bushes were in full bearing. They were growing in clumps, of which measurements were taken by the botanical expert who accompanied the party, and the plants were found to be ten feet high, while each clump measured about fifteen yards in circumference. This is almost phenomenal for cotton. They carried a very heavy crop. The cotton which they bore is silky and long in the staple, and even locally fetches a high price.

The provinces of Kano and Katagum are full of cotton, which is grown with care in fenced enclosures. In Zaria, every town and village has its cotton fields. The people thoroughly understand its cultivation, and it is reported that "the capabilities of the country for the production of cotton are enormous."

The opinion of a cotton expert, who passed through Nupe and some other districts in 1904, was that Northern Nigeria held out better prospects for the cotton industry than any other West African colony.

I have dwelt at some length upon the question of cotton, as it offers, perhaps, a prospect of the creation of the first large export industry of the Protectorate, and there is no need to insist upon the importance of feeding the looms of Lancashire with home-grown raw material. There are, of course, many other prospective industries, which should include all forms of tropical agriculture. The leather trade and ostrich farming are also industries to be developed.

There has been no time for the systematic exploration of the mineral resources of the country. The highlands to the north of the Benué have an historical reputation, and silver and tin ores are known to exist in them in some quantity. Antimony also occurs, and small quantities of monozite and other valuable thorium-bearing minerals have been found. Iron ores are common throughout the Protectorate; and smelting is one of the oldest industries of which local records have been preserved. A small survey was sent out in 1904, but the discovery of minerals takes time, and the country must be more fully open to European enterprise before its true mineral capacity can be gauged.

Enough has, I think, been said to show that with the forest-bearing slopes and valleys of the southern provinces, the mineralised, though as yet unexplored, belt of highlands, which at the back of these traverses the country from west to east, and the open agricultural plains of the northern districts, the Protectorate contains in itself all the primitive elements of a valuable trade. Add to this that the population, though much depleted now, is to be counted in millions, who, under conditions of peace and security, are likely to show a rapid increase, and that from the earliest times their numbers have been made up of agriculturists, herdsmen, and traders; and it will be understood that there was a substantial foundation for the North African proverb which said that, "As tar cures the gall of a camel, so poverty finds its cure in the Soudan."

CHAPTER LIII

THE DEVELOPMENT OF TRADE

FROM the point of view of a development which should bring the country into touch with the outer world, the trade of Northern Nigeria may at once be divided into two branches, the internal and the external. In proportion as the internal trade is active and widespread, local life will evidently be nourished, and the native populations will attain to a prosperity in which, if they desire to do so, they can restore the old position of Negroland, by attracting, for the gratification of their own wants, a steady volume of trade from other nations.

We have seen that in the Middle Ages the trade of the West African Soudan bore no mean proportion to the relatively limited trade of the civilised world. It is probable that, as the nations of the Soudan recover their ancient prosperity under a just and enlightened rule, they may contribute again in equal proportion to the now enlarged volume of the world's commercial movements.

Clearly, if we look to the millions of Nigeria to become our customers, it is of great importance that they should be rich and prosperous themselves. From this point of view the internal trade movements of the country have a general, as well as a local interest, and it is satisfactory to find that with every year of British administration the value and convenience of open roads is being more widely appreciated by local traders, and trade is proportionately increasing. It consists largely, as in other parts of the world, of an exchange of the manufactures of the towns for the raw material of the country, and is carried on by the direct operation of barter, supplemented by a currency in cowries.

All trade at present is caravan-borne, partly by means of transport animals, partly by human carriage. A man carries usually about seventy pounds, and in order to deliver this weight of goods in distant portions of the Protectorate he may have to walk for several months. When this has to be done through disturbed countries the risk to life and property is of course great, and to minimise the risk, caravans in old days travelled in great strength, sometimes numbering several thousand persons. The passage of such bodies of men through a country unprepared for their reception was in itself likely enough to provoke disturbance, and it was the habit of the rulers through whose territory they passed to compensate themselves for damage by the exaction of very heavy tolls.

The main routes of trade ran generally north and south through the western portion of the Protectorate, where Ilorin at one end counterbalanced Kano at the other, and east and west through the northern states, where the caravans travelling from Tripoli to Kano usually entered the territories of Haussaland *viâ* Lake Chad and Kuka. Upon these main routes Fulani toll stations were established, while the by-roads were rendered impracticable by the brigandage of pagan tribes. The position of a trader was not always enviable under the circumstances. Nevertheless, the whole of the territories were traversed by a network of caravan routes. Besides those which ran from Kano to Ilorin in the south-west, there were others, more dangerous and less frequented, which carried goods to Yola in the south-east. Kano, which was itself a manufacturing centre, and was also a receiving centre for European goods from the Mediterranean coast, sent local manufactures and European products to the country districts, receiving raw materials in exchange. Ilorin, which was not itself so much a manufacturing as a receiving centre, distributed the goods of Kano through the coast districts, and supplied the returning caravans with European goods in exchange.

These caravans were, however, confined to the interior. They were not allowed to pass through Ilorin in the south-west, but were obliged to receive from the Ilorin middlemen any goods which they desired to purchase from the coast. Similarly Lagos traders from the coast were prevented from passing to the north. Ilorin held the position of a buffer trade state, in which the whole of the exchange trade was done by local brokers. An equally impassable barrier existed on the south-eastern frontier. The greater part of the southern pagan belt was entirely impenetrable by peaceful caravans. There existed only one or two roads by which it was possible to cross it, and on those the tolls were so extortionate that the exactions on the road amounted to half the goods of the caravan. A similar exaction was made on the return journey, and, in addition, there was all the risk of murder and pillage. This trade was directed towards what is now German territory, but the dangers of the road rendered it practically impossible. On the northern frontier, trade from Tripoli *viâ* Chad to Kano took some months for the journey, and cost about £50 per ton of merchandise carried, in addition to heavy risks of pillage and murder in the desert.

Since the introduction of British government the roads of the Protectorate have been rendered practically safe, and traders travel singly or in couples where caravans used to think it necessary to travel in strength. The tolls, though still retained in principle, have been reduced to a relatively small percentage upon the value of goods carried, and the safety of the roads has now thrown open the passage to the coast. An experimental down journey was made by an Arab trader from Tripoli in the early part of this year. He took a caravan of eighteen oxen from Kano to Zungeru, and was amazed at the security and convenience of a road which he had believed to be impassable. He went on personally to Lagos, and thence by sea to Tripoli, his own prediction being that he would be the "first of many" who would take this road when he had reported its advantages and security in Tripoli. His calculation was that goods could be carried between the Lagos coast and Kano in forty days without risk, whereas, between Tripoli and Kano, the journey extended sometimes to seven months, with the risks of the desert in addition. It has since been reported that the arrival of this Arab in Tripoli, and the account which he has given of his journey, has created a great sensation in commercial circles there. It remains still to be seen how much of the northern trade will in this way be diverted to the British coast.

The facilities which have been given by the new order of things to caravans travelling southward towards the coast have, of course, been reciprocally extended to traders travelling northward from the coast to the interior, and upwards of four thousand trade licences were this year issued by the British Government in Ilorin to petty traders, many of whom flocked from the coast provinces into the town. The British Resident of Ilorin reports that whereas, in old days, no Yoruba trader was to be found upon the left bank of the Niger, there is now no market of importance in Northern Nigeria in which they are not to be found. This, if correct, is in itself extremely satisfactory. It prepares the way for an easy flow of trade from the coast to the interior, and the impetus which has already been given to the trade of the coast colonies is clearly marked in their annual returns.

The question of caravan tolls is an interesting one, upon which the permanent policy of the British Administration is still open to consideration. It seems fair that all trade profiting by the safety of the roads, and the new markets opened to its activity, should bear a share of the expense by which this state of things is brought about. But, on the other hand, the undesirability of placing any restriction upon the movements of trade is keenly recognised. It is to be desired on all sides, that the cumbrous and extravagant system of caravan traffic may soon be superseded by a more convenient form of transport. With the introduction of railroads, and the extension of a steam service upon the rivers, the question of caravan tolls will probably fall into abeyance. Throughout the interior of the Protectorate the reduction of these tolls has given universal satisfaction, and the steady increase in the amount collected — notwithstanding the fact that by-roads, which have no toll stations, are now so safe as to be frequently used for the purpose of evading all tolls — gives unmistakable indication of the increase in the volume of internal trade.

The question in which European traders are interested is, of course, the development of an export trade. This rests, I have tried to show, in the first instance, upon internal prosperity. The direct object of the administration is to promote prosperity by the peaceful organisation of the country under just laws, the maintenance of order, and the opening of communication with the outer world. When these objects have been attained, the administration may be regarded as having done its part. It holds the field in the interests alike of the native and the European. It is for European trade itself to do the rest.

The wealth of opportunity cannot be doubted, and private enterprise is already following close upon the heels of established government. The returns of European trade with the Protectorate are not at present published in a form which makes accurate figures attainable, but the two European firms who do the principal trade have for the last year given incomplete figures, which reach a total of about £300,000. This is exclusive of European trade done for Government through the Crown Agents, and also of trade of which the values in European goods done by native traders are not known. Some £60,000 worth of British cottons are estimated to have been imported last year by petty native traders living at Ilorin. The trade is entirely exclusive of trade spirits, which are not admitted into Northern Nigeria, and small as its total is at present, it equals already about half the trade which was done forty years ago with all the West Coast settlements together.

This is not a despicable beginning when it is considered that there are at present but two English firms who have established operations in the country, and that they have not yet taken possession of the field which has been opened by the extension of British administration to the northern provinces and to Bornu. It must be understood that in entering the northern states we enter regions of civilised industry which bear no comparison with the peoples of the coast, and which have already markets susceptible of indefinite expansion.

Over the greater part of the territories the native population are reported as being eager to buy English agricultural implements. Some dissatisfaction has been felt with the bad quality of English cloth which has been introduced, and a consequent impetus has been given to native dyeing and weaving industries, but for good cloth there is a ready sale. Hardware, needles, thread, writing paper, mirrors, and many other articles of English manufacture, are keenly appreciated, and since the superiority of the road from Lagos to Kano has been demonstrated over the desert route to Tripoli, it is to be hoped that English goods will before long take the place in the market of Kano which has hitherto been held by other European goods imported through the Mediterranean coast. Tea, of which the stimulating quality is recognised by the Tuaregs of the desert, under the name of "Water of Zem-Zem," has now largely taken the place of coffee with the richer class of Mohammedans; and European provisions are readily bought in the northern states.

Here a wide market evidently waits. Two main obstacles are opposed to the rapid development of trade.

One is a radical difficulty which the development of intercourse and the promotion of native prosperity can alone remove. Natives are ready to buy, but they do not possess in sufficient quantity a marketable equivalent for European goods. Native manufactures have no value in European markets. Horses and cattle are too cumbersome for export. Cowries are only locally useful. Exchange must therefore be based solely on produce which has value in European markets, and which is sufficiently portable for export under present conditions. Even this to be profitable must be in bulk, and retail trade is impracticable while small payments have to be made in kind. The same difficulty attaches to the collection of Government taxes, which for the present have to be paid for the greater part in kind. The solution evidently is to be found in the encouragement of a surplus production in native industries of which the produce can be profitably exported, combined with the introduction of a cash currency as a medium of general exchange. In this way native existing industries of the kind most valuable to Europe will, by a natural process, be expanded, and new ones will be sought which will gradually extend the basis of an export trade. The stimulus to this movement will be supplied by the desire to possess articles procurable only with the required forms of produce, and though the operation of the movement may require time, it may on the whole be trusted to correspond with the amount of enterprise displayed on the part of European firms in introducing new commodities to the native markets. Already, as has been seen, a good deal has been done by the administration in the direction of introducing a cash currency, and silver coins are coming into general use.

It has been seen, in describing the early history of the Royal Niger Company, that its founders looked to the northern states of Haussaland for the ultimate success of its trading operations. Here they expected to meet with returns which should repay all the administrative expense of opening the northern country to British influence, and there is no reason to suppose that they were mistaken. The realisation of their ideal is now attainable. The burden of administrative expense has been assumed by the British taxpayer. The country has been opened, not only to one firm, but to all legitimate British trade, and it is for British trade to develop the wealth of the markets which at that time were beyond its reach.

The second obstacle to the development of trade is easier to remove than the first. It is the obvious difficulty of transport which arises from the very nature of an extended trade. The existing system of human carriage, if the most natural to a semi-civilised society, is absolutely opposed to any large commercial movement. Were it possible to obtain carriers for the transportation of goods in bulk, armies of men would be required, who would destroy, by the mere fact of their passage, the country over which any large produce trade was in operation. The time required for such transport would be prohibitive, and the cost, as calculated in Northern Nigeria under present circumstances, would be two shillings per ton per mile, as opposed to the fraction of a penny for which certain classes of goods would be carried by rail. Add to this that heavy machinery, such as may be required for mining, cotton pressing, &c., cannot be transported at all by human carriage, and it is evident that the present system of carrier transport is hopelessly condemned. Were there no other argument against it, the mere fact that every man who is employed as a carrier represents so much labour taken away from production is itself a sufficient reason for regarding the system as the most costly and unprofitable that can be employed. Human carriage is a concomitant of slavery. With the abolition of slavery it becomes impossible.

One of the first endeavours of the administration has been so to improve the main trade routes of the Protectorate as to render them fit for the more general employment of animal transport, and between Zungeru and Kano a fairly good cart road, fit for the employment of wheeled vehicles, will soon have been completed. The opening of navigable waterways has also already placed some rich districts within easy reach of European trade, but the urgent need of the Protectorate from every point of view, political and commercial, is obviously for the introduction of railways. These need not in the first instance be expensive. The country is generally open, the gradients of the main routes are easy, and there are no impassable obstacles which call for costly engineering works. The development of trade must be necessarily gradual, and in order to keep pace with it, a railway so light as to be little more than a tramway, along which waggons could be drawn by steam, might, in the first instance, be laid from a navigable port on the Niger to Zungeru, and thence along the route which has been cleared for the construction of a cart-road to Zaria and Kano. This is the caravan route which traverses some of the richest and most populous districts of the country. When the markets of this district had been worked, it would perhaps be time enough to extend a similar cheap service from Kano to the capital of Bornu. If the trade which resulted were sufficient to justify further expense, the construction of more solid railways would rapidly follow. Transport in a peaceful country is not in truth a difficulty. It is little more than a calculation of profit and loss.

The administration of Northern Nigeria is but five years old. Its duty has been to bring under control a congeries of states, of which the internal disorders necessitated, in the first instance, a resort to the plain argument of military conquest. The administration has not in the short period of its existence been able to do more than to affirm the conquest of the country, and to create a skeleton of the machinery of government which it will be for time to bring to its full perfection. But a beginning has been made. The framework of administration has been established in all the provinces. A territory which we found in chaos has been brought to order. The slave trade has been abolished within its frontiers. Its subject races have been secured in the possession of their lives and property. Its rulers have been converted with their own consent into officials of the British Crown, and are working sympathetically to promote an order of things that shall render a return to old abuse impossible. There has been no great shock and no convulsion, only into the veins of a decadent civilisation new blood has been introduced, which has brought with it the promise of a new era of life.

Thus a territory has been opened, in which the genius for administration, and the adventurousness in trade, which have always characterised the British people, have once more the opportunity of working side by side to the accomplishment of great national results. It is a union which in times past brought the British Empire into existence. It gave us India, it gave us Canada, and though these are great names, there is a reasonable ground for hope that the chapter of Imperial history which has been opened in the interior of West Africa will not prove unworthy of the rest.

INDEX

250311-2-20-50W